READING THE *LET*
YOUNGER: AN

M000265632

This is the first general introduction to Pliny's *Letters* published in any language, combining close readings with broader context and adopting a fresh and innovative approach to reading the letters as an artistically structured collection. Chapter 1 traces Pliny's autobiographical narrative throughout the *Letters*; Chapter 2 undertakes a detailed study of Book 6 as an artistic entity; while Chapter 3 sets Pliny's *Letters* within a Roman epistolographical tradition dominated by Cicero and Seneca. Chapters 4 to 7 study thematic letter cycles within the collection, including those on Pliny's famous country villas and his relationships with Pliny the Elder and Tacitus. The final chapter focuses on the 'grand design' that unifies and structures the collection. Four detailed appendices give invaluable historical and scholarly context, including a helpful timeline for Pliny's life and career, detailed bibliographical help on over thirty popular topics in Pliny's *Letters* and a summary of the main characters mentioned in the *Letters*.

ROY K. GIBSON is Professor of Latin at the University of Manchester and the author of a commentary on Ovid, *Ars Amatoria* 3 (Cambridge, 2003) and *Excess and Restraint: Propertius, Horace and Ovid's Ars Amatoria* (2007). He is co-editor with Ruth Morello of both *Re-imagining Pliny the Younger* (2003) and of *Pliny the Elder: Themes and Contexts* (2011). He plans to work next on a commentary on Pliny, *Letters* Book 6.

RUTH MORELLO is Lecturer in Latin at the University of Manchester, and co-editor with A. D. Morrison of *Ancient Letters: Classical and Late Antique Epistolography* (2007). Also in collaboration with Roy K. Gibson, she is co-editor of *Re-imagining Pliny the Younger* (2003) and of *Pliny the Elder: Themes and Contexts* (2011). She is currently working on a monograph on representations of Julius Caesar in the literature of the triumviral and early imperial periods.

READING THE *LETTERS* OF PLINY THE YOUNGER: AN INTRODUCTION

ROY K. GIBSON AND RUTH MORELLO

CAMBRIDGE
UNIVERSITY PRESS

CAMBRIDGE
UNIVERSITY PRESS

University Printing House, Cambridge CB2 8BS, United Kingdom

Cambridge University Press is part of the University of Cambridge.

It furthers the University's mission by disseminating knowledge in the pursuit of education, learning and research at the highest international levels of excellence.

www.cambridge.org
Information on this title: www.cambridge.org/9780521603799

© Roy K. Gibson and Ruth Morello 2012

First published 2012
First paperback edition 2015

A catalogue record for this publication is available from the British Library

Library of Congress Cataloguing in Publication data
Gibson, Roy K.
Reading the Letters of Pliny the Younger : an introduction / Roy K. Gibson and Ruth Morello.
p.   cm.
ISBN 978-0-521-84292-1 (hardback)
1. Pliny, the Younger. Correspondence – Criticism, Textual.   2. Pliny, the Younger – Criticism and interpretation.   3. Letter writing, Latin – History – To 1500.   I. Morello, Ruth.   II. Title.
PA6640.G53   2012
876´.01 – dc23   2011042605

ISBN 978-0-521-84292-1 Hardback
ISBN 978-0-521-60379-9 Paperback

FOR
David Delaney-Gibson
and
Jim Petch

Contents

Acknowledgements

This book began as a conversation on a train on the way back from a conference in 1998. An unsuspected shared enthusiasm for Pliny led to a small conference in November 2000 at Manchester on this understudied – and in those days also largely unloved – author, and soon to the idea of a jointly authored book on Pliny. Along the way – with surreptitious agenda – we organized a series of conferences designed to bring to Manchester scholars who were well informed about subjects and authors important for understanding or contextualizing Pliny: Ancient Letters (2004, with our colleague Andrew Morrison); Pliny the Elder (2006, with our colleague Mary Beagon); and Suetonius (2008). To all those from whom we learnt so much at those conferences, we express our gratitude.

Work on the present book began in earnest around 2005, and since then we have incurred more debts to the patience and acumen of friends and colleagues than we can ever repay. We benefited greatly from comments offered by John Henderson Stanley Hoffer, and Gareth Williams, who kindly identified themselves as the readers for the Press. In addition, the entire manuscript has been read, and considerably improved, by Tony Woodman, Chris Whitton, Jim Petch, and Spyridon Tzounakas. We have also profited from the generosity of Tony Birley, John Bodel, Amanda Claridge, Jennifer Ebbeler, Dan Harmon, Niklas Holzberg, Regina Höschele, Eleanor Winsor Leach, Ilaria Marchesi, Carole Newlands and Roland Mayer. Audiences at the University of Madison, Wisconsin, and at Kings College London made suggestions which changed our thinking on important points; particular thanks are due to Laura McClure, Jim McKeown and William Fitzgerald.

Roy Gibson would like to offer additional thanks to Graham Burton (who gifted him with several volumes of Syme's *Roman Papers*), as well as to Paolo Braconi of the University of Perugia and Claudio Veschi of the Comune di San Giustino, who very kindly showed him around the nearby site of Pliny's villa (and the museum at Celalba).

We both have particular reason for gratitude to the Arts and Humanities Research Council, which funded invaluable periods of research leave. Sincere thanks are due also to our colleagues at Manchester for help (and forbearance) of various sorts, especially Alison Sharrock and Andrew Morrison. We are very grateful to Rita Wolff, who kindly allowed us to use her painting of Pliny's Laurentine villa for the cover of this book (and also to Pierre du Prey, who put us in touch with the artist). Warm thanks are offered also to Catherine Delaney, who drew the map of 'Pliny's Italy' for us. Liz Hanlon and the staff of Cambridge University Press have been unfailingly patient and helpful during the lengthy gestation of this book. Particular thanks are due to Michael Sharp for his always swift and helpful support and advice. We are also very grateful to Malcolm Todd, who copy-edited the book, for his professional acumen, sharp eyes and patience with a pair of often dilatory authors.

Finally, we would like to offer heartfelt thanks to our families, who have encouraged and supported us. This book is dedicated in particular to David Delaney-Gibson and Jim Petch.

Translations of Pliny are taken or adapted from John Delaware Lewis, *The Letters of the Younger Pliny Literally Translated* (London, 1879). Translations of other texts are either our own or taken (or lightly adapted) from duly credited sources (usually the relevant Loeb Classical Library volume). The text of Pliny's letters is that of the Oxford Classical Text. Abbreviations of ancient texts largely follow the conventions of the *Oxford Classical Dictionary*, 3rd edition.

Abbreviations

AE	*L'Année epigraphique*, Paris, 1888–
CAH 11²	A.K. Bowman, P. Garnsey, and D. Rathbone (eds.), *The Cambridge Ancient History*, 2nd edition. Vol. xi: *The High Empire, AD 70–192*, Cambridge, 2000.
CIL	*Corpus Inscriptionum Latinarum*, Berlin, 1862–
ILS	H. Dessau, *Inscriptiones Latinae Selectae*, Berlin, 1892–1916.
*PIR*²	E. Groag, A. Stein, L. Petersen, and K. Wachtel (eds.), *Prosopographia Imperii Romani*: A–B (Berlin, 1933); C (1936); D–F (1943); G (1952); H (1958); I–J (1966); L (1970); M (1982); N–O (1987); P (1997).
RP 1–7	R. Syme, *Roman Papers* 1–2, ed. E. Badian (Oxford, 1979); 3, ed. A.R. Birley (Oxford, 1984); 4–5, ed. A.R. Birley (Oxford, 1988); 6–7, ed. A.R. Birley (Oxford, 1991).
TLL	*Thesaurus Linguae Latinae*. Leipzig/Stuttgart, 1900–

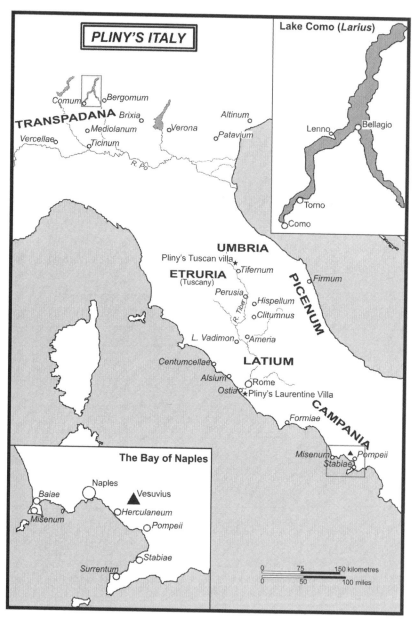

Pliny's Italy. Drawn by Catherine Delaney.

Introduction

Books 1–9 of Pliny's *Letters* contain 247 letters to various friends, acquaintances and family members, while Book 10 adds another 121 letters exchanged between Pliny and the emperor Trajan. It is conventional for critics – including the authors of this book – to refer to this vast assemblage of (mostly) short items as a 'mosaic'. The metaphor is useful, since it conveys the idea that an artist's assembly of small and variegated individual 'fragments' can create both discernible local patterns and – when viewed from a suitable perspective – a big picture. However, what the static 'mosaic' metaphor cannot convey is the sense of constant shifting movement inherent in the process of actually reading Pliny. To convey this aspect of the *Letters*, a new metaphor is needed: 'shake Pliny's kaleidoscope, and no second peek will ever exactly repeat the patterning'.[1] John Henderson's image of the kaleidoscope conveys well an aspect of reading Pliny, the sense that an almost infinite number of configurations and connections is available for the reader of the *Letters*. In the preface to his magisterial commentary on Pliny, A.N. Sherwin-White hints from a different direction at the same feature of the work, in a disarming confession that 'After sixteen years of study I still continue to discover links and parallels within the letters that had hitherto escaped me.'[2]

Some generators of the kaleidoscopic experience are easy to suggest, but hard to define precisely. Although Pliny, as has often been noted,[3] tends to confine his letters to a single topic, the truth of this observation can be overplayed. In fact, Pliny often manages to cluster a large number of apparently 'minor' issues rather deftly around his main topic, with the result that a single epistle can display potentially significant connections – on a wide variety of subjects – with a good number of other letters elsewhere. Or, as Sherwin-White phrases the matter from the commentator's

---

[1] Henderson (2002a) xi, 195 n. 5. [2] Sherwin-White (1966) v.
[3] E.g. by Sherwin-White (1966) 3–4, with a list of exceptions.

perspective, 'the illuminating parallel [for a letter, group of letters or even paragraph] often lurks unnoticed in a letter about a different topic'.[4] The word 'unnoticed' here is not without its own significance, since it says something about the fabric of Pliny's text and its tendency to treat certain topics in a manner that is best described as unemphatic.

At any rate, the letters are strongly interconnected, but the connections one detects – the picture glimpsed in the kaleidoscope – depends on the topic one chooses to emphasize at any given moment. Choose a different topic, and new configurations will appear. And, despite the impression of repetitiveness which a first reading of the *Letters* can leave,[5] further readings will reveal – through fresh attentiveness to Pliny's unemphatic mode of presenting his material – that the collection manages to pack in an astonishing array of subject matter over its 368 individual items.

All of this, of course, presents a problem for a modern volume billed as an 'Introduction' to the *Letters* of Pliny. How can one hope to introduce a kaleidoscope? Or cover such a vast assemblage of topics? Setting aside – for the moment – a sense of despair, it can readily be admitted that the present book is very far from exhaustive even within its remit of 'introducing' the *Letters*. Instead we aim for representative coverage – and in two senses. First, we cover a range of methods of reading the *Letters*. Secondly, we tackle a selection of key themes and topics present within the corpus. It is the combination of these two approaches that gives this volume its title: *Reading the Letters of Pliny the Younger: An Introduction*.

There is no one method of reading the *Letters*. Readers may choose to read the entire collection in sequence from 1.1 to 10.121, or to concentrate on a single book of letters, or to select favourite letters for individual attention. Alternatively readers may focus on groups and cycles of letters connected by shared theme, addressee or recurring persons of note.[6] Each of these reading methodologies is applied to Pliny's *Letters* in the course of this book. In Chapter 1 ('Reading a life: *Letters*, Book 1') we adopt the most popular approach of all for tackling letter collections, ancient or modern, and attempt to read Pliny for the story of his life; but with a particular focus on what this process brings to our understanding of Book 1. We follow up in Chapter 2 ('Reading a book: *Letters*, Book 6') with a detailed study of one of Pliny's individual books as an artistic entity in its own right, while in Chapter 3 ('Epistolary models: Cicero and Seneca') we pause to review Pliny's acknowledgement of his literary models. Next we study

---

[4] Sherwin-White (1966) v.   [5] On the repetitiveness of letter collections as a genre, see Chapter 6.
[6] On this variety of ways of reading Pliny, see Marchesi (2008) 16–27.

letters connected by repeated appearances of the same individuals, whether as prominent characters within the letters (Chapter 4 'Pliny's elders and betters') or as addressees of the letters (Chapter 5 'Pliny's peers: Reading for the addressee'). In Chapter 6 ('*Otium*: How to manage leisure') we tackle letters connected by one of the key themes of the correspondence, while in Chapter 7 ('Reading the villa letters') we adopt the habits of the anthologist and pick out a handful of Pliny's most famous letters for study.

In the book as a whole we maintain an emphasis on the value of reading Pliny in sequential order – particularly at the level of the individual book or the collection as a whole – over the more common method of creating an anthology of some of the more famous letters. We believe that we do a disservice to Pliny by stripping his most attractive letters from their original context, namely as part of a deliberately sequenced and artistically constructed book or cycle of letters. Nevertheless, in Chapter 7 and elsewhere we recognize the openness of the *Letters* even to the piecemeal approach represented by the anthology.[7] Finally, in the closing chapter ('The grand design: How to read the collection'), we raise our sights to the entire ten-book collection and look at Pliny's designs for *re-reading* his *Letters* as a single literary unit.

Alongside tackling various approaches to reading the *Letters*, this volume, as promised earlier, aims to introduce some important subjects and themes present in the correspondence. Chapters 4–7 form a loose quartet of two pairs, where the first pair joins a study of Pliny's relationships in regard to the older (and eventually younger) generations (Chapter 4) to a study of Pliny and his peers (Chapter 5). The second pair joins a study of one of Pliny's greatest obsessions – the proper use of *otium* (Chapter 6) – to an in-depth study of one of the contexts for Pliny's *otium*, namely his famous country villas (Chapter 7). As 'topic' chapters, these studies must be understood as representative rather than exhaustive of the possibilities for criticism offered by Pliny's correspondence. We might as easily have chosen – or, had space allowed, included – other equally potent areas to focus on, such as Pliny's relations with women, the Domitianic 'Stoic' opposition or slaves, or his theories on oratory and rhetorical style, etc.[8] Nevertheless the four areas chosen for detailed study are notable for their ability to draw in major portions of the correspondence effectively.

---

[7] See e.g. pp. 36–7, 45–7, 66–7, 201–2, 234–6, 244–7, where the anthologizing habit is discussed.

[8] The first two are well covered by Carlon (2009), and appear as subjects also in Chapters 1 and 2 of this volume; for aspects of slavery in Pliny, see e.g. de Neeve (1992), Hoffer (1999) 50–4, Gonzalès (2003). For Pliny on oratory and rhetorical style, see e.g. Gamberini (1983) 12–57, Cova (2003), Cugusi (2003), Marchesi (2008) 97–143.

Pliny's relations with the 'Stoic' opposition, or with women, and his theories on rhetorical style – and several other 'popular' topics – receive occasional comment over the course of the book. Readers who wish to know more on these and other subjects in Pliny's correspondence should consult Appendix 3. Here we provide bibliographical help (and lists of relevant letters) on a select number of favourite aspects and topics, ranging from the eruption of Vesuvius and the *Panegyricus* (both touched on briefly in this volume), to the Latinity and style of the *Letters*, Christians, dolphins, and provincial government (each allotted incidental mention only in the course of the volume). In this way we hope to balance detailed treatment of selected 'representative' topics with a briefer indication of the wider array of subjects associated with the detailed study of Pliny.

Nevertheless, one topic listed in Appendix 3 – given only very indirect treatment within this volume – calls for some further (brief) comment. This is the hoary topic of 'revision and authenticity' in the *Letters*. In the succinct formulation of Ilaria Marchesi, Pliny's epistles 'are what we are accustomed to call private letters: however stylistically (re-)elaborated, they display all the features we expect of a real correspondence' (2008, 12). Beyond further amplification of this point (not attempted here), little of genuine critical value can be added to the issue (which indeed gives all the appearance of being, for the moment at least, a critical dead end). Given the prominence which Pliny allots within the correspondence to the revision of his many speeches and poems before publication, it would be surprising if he did not also revise his letters prior to publishing them. But at the extent of that revision we can only guess, with little prospect of critical consensus on the issue. It should be added that in the chapters which follow, we have found it possible to treat Pliny's individual books and even the entire ten-book collection as contrived artistic entities. However, this does not imply or require a belief that Pliny composed the *Letters* as a separate literary work without reference to actual letters sent to actual addressees. Relevant here are the comments of Alessandro Barchiesi on old controversies about poetry books, where 'people would even deny that the *Odes* were a legitimate book because Horace presumably did not write his poems *after* designing the book. *But this is to exorcize the amount of bricolage, improvisation, and workmanship that goes into literary practice*' (emphasis added).[9]

A volume of 'Introduction' to Pliny's *Letters* needs, we trust, little in the way of justification. Pliny has, since the 1960s, possessed all the modern

---

[9] Barchiesi (2005) 338.

markers of a canonical classical author: an authoritative Oxford Classical Text (R.A.B. Mynors, 1963) and a full commentary (A.N. Sherwin-White, 1966). Discussion of the author in journals and book chapters has maintained a respectable rate since that time, without (so far) quite achieving positive critical momentum. The reasons for this are not hard to find. Like, for example, Herodotus, Pliny has tended to attract a strikingly diverse set of scholarly communities: prosopographers, social historians, political historians, legal historians, economic historians, architects, garden designers, archaeologists, and – of course – literary critics of all hues.[10] Each sub-group has tended to concentrate on a particular set of letters or concerns, and few scholars have felt it incumbent upon them to read the Plinian literature either entire or even much beyond their particular specialism. One result is that, as a rule, the journal literature is – unlike that written, for example, on republican and imperial poetry – far from cumulative: the scholarly landscape here more resembles a collection of isolated communities than some great urban centre dominated by competing superstructures of various kinds. This is a tendency no single book can hope to reverse; but in Chapter 7 in particular we seek to demonstrate the value of integrating archaeological and historical approaches with the literary.

Nevertheless, if the journal literature has not yet achieved positive critical momentum, the reverse is true of the literary-historical study of Pliny in monograph form. Since 1997 we have witnessed the publication of no less than ten important monographs on the epistolographer, including works in German (Ludolph 1997, Beutel 2000, Lefèvre 2009), French (Gonzalès 2003, Wolff 2003, Méthy 2007) and English (Hoffer 1999, Henderson 2002a, Marchesi 2008, Carlon 2009), not to mention edited collections.[11] From these works taken as a whole there is gradually emerging the conviction that Pliny is an extremely sophisticated writer of considerable stature, whose work handsomely repays close reading. Taken individually, each of these works examines various – sometimes specialist – literary or literary-historical aspects of the author, such as (to take a few examples) Pliny's presentation of his own image, the workings of literary allusion in the text, or the moral and philosophical principles implicit in the author's practice and assertions.[12] A work of more general literary-historical introduction

---

[10] For a demonstration, see Appendix 3.
[11] Castagna and Lefèvre (2003) and Morello and Gibson (2003).
[12] For a useful summary of the main emphases of these contributions, esp. Ludolph (1997), Hoffer (1999) and Henderson (2002a) – plus the edited collections of Castagna and Lefèvre (2003) and Morello and Gibson (2003) – see Marchesi (2008) 1–11.

has an obvious role to play in this landscape.[13] Not least because Pliny, despite his reputation for 'easy' and clear Latin – and hence his frequent (and ultimately somewhat misleading) employment in the intermediate stages of learning Latin – is hardly an author who is self-explanatory. His 'difficulty' as an author becomes especially clear, in fact, when his *Letters* are read in their original book format from Book 1 through to Book 10, rather than in the bite-size chunks characteristically offered in an anthology. If he is to be studied seriously, he requires readers equipped with a surprisingly large amount of basic information about his life and career, his addressees and about the design and workings of the collection in its literary context and tradition. The hope is that the present volume will provide, under one cover, access to this kind of information, otherwise liberally scattered amongst more specialist publications.

The appendices at the end of this book – of which one has already been mentioned – have a special role to play in the provision of some of this basic information, and readers new to Pliny might begin here. Appendix 1 provides a timeline of major events in Pliny's life and in the lives of his friends and in society at large, along with a transcription and brief discussion of the great Comum inscription (source for so much of our knowledge of Pliny's official career and testamentary benefactions). A thorough familiarity with this timeline is assumed for the reader of this book, so that references to, for example, Pliny's praetorship assume the knowledge that this post was held under Domitian in the early 90s AD, etc. Many incidental references made in the course of the book will lack immediate comprehensibility without basic knowledge of the kind imparted in the timeline. In Appendix 2 we provide a book-by-book catalogue of the addressees and contents of *Letters* 1–9. (Space forbids a catalogue for the 121 letters of Book 10.) An explanation of the purpose – and the limitations – of the catalogue or index is in order. As with the study of many letter collections (or indeed miscellaneous poets such as Martial), the generation of critical momentum usually requires that frequent reference be made to a very wide range of individual letters (or poems). We do not assume close familiarity in the reader with each of Pliny's 247 letters in Books 1–9; on the other hand, it would be both tedious and repetitive for the reader if we paused to indicate the addressee – and to summarize the contents – of each letter to which we

---

[13] Marchesi (2008) 1–4 acutely notes that much of this recent Plinian criticism has been concerned with the author and his strategies for self-promotion and censorship, and characterizes her own work as text- rather than author-centred, where the *Letters* themselves are the final object of interpretation, rather than any service that these texts may have performed for their author in the context of his society (2008, 5). The present volume employs both of these approaches.

make reference. The catalogue in Appendix 2 is offered as a partial solution to this problem: consultation of its contents will provide a brief indication of the addressee and main theme(s) of each letter (or act as a mnemonic for readers already familiar with the text). The key feature here is quick access to the requisite information, and is of course not designed to substitute for (knowledge of) the text itself.

Conversely, readers may use the catalogue in Appendix 2 as a way of familiarizing themselves with the contents of individual books, or indeed of identifying individual letters (and locating their position). Here we return in a little more detail to the issue of Pliny's 'unemphatic' mode of presentation. As already suggested above, a good number of Pliny's letters often initially appear rather similar to one another, and distinguishing features – such as specificities of fact, figure and date – often seem to be avoided in the letters. Furthermore, Pliny strives for a consistency of tone and a moderation of language. The total effect is quite deliberate on Pliny's part, but from a modern reader's point of view one result is that individual letters – the anthologists' favourites aside – may lack strong distinctiveness. In this context, our catalogue is in part designed to aid readers' memories. (The ancient 'indices' to Pliny, discussed in Chapters 2 and 5 and in Appendix 2, may well have performed similar services in antiquity.) Nevertheless, there are some obvious limitations. As noted above, Pliny's letters contrive to smuggle in an astonishing variety of subject matter, despite their apparent commitment to the discussion of a single subject. Our brief summaries cannot do justice to this aspect of the *Letters*, and consequently some features of individual letters will be invisible. Nor can a summary of a letter be fully objective, and we have repeatedly crossed the line between report and interpretation. In addition, our catalogue cannot indicate the relative size of individual letters and thus indicate those which Pliny marks out as especially important through their sheer length.

Appendix 4 provides extremely brief information – for orientation purposes only – on a very select number of correspondents or figures named by Pliny in the *Letters*. For more information, including their full nomenclature and a list of letters where each is either named or receives a letter, see the 'Biographical Index' at the end of the second volume of Radice's Loeb edition of Pliny (1969) or – preferably – the onomasticon of Birley (2000a).[14] The provision of such information is necessary in view of the

[14] Radice (1969) 2.557–86 and Birley (2000a) are gratefully acknowledged as the source of the information condensed in Appendix 4.

fact that over 100 persons receive letters from Pliny – and this without mentioning the relatively large number of other characters living or dead named in the text of the letters.[15] The result – from the reader's perspective – is a not inconsiderable cast of characters.

---

[15] However, it can be surprising to learn that more than half of the *Letters* in Books 1–9 – slightly less in Book 10 – are free of names other than those of the correspondent and of Greek or Latin authors; see Birley (2000a) 22.

CHAPTER I

Reading a life
Letters, *Book 1*

As noted in the Introduction to this volume, Pliny's *Letters* can be approached in a variety of ways, ranging from reading all ten books of the collection in strict sequence to picking out individual favourites for special attention. In this opening chapter, however, we try out the most popular methodology of all for approaching letter collections, of whatever era, and read the correspondence for the story of the author's life. We endeavour to help readers make sense of how Pliny shapes his 'autobiography'. Much will be learnt about the structure and workings of Pliny's collection, including the fact that the *Letters* – despite initial appearances – are relatively hospitable, by *ancient* standards, to readers interested in a narrative of Pliny's life. Nevertheless, they are most welcoming to the returning reader who has read all ten books of letters and now starts the collection again from the beginning. For much key information is withheld till the closing books of the *Letters* – in such a way that a dynamic of re-reading becomes crucial to grasping the full potential of the collection.[1] It is the job of this chapter in due course to perform this act of re-reading for our own audience.

However, we do not tackle Pliny's life in isolation from his times. We read the *Letters* against the wider historical record and ask what Pliny puts in, what he leaves out, and what he delays for later revelation. The result will be a deeper appreciation of the images which Pliny wishes to create both of himself and of his era. It will also emerge that, for all their careful crafting, the *Letters* are not necessarily a coherent piece of self-justifying propaganda. Pliny's own later autobiographical revelations may be turned against his earlier self-images.

For reasons to do with the structure of Pliny's *Letters* (on which more below), our reading of Pliny's life will concentrate largely on a single book

---

[1] For this as a persistent feature of the collection – where later books (esp. 9 and 10) belatedly reveal important information or invite a re-reading of earlier books – see above all Chapter 8; cf. Murgia (1985) 198–200, Leach (2003) 162–3, Marchesi (2008) 239–40.

9

(Book 1). We begin, however, with an investigation of the relationship between letters and autobiography, since that relationship is not entirely straightforward, particularly in the case of ancient letter collections.

LETTERS AS AUTOBIOGRAPHY

Why do we read letter collections for the story of the life?[2] Modern audiences, it is often claimed, experience impulses to discover some form of unity within texts they read, above all a kind of broadly conceived 'narrative' unity.[3] This is a credible claim, since even ancient texts which offer no formal narratives to their readers – such as satire, love elegy and didactic – continue to attract attempts to examine or trace the stories which apparently lie at their base.[4] In the case of collections of letters the rich supply of personal information found in individual letters offers the possibility of a narrative unity based around a complete story of the letter-writer's life. Readers may interpret and rearrange the personal data so as to produce a satisfactory 'life' in chronological order, while biographical information 'lost' between letters beckons alluringly with a siren call, inviting readers to fill the gaps.[5]

Certainly, as regards modern letter collections, the marketing techniques of contemporary booksellers evince an expectation that we will want to read letters for the life-story which they apparently contain. Published correspondence is frequently found within the 'Biography' sections of the stock, while editors repeatedly adopt the playful title 'A Life in Letters' for the epistolary collections of prominent figures from the worlds of literature and the arts. In this limited but powerful sense letter collections are viewed in a relatively uncomplicated way as a form of autobiography.[6] And it can hardly be doubted that Pliny's *Letters* offer rich material for what is – by ancient standards – a relatively detailed life-story, from his birth seventeen or eighteen years prior to the eruption in AD 79 of Vesuvius (6.20.5) to

---

[2] For a more detailed investigation of the autobiographical potential of ancient letter collections (and modern attempts to realize that potential), see Gibson (2012).

[3] See e.g. Sharrock (2000), esp. 16–17, 32–3.

[4] See e.g. Gowers (2003) on Horace *Satires* 1, Breed (2009) on Propertius, Lee (2008) on Tibullus, Sharrock (2006) on Ovid's *Ars Amatoria* and Tola (2008) on Ovid's *Tristia*.

[5] Cf. Trapp (2007) 342 on the Ciceronian letter collections, also Morello and Morrison (2007) xii. Nevertheless, for criticism of the idea that we inevitably construct narratives out of lives, see Strawson (2004).

[6] For the importance of autobiography as an organizing concept in modern thought, see Marcus (1994). The modern literature on autobiography is vast; for two classic investigations, see Lejeune (1989), Sturrock (1993).

his appointment and tenure as governor of Bithynia around the year IIO (10.15–121).[7]

But how closely do letter collections fit a definition of 'autobiography'? Definitions of biography and autobiography – not to mention the question of the origins and development of these genres – are inevitably somewhat controversial.[8] In the useful working definition offered by Glenn Most, 'what distinguishes autobiography from all other kinds of first-person narrative is that it alone is addressed on principle to people the speaker has never met'. This, he adds, is why autobiographical narrative often is obliged to cover the subject's 'life from birth to the time of narration'.[9] Most ancient and modern letter collections fail to meet this definition on several counts. A published collection may in some sense be addressed to people the letter-writer has never met, but the constituent members – the individual epistles – are usually addressed to people he or she knows well (many intimately). Hence not only is there no overt attempt to provide a systematic narrative of life from birth to present time, but even within individual letters otherwise revealing autobiographical information may be omitted or be the subject only of allusion – since it is already known to the addressee.

Editors of modern correspondence characteristically attempt to overcome these limitations by providing both copious annotations to individual letters and substantial 'connective tissue' between groupings of letters, often in the form of consolidated biographical information and other relevant facts which give the context for the period of time covered by any set of letters then printed. However, in a revealing comment, one recent editor, referring to a separately published biography of the letter-writer whose correspondence he is annotating, suggests that 'any reader who wishes to get the most out of the[se] letters should most certainly have read this biography, or at least its relevant chapters, before embarking on the present volume' (Hardy (2004) xxv). In Pliny's case, of course, no separate ancient biography survives, nor is it the practice of ancient editors or writers to add anything substantial in the way of contextual material

---

7 Our relative ignorance about the life of Tacitus makes an interesting contrast; see Griffin (1999) 140–2, 157–8. For a schematic presentation of the order of events of Pliny's life, see Appendix 1; for the life of Tacitus, see Birley (2000b). For the relationship between Pliny and Tacitus, see Chapter 5.

8 On the development and character of ancient biography and autobiography, see Momigliano (1993), Burridge (2004) and Reichel (2005), also Most (1989) and Pelling (2009).

9 Most (1989) 122 and n. 32. Note also the 'normative' modern definition offered by Lejeune (1989) 4, 'a retrospective prose narrative written by a real person concerning his own existence, where the focus is his individual life, in particular the story of his personality'. Pliny's *Letters* fail this definition also on several counts.

beyond a prefatory epistle.[10] Such 'connective tissue' as Pliny does supply comes rather in the form of information revealed later in the collection (and which invites a re-reading of earlier books with such information in mind).

Letters, then, are not 'autobiography' in any straightforward way. In the case of ancient letter collections it is also clear that not every reader approached published correspondence for a narrative account of a life's events. In a notorious passage, ps.-Demetrius insists that revelation of character is the characteristic virtue of the epistle (*Eloc.* 227),[11] and – with no less notoriety – ancient biographers such as Plutarch and Suetonius appear to have been rather sparing in their use of a subject's letters.[12] Yet we need not be overawed by these facts. Cornelius Nepos, for one – in a passage to which we shall return later in the book – hails Cicero's letters to Atticus as virtually the equivalent of a history of the times through its depictions of the leading figures. This is clearly untrue, but all the more interesting for it: Nepos is willing to mistake letters for a narrative of the period, including the autobiographical narrative of Cicero himself.[13] Nevertheless, we may note that Cicero seems not to have depended on his letters to communicate his life-story to a larger public, and did not even ensure that his letters were published during his own lifetime.[14] Rather he depended on his speeches and dialogues, and above all on such first-person poetic efforts as the *de Consulatu suo*.[15]

More dramatic evidence of the connection made by some readers between letter collections and autobiographical narration comes from some well-known instances of the insertion of spurious letters into pre-existing *corpora*. Such additions, for example to the Hippocratic letter collections, are designed precisely to fill in chronological and biographical gaps in the

---

[10] In Book 9 of the *Letters*, nevertheless, Pliny lets it be known that Voconius Romanus and Sardus are engaged on biographical works whose subject is himself (9.28.3, 9.31.1). Perhaps something was also expected from his protégé Suetonius.

[11] Pliny's early description of his Laurentine villa may cater to this reading tendency. By the time readers reach 2.17 they will not yet have gathered all the information needed to form a judgement; the detailed tour here of the villa – assimilated in ancient thought to its owner's character (see Chapter 7) – perhaps provides the reader with a short-cut.

[12] As Trapp (2007) 335–8 suggests, this may be due to a fear that the informal style of letters might undermine the higher generic standards of biography.

[13] Nep. *Att.* 16.3–4 *quae qui legat, non multum desideret historiam contextam eorum temporum. sic enim omnia de studiis principum, uitiis ducum* ... , 'The reader would little need a continuous history of the period. For they offer so full a record of everything to do with statesmens' policies, generals' failings ...' (trans. N. Horsfall). For further discussion of this important paragraph, see below pp. 77, 83–4, 136–7.

[14] White (2010) 31–61; see also Chapter 3 of the present volume.

[15] See Gibson and Steel (2010) 119–25.

existing text.[16] These instances of individual insertion are already well along the intellectual and artistic path to the creation of entirely spurious[17] or fictional books of letters. Written purposely as collections, the fictional correspondence authored by (for example) Alciphron or Aelian – such as their *Letters of Courtesans* or *Rustic Letters* – is clearly designed to offer a reader the pleasure of putting together various narratives on the basis of events adumbrated over a course of single letters, or even 'the chance to try his or her hand at *ethopoieia*', i.e. the imaginative re-creation of character.[18] However, the potential for letters to form an 'epistolary biography' seems to have been grasped most firmly by the authors of deliberately planned pseudepigraphic collections, above all the (probable) first-century AD author of the *Letters* of Chion of Heraclea.[19] These seventeen chronologically ordered letters, which purport to have been written by Chion in the fourth century BC, tell the autobiographical story – and accompanying character development – of their 'author's' journey from self-indulgent aristocratic youth to philosophical tyrannicide.[20] Here most clearly, as Michael Trapp remarks, 'Letters... emerge as interestingly poised on the margins of biography.'[21]

PLINY'S *LETTERS* AS AUTOBIOGRAPHY

Letter collections, then, are not to be equated with 'autobiography'; but clearly they possess autobiographical potential. In practice, as we shall see, the realization of autobiographical potential within ancient letter collections varies enormously from author to author. But, as suggested earlier, Pliny's *Letters* prove relatively hospitable, by the standards of ancient letter collections, to readers attempting to follow the author's life.

This will not be immediately apparent to a modern reader. At first sight the text – as put together and published by Pliny in its format of nine

---

[16] See Hodkinson (2007) 287. For an excellent overview of surviving ancient letter collections – including many of the collections mentioned here – see Klauck (2006) 103–82.

[17] For letter collections written for spurious attribution to historical figures, see Rosenmeyer (2001) 193–233.

[18] Rosenmeyer (2001) 255–338, with quotation from 306–7; cf. König (2007a) 269–72. Similarly, Horace's *Epistles* 1 offers readers the chance to reconstruct the story of the poet's moral progress; see Morrison (2007) and cf. Ferri (2007).

[19] On these letters, see further Trapp (2003) 30–1 and, in rather more detail, Rosenmeyer (2001) 234–52; for a translation of the letters, see Rosenmeyer (2006) 82–96. On the Greek 'epistolary novel' (a category within which the *Letters* of Chion are often included), see further Holzberg (1994), Rosenmeyer (2001) 133–233, Hodkinson (2006).

[20] See Trapp (2007) 344–6; but for a revisionary reading of Chion's character development, see Penwill (2010).

[21] Trapp (2007) 347. For the possibility that Roman audiences were familiar with a genre that cast autobiography in epistolary form (albeit usually in a single letter), see Bollansée (1994).

(or ten) books of correspondence[22] – offers a series of autobiographical fragments in a sequence which is chronologically unruly in a double sense. First, narratives of, and references to, Pliny's youth and early manhood appear in unpredictable places over the course of the collection (although even here some patterns can be detected).[23] Secondly, we are warned in the very opening epistle (*collegi non seruato temporis ordine*, 'I have collected [my letters] without preserving the order of dates', 1.1.1) that letters reflecting his current life will be arranged without regard to chronological – i.e. narrative – order.[24] Readers may wish to reconstruct Pliny's life from these 'disordered' autobiographical fragments,[25] but Pliny himself appears to be making the job rather difficult.

This 'problem', however, needs to be viewed within the context of principles of arrangement for letter collections in general in the ancient world. (And, as we shall see later, Pliny's claim to have no regard for chronology is true only in a rather limited sense.) It appears that it was usual for an author or his editors to publish correspondence grouped by addressee or 'dossier' of related letters.[26] Such editorial methods further hindered the ability of letters to form an 'up to the present moment' autobiographical narrative, and in two ways. First, letters to a single correspondent or on a set of related matters might necessarily give only a very narrow sense of

---

[22] On Book 10, see Chapter 8 and Appendix 1.

[23] E.g. Book 7 offers a brief and suggestive, but within its own terms fairly complete, 'narrative' of a distinct period of Pliny's life, i.e. his early political career up to 97 or so; cf. 7.4, 7.11.3–5, 7.14, 7.16.2, 7.19.10, 7.27.14, 7.31.2, 7.30.

[24] For the tradition of asserting random order (with varying degrees of disingenuousness) in miscellaneous works, cf. Plut. *Mor.* 629d, Gell. *NA praef.* 2–3, Clem. Al. *Strom.* 6.2.1, Phot. *Bibl.* 17.119b.27–32 (Pamphile); König (2007b) 44, 44 n. 3, 61–2.

[25] In the terms of modern literary criticism, readers wish to impose a *fabula* (narrative chronological reconstruction) on the plot (events as disposed and narrated in the original text); for these terms, see further Lowe (2000) 3–16.

[26] For example, letters are collected by addressee in Cicero's *ad Atticum*, in the letters of Seneca to Lucilius, in much of the highly varied correspondence of Fronto (e.g. *ad Marc. Caes.*, *ad Verum*: see Champlin (1974)), and in Books 1–7 of the letters of Symmachus, where blocks of letters to single addressees are arranged consecutively (Matthews (1974), Sogno (2006) 59–63). As for dossiers, the correspondence of Fronto preserves several examples, e.g. *ad Amicos* 1, *de Feriis Alsiensibus*. Cf. Book 10 of the letters of Ambrose, which collects letters and documents relating to the author's dealings with a series of emperors (Liebeschuetz (2005) 31–43), also Books 6 and 7 of the letters of Sidonius, which collect letters to bishops (Harries (1994) 7–11), and the letters of Augustine, where many manuscripts open with a portfolio of letters involving Volusianus and Marcellinus (Ebbeler (2012) 'Introduction'), etc. Both principles of arrangement are already on display in the Ciceronian collection we know as the *ad Familiares*; cf. e.g. Book 3 (thirteen letters to Ap. Claudius Pulcher); Book 13 (seventy-nine letters of recommendation on behalf of various friends); and Book 14 (twenty-four letters to Terentia and her family). But for the arrangement of this collection largely by correspondent, see White (2010) 51–61. For the extremely complex situations observable in the manuscript traditions of Jerome and Paulinus of Nola, see Cain (2009), esp. 13–42, 223–8, and Conybeare (2000) 161–5.

the writer's larger unfolding life; and secondly letters even to a single correspondent might be arranged in a sequence other than the chronological.[27]
Where correspondence to one addressee is both sufficiently ample over
time and largely arranged by chronology – as with Cicero's letters to Atticus or (apparently) Seneca's to Lucilius – then the reader could potentially
gain a (restricted) sense of the playing-out of the writer's life. But of course
the vast majority of Cicero's collections circulating in antiquity were not
like this,[28] and Seneca's philosophical epistles are notoriously reticent about
the major events of his 'outer' life and carefully avoid the provision of more
than one or two dates.[29] At any rate, the frustration of readers with, for
example, Cicero's *ad Familiares* and the correspondence of Augustine –
as texts with lamentably unrealized autobiographical potential – can be
judged from various attempts made since early modern times to break
up the original manuscript groupings, and to rearrange them along more
strictly chronological lines.[30]

It is thanks to the massive labours of these modern editors – such as those
of Shackleton Bailey on the *ad Familiares* – that we can use ancient letter
collections to follow historical events and trace the course of the authors'
lives; but in a majority of instances it is somewhat against the grain of
the original format of the collections that we do so. Pliny's *Letters*, often
carefully imprecise about the date of individual epistles (see below), are
not susceptible to the large-scale chronological rearrangements imposed
by editors on the *ad Familiares* or the letters of Augustine. Yet, if as resis-
tant as any Augustan poetry book to the re-ordering of individual pieces,
Pliny's books offer less resistance to the reader attempting to realize the
autobiographical potential of the *Letters*. For they are arranged – strikingly,
by ancient standards – neither by addressee nor by portfolio, but on the
principle of thoroughgoing variety of addressee and subject matter.[31] As

---

[27] See Beard (2002) on the letters to Tiro in *Fam.* 16. The collections of e.g. Fronto, Symmachus and
Augustine likewise often display little commitment to ordering by chronology within groups of
letters arranged by correspondent.

[28] For a useful inventory of the contents of all sixteen books of the *ad Familiares* and their varying
principles of arrangement, see Shackleton Bailey (1977) 1: 20–3; for a catalogue of the many lost
Ciceronian letter collections, see Nicholson (1998) 76–8, also White (2010) 171.

[29] See Griffin (1976) 4, Edwards (1997) 23–4 = (2008) 84–5.

[30] For the chronologically driven dismemberment of the books of the *ad Familiares*, see Beard (2002);
for the similar re-ordering of Augustine, see Ebbeler (2012) 'Introduction'. Other ancient letter
collections to endure a comparable fate include those of Fronto, Ambrose (Zelzer (1990) xxxiv–
xxxix, lxi–lxvii), Jerome (Cain (2009) 16 n. 13) and Paulinus of Nola (Conybeare (2000) 164); cf.
the history of the letter collections of Erasmus, discussed at Jardine (1993) 148–56. On the whole
subject, see further Gibson (2012).

[31] Cf. esp. Marchesi (2008) 16–22. (The obvious exception is Book 10, with its dossier of letters to and
from Trajan.) The late-antique letter collections of Ambrose and Sidonius, arranged (for the most

such, Pliny's *Letters* are not subject to the limitations imposed on auto-biographical narration by other more common forms of arrangement. Of course, the reader must still contend with the non-chronological arrangement of letters. However, while letters within individual books are ordered without regard to chronology, Pliny's books *as a collection* largely preserve the order of events in his adult life from late AD 96 to 100 (Books 1–2), through his consulship of 100 (as advertised in Book 3) and nomination to the post of augur in 103 (retrospectively narrated in Book 4), to his term in Bithynia-Pontus (the bulk of Book 10).[32] That is to say, Pliny's claim in letter 1.1 to have no regard for chronology holds good only for the contents of individual books[33] – and even here some qualifications need to be added. For, as will become evident in Chapter 2, the correspondence includes numerous 'cycles' of letters on a developing theme which invariably preserve chronological sequence within themselves, whether sustained within a single book or across several.

In sum, Pliny's individual books appear to progress forward unit by unit according to identifiable (if overlapping) periods of time. In this sense, the *Letters* as a corpus preserve the large-scale chronological progression of the letters of Cicero to Atticus (or Seneca to Lucilius), while rejecting the principle of a single addressee. But within individual books Pliny adopts a scheme of a varied but meaningful order that may have been learnt from certain books of the *ad Familiares*,[34] but might equally well have been picked up from the typically fragmented 'narrative' styles of Horace's *Epistles* (or even Roman love elegy). More will be said on this topic of significant non-chronological ordering in Chapter 2.[35] All that remains, here, is to draw the conclusion that if we seek to read the *Letters* for the

part) according to the same principle of variety in nine or ten books, have long been suspected of coming under the influence of Pliny's *Letters*; see Cain (2009) 18–19, Gibson (forthcoming a), both with further references.

[32] Note that in the *Panegyricus* Pliny rejects the more common encomiastic method of praise under individual headings and adopts a broadly chronological structure; see Innes (2011).

[33] For the dates covered by Pliny's individual books, see pp. 19–20, 51–3 and Appendix 1. For a letter collection which offers the radical disordering which Pliny appears to promise in letter 1.1 – but 'fails' to deliver in the books which follow – one must look to e.g. the pseudonymous late-antique letters of Phalaris; see Rosenmeyer (2001) 225–9.

[34] E.g. the letters to Tiro collected in *Fam.* 16 display, in their original (non-chronological) manuscript order, a distinct design: two groups of eleven letters from separate periods (50–49 and 45–44 BC) are placed on either side of a central group of five focusing on the pivotal moment of the manumission of Tiro. This central group of letters belongs to 53 BC – the probable date of Tiro's manumission – and is thus markedly out of chronological sequence within the book; but the artistic gain from placing the manumission in a central position is clear. See Beard (2002) 131–43.

[35] See also Chapter 5 for an attempt to read Pliny's *Letters* on the 'Ciceronian' principle of collection of letters by addressee.

story of Pliny's life, we are *not* reading entirely in opposition to the text as it was assembled for circulation in antiquity.

One further consequence of Pliny's scheme of organization for the collection is the creation of 'pools' of time – pools into which late-revealed fragments of autobiographical narrative can then be dropped.[36] For example, as will be shown in more detail later in this chapter, the period encompassing late 96 and 97 was filled with events of great personal significance for Pliny, quite apart from the assassination of Domitian in September 96. This time period corresponds roughly with the dates for Book 1 of the correspondence (see below). However, no clear reference to some of the most important of these events is offered until Book 9 and the opening letters of Book 10. One letter in particular (9.13) contains key information on Pliny's political (and domestic) life in AD 97. Of course, it falls ultimately to the reader to integrate these autobiographical fragments positioned at opposite ends of the collection. However, Pliny has clearly not made it difficult for the reader to perform this task, since the events of letter 9.13 can be mentally carried back by the reader for insertion within the pool of time represented by Book 1. (This is in fact the act of 're-reading' the collection mentioned earlier as intrinsic to the operation of the *Letters*.)

Other difficulties presented by the *Letters* to the reader wishing to follow Pliny's life-story are characteristic of letter collections in general, however they may be arranged. Flickering references to people, events and places must be decoded, and narrative gaps between letters must be filled. The gaps between autobiographical fragments are easier for the reader to deal with in one sense, since it is precisely the holes in the story which pull the reader in and provide the *Letters* with much of their dynamism. As Altman (1982) 172 remarks more generally of the European epistolary novel, 'The more fragmented and disconnected the narrative appears, the more actively the outside reader seeks to discover the connections.'[37] Indeed the gaps in Pliny's life can perhaps be accounted one of the most attractive features of his correspondence, at least to judge by one aspect of the reception of the *Letters*. For Pliny, despite an often uneventful life free from hardship and major obstacles, has enjoyed a popularity in the sub-genre of modern historical fiction that is as vigorous as it is occasionally surprising. The

---

[36] Pliny shows some awareness of the attractions of publishing biographical writing *in serial form*, at 3.10.3.

[37] Altman (1982) 167–84 offers a classic account of the tension between the narrative discontinuity inherent in the epistolary form and the reader's attempts to perceive (or the author's attempt to foster) continuity.

allure of filling the gaps which he leaves in his epistolary autobiography is perhaps part of the explanation of this phenomenon.[38]

One resource available to Pliny's contemporaries for supplementing the life-story of the *Letters* and decoding the allusions is, alas, no longer available to us: Pliny's many other publications, particularly his speeches of various kinds and his poetry. Only the *Panegyricus*, his speech of thanks to Trajan on the attainment of the consulship in AD 100, survives, along with some scraps of poetry.[39] No doubt these works provided some biographical illumination. But one comment can be added on these long-perished works. Pliny's frequent references to them in the *Letters* effectively transform the collection into the nerve centre not only of his autobiographical narratives, but also of his putative *Collected Works*. For the flexibility of the letter format allows Pliny repeatedly to make reference to his other prose and verse publications. By contrast, neither the *Panegyricus*, nor his many published speeches to court and senate, perhaps not even his poetry could make generically appropriate sustained reference to the *Letters* or to each other.

By way of illustrating how Pliny's letters may be read for the story of his life, and of demonstrating the autobiographical potential latent in the particular character of Pliny's individual books (and the structure of his collection), we concentrate for the remainder of the present chapter on the material contained in perhaps the most fascinating of Pliny's books (in autobiographical terms), Book 1. Of course, as implied at the beginning of this chapter, there are other ways to read Pliny than for the life, and in Chapter 6 we return to Book 1 and read many of the same letters more thematically as a meditation on *otium*. But here in Chapter 1, as promised, we read Pliny's autobiographical material against the historical record, asking what he leaves in, what he leaves out, and what he delays for

---

[38] Pliny's presence at the eruption of Vesuvius and his role as an early persecutor of Christians have also played their part here. For some examples of this fiction, see Monsigny (1988), Bell (2002), (2008), Harrington (2006), MacBain (2010), and note especially Pliny's appearance in the *Roman Mysteries* series of Caroline Lawrence, e.g. Lawrence (2001), (2003), (2007) 73–8, 93–6 – later filmed and shown on BBC television as part of *The Roman Mysteries*, Series 1–2 (Lawrence (2008–9)). For a particularly entertaining example of a novelist filling a gap in Pliny's life, cf. Harris (2003) 172–3, using Pliny's virtual silence about his natural father to good effect: 'Life had knocked [Pliny's mother] about enough as it was – humiliated by her wastrel husband and his ghastly mistress, then left widowed with a boy to bring up.' Contrast the more hostile portrait in Bulwer-Lytton's *The Last Days of Pompeii* (quoted below p. 114 n. 39). For the reception of Pliny, see further Appendix 3.

[39] On the *Panegyricus*, see esp. Roche (2011c) and Appendix 3. For Pliny's lost speeches, see Sherwin-White (1966) 91, 334; on Pliny as poet, see Gamberini (1983) 82–118, Marchesi (2008) 53–96, Appendix 3, and cf. Courtney (1993) 367–70 on the surviving lines. The *Letters* nevertheless preserve the memory of these lost works; see Mayer (2003).

future revelation. However, Pliny's narrative of his life cannot be discussed without a brief review first of the dating of his books.

DATES FOR BOOK I

Dates for Pliny's books were first convincingly established by Mommsen,[40] and have been subject to further refinement by Sherwin-White and Syme, among others.[41] As will be seen in Chapter 2, evidence for particular book dates can appear flimsy on closer inspection; yet the entire system has never been convincingly overthrown (indeed it has proved remarkably resilient to serious criticism). And a brief look at dates for Books 1–2 will suggest why. Many of the letters here – in fact the majority – are formally undateable, in the sense that they contain no absolutely certain references to externally verifiable events, whether contemporary or from the recent past. Nevertheless, those relatively few letters which do contain references to such events appear to be fixed by the latter to dates roughly between late 96 and 100. Contrariwise, there appear to be no certain references in Books 1–2 to contemporary events after the year 100 (or possibly 101). And, as often in Pliny's books, dates for individual books are chronologically progressive, but contain overlaps, whereby a date of late 96 to early 98 appears to be suggested for Book 1 (with one probable exception in 1.10; see below), and of late 97 to 100 for Book 2.[42]

In effect, the minority of dateable letters influences our reading of the undateable letters, whereby readers will have to make a special critical effort to avoid the assumption that the latter are contemporary with the former. Pliny's consummate skill in manoeuvring a reader towards this position is much to be admired. For all we know, many of the undateable letters in Books 1–2, for example, were written in the year 106,[43] yet their seamless integration into books which contain letters which demand to be dated to 96–100 inevitably influences how all the letters of Books 1–2 will be read. Here we may contrast the letter collections of Cicero and late antiquity. In the books of the *Ad Familiares* or of the collections of, for example,

---

[40] Mommsen (1869) 31ff. For bibliography on the chronology of the letters, see Appendix 3.

[41] See Appendix 1.

[42] See Sherwin-White (1966) 27–30 for a detailed consideration of the evidence. The dating of individual letters for Books 1–2 of Pliny's collection, of course, tells us nothing about dates of publication, other than that e.g. Book 2 was published after 100: we simply do not know how long after; cf. Syme, *RP* 5.478 [= (1985b) 176]. Vidman *PIR*² P 490 asserts a consensus of 106 for the publication of Pliny's earliest books (cf. Syme (1958) 663); but for other views, see e.g. Marchesi (2008) 12 n.1 on the conclusions of Bodel (unpublished), Woodman (2009) 31–5.

[43] For sensible remarks on revision, see Hoffer (1999) 17–18, 26–7, 87.

Symmachus and Sidonius Apollinaris, letters of widely differing – and *noticeably* differing – dates often sit next to one another.[44] As a result, the reader of these books can soon dispense with the idea that they are united by date and time; but a reader of Pliny cannot.

Finally, since they play a role in the discussion below, something brief should be added about the first fourteen letters of Book 10.[45] This sequence contains the so-called 'private correspondence' with Trajan from the years 98–102, and it prefaces the 107 items of official Bithynian correspondence with the emperor from about a decade or so later. Controversy still rages about who compiled and published Book 10, whether a posthumous editor such as Suetonius (the older and dominant view) or Pliny himself. In the final chapter of this book and in Appendix 1 we argue for artistic design in the arrangement of Book 10.

PLINY'S LIFE IN BOOK 1

What do we learn from a first complete reading of Book 1 about the author and his life so far?[46] At this early stage in the collection, Pliny is careful to avoid overwhelming the reader with a mass of personal information and details. Yet, as will become clear, enough hints and allusions are provided to whet the reader's appetite for further revelations in the succeeding books of correspondence implicitly promised in the first letter of the collection: *ita enim fiet, ut eas quae adhuc neglectae iacent requiram et si quas addidero non supprimam*, 'The result, in that case, will be that I shall hunt up such other letters as still lie neglected, and if I write any fresh ones, I will not withhold them' (1.1.2). Indeed the promise here of the addition of 'neglected letters' – i.e. unpublished letters whose 'proper' home would otherwise be in Book 1 – acts precisely as an invitation to interested readers to press on in expectation that the biographical and narrative gaps of Book 1 will be (ultimately) filled.

At any rate, we learn that Pliny is by origin a (wealthy) member of Comum's local elite who retains strong ties with his *patria* (1.3, 1.8, 1.14.4,

---

[44] For Cicero, see above p. 16 n. 34, and below pp. 52–3 (where Cicero's habits of dating his letters are discussed). For e.g. Sidonius, see Harries (1994) 16 and van Waarden (2011) on Book 7 of Sidonius (and on the effect intended by this noticeable difference in dating).

[45] For a survey of these neglected letters, see Millar (2004a) 25–6, 29–30, 32–4. They are united by the fact that all were written to Trajan while he was away from Rome; by contrast, the later letters of Book 10 belong to Trajan's single period of extended residence in Rome.

[46] For a catalogue of the contents and addressees of letters in Book 1, see Appendix 2. The debt of the analysis below to Hoffer (1999) is warmly acknowledged. For an attempt to read Book 1 rather differently, as an artistically arranged display of personal virtues and activities, see Ludolph (1997) 91–193.

1.19), that he has a mother-in-law with Umbrian connections (1.4; cf. 1.18.3), and that he is an advocate with a long history of successful practice and currently much in demand for legal and other services of a social nature (1.5.4–7, 1.7, 1.9, 1.18, 1.23). Of Pliny's own 'official' career so far we learn little directly. At 1.10.2 we gather that Pliny did his military service (i.e. as military tribune) many years ago in Syria, and in 1.23, in a reply to a correspondent on the proper conduct of a political office, it is revealed that Pliny was at some point in the past tribune of the plebs. Nevertheless, some significant facts emerge. In 1.14.3–4 Pliny speaks in tones of personal patronage about one who has reached the office of praetor (1.14.7): an indication of Pliny's own position and possible prospects. More importantly, letter 1.10 drops strong hints about Pliny's current employment.[47] Here, writing in praise of the philosopher Euphrates, a friend from Syrian days, Pliny complains of the time he must spend on his exacting but tedious duties away from his friend:

nam distringor officio, ut maximo sic molestissimo: sedeo pro tribunali, subnoto libellos, conficio tabulas, scribo plurimas sed inlitteratissimas litteras. . . . [Euphrates] me consolatur, affirmat etiam esse hanc philosophiae et quidem pulcherrimam partem, agere negotium publicum, cognoscere iudicare, promere et exercere iustitiam, quaeque ipsi doceant in usu habere. (1.10.9–10)

For I am engrossed in the discharge of an office as highly irksome as it is important. I sit on the bench, countersign petitions, make up accounts, and write a vast number of most unliterary letters . . . [Euphrates] consoles me, and goes so far as to assert that it is a function, and indeed the noblest function of philosophy, to conduct public affairs, to investigate, to judge, to exhibit and exercise justice, and to put in practice what these very philosophers teach.

The description of these tasks allows a skilled contemporary reader to infer – without being informed directly – that Pliny is currently a prefect in the treasury of Saturn.[48] This post entailed a significant amount of the administering of justice, particularly in the complicated area of inheritance law (Pliny's main sphere of legal expertise).[49]

The reference to Pliny's duties is made elegantly in passing, but the choice and positioning of the letter is quite deliberate. In context, the complaints about overwork are meant to form one half of a contrasting pair with letter 1.9, where Pliny describes the leisure of his life at the Laurentine villa as

---

[47] On this letter, see also Chapter 6.

[48] Sherwin-White (1966) 110. Belated confirmation can be found in the similar – if unmemorable – language which Pliny uses explicitly to describe his duties in the treasury of Saturn at 10.9 *districtum*, *Pan.* 91.1 *laboriosissimo et maximo*.

[49] See Millar (2004b) = (1964); cf. Sherwin-White (1966) 110, 562.

a rest from his round of pressing personal and domestic obligations. This characteristic swing of the pendulum between *otium* and *negotium* will be a topic of brief investigation in Chapters 2 and 6;[50] but we can suggest here that the juxtaposition of the two letters also sets up a biographical conundrum alongside the evident thematic contrast. As already noted, the bulk of the letters in Book 1, where they can be dated, seem to belong to the reign of Nerva. During this period Pliny apparently held no public position, after demitting office at the *aerarium militare* or military treasury in 96, perhaps just prior to the death of Domitian (see further below). In this context, letter 1.10 appears to belong to the reign of Trajan, since Pliny commenced his duties at the treasury around or some time after the death of Nerva in January 98.[51] The reader intent on finding out about Pliny's life will inevitably ask, after a suitable pause to appreciate the artistic contrast with 1.9, how the complaints about being overwhelmed by work in letter 1.10 match up chronologically with his private *otium* and freedom from onerous employment in the preceding letter and elsewhere in the book (e.g. 1.7, 1.9, 1.13, 1.22). These problems can be solved by readers positing the fact that letter 1.10 postdates the others: an eventuality for which we have been prepared by Pliny's insistence that his letters have not been arranged chronologically. But any passing difficulties that this might create are outweighed by one signal benefit. The reader who is competent to decode the reference to the duties of a prefect of the treasury of Saturn will also be equipped to infer that Pliny is 'destined' for the consulship. For such prefects enjoyed a high success rate in the journey to the summit of the *cursus honorum*.[52] The positioning of letter 1.10 somewhat outside of its 'natural' sequence – it might find a more convenient home in Book 2 – is a deliberate first act in the creation of a narrative about the onward march of Pliny's career. The interested reader is primed to look for further instalments in the books to come.

More broadly autobiographical – in the sense of evidence for the author's personal interests – is Pliny's focus in Book 1 on *studia*: intellectual and especially literary activity in the broadest sense.[53] Thus, for example, letter 1.3 urges a friend to concentrate on his writing; 1.6 finds Pliny writing even while out hunting; 1.9 praises Pliny's Laurentine villa as a haven for the Muses; 1.10 celebrates the extraordinary flourishing of *liberalia studia* in the

---

[50] See also Chapter 6 for an egregious contrast between the *otium* of 8.8 and the *negotium* of 8.9.
[51] See Syme (1958) 658–9, Sherwin-White (1966) 75–8, Vidman *PIR²* P 490 (p. 206).
[52] Cf. the clear implications of 9.13.11, 23 (both quoted below in connection with Publicius Certus), and see Syme, *RP* 4.320–1 [= (1984) 55–6] (although the evidence here cited postdates Pliny).
[53] On the concept and practice of *studia* in Pliny, see Méthy (2007).

guise of the presence of the philosopher Euphrates; 1.13 celebrates the year's bumper crop of poets in Rome; 1.16 offers a eulogy of the varied literary talents of Pompeius Saturninus; 1.20 discusses at extended length issues of style in forensic oratory, and 1.24 is a letter on behalf of a friend who is explicitly identified as a writer, namely Suetonius. Such is the importance of literary matters in Book 1 that it is through their lens Pliny chooses to allude to some important events in his own life. For example, Pliny's dedication of his library at Comum and setting up of an alimentary scheme there 'for the support of children born of free parents' (1.8) – an act designed to win imperial favour[54] – are mentioned in the context of sending a speech on these subjects to a friend. Likewise, as we shall see later, the lengthy discussion of the style of an otherwise unidentified speech in 1.2 almost certainly carries an oblique allusion to the most important event in Pliny's political life in the period 96–8.[55]

If we now ask, as promised, what potential autobiographical material Pliny leaves out of Book 1, we will begin to see that the expression of intense personal interest in literature identified above has a particular role to play in the larger 'message' of the book. First, a small digression on the events of 96–8 is necessary.

PLINY'S LIFE IN BOOK 1: THE HISTORICAL CONTEXT

The period encompassing late 96 to early 98 was one of varied and often intense activity both for Roman society in general and for Pliny personally.[56] September 96 saw the assassination of Domitian and the accession of the elderly Nerva, who despite his track record as a Domitianic loyalist was likely to favour stability over everything else.[57] Turmoil and excitement among the elite inevitably followed. The return of those who had been exiled by Domitian was keenly anticipated, while the dead emperor's erstwhile supporters necessarily feared for their own fortunes in the new era. The assassination of Domitian had been a boudoir affair rather than a

---

[54] See Hoffer (1999) 93–104; cf. *CAH* 11².116–17. For Pliny's benefactions in general, see Duncan-Jones (1982) 27–32, and Appendices 1 and 3 in this volume.

[55] Perhaps Pliny has already warned us that few letters in Book 1 will contain letters on his 'professional' life by referring to the 'vast number of most unliterary letters' (1.10.9, quoted above) – i.e. ones unsuitable for inclusion in a collection of letters written 'with rather more than usual care' (1.1.1) – composed in connection with his treasury posting. For discussion of *cura*, 'care' as Pliny's principle of selection from among his letters, see Chapter 8.

[56] For a fuller narrative of events and critical reflection on the sources, see *CAH* 11².84–96; cf. Syme (1958) 1–18, 627–36, Birley (1997) 35–7, Bennett (2001) 42–52, Grainger (2003) 45–108.

[57] See Murison (2003).

popular revolt, and the dissatisfaction of some groups was inevitable. In particular, the reaction of the military was ominous, and the following year brought discontent with Nerva into the open. In October 97 the Praetorian Guard – perhaps already foiled in an attempt to replace Nerva with their own candidate – rioted, demanding the execution of the killers of Domitian. The impotent Nerva was forced to adopt Trajan as his partner and successor. In the words of Syme, this was a 'masked *coup d'état*, not without surmise of conspiracy' (*RP* 7.519),[58] where the succession was secured largely on the brute fact of Trajan's control of the legions on the Rhine. The real threat of civil war was now averted, and Nerva subsequently died, perhaps fortunately, in the first month of 98. The new emperor would not set foot in Rome until the autumn of 99.

Many of these events are completely omitted by Pliny from Book 1, some are viewed only from an oblique angle, while others are the object of fleeting or cryptic reference. Thus we find no letter to an anxious correspondent in faraway Comum on the assassination of Domitian, or on the discontent of the military, the adoption of Trajan[59] or the death of Nerva.[60] Rather, a correspondent in Comum receives a letter – prominently placed in the collection – enquiring about the delights of the addressee's villa and urging him to accomplish some immortal work of literature (1.3). Such reports as we do gain of contemporary affairs are carefully restricted by Pliny to events which affect himself and his friends very directly. Thus we hear of the suicide of Corellius Rufus, where an anecdote is told of the pain-wracked man's (successful) determination to outlive Domitian (1.12.6–8; cf. also 1.18.3), and we encounter letters which underline Pliny's long-standing connections with such members of the Domitianic 'Stoic opposition' as Iunius Mauricus and his brother Arulenus Rusticus (1.14)[61] and with the philosopher Euphrates (1.10), now returned to Rome – it is understood – after the revocation of Domitian's ban on philosophers.[62] Even here a tone

---

[58] Cf. Berriman and Todd (2001), and Eck (2002), also Hoffer (2006) 74–7.

[59] In Book 2 Pliny refers first to Nerva (2.1) then to Trajan (2.11) as simply *Caesar*, which emphasizes continuity in the office of emperor instead of the turmoil which led one to succeed the other. A rather different approach is taken in the *Panegyricus*; cf. Hoffer (1999) 143.

[60] By contrast, a letter of congratulation to Trajan on his accession opens Book 10; on Pliny's handling in 10.1 of the imperial transition, see Hoffer (2006). Similarly in Book 2, Pliny makes no mention of Trajan's spectacular entry into Rome in autumn 99 (*CAH* 11².102–3): this is reserved for *Pan.* 20–4, with a very oblique reference also in letter 3.7.7. (For the excitement created by anticipation of Trajan's return, cf. Mart. 10.6–7.) On Pliny's analogous strategy of silence over the Dacian wars, see pp. 51–2.

[61] On this grouping, see below pp. 27–8 in connection with Pliny's attempted prosecution of Publicius Certus.

[62] See Hoffer (1999) 120. An example of a weakly suggested narrative is found in the sequence 1.5, 1.10, 1.14: in the first Pliny is waiting for the return of the Stoic exile Mauricus, in the second an

of friendly (disingenuous?) optimism is maintained. Corellius is said to pass away *florente re publica*, 'while the state prospers' (1.12.11),[63] where it is part of Pliny's design to suggest the immediate improvement and stability of political conditions after the death of Domitian.[64] In fact these months were characterized by great uncertainty and fear of further chaos.

How could Pliny avoid fuller, perhaps even more honest references to the dramatic events of 96–8 in his correspondence? After all, these events will have impinged on him personally as an ambitious and well-connected senator. Quite apart from the need for Pliny to avoid putting potentially risky opinions on paper, we need to take seriously his short but significant assertion in the opening letter: *neque enim historiam componebam*, 'since it was not a history I was compiling' (1.1.1). In context this is appended to the revelation that the letters are not chronologically ordered.[65] But, as the reader progresses further through the collection, the assertion apparently broadens its scope to include the general omission from the letters of numerous contemporary political events.[66] For a fuller story readers will have to turn to the *Panegyricus* (5–12), where the narration of affairs of state in chronological order is apparently more appropriate both contextually and generically (and arguably somewhat safer too).[67]

Nevertheless, Pliny's choice of literary studies as an area for autobiographical emphasis in Book 1, noted earlier, turns out to be highly charged when read against the political developments of the period.[68] The purpose of this emphasis is to suggest that – now Domitian is dead and open speech has returned – the elite may concern themselves once more with the 'proper' business of civic society (including the writing of letters).[69]

---

exiled philosopher is found (back) in Rome, apparently joined in 1.14 by Mauricus himself. For such informal sequences, see Chapter 2.

[63] Similarly Verginius Rufus – the report of whose death is artificially delayed until Book 2 (see below) – is said to leave behind a stable Nervan regime (2.1.3) and to pass away *in altissima tranquillitate*, 'in the most perfect composure of mind' (2.1.4). The body politic did not share this composure.

[64] As Hoffer (1999) 140–3 notes, Pliny makes the suicide of Corellius symbolize the transition from Domitian to Nerva by allowing the impression that Corellius died not long after Domitian's assassination in 96; cf. esp. 1.12.8. In fact Corellius survived well into the reign of Nerva, as we learn at 7.31.4. For similar effects contrived for the meeting with Regulus in 1.5, see Hoffer (1999) 81–3, also 164, 173.

[65] For chronological narration as a key component of historiography – the primary object of Pliny's rejection at 1.1.1 – see Woodman (1989) 135.

[66] However, for the way in which the text of letter 1.1 nevertheless emphasizes generic similarities with historiography, see Tzounakas (2007). For Pliny's dialogue with historiography, see Traub (1955), Ash (2003), Marchesi (2008) 144–206, and Appendix 3.

[67] For the political narratives of the *Panegyricus*, see Roche (2011a).

[68] Cf. Hoffer (1999) 9–10, 27, 142–3.   [69] Cf. esp. 3.20.10–12.

Pliny's emphasis on the flourishing of literature is indeed the letter-writer's way of reflecting history without writing it: Rome has literally come to life again, now that the tyrant is gone. In the words of the sentence which opens letter 1.10: *si quando urbs nostra liberalibus studiis floruit, nunc maxime floret*, 'If ever the polite arts flourished in our city, they are particularly flourishing now.'[70] And of course Pliny's own efforts as patron and writer have a prominent role in this 'renaissance'. In sum, Pliny's emphasis on the rebirth of literature at Rome allows him to promote an ideologically charged picture of the rebirth of civil society.[71] No room here for gloomy reflections on the power of the military and the instability inflicted by them on Rome, or indeed for the pessimism about literary endeavour itself which is apparently expressed by Tacitus in the *Dialogus*.

Nevertheless, despite this apparent optimism, the angle adopted by the *Letters* here for catching the reflection of history also possesses one notably combative aspect. If the months between September 96 and January 98 were a demonstration of the might of the military in Rome – the violence of the Praetorian Guard and the threat of the legions massed on the Rhine which saw Trajan to power – then Book 1 of the letters responds with a picture of a society where polite letters flourish, and the military has little place or influence. Indeed, this is something of a keynote for the *Letters* as a whole, where even Trajan – the consummate military man – is made to appear largely in the guise of *ciuilis princeps*.[72]

Pliny's decision to concentrate on creating an atmosphere of civil renaissance in Book 1 also has personal advantages. As Stanley Hoffer (1999) 55 has suggested, a keynote of the book is introduced in the first sentence of letter 5: 'Have you ever seen anyone more cowed and abject than Marcus Regulus since the death of Domitian [*post Domitiani mortem*]?'. The clock in this book starts ticking precisely at the moment of Domitian's death. Even the hated Regulus – of whom more below – is a thoroughly changed man after the assassination of the tyrant. Under these circumstances what need here in Book 1 to highlight (potentially troubling) facts immediately

---

[70] Cf. the opening of 1.13: 'The present year has brought us a great supply of poets: during the whole month of April there was hardly a day when someone did not recite. I am glad that learning flourishes, that men of genius come forward and show themselves . . .'. The gifted poets and writers of Flavian Rome might disagree with Pliny's narrative of a sudden renaissance; see further Hoffer (1999) 161–3, 170.

[71] Cf. Tac. *Agr.* 3.1–2, also (more broadly) Woolf (2003) 212–21.

[72] Cf. below p. 147 n. 44 and see further Chapter 2 and Appendix 3. The point is made with particular force for Book 10 by Noreña (2007). For Trajan's trademark cultivation of *ciuilitas*, see *CAH* 11².102–6; but for Trajan's career as not especially marked by military service prior to 97, see Eck (2002).

ante Domitiani mortem – other than those which might hint at noble behaviour under the previous regime (1.5, 1.12, 1.18)? Pliny's record and offices held under Domitian might be best reserved for treatment rather later in the collection, as notably in Book 7, for example, when the consular orator's worth has been more fully established.[73] More will be said on Book 1 and Pliny's record under Domitian at the end of the present chapter.

LATER AUTOBIOGRAPHICAL NARRATIVES: RE-READING BOOK 1

After asking what Pliny puts into Book 1 and what he leaves out, we now turn at last to the question of what events in AD 96–8 he delays for later revelation in the course of the collection. For example, Pliny's old *tutor* Verginius Rufus opened the year 97 as consul, only to die later the same year from injuries sustained before taking up the office. Pliny, however, delays the narrative of his public funeral till the first letter of Book 2, apparently so as to allow the contemporaneous death of his other consular patron, Corellius Rufus, to take centre stage in Book 1 instead (1.12).[74] Both were active participants in Nerva's notorious gerontocracy,[75] and are kept apart as a mark of honour to each. Likewise the subject of later revelation is Pliny's farewell to the poet Martial on his departure from Rome in early 98. Pliny reveals his involvement with this Domitianic panegyricist – and his payment of the traveller's passage to Spain – only at the end of Book 3 when reporting the death of the poet (3.21.2).

Both of these events – as suggested earlier – can be carried back mentally by the reader to the pool of time accommodated by Book 1 and dropped in. Neither, however, will cause so big a ripple as an affair whose narration is delayed till the other end of the collection. That affair is Pliny's attack in the senate on one Publicius Certus, later written up and published as a speech apparently entitled *de Heluidi ultione*. Nerva did not encourage senators to rake over the glowing ashes of the Domitianic era;[76] but Pliny carried on regardless and picked out for attention a man who had been, under the previous regime, one of the prosecutors of Helvidius the Younger. The latter had been a prominent member of a loose grouping of senators, briefly mentioned earlier, allegedly inspired by Stoic ideals to oppose the

---

[73] See above p. 14 n. 23 for the relatively full record in Book 7 of Pliny's political career up to 97.

[74] Cf. Sherwin-White (1966) 143.

[75] *CAH* II².89: 'elderly, cautious men of [Nerva's] own generation, whose distinguished careers lay in the period before Domitian's worst excesses'; see further Chapter 4.

[76] See *CAH* II².88–9.

emperor.[77] He was executed by Domitian in 93, along with Arulenus Rusticus and Herennius Senecio.[78]

The Certus affair was the most significant event in Pliny's political life in the years 96–7. Its complete omission from Book 1 must initially have startled Pliny's contemporaries. It is true that there is one possible reference in the second letter of Book 1; but, as suggested earlier, it is highly oblique. Here Pliny sends an addressee a copy of an (apparently forensic) speech, whose significance is strongly underlined both by Pliny's pride in its style (1.2.1, 3) and the position of the letter at the very front of the collection proper, but whose subject matter he does not identify. Readers who press on with their reading of the entire correspondence will reach letter 9.13 and perhaps return to conclude that the work mentioned in 1.2 must be the *de Heluidi ultione*.[79] Yet, for the moment, Pliny declines to spell the political circumstances out, and prefers to concentrate instead on the more purely literary matter of the style adopted in the speech.[80] (This is part of the emphasis in Book 1 on literary matters.)

A full narrative of the Certus affair, as hinted above, emerges belatedly only in letter 9.13.[81] The immediate pretext for this letter is that an aspiring orator, who has been reading the published speech, has requested that Pliny 'write . . . in detail on such matters as are not contained in the books, and on the background to them, in short, as to the whole process of an affair which you were too young to witness' (9.13.1). This provides Pliny with an opportunity to inspect a pivotal moment in his career, and to make sure that his readers understand its significance and interpret it correctly. More importantly, for the present chapter, letter 9.13 constitutes, in some ways, the missing heart of Book 1. Much could be said about its effect on a re-reading of the book; but here we pick out only the most prominent of the main features which make a revisionary visit necessary. That feature is

---

[77] Pliny places repeated emphasis on his links with this group throughout the *Letters*; see Carlon (2009) 18–67, also Beutel (2000) 220–37 and Appendix 3. For the characters in the group, see Syme, *RP* 7.568–87.

[78] For a clear narrative of events surrounding their execution in 93 (not provided by Pliny) see Carlon (2009) 27–34.

[79] For the deliberate literary links created between 9.13 and 1.2, see Marchesi (2008) 36–9. Pliny makes no explicit reference to the *de Heluidi ultione* prior to 4.21.3. For speculation on the order in which Pliny's speeches were published in the period 96–101, see Sherwin-White (1966) 91.

[80] In this sense 1.2 delivers the earliest possible warning that we must be prepared to read on if we wish to solve some of the problems which Pliny's characteristic allusiveness creates, and must even be prepared to seek out Pliny's other publications (an opportunity, as noted earlier, largely unavailable to us now). For the functions of Pliny's references to unnamed speeches in these respects, see Mayer (2003) and Morello (2003).

[81] On this letter, see also Beutel (2000) 187–200, Carlon (2009) 58–64, Lefèvre (2009) 66–76, Whitton (2011), Whitton (2012).

the atmosphere of political menace so effectively conveyed throughout the letter. Particularly significant are the words of counsel allegedly received from one consular, whose purpose was to restrain Pliny from acting rashly in the light of the uncertainty of the future:

interim me quidam ex consularibus amicis, secreto curatoque sermone, quasi nimis fortiter incauteque progressum corripit revocat, monet ut desistam, adicit etiam: 'notabilem te futuris principibus fecisti' (9.13.10)

Meanwhile one of my friends of consular rank deeming me to have proceeded with too much daring and rashness, reproved me in some private and anxious words, recalling me and warning me to stop. He went so far as to add, 'You have made yourself a marked man in the eyes of future emperors.'

Likewise important are the warnings of an unnamed figure, who ultimately draws attention to the powerful friend with armies in the east that Certus can apparently rely on:[82]

'quid audes? quo ruis? quibus te periculis obicis? quid praesentibus confidis incertus futurorum? lacessis hominem iam praefectum aerarii et brevi consulem, praeterea qua gratia quibus amicitiis fultum!' nominat quendam, qui tunc ad orientem amplissimum exercitum non sine magnis dubiisque rumoribus obtinebat. (9.13.11)

'What daring is this? Where are you heading? What dangers are you throwing yourself in the way of? Why trust to the present state of things, while still uncertain about the future? You are attacking a man who is already prefect of the treasury, and who will shortly be consul; a man, besides, supported by such influence and such connections!' He named a certain person, who at that time commanded a powerful army in the East – not without strong and suspicious rumours being connected with him.

It is precisely this air of menace and uncertainty which is absent from Book 1. And if readers now return to re-read to Book 1 in the light of this long-delayed information, some may find there much to admire in Pliny's carefully crafted image in troubled times of an optimism, a confidence and an enthusiasm for the literary renaissance. But others will surely find much to query in the 'failure' to reflect the dark side of Nerva's reign.

However, for all the fullness of the information now provided by Pliny for the benefit of the young orator, it is clear that there are some large gaps in the narrative which Pliny either does not fill or passes quickly over,

---

[82] For the probable identity of the person in question (M. Cornelius Nigrinus Curiatius Maternus) and his role in the events of 97, see Eck (2002), also *CAH* 11².90.

even at this late stage. He alludes, very briefly, to the fact that while the senatorial motion to prosecute succeeded, the prosecution itself never took place, apparently because the conciliatory Nerva simply failed to respond to the motion.[83] The rather limited scale of his triumph receives no emphasis from Pliny; but the reader trying to reconstruct Pliny's life may draw rather more pessimistic conclusions from this outcome.[84]

Kept even more obscure is the personal effect of the attempted prosecution on Pliny's career. The passage from 9.13.11 quoted immediately above attests to the routine expectation that a man holding a post in the treasury of Saturn can in due course expect promotion to the consulship. Pliny himself later comments on the outcome of the trial for Certus, who of course held a post at the treasury at the time of the trial: *obtinui tamen quod intenderam: nam collega Certi consulatum, successorem Certus accepit*... 'I obtained what I had aimed at. For the colleague of Certus got the consulship, and Certus himself was superseded' (9.13.22–3). That is to say, Certus' colleague at the treasury got his consulship, while – thanks to Pliny – Certus suffered the indignity of merely being succeeded in his post in the treasury (i.e. did not obtain the consulship).[85] What Pliny does not say here is that this successor at the treasury was himself (alongside Cornutus Tertullus), who in turn became a safe bet for the consulship.[86] Cornutus Tertullus in fact appears earlier in the letter revealed as guardian to the daughter of Helvidius and as one of the few speakers in the senate who supported Pliny's motion for attempted prosecution (9.13.15–16). By this stage of the correspondence, readers will be familiar with the *pari passu* careers of Pliny and Tertullus – Pliny strongly emphasizes the fact in 5.14 – and so may be able to work out, with a little effort, that both Pliny and Tertullus benefited from this attack on Certus by their own promotion to the treasury.[87] That is to say, the correspondence, while not entirely open with the reader, does not appear

---

[83] *Epist.* 9.13.22, with *CAH* ii².88 and n. 31.

[84] The trial of Marius Priscus, narrated at considerable length in Book 2 (2.11–12), may provide the reader with a similar pretext for dark thoughts. Pliny refers to Priscus' trial again – with great pride – also in Book 3 (3.9.2, 4), Book 6 (6.29.9), Book 10 (10.3a), and in the *Panegyricus* (76.1–3). But later generations would come to disagree with Pliny's estimate of the importance of the trial: the leniency of Priscus' sentence would become proverbial (Juv. 1.47–8; cf. 8.119–20). It has been argued that the outcome of the case created in Pliny's co-prosecutor Tacitus a pessimism about the rhetorical arts which found expression in his *Dialogus*; see Syme (1958) 465, Mayer (2001) 7–8, 27 (but denied by Goldberg (2009) 79).

[85] Cf. Syme, *RP* 7.579; but for the view that illness (and death) snatched the consulship from Certus, see Griffin (1999) 154 n. 52.

[86] For a variety of views on the exact sequence of events, see Syme (1958) 658, *RP* 7.564–5, Sherwin-White (1966) 491, *CAH* ii².88.

[87] For Cornutus Tertullus, see further Chapter 5.

to be a coherently crafted piece of self-justifying autobiography.[88] (Or is that the intended impression?)

In place of the more serious and weighty attack on Certus, Book 1 offers instead – quite deliberately – a narrative of something of a sideshow in the aftermath of Domitian's assassination and the return of the exiles to Rome, namely the attempt of Regulus to effect a reconciliation with Pliny (who is allegedly considering Regulus' prosecution). The senatorial Regulus was Pliny's main rival in the Centumviral courts, and, although an informer under Nero, had little involvement in the Domitianic 'terror', beyond some support for the prosecution of Arulenus Rusticus, later pamphlets deriding the memory of the latter and of Herennius Senecio (1.5.2–3) and an alleged attempt to trap Pliny into saying the wrong thing in the Centumviral court (1.5.4–7). Throughout the letter, both in reported conversation with others and to his addressee, Pliny insists that the decision to prosecute Regulus must wait on the return of the Stoic Mauricus from exile. A perusal of later books in the collection will reveal no reference to such a prosecution.

Given the emphasis on literature in Book 1 and the promotion of the image of Pliny as successful man of letters here, it is tempting to accept Sherwin-White's explanation of Pliny's preference for narrating his dealings with Regulus instead of those with Publicius Certus: 'The reason why the subject of this letter was not employed in Book I or II is evidently that its theme overlapped too extensively with his recently published book. Hence he preferred to include the Regulus affair in Book I.5, and this is revived as an historic incident for IX' ((1966) 499). That is to say, Book 1 has been shaped with Pliny's other literary publications in mind, namely his *de Heluidi ultione*. This pattern is repeated in Book 3 with respect to the *Panegyricus* and the achievement of the consulship. Here Pliny, rather than place great emphasis on how he reached the consulship, or his joy in achieving it, or its significance, simply refers his reader to his speech of thanks to the emperor (3.13, 3.18), where information on both may easily be found. In any case, Regulus, while perhaps a minor delinquent compared to Publicius Certus in political terms, is for Pliny's *Letters* an important thematic strand, and one which will be pursued up to Book 6, where the death of this great rhetorical rival is at last recorded.[89] It ought to be added that it is perhaps precisely because Regulus is a minor delinquent compared

---

[88] Similarly, 9.13.3 might allow the inference that Pliny's affection for the executed Helvidius was largely posthumous; see Carlon (2009) 60–1, 67.

[89] See Chapter 2. On the Regulus theme in the correspondence, and its origins in Book 1, see Hoffer (1999) 55–92, Méthy (2007) 142–51, Lefèvre (2009) 50–60.

with Certus that he has been judged a more appropriate subject for Book 1's optimistic tone.

It is not only events in the public sphere which Pliny conceals or delays for later revelation. His wife, the daughter of Pompeia Celerina, passed away in late 96 or early 97, and Pliny himself fell rather seriously ill in 97. He may then have entered into a new marriage in or before 98, in keeping with the encouragement of the Augustan marriage laws. Information on all three of these domestic events is revealed, once again, only at the end of the collection. News of the death of the earlier wife in fact emerges in the same letter in Book 9, just considered, which narrates the attempted prosecution of Certus. Here Pliny tells us that, following his decision to avenge Helvidius' death, he decided to inform various surviving members of Helvidius' family, including the dead man's wife:

quamquam tum maxime tristis amissa nuper uxore, mitto ad Anteiam (nupta haec Heluidio fuerat); rogo ut ueniat, quia me recens adhuc luctus limine contineret. (9.13.4)

Though I was at that time particularly distressed, having lately lost my wife, I sent to Anteia (the widow of Helvidius); I asked her to come to me, since my still recent bereavement kept me within doors.

Later in the same letter, Pliny again reverts briefly to these sad circumstances in the course of identifying one of the (opposing) speakers in the senatorial debate over the prosecution of Certus as the stepfather of the wife who had just passed away (9.13.13).

The references to the dead wife are made incidentally, but their retrospective effect on the reader of Book 1 must (again) be profound. Certainly a reader finishing Book 9 and returning to Book 1 will read the latter in a new light, and may now wonder what else Pliny has not seen fit to pass on to the reader in the early books of the collection. In particular, the reader will now grasp the reason for the prominent award of fourth position in Book 1 to a letter for Pompeia Celerina, the deceased wife's mother. This in fact will be the only letter addressed to her in the entire correspondence. The subject of 1.4 – Pompeia's many splendid properties on the Via Flaminia – can now be seen to reinforce and partake in Pliny's reticence on the subject of his wife's death in Book 1.[90] No doubt the Pliny of the early books felt that he was insufficiently well established and in credit with the reader to introduce the topic of purely private and domestic grief.

---

[90] On Pompeia Celerina, see Carlon (2009) 106, 119–23; for the possible political significance of the localities in which she owns properties, see Hoffer (1999) 52–3.

Later in the collection, Pliny, now long established with the reader and having been consul long since, will document episodes of ill health for his new wife, Calpurnia (in Book 6; see Chapter 2), and in an astonishingly confident display of intimacy will include in Book 8 letters on Calpurnia's miscarriage.[91] Nevertheless, Pliny's reticence also has an artistic role to play in Book 1, since the inclusion of a letter on this tragic subject might have interfered too obviously with the theme of rebirth under the new emperor. In this context it is more effective that reports of the deaths of intimates be confined to the elderly and politically heavyweight (and male) – such as Corellius Rufus in 1.12 and Verginius Rufus in 2.1 – who triumphantly survived in old age into the reign of Nerva.

No doubt omitted for similar reasons was news of Pliny's own serious illness in 97. Again, details of this episode are revealed only at the other extremity of the collection, this time in Book 10. For in the pre-Bithynian imperial correspondence which opens Book 10 is included a letter of request for a grant of Roman citizenship to the 'medical therapist' – part of a series on the subject – who treated him during his terrible illness.[92] Again, the reader of Book 10 may now go back to read Book 1 in a revised light, and once more admire the reticence of Pliny and the artistry of a book which managed to convey a message of hope and optimism despite Pliny's own personal difficulties.[93]

Another letter early in Book 10 reveals the third of the important omissions of personal details from Book 1 indicated above. Letter 10.2, a note of thanks to Trajan (apparently written in 98) for the grant of the *ius trium liberorum* includes the revealing statement that Pliny was still childless after two marriages.[94] From this it is possible to conclude that he had married Calpurnia soon after the death of the daughter of Pompeia Celerina. Of this new wife, no mention is made until the first letter of Book 4

---

91 For Book 8 as the portion of the *Letters* in which Pliny also most fully develops his rhetoric of metaphorical paternity to protégés, see Bernstein (2008a).

92 10.5.1–2 *proximo anno, domine, grauissima ualetudine usque ad periculum uitae uexatus iatralipten adsumpsi . . .* , 'Last year, sir, being afflicted by a severe disease, so that my life was in danger, I engaged a medical therapist . . .'. The date of 97 appears to be guaranteed by 10.8.3, where the illness is said to take place during the reign of Nerva, but before Pliny's assumption of the post of prefect of the treasury of Saturn in 98.

93 Alternatively the reader may ask why Pliny did not choose to turn his own recovery from serious illness into an allegory for the return of political health, perhaps along the lines of Tac. *Agr.* 3.1–2.

94 Cf. esp. 10.2.2 *eoque magis liberos concupisco, quos habere etiam illo tristissimo saeculo uolui, sicut potes duobus matrimoniis meis credere*, 'And all the greater is my longing for children, whom I wished to have even in that dismal past era, as you may judge from my two marriages.' For the argument that this passage refers to one past marriage and one current marriage (under Trajan in 98), rather than to two past marriages under Domitian (*contra* Sherwin-White (1966) 264, 559, also Syme, *RP* 7.510, Vidman *PIR²* P 490 (p. 206)), see Hoffer (1999) 232–3, Birley (2000a) 2–3.

(conventionally dated to 104–5), i.e. perhaps as much as six years after the event. Once again, a letter published late in the collection may prompt a reader to go back and read the earlier books with renewed interest. If the previous wife, to judge from her mother, embedded Pliny further in the local elites of Umbria, then the marriage to Calpurnia now strengthened the senator's ties to his home town of Comum. As such the reader may view those letters which emphasize personal links to Comum with a fresh eye (starting from 1.3). Likewise of fresh interest in respect to Calpurnia will be such marriage-themed letters as the recommendation of a Northern Italian bridegroom for the daughter of the Stoic Arulenus Rusticus in 1.14, and more obviously the first appearance in 1.12 of Hispulla, wife of Corellius Rufus and probable relation of Calpurnia Hispulla, aunt of Calpurnia. Quite apart from Pliny's sense of tact towards his former mother-in-law and dead wife, Calpurnia is no doubt excluded also because Pliny did not want to intrude his own domestic and emotional life into 'the introductory books 1–3 with their serious, political, and masculine emphasis'.[95]

There is, however, one personal omission from Book 1 which is not reserved for later treatment *anywhere* in the collection. It was noted earlier that a series of letters in Book 1 comments on Pliny's *otium* or freedom from onerous employment. These letters correspond in time to the year 97, when Pliny held no public post (while the complaints of letter 1.10 on overwork correspond to 98 or later). One particular letter from this series invites closer attention in the post-Domitianic context of the book. In 1.9 Pliny complains of wasting time at Rome attending such elite mundanities as weddings and the witnessing of wills, and praises the leisure of life at his Laurentine villa: *o rectam sinceramque uitam! o dulce otium honestumque ac paene omni negotio pulchrius!*, 'what a true and genuine life, what sweet and honourable leisure, one might almost say, more attractive than occupation of any kind' (1.9.6). As noted by Hoffer (1999) 112, apparently this 'life of leisure stretches an indefinite extent into the past'. Cleverly erased, as a result, from both the book and the attention of its readers is any thought of the onerous public office which Pliny had demitted so very recently in 96, perhaps just before the death of Domitian (and the start of Book 1).[96] That post is prefect of the *aerarium militare* or military treasury. Pliny's

---

[95] Hoffer (1999) 233, who points out, too, that Pliny delays introduction of his career as a poet also until Book 4.

[96] The normal assumption is that Pliny held the originally triennial (Dio Cass. 55.25.2) post of prefect of the military treasury from the beginning of 94 to sometime in 96, somehow laying office down before the assassination of the emperor on 18 September of that year; see Sherwin-White (1966) 75, 768–9, Vidman *PIR*² P 490 (pp. 205–6). However, Birley (2000a) 14–16 holds out the possibility that Pliny occupied the post under Nerva.

tenure in this significant post under Domitian is known only from the great Comum inscription (*CIL* 5.5262),[97] and from an inscription set up by the citizens of Vercellae (*CIL* 5.5667): it is not mentioned at any point in the *Letters* (or indeed in the *Panegyricus*). Pliny's silence has naturally aroused suspicion. Syme, in fact, makes the fact that he held this post central to a demolition both of Pliny's narrative elsewhere in the *Letters* of imminent political dangers during the latter stages of Domitian's reign, and of Pliny's insistence at *Pan.* 95.3–4 of a stalled career under the hated emperor.[98] Certainly a man whose career apparently flourished in the last tyrannical years of Domitian has no overwhelming need to draw attention to that fact in a book which celebrates political rebirth under a new emperor and which turns a friendly blind eye to contemporary chaos and instability. And letter 1.9 – with its emphasis on extended leisure and its attractions – partakes in Pliny's silence about his potentially awkward immediate past.

---

[97] For the inscription in full and further brief discussion of the treasury posting, see Appendix 1.

[98] Syme's classic piece of debunking at *RP* 7.564–5 is worth quoting in full:

> The praetor avows . . . one other action in this momentous year [93]. He visited Artemidorus in the suburbs when an edict removed philosophers from the city. That called for courage, so he avers. The thunderbolts had fallen in near vicinity to his person (3.11). Pliny survived unscathed. Indeed he prospered, for all his declaration that he now called a halt in his career (*Pan.* 95.3–4). The inscription contradicts. Pliny was one of the prefects put in charge of the *Aerarium Militare* (presumably from 94–96, inclusive). That fact discredits another allegation: the incriminating document from the hand of Mettius Carus (his opponent in the prosecution of Massa) found among state papers after the assassination of Domitian (7.27.14).

See also e.g. Shelton (1987) 129–32, Ludolph (1997) 44–9, Strobel (2003).

CHAPTER 2

Reading a book
Letters, *Book 6*

In the Introduction to this volume, we outlined a number of the ways in which Pliny's *Letters* may be approached, according to whether readers choose, for example, to focus on cycles of letters, or to read the whole collection, a single book, or selected favourites. In the body of Chapter 1 we adopted the strategy of reading the *Letters* for the story of Pliny's life, and focused particularly on Book 1. The concentration on a single book was justified by an observation made about the particular structure given by Pliny to the collection as a whole. Individual books, while displaying overlaps in time with their immediate fellows, cover chronological periods that are relatively distinct, and as a collection move forward in time from the aftermath of Domitian's assassination (in Book 1) to Pliny's tenure in Bithynia (in Book 10). Under this scheme individual books represent 'pools' of autobiographical time – into which contemporary events revealed later in the collection can be 'dropped'.

The present chapter likewise focuses on a single book; but more intensively, and for different reasons. As noted already, again at the beginning of Chapter 1, in this volume we value the reading of Pliny in sequential order, particularly at the level of the individual book (or the entire collection). Here, however, we do not analyse Book 6 with a view to reconstructing the story of Pliny's life in the period AD 106–7 (the conventional date for this book). Rather, we study the book as a whole for evidence that it invites appreciation as a piece of workmanship in its own right. This is despite the fact that Pliny's books of letters, like (for example) the poetry books of Martial, while clearly constructed and put together by the author, have usually been assumed to be largely devoid of meaning or design.[1] In Pliny's case, readers have perhaps taken too seriously the claim made in 1.1 that the letters have been ordered 'just as each came to hand' (a passage to which

---

[1] See Barchiesi (2005) 324, with analysis of Martial and Pliny at pp. 324–32. For a comprehensive introduction to the reading of ancient poetry books, with particular reference to Martial, see Höschele (2010) 8–68.

we shall return later). In Chapter 1 we have already seen that the claim of non-chronological ordering made in the very same sentence is somewhat misleading.

One incidental, but significant, result of the undervaluation of Pliny's books as individual entities has been the proliferation of anthologies of the *Letters*. In the late nineteenth and twentieth centuries, most readers who encountered Pliny normally did so in the medium of a 'Selected Letters' rather than in editions of single books. There have been several exceptions to this rule, such as J.E.B. Mayor's 1880 edition of Book 3, which in turn inspired John Henderson's 2002 monograph on the same book of Pliny.[2] And Sherwin-White was well aware of the character of individual books and connections between them – even if he did not allow these things prominence in the body of his commentary on Pliny (and indeed went on to produce a widely used anthology of Pliny's *Letters*).[3] But, for most readers approaching Pliny for the first time, the anthology has been the normal point of entry to his text.

In this context, it would prove of great interest if Pliny's books did show evidence of design. Any architecture uncovered might not only prove aesthetically meaningful in itself, but could also be taken as an indication that Pliny meant his books to be read as artistic units. That is to say, alongside the activity of selecting letters for particular attention – or, as in Chapter 1, scanning individual books for autobiographical material – we may find ourselves invited to situate letters within their immediate context as members of an artistically arranged series with a meaningful structure and beginning and end. As others have argued in the analogous case of Martial, the individual items which make up a book perhaps offer up their full meaning only when read within the context which the author arranged for them.[4]

---

[2] For other attempts to read Pliny's books as artistic or thematic entities, see e.g. Radicke (1997) on Book 3, Fitzgerald (2007a) on Book 7, Bernstein (2008a) on Book 8, and above all Ludolph (1997) on Book 1 (cf. Hoffer (1999)).

[3] See especially Sherwin-White (1966) 27–50, 65–9; for the anthology, see Sherwin-White (1969a). The edition of Book 10 produced by Williams (1990) excludes the opening fourteen 'private' letters to Trajan.

[4] See Lorenz (2004) 256–7, citing Fowler (1995). Martial is a particularly good parallel for Pliny, since he displays a marked fondness for constructing cycles of thematically related items, and for allowing subtle connections between adjacent pieces which otherwise differ strongly in content. For the importance of cycles within Martial, after Barwick (1958), see e.g. Lorenz (2004) 256–7, Fitzgerald (2007b) 107, with further reading at 221 n. 1. For similar cycles in Pliny Book 6, including series of letters on Calpurnia, Trajan and the trials of provincial governors, see below. For subtle connections between adjacent items in Martial, see Lorenz (2004) 261–2, 265 etc.; for parallels in Pliny, see Marchesi (2008) 26–52.

As a test case for the discovery of significant design in Pliny, we have chosen Book 6. This is a unit full of letters that are well known, e.g. for the light they shed on Pliny's domestic life (as in the two letters to his wife Calpurnia, 6.4 and 6.7) or for their narration of a historical event (as in the two 'Vesuvius' letters, 6.16 and 6.20). As a result, letters from this book have tended to be excerpted for use in the anthologies of Pliny's letters mentioned earlier, rather than read within the surrounds of Book 6. By returning these and other letters to their original context, we aim to demonstrate the critical advantages to be gained from reading Pliny's letters 'by the book'. We should add that we have chosen this particular book also because, while much of the collection – and indeed the present volume – obsesses about *otium* and its problems of time management, Book 6 is Pliny's *negotium* book *par excellence*. Here we see Pliny in the mode for which he cared most fervently: as consular orator, doyen of Rome's courts.[5] (Pliny's *otium* book *par excellence* – Book 7 – will be the object of separate study in Chapter 6.[6])

In the opening two sections of the chapter, we uncover a symmetry between the opening and closing sequences of letters in Book 6, and argue that this newly discovered patterning constitutes evidence of a deliberate design for the book and – as such – an invitation to read the book as an artistic product. In the following section we pause to look at other ways of reading Pliny's letters. We point out that clues provided by the ancient 'indices' to Pliny's books suggest that respect for reading single letters in isolation goes back to antiquity itself; but that the same indices also affirm the importance placed on the ordering and unity of individual books of letters. In the fourth section, we begin to focus on Book 6 as a whole and look at the range of correspondents addressed by Pliny here,[7] at the contemporary context for the letters (in AD 106–7) and at the ways in which Pliny makes the book distinct from its fellows, particularly from Books 5 and 7. In the next section – the heart of the chapter – we offer a reading of the first half of Book 6, particularly looking out for significant connections between letters, along with meaningful juxtapositions, specific thematic emphases, and formally or informally sustained internal narratives. In the sixth and final section of the chapter we concentrate on a series of letters strung out across Book 6 which, as a loosely connected cycle, do much to

---

[5] For Book 10 as another significant unit of *negotium*, see Chapter 8.

[6] In what follows, many of the issues raised at the level of the individual book will reappear in Chapter 8 when we turn our attention to the reading and (especially) re-reading of the entire collection as an artistic production.

[7] For a catalogue of the contents and addressees of letters in Book 6, see Appendix 2.

give the book both point and character. The goal of the chapter as a whole is a deeper appreciation of Pliny's consummate skill as a literary artist.

THE DISCOVERY OF SYMMETRY: READING FROM THE END OF BOOK 6

In attempting to read Book 6 as an artistic unit, it must be admitted straightaway that critical emphasis on the ancient book as aesthetic entity – particularly on the poetry book – has not always proven benign in its effects. Alessandro Barchiesi has written on Latin scholarship of the 1970s and 1980s and its 'search for the perfect book', arguing persuasively that such scholarship, with its drive for geometric perfection, has served to distort our understanding of Augustan poetry. Horace, for example, is clearly aware of the possibilities of the book unit, but also seeks to foster 'performative autonomy' for each of his odes.[8] Later in this chapter, in fact, we shall uncover ancient evidence for ways in which Pliny's collection allows a similar autonomy to individual letters. Yet, for now, we toss critical caution to one side and argue for a species of geometry in Pliny. Whether our 'perfect' Plinian book serves to distort the letters of Book 6 to the same extent as the schemes inflicted on the poetry books of Horace or Propertius, we leave to the reader to judge.

The fourth letter from the end of Book 6 (6.31) provides an account of Pliny's stay at Trajan's villa near Centum Cellae on the coast not far north of Rome, where he serves as a member of a panel which hears a number of trials alongside Trajan himself. No reader of this letter will have any reason to think back to the numerical fourth letter of the same book, where Pliny writes to the ill Calpurnia as she convalesces in Campania (6.4). In the third letter from the end (6.32), Pliny announces his intention to provide a correspondent's daughter with a dowry. This letter has its own links with 6.26, where Pliny writes to another *amicus* on the marriage of his daughter. However, gifts of any kind conveyed specifically on women are rare enough in the correspondence to prove memorable, and the reader might think back to 6.3, where Pliny discusses the gift of a farm to his old nurse and arranges for the addressee Verus to take better care of the property. Nevertheless, there are no strong verbal links between 6.32 and 6.3, and the reader may find little significance, as yet, in the connection between them. In 6.33, the penultimate letter of the book, Pliny writes to Voconius Romanus on his recent speech *pro Attia Viriola*, where Pliny

---

[8] Barchiesi (2005) 320–1, with references to further literature; cf. Lorenz (2004) 259 on Martial.

took up the cause of a daughter recently disinherited by her elderly father almost immediately after his remarriage.⁹ The epistle opens with exuberant quotation from Vergil and the declaration that Pliny's speech is perhaps his greatest ever:

'Tollite cuncta' inquit 'coeptosque auferte labores!' seu scribis aliquid seu legis, tolli auferri iube et accipe orationem meam ut illa arma diuinam (num superbius potui?), re uera ut inter meas pulchram; nam mihi satis est certare mecum. (6.33.1)

'Throw your tasks aside, off with your works begun!' Whether you are reading or writing, 'throw it aside', 'off with it', is the order, and take in hand *my speech*, divine like those arms of Vulcan (would it be possible to speak more boastfully?). Well, in sober truth, an excellent one for a production of mine, and it is enough for me to compete with myself.

As an inheritance dispute the case was tried, as Pliny goes on to tell us, at a special session of the Centumviral court where all four panels of jurors combined to hear the case (6.33.3). Here the reader receives a strong prompt to think back to the second letter of the book, where the death of Regulus, the former leading orator of the Centumviral court, is announced:¹⁰

Soleo non numquam in iudiciis quaerere M. Regulum; nolo enim dicere desiderare . . . sed utcumque se habent ista, bene fecit Regulus quod est mortuus: melius, si ante. (6.2.1, 4)

Not infrequently I find myself looking out for M. Regulus in our law courts; though I could not say I longed for him. . . . But, however all this may be, Regulus did well to die, and he would have done better if he had died sooner.

The death of Pliny's greatest rival in the Centumviral courts in the second letter of the book is matched in the book's penultimate letter by a report of Pliny's 'greatest ever speech' delivered in those same courts. This is hardly a coincidence. Indeed, the barb could hardly be more pointed: rhetoric in Rome's most prestigious public court, specifically Plinian rhetoric, reaches new levels of brilliance following the death of its former (and, according to Pliny, deeply compromised) doyen.¹¹

---

⁹ For a possible connection between Attia Viriola and Trajan (himself an important feature of Book 6), see Carlon (2009) 113, 132–4.

¹⁰ For Pliny's rivalry with Regulus in the Centumviral court, cf. 1.5.4–7, 4.7.4–5. For Regulus' leading position in that court under Domitian, cf. Mart. 6.38, and see Syme (1958) 101ff. For the start of Pliny's engagement with Regulus already in Book 1, see above pp. 31–2.

¹¹ In a repetition of the contrast between Plinian optimism and Tacitean pessimism already glimpsed in Chapter 1, Pliny's verdict here can be set over against the gloomy assessment of the worth of oratory in this same court put into the mouth of Maternus at Tac. *Dial.* 40.2; cf. Marchesi (2008) 133–4. (Note that one of the other characters in this work, Messalla, is a half-brother of Regulus; cf. *Dial.* 15.1.) For Pliny's dialogue with the *Dialogus*, see Murgia (1985), Hoffer (1999) 175–6, Marchesi

Furthermore, the legal issue at the heart of letter 6.33 – a marriage in old age which provokes the disinheritance of a daughter (6.33.2) – will remind the reader of the living Regulus' own intention, announced as recently as Book 4, to remarry in old age. That declaration had elicited lavish disgust from Pliny (4.2.6–8).

The fact that 6.2 and 6.33 are placed in mirror position at opposite ends of the book – allied to the now significant observation that letters on gifts to women are found in third position also at either end of the book – should motivate the reader of the book's final letter to be on the lookout for links with letter 6.1. The final letter offers congratulations to one Maximus for putting on a gladiatorial show in memory of his wife, and ends with a note of commiseration about the late arrival of the African panthers for the event. This is arresting, as Pliny rarely takes an interest in the details of public spectacles, and is indeed more likely to express hostility (4.22, 9.6). The motivation for including this letter is clearly Ciceronian: Sherwin-White (1966) 401 notes 'the parallels with the letters of Cicero and Caelius about beasts for aedilician games, *ad Fam.* 2.11.2, 8.8.10, 8.9.3'.[12] This is all significant in itself of course, since Cicero is a key figure for Pliny; see Chapter 3.

That Book 6 also opens with a strong Ciceronian epistolary motif has been less obvious to readers – in part, perhaps, because of an unwillingness to entertain the idea of a Pliny who plays on the names of his addressees. Readers of the immediately preceding book will be aware that Pliny has recently made the long trip to his home town of Comum (5.7, 5.11, 5.14), and the opening words of 6.1 announce Pliny's return from the Transpadane regions (*Quamdiu ego trans Padum... postquam ego in urbe*, 'so long as I was on the other side of the Po... but now that I am in Rome', 6.1.1). The letter goes on to report that Pliny now misses his addressee even more keenly, and he asks that the latter (who is at his estates in Picenum) follow him to Rome. The addressee here is in fact Pliny's old friend Calestrius Tiro: a circumstance which allows a witty allusion to the Ciceronian Tiro via the deployment of some notably passionate language about missing the absent addressee. Such language is not uncharacteristic of Pliny (cf. e.g. 6.26), but a little surprising in reference to a correspondent in whom Pliny has shown no interest since letter 1.12.[13] Note particularly:

(2008) 97–143, Edwards (2008), Johnson (2010) 63–73, Whitton (2012), also Appendix 3. For the *Dialogus* in its context, see Dominik (2007), Goldberg (2009).

[12] See further Marchesi (2008) 225.

[13] For Calestrius Tiro, see further Chapter 5. For conventions of naming in the collection, see Appendix 2.

... ipsa loca in quibus esse una solemus acrius me tui commonent ... **desiderium** absentium nihil perinde ac uicinitas acuit ... eripe me huic tormento. ueni, aut ego illuc unde inconsulte properaui reuertar ...

... the very places where we are usually together bring you more keenly to mind ... nothing sharpens longing for absent friends so much as proximity ... deliver me from this torture. Come, or else I shall return to the place I rashly hurried from ...

Pliny is arguably creating a reminiscence of Book 16 of the *ad Familiares*, where sorely missing the Ciceronian Tiro is a dominant theme of the opening letters of the book. The opening letter in modern editions of *Fam.* 16 – in fact the third letter in the original manuscript order (see below p. 52) – gives the general tone of the correspondence:[14]

Paulo facilius putaui posse me ferre **desiderium** tui, sed plane non fero et, quamquam magni ad honorem nostrum interest quam primum ad urbem me uenire, tamen peccasse mihi uideor qui a te discesserim ... (16.1.1)

I thought I could bear the longing for you quite easily, but plainly I cannot bear it; and although it is highly important, in view of the honour I have in prospect, to reach Rome as soon as possible, still I think it wrong to have left your side ...

The context is Cicero's return to Rome in 50 BC from Cilicia, and he writes en route to Tiro, who has been left behind ill at Patrae. The theme of how much Cicero misses Tiro as he returns to Rome is then repeated throughout the sequence of letters which opens *Fam.* 16. Pliny, it can be argued, has skilfully mapped onto his own life a return to Rome which also includes a passionate longing to see (his) Tiro again.[15]

Some missing Ciceronian panthers at the end of Book 6 have motivated the discovery of a sorely missed Ciceronian Tiro at its outset; Pliny's best ever speech in the Centumviral courts in the book's penultimate letter is

---

[14] Cf. also Cic. *Fam.* 16.1.3 *nos ita te desideramus ut amemus. amor ut ualentem uideamus hortatur, desiderium ut quam primum*, 'I miss you like one who loves you. Love urges that I see you restored to health, longing that it be as soon as possible.'

[15] Pliny's persistent punning on the names of his addressees is a subject which deserves separate study. For a suggested reference to the Ciceronian Tiro via the Plinian counterpart in letter 9.5, see Beard (2002) 124 n. 67; cf. Henderson (2002a) 212 n. 32 on 3.6. Cf. also 1.6.2 (to Tacitus on the stimulating effects of silence), 1.9 (to Fundanus on Pliny's *fundus*, 'estate'), 1.18 (to a notably anxious Tranquillus: Hoffer (1999) 213), 3.16 (to Nepos on the *neptis*, 'granddaughter' of Arria), 3.21 (to Priscus on the *mos antiquus*, 'ancient custom', adopted by Pliny), 7.3 (to Praesens on his absence from Rome), and Marchesi (2008) 102, 250 (various examples of punning on Secundus). A particularly complex example is found in 4.27: Pliny writes to Pompeius **Falco** about the poetry of Sentius **Augurinus** – in a book where Pliny has announced his own rise to an augurship (4.8) – and where Augurinus' own poetry is about Pliny himself, but C. Plinius **Secundus** says he has forgotten the ***secundus uersus***, 'second verse'. For ancient interest in names and their potential significances, 'even in the highest genres of literature', see Woodman and Martin (1996) 491–3.

found to match the death of his greatest rival in the same courts in letter 6.2; and gifts conveyed on women can be discovered in third position at either end. The symmetry here is presented in an understated manner, and receives only delicate signposting; but its presence is unmistakable.

THE SIGNIFICANCE OF SYMMETRY: RE-READING THE BOOK

Thematic symmetry at the opening and close of a book of letters, such as that found in Pliny Book 6, is not without precedent in pre-existing collections. The editors of Cicero's letters to Atticus gave some thought to the beginnings and endings of books, as for example in Book 3, where the first and last letters, in a species of 'ring composition', use similar language to reinforce the shared theme of longing for reunion with Atticus during Cicero's months of exile.[16] Those with immediate control over their own material might accomplish even stronger effects, such as Seneca's deliberate framing of the opening book of his philosophical correspondence.[17] More thoroughgoing symmetry can be detected in Horace *Epistles* 1, whereby the first and nineteenth poems are linked by their joint address to Maecenas, while the second and eighteenth are similarly both addressed to Lollius.[18] The presence of similar artistic patterning in Pliny's sixth book perhaps ought not to surprise us, at least if we have picked up the signal given in the very first letter of Book 1. Here, as suggested in the final chapter of this book, Pliny alludes to Ovid's self-undermining claim to the random ordering of his *Epistulae ex Ponto* in such a way as to convey to the astute reader the message that Pliny's own assertion of the artless disposition of letters is also likely to be entirely misleading (*collegi . . . ut quaeque in manus uenerat*, 'I collected [them] . . . just as each came to hand', 1.1.1; cf. Ov. *Pont.* 3.9.53 *postmodo conlectas utcumque sine ordine iunxi*, 'later I collected [the letters] and put them together somehow, without order').[19]

Nevertheless, one critic has acutely observed that 'it is remarkable how seldom such [symmetrical] schemes illuminate the most salient questions about the book[s]'.[20] But this misses a much broader point, at least so far as Pliny is concerned. For Pliny's books, as suggested at the outset of the chapter, have generally not been credited with much in the way of

---

[16] Beard (2002) 126–7.

[17] See Richardson-Hay (2006) 23–9 on the thematic and verbal interactions between letters 1 and 12, embracing the topics of time, freedom and death.

[18] See further Mayer (1994) 48–51. Cf. Giannotti (2001) 30–1 on Sidon. *Epist.* 3.

[19] For the argument, see Marchesi (2008) 20–1.   [20] Hutchinson (1984) 99; cf. Hutchinson (2008).

significance. However, patterning in the frames to Book 6 would appear
to act as a signal that this is 'an aesthetically organized collection that is
more than the sum of its parts, where meaning resides as much in the
interrelationship of the [letters] as in individual [letters]'.[21] We adapt here
the words of Kathryn Gutzwiller from a landmark collection on the new
epigrams of Posidippus. What proved particularly interesting about these
epigrams was their discovery in a format that constitutes the earliest Greek
poetry book currently known. Immediately a number of questions presented themselves: did Posidippus himself or a later editor create the book?
In either case, does the arrangement of the epigrams within the book possess aesthetic significance? Gutzwiller herself confidently argued that 'The
more clearly and extensively the collection promotes recognizable themes,
to the greater degree that structural arrangement emphasizes these themes,
and the more frequently these thematic messages appear in key epigrams
at points of opening, closing, and transition, then the more likely we are
dealing with a purposely constructed, or author-edited, poetry book.'[22]
The situation in Pliny is strongly analogous: the structural arrangement of
Book 6, in its opening and closing letters, is designed to draw attention
not only to the importance of the Ciceronian model of letter-writing; but
also to the theme of Pliny's flourishing legal career, via the symmetrical
placing of letters on the death of Regulus and the renaissance of oratory in
the Centumviral courts. This theme, as will be seen at the chapter's end, is
perhaps the dominant feature of Book 6.

In sum, the symmetry on display at *Letters* 6.1–3 and 32–4 is important
largely for the broader hint it provides, namely that the letters are offered
for consumption as books. In particular, we emphasize that the emergence
of the symmetry of Book 6 only at the book's end constitutes an invitation
to re-read, to look for significant order within the book. Later in the
chapter we will indeed adapt the perspective of the second- or third-time
reader, and read a sequence of letters from Book 6 with an eye to unity
and development. At any rate, the belated revelation of symmetry in Book
6 also parallels the larger arrangement of the nine-book collection as a
whole, where the appearance of a symmetry between the last letter of the
collection and the first (9.40, 1.1) – as we will see in this volume's final
chapter – signals a fresh invitation to re-read the entire correspondence
with an eye to an artistic design.[23] (Likewise analogous is a feature of
the collection uncovered in Chapter 1, where we argued that letters in

---

[21] Gutzwiller (2005a) 288.   [22] Gutzwiller (2005a) 289.
[23] For an important attempt to theorize the process of re-reading in linear order, applied to the elegist
Tibullus, see Lee-Stecum (1998).

Books 9 and 10 containing delayed autobiographical information acted as invitations to re-read Book 1 in a new light.)

Nevertheless, for all that, it is worth underlining once more the fact that Pliny has chosen a relatively delicate method of signposting the importance of the individual book within his collection. He has evidently decided not to fracture the documentary appearance of the collection more emphatically, for example by referring to the progress of his books. This is a strategy more freely adopted by poets such as Martial, who comments in epigram 1.16 on the building of a book out of miscellaneous items.[24] Later letter-writers use it too, such as Sidonius Apollinaris, who models his nine-book collection explicitly on that of Pliny, and within the text of his letters frequently comments on their status as a (growing) collection of books.[25] Pliny evidently refused the idea of such open metaliterary comment, although it is arguable that he makes such comments implicitly.[26] In particular, it is hard to resist the conclusion that Pliny's discussion of his books of poetry is a way of broaching similar issues thrown up by his letters, particularly in letter 8.21 where he betrays an acute sense of the difference between the reading of selected pieces and the reading of an entire book.[27]

BOOKS VS ANTHOLOGIES: THE ANCIENT 'INDICES' TO PLINY'S LETTERS

In Chapter 1 we paused briefly to indicate that there were ways to read Book 1 other than for the story of Pliny's life. Similarly here, we admit – despite the evidence now uncovered for artistic design within Book 6 – that we cannot insist that Pliny's letters be read only within the context of their original books. Given the variety of approaches to the *Letters* in the present book, it would (at the very least) be inconsistent to do so. In fact, before exploring the reading of a single book of Pliny, it is time to consider evidence which suggests that the collection, as it existed in antiquity, allowed a measure of autonomy to individual letters. In other words, Pliny's *Letters* might very well cater to anthologizers, as well as to

---

[24] On this epigram, see Fitzgerald (2007b) 88–93.

[25] Cf. esp. Sid. Apoll. 9.1.1; also 4.10.2, 5.1, 7.12.1, 7.18, 8.1, 8.16, 9.11, 9.16.

[26] See Barchiesi (2005) 330–1 on 9.40.1 *scribis pergratas tibi fuisse litteras meas, quibus cognouisti quemadmodum in Tuscis otium aestatis exigerem,* 'You write that you found my letters very pleasing, from which you learnt how I spend my leisure time in summer at my Tuscan villa.' In this final letter of the nine-book collection, it is hard not to widen the reference of the addressee's pleasure in letters to Pliny's entire epistolary corpus; see also Chapter 8.

[27] Cf. 2.5.10, and see further Chapter 8 for the significance of letter 8.21. For Pliny's consciousness of the book as the privileged medium for poetry, see Höschele (2010) 46–52.

readers who pick up on the signals of the importance of the book. That evidence is to be found in the ancient 'indices' (so called) to Pliny.[28] Yet, as we shall soon see, the very same evidence also points to the importance of Pliny's books as artistic products.

Indices to individual books of Pliny are preserved in one branch of his manuscript tradition, and may originally have consisted of the *nomen* and *cognomen* of the addressee plus the opening words of each epistle.[29] More specifically, indices for Books 1 to 5 survive in a ninth-century manuscript,[30] but their existence can be traced back to the late fifth century, since one survives for Book 3 in the famous late-antique manuscript preserved in fragmentary form as New York, Pierpont Morgan Library M.462.[31] This index, which prefaces the book, consists of a list of the addressees' *nomina* and *cognomina* and the opening three or four words of each epistle, where the names transcribed in red ink alternate with the opening words transcribed in black ink on the line below (and indented to the right), in sequence from first letter to last.[32] This layout allows a reader to pick out individual epistles with relative ease,[33] and so potentially provides an alternative way of reading the letters other than in a linear fashion from a book's first epistle to last.[34]

It is perfectly possible that these indices are a product of someone working on the epistles after Pliny. John Bodel argues, more persuasively, that they are ultimately the product of the author himself.[35] Certainly Pliny will have been familiar with the epistolary prose prefaces to the first four books of Statius' *Siluae*, where the author effectively catalogues the running order of his poems and associated subjects and addressees.[36] If the indices

[28] Given the nature of these paratextual features, 'tables of contents' might be a better term; for a study of tables of contents in Latin literature, see Riggsby (2007).

[29] For these indices, see, in addition to the items cited below, Appendix 2 and Gibson (2011b). For an account of Pliny's complex manuscript tradition and its separate nine-book and ten-book branches, see Reynolds (1983) 316–22.

[30] For a complete transcription, see Robbins (1910) 476–8.   [31] See Reynolds (1983) 317–18.

[32] See the annotated transcription and facsimile of Lowe and Rand (1922) 24–5, Plates II–III. Other methods of distinguishing individual letters were available: the index for e.g. Book 4 preserved in a medieval ms. numbers the letters in sequence; see Robbins (1910) 477.

[33] And so allows for easy excerption of favourites? The rediscovered Posidippus collection has done much to alert attention to the frequency with which readers designed their own 'unofficial' collections of texts; see e.g. Barchiesi (2005) 337–8, Johnson (2005), Krevans (2005), Krevans (2007). For evidence of excerption in Pliny's mss., see Reynolds (1983) 318–19, 321–2, also Stout (1954) 57, Mynors (1963) xi–xii. For the transmission of Pliny's letters, see Appendix 3.

[34] Martial attributes a similar function to the *tituli* which preface each item in Book 13 (13.3.7–8; cf. 14.2), although it is evident that the book also responds to a linear reading; see Höschele (2010) 62–5.

[35] Bodel (unpublished), Chapter 2.

[36] On Statius' prose prefaces and their antecedents, see Coleman (1988) 53–5, Johannsen (2006) 240–301, Newlands (2009). For the parallels between Statius' epistolary prefaces and Pliny's cover letters,

do go back to Pliny, then we have here evidence that the author catered for readers interested in individual letters as autonomous texts. If, on the other hand, they are the product of late-antique readers of Pliny, then we see that the desire to read the letters in this fashion developed early. And it must be admitted that some letters do respond well to excerption (as we shall see in our survey of Book 6 below). Many are complete enough in themselves, and do not cry out for the support of others in the collection, at least in order to make a basic kind of sense.[37]

Yet, for all that, the indices of Pliny's books do not promote one style of reading alone. For not only do indices allow readers quick access to individual letters, but they also encourage the preservation of the order of the book for future readers. More importantly, the indices, by listing each letter in a book from first to last, offer immediate visual evidence and confirmation of the importance of the book as a unit of authorial composition and audience consumption. In sum, an index visually encapsulates the tension between the desire to pick out individual letters for reading in isolation, and the necessity of seeing individual letters as part of a larger literary whole.[38] In the present chapter, encouraged by the additional discovery of artistic design in the opening and closing sequences of Book 6, we strongly emphasize the importance of that larger literary unit. Nevertheless, later instalments in this volume, such as Chapter 7, pick out some of the anthologists' favourites (albeit without reading them in complete isolation from the book context), or – as in the case of Chapter 5 – experiment with reading for sequences of letters joined by a shared addressee.

BOOK 6: CORRESPONDENTS, CHARACTER AND DATES

It is time to turn our focus to Book 6 as a whole. We begin with some basic information on the size, addressees and distinctive emphases of this book (and, later, its dates).

With the exception of the massive Book 10 (58 OCT pages, 121 letters), the individual books of Pliny's collection are all roughly the same length

---

see Janson (1964) 106–7 and Pagán (2010) (who emphasizes particular links with letter 3.5 and its list of works written by the Elder), also Morello (2003) 196–201. If Ovid produced an index for his *Epistulae ex Ponto*, this would give extra point to his closing declaration in Book 3: *Musa mea est index nimium quoque uera malorum*, 'My poetry is only too true an index to my troubles' (3.9.49). For the significance of this passage in relation to Pliny, see Chapter 8.

[37] Cf. Ash (2003) 211–13.

[38] Cf. the similar tensions between reading the whole and searching for individual items introduced by the 'index' or *summarium* which prefaces the Elder Pliny's *Natural History* as Book 1; see Doody (2010) 92–131. See also the highly suggestive remarks of Krevans (2007) 138–41 on comparable tensions evident in ancient collections of epigrams, also Fitzgerald (2007b) 92, 105 on Martial.

(i.e. around 30–34 OCT pages apiece), although the number of letters within each book varies between twenty (Book 2) and forty (Book 9). Book 6 contains thirty-four letters and addresses twenty-seven different correspondents.[39] All the addressees are male, with the exception of letters 6.4 and 6.7, which are addressed to Pliny's wife. Just over three-quarters of those addressed receive a single letter in Book 6; one addressee, Tacitus, is privileged with three letters (6.9, 6.16 and 6.20), while five others – including two close relatives – receive two letters apiece.[40] The majority of these favoured addressees are prominent elsewhere in the correspondence, with the exception of Calpurnia, who receives only a single further letter – although she is the subject of numerous letters to her grandfather and aunt and reappears in the final letters of Book 10.

Such figures – rather indigestible by themselves – suggest something of the 'centre' and 'periphery' of Pliny's mass of correspondents. In particular, it is worth making the point that Pliny's favoured addressees – as elsewhere in the collection – are a mixture of close personal or family connections, alongside the obscure, and the great of the day with whom Pliny had a particularly warm relationship. Neither Book 6 nor any of its fellows is addressed primarily to the luminaries of the day; rather they offer a spectrum of the members of the senatorial and equestrian or local elites (where Pliny is rarely outshone).[41] This is not to say that Pliny's Book 6 lacks for addressees of standing,[42] and several important figures of the day emerge as addressees, including the aristocratic and well-connected Julius Servianus (6.26),[43] the eminent Minicius Fundanus (6.6) and the emerging young aristocrat Ummidius Quadratus (6.29).

If Book 6 emerges as fairly typical in many respects of Pliny's units of correspondence, then it also clear that Pliny has gone to some lengths to make the book thematically distinctive, at least so far as it is compared with Books 5 and 7.[44] For example, as hinted earlier, Pliny's announcement in the

---

[39] Sherwin-White (1966) 65–9 on 'Selection and Distribution of Correspondents' remains essential reading; cf. Birley (2000a) 17–21. Note that over half of the letters in Books 1–9 are addressed to just twenty-eight correspondents; see Birley (2000a) 19.

[40] The family members are Calpurnius Fabatus (6.12, 6.30), Pliny's grandfather-in-law, and Calpurnia. The other recipients of a pair of letters are the obscure equestrian Cornelius Ursus (6.5, 6.13) plus two intimates who will – along with Tacitus – receive close attention in Chapter 5: Calestrius Tiro (6.1, 6.22) and Voconius Romanus (6.15, 6.33).

[41] For development of this point, see Syme (1958) 87–8, *RP* 5.463–5 [= (1985a) 345–7].

[42] Of the book's twenty-seven addressees, up to eleven (and possibly twelve if the Maximus of 6.34 is included) are of senatorial rank, of which group perhaps seven had reached the consulship by the date of the termination of the book (106–7).

[43] On this important figure (and his role in Pliny's de-emphasis on the military aspect of Roman society), see further Chapter 5.

[44] On the varied colour and tones of Books 5–7 as a sequence, see esp. Sherwin-White (1966) 48–9.

opening letter of Book 6 of a return to Rome from the Transpadane regions caps a sequence of letters in Book 5, where Pliny first involves himself in the affairs of Comum from afar (5.7, 5.11) before making a journey there in 5.14. That letter ends with the need to make preparations for the long journey back to Rome, and that notion is sustained, at least in a purely thematic sense, in the formally unrelated letter 5.21, where Pliny writes from outside Rome to a correspondent who awaits Pliny's return to town (5.21.1). Letter 6.1 settles the writer firmly back in Rome, and this is a prelude to a shift in the scenery for Book 6. For here there are no letters which are either set in or envisage a scenario in Comum (with one exception[45]) – and indeed no mention of the Tuscan villa 150 miles north of Rome which had appeared so prominently in letter 5.6. Rather the focus moves noticeably southwards, particularly to Campania.[46] The distinctiveness of the geographical focus of Book 6 is further confirmed in Book 7, where Comum makes a return to prominence. Here is recorded the journey of Calestrius Tiro up through Italy on the way to his provincial appointment in Baetica and diversion – at Pliny's request – to Comum in order to officiate at the manumission of some slaves belonging to Calpurnius Fabatus (7.16, 7.23, 7.32).[47] Pliny does not travel there himself in Book 7, but becomes involved in the management of his own estates there and the affairs of the locality (7.11, 7.14, 7.18). After an absence in Book 6, then, Comum as physical backdrop returns with greater force in Book 7, which in turn allows the focus on Campania and neighbouring regions in Book 6 to emerge even more distinctly.[48]

Despite the geographical focus on the Roman playground of Campania, Book 6 – with attractive paradox – is dominated, as noted earlier, by *negotium* (and Book 7 by its polar opposite). The series of letters on senatorial business, the courtroom and associated 'public affairs' so prominent in Book 6[49] slows to a trickle in Book 7 (7.6, 7.10). Not unconnected is Book 7's emphasis on the theme of unwanted distraction by *negotia* (e.g. 7.2,

---

[45] The one letter to involve Comum (6.24) sees Pliny relate a story told to him at an unspecified date while sailing on the lake there. For Pliny's relationship with Comum, see Appendix 3.

[46] In 6.4 the ill Calpurnia is found recuperating in Campania (and again at 6.7); in 6.10 and 6.31 Pliny is on the coast not far north of Rome at Alsium and Centum Cellae respectively; in 6.14, Pliny arranges a visit to Formiae in Latium; letters 6.16 and 6.20 revisit the scenes on the Campanian coast of AD 79; in 6.18, Pliny agrees to act as advocate for the Picenum town of Firmum; in 6.25, Pliny is asked to intervene in the case of someone who has gone missing in Umbria not far from Rome; letter 6.28 relates the visit of Pliny to a friend's villa in Campania; and letter 6.30 deals with the management of an estate in Campania.

[47] On this sequence of letters, see Chapter 5.

[48] The Campanian focus of Book 6 is allowed to continue (without emphasis) into the early letters of Book 7; cf. 7.3.1, 7.5.

[49] Cf. e.g. 6.2, 6.5, 6.6, 6.9, 6.11, 6.13, 6.18, 6.19, 6.22, 6.23, 6.27, 6.29, 6.31, 6.33.

7.15, 7.30) and concomitant focus on the employment of leisure (7.3, 7.9, 7.13); see further the section on Book 7 in our study of *otium* (Chapter 6). Book 6, by contrast, contains many examples of affairs which in other contexts might be described as 'distractions', including not only court cases and senatorial business or elections, but a betrothal, a dowry, and issues of the management of estates and requests for aid. However, in the context of Book 6 Pliny prefers to work his way equably through them and to describe them to his correspondents, not of course without complaint (6.4.1, 6.18.1). Perhaps negative comments in Book 7 on 'distractions' serve the further function of making it clear to the reader that Pliny will not repeat here the subject matter of Book 6. This contrast between the books is replayed in the literary arena, where Book 7 devotes a series of memorable letters to specifically literary matters[50] – the province of most concern to a man focused on *otium* – while Book 6 is noticeably lighter in this regard.[51]

In Book 7, furthermore, Domitian casts a long shadow,[52] while in Book 6 we rarely look back to the Domitianic era after the 'obituary' letter for Regulus at 6.2 (as if this itself were the dawn of a new age!).[53] Instead this is Trajan's book, and he is shown intervening *in absentia* to resolve senatorial matters (6.13, 6.19), before turning up in Italy to deal with a trial in person (6.22). The sequence continues with advice to a correspondent on what subject he as consul designate should include in his speech to the emperor (6.27), where 'the recent achievements of our illustrious emperor' – i.e. his new military successes – are highlighted as a felicitous subject (6.27.5). The sequence is crowned with a celebration of the splendour of the new regime and a sustained sojourn in the presence of Trajan himself in 6.31. The emperor's *humanitas* is emphasized (6.31.14–15), and the letter ends with a detailed description of the imperial harbour at Centum Cellae where, as Saylor (1972) suggests, the harbour is a metaphor for the bulwark of Trajan himself.[54] Book 5 also has relatively little to say about earlier

---

[50] Cf. e.g. 7.2, 7.4, 7.9, 7.12, 7.13, 7.17, 7.20, 7.25, 7.30, 7.33.

[51] Cf. 6.15, 6.16, 6.20, 6.18, 6.21, 6.33. Book 5, it may be noted, mixes literature and legal affairs with more equality than either Book 6 or Book 7.

[52] Letter 7.19 records the serious illness of Fannia – wife of Helvidius Priscus, daughter of Thrasea Paetus – previously exiled under Domitian; 7.27 relates an incident involving a threat to Pliny's life under Domitian; and 7.33 informs Tacitus of Pliny's role in the hazardous prosecution (with Herennius Senecio) of Baebius Massa, also under Domitian. On Pliny's association with these figures of the 'Stoic' opposition, see p. 28 n. 77.

[53] Domitian and other Bad Emperors appear briefly or by implication only at the end of 6.24 (where Fannia is mentioned), in a broad allusion at 6.27.3, and in a quotation from Thrasea Paetus at 6.29.1.

[54] Similarly two of Martial's books are characterized as especially 'imperial' (Books 5 and 8), although Pliny of course avoids the explicit marking adopted by the former in his prefatory poem or prose

times – certainly by comparison with Books 3 and 4 – but there is no concomitant emphasis on the figure of Trajan, who features only once (5.13.7–8).[55] Mentions of the emperor are similarly infrequent in Book 7, and he makes notable appearances only in letters 7.6 and 7.10 (on the trial of a Bithynian governor).[56]

The relative prominence of Trajan in Book 6 is related to the apparent date of the book. Trajan left Italy to conduct the first Dacian war in March 101, and returned to celebrate his triumph in December 102.[57] He was not to stay long and in June 105 left to prosecute the second Dacian war. The enemy leader Decebalus was dead before the end of 106 and Trajan returned to Rome before the summer of 107. (The victories would soon be celebrated on Trajan's famous column.) The conventionally accepted date for Book 6 is in fact 106–7, i.e. precisely during the period of Trajan's final victory in Dacia and subsequent return to Rome. In keeping with this, the series of Trajanic letters outlined above constructs a strong thematic sequence which rides on the back of a rather weakly suggested temporal sequence. Here the Emperor, at first apparently absent from Rome (6.5, 6.13, 6.19), returns to Italy to resume normal administration (6.22).[58] The sequence builds to a crescendo where Pliny – and the reader – find themselves ever closer to Trajan, finally to bask in the sunshine of his presence in a letter near the end of the book where his return from Dacia is explicitly marked (6.31.8–9). Nevertheless Pliny's attitude to the *princeps* throughout is optimistic and deferential, without servility or bombast. Pliny does not include a letter addressed, for example, to a fellow senator on the triumphant return of the *princeps* to Rome. Similar opportunities had been eschewed on Trajan's entry into Rome as emperor in autumn 99 (in Book 2), and on Trajan's triumphal return from the first Dacian war in 102 (in Book 3).[59] Arguably this is part of a deliberate strategy on Pliny's part – and one agreeable to many fellow members of the senatorial elite and even Trajan himself – of

---

introduction (Mart. 5.1, 8 *pref.*, 8.1). For a comparable 'zooming in' technique adopted by Martial in Book 5 in relation to the figure of the emperor, see Garthwaite (1998).

[55] For Domitian and tyranny in Book 5, cf. 5.1.5–6, 7–8, and rather more distantly 5.5 and 5.8.

[56] Some statistics on the frequency of the terms *Caesar* and *princeps* in reference to Trajan back up these impressions. Book 5: *princeps* 2 (5.13.7, 8), *Caesar* 0. Book 6: *princeps* 8 (6.2.4, 6.13.2, 6.19.3, 6.27.1, 2, 5; 6.31.2, 13), *Caesar* 11 (6.5.5, 6.22.2, 5; 6.31.1, 4, 5, 6, 8 *bis*, 11, 14). Book 7: *princeps* 3 (7.6.8, 10, 14), *Caesar* 3 (7.6.1, 6; 7.10.2). For Book 3 as also a unit in which Trajan is given prominence, see Henderson (2002a) 148–52.

[57] For the dating of events, cf. Appendix 1 and see *CAH* 11².109–13; for other versions and qualifications, see Sherwin-White (1966) 382, Bennett (2001) 102, Millar (2004a) 26, 34.

[58] On the date of 6.22, see Sherwin-White (1966) 381–2, 382.

[59] Cf. pp. 23–7 with n. 60 on the treatment of emperors in Books 1 and 2. For Pliny's strategy of virtual silence over the Dacian wars, see Syme, *RP* 6.142–9 [= (1964)].

downplaying the military element in Trajan's image in favour of emphasis on the *ciuilis princeps*. When Trajan does return in Book 6 it is to play his part in the legal and civil life of Rome and the empire (as also with his presiding role in the trial of Priscus before the senate in Book 2).[60]

Nevertheless, for all the satisfactory interplay between known events and thematic sequences in Book 6, letters which can be positively tied to 106–7 are in the minority in this book. Sherwin-White, a dating optimist, can discover no more than nine letters which display secure references to these years,[61] although even here some of the evidence is suggestive rather than conclusive.[62] However, as argued in Chapter 1, whatever the actual date of individual letters, Pliny has engineered a situation in which it is difficult for readers to resist the (alluringly painless) critical assumption that a book's formally undateable letters roughly share a date with the more firmly dateable members.

It is worth adding here an observation – more positively – on what the omission of dating evidence from two-thirds of the letters in the book allows Pliny to achieve. The omission of such evidence grants him the freedom to position, according to primarily artistic demands, those letters which are not part of an identifiable sequence. The result is that Pliny can – without disturbing the sensibilities of his readers – arrange many of his letters with the same freedom as an Augustan poet. By contrast, the Tiro letters of *ad Familiares* 16 (introduced earlier in this chapter) presented Cicero's readers with a temptation to re-order which they apparently could not resist. Arranged by their first editors in a distinct thematic rather than chronological order (as noted in Chapter 1, p. 15 n. 28), the letters were eventually repositioned by early modern editors in their 'proper' narrative order so that (for example) the third letter in the manuscripts became the first letter in printed editions, where it has assumed ever since the numeration 16.1.[63] The reasons are not far to seek, since numerous letters

---

[60] A Dacian 'triumph' letter is found at 10.14 – although in the book as a whole Pliny plays up the civil aspects of the emperor; see Noreña (2007) 258–61. For Pliny and Trajan, see Appendix 3.

[61] See Sherwin-White (1966) 36–7, who adds 'a place in this book fits twelve others very well'. By this is meant that some letters in Book 6 clearly take place after events referred to in preceding books (themselves not always securely dateable).

[62] Letter 6.31.8–9 implies that Trajan's *consilium* at Centum Cellae takes place after his return from Dacia, and the context appears to be summer in 6.31.15; hence an assumption – not beyond doubt – of a date of summer 107. Letter 6.10, with its reference to the tenth anniversary of the death of Verginius Rufus, is more firmly dated to 107. This letter refers to a stay at Alsium on the Tuscan coast and could be used to shore up the same date for the visit to Trajan's *consilium* further up the same coast; but, again, hardly beyond doubt (see further below on this letter). A date of 107 for letter 6.27 depends on the identification of the addressee with Vettenius Severus, suffect consul in May–August 107 (although other candidates are possible; see Birley (2000a) 100 s.v.).

[63] See Beard (2002) 131–2. Cf. more broadly Gibson (2012).

give some indication of dates and places of composition either within the body of the text or at the epistle's end (i.e. in the *adscriptio*).[64] As already hinted in Chapter 1, letters are thus often *identifiably* out of chronological sequence. Pliny made sure not to trouble his own readers with similar distractions,[65] and his books of letters have consequently retained the shape and order he designed for them.

RE-READING IN SEQUENCE: BOOK 6.1–17

Space does not allow a complete sequential reading of the entire book. Instead, we aim to cover a representative sample, reading the first half of the book in linear fashion.[66] In so doing we hope to see emerge the difference between reading letters in isolation and reading them in terms of the interrelations revealed with their immediate fellows. In the process the importance of Pliny's 'filler' letters – the 'insignificant' items normally omitted from anthologies – will become clear.[67] Naturally the strictly linear reading will be interrupted from time to time, in order to discuss links with letters which appear rather later in the book or elsewhere in the collection. In so doing, we adopt – as promised earlier – the perspective of the reader approaching the book for the second time or more, i.e. one who harbours expectations of artistic developments. Finally, we end with a detailed reading of the most significant 'cycle' within the book – the cycle focused on Pliny's legal career and the death of Regulus, which begins in 6.2 and ends in the penultimate letter of the book. Here the insistent focus on the linear reading of Book 6 will disappear, and there will emerge a difference between reading a letter within its immediate context and reading the same letter for connections with more widely spaced thematic fellows within a book.

The reader of the final three letters of Book 6 who has spotted the links with the three opening epistles will return to the first letter of the same book to be reminded that internal symmetry does not entail that the book look entirely inward and ignore its immediate predecessor:

---

[64] Roughly one-third of Cicero's surviving correspondence gives the co-ordinates of composition, dispatch or receipt of a letter, with reference to place and/or date (usually day and month, rarely year); see the comprehensive analysis of Rossi (2010) 34–122, who notes that such co-ordinates are most likely to be given by Cicero when on the move, also White (2010) 75–6.

[65] Cf. e.g. the avoidance of explicit markers of time at 4.13.1–3. For the rarity of dates within the collection, see Chapter 4 on the Vesuvius letters.

[66] Our model here is Lorenz (2004), esp. 259–60.

[67] The centrality of a 'filler' letter is the subject of Henderson (2002a), who argues for the neglected 3.6 as key to understanding the themes of Book 3.

So long as I was on the other side of the Po, and you were in Picenum, I missed you less [*minus te requirebam*]; but now that I am in Rome, while you are still in Picenum, I miss you a great deal more; whether it is that the very places [*ipsa loca*] where we are usually together bring you more keenly to my mind; or else that nothing sharpens longing for absent friends [*desiderium absentium*] so much as proximity . . . (6.1.1)

The book begins here by looking back to Pliny's journey to Comum in Book 5. But we also look forward into the heart of Book 6, since Pliny marks the importance of the central Italian location with a typically unobtrusive phrase (*ipsa loca*) which will recur in loaded contexts later in the book, both in reference to the former villa of Verginius Rufus at Alsium (*ipse mihi locus*, 6.10.1: quoted more fully below) and the emperor's villa at Centum Cellae (*locus ipse periucundus fuit. uilla pulcherrima cingitur . . .*, 'the place itself was particularly delightful. The loveliest of villas is surrounded . . .', 6.31.14–15).

Also programmatic is the phrase *desiderium absentium*, since the theme of separation and the desired return of an addressee bulks large in Book 6, particularly in the first ten letters. The motif of separation, of course, is fundamental to the epistolary genre; without it one usually has no reason to write a letter.[68] But in this opening suite of letters its cumulative weight is strong, and gathers its momentum from such repeated terms as *desiderium* and cognates, *requiro*, and the phrase *praecipue cupio esse*. The effect is to unite an otherwise thoroughly heterogeneous group of Plinian acquaintances. Thus Pliny misses Regulus in court – up to a point ('Not infrequently I find myself looking for M. Regulus in our law courts; though I could not say I longed for him [**desiderare**]', 6.2.1). Calpurnia receives two passionate letters lamenting her separation from Pliny in Campania (6.4.2–3, quoted below p. 57; **nos requiris** . . . *ad* **desiderium** *tui accendor*, 'you miss me . . . I am inflamed with a longing for you', 6.7.2). In 6.6 Fundanus, like Tiro in 6.1, is away and Pliny urgently desires his presence in Rome – although now for the immediate and practical purpose of aiding Pliny in the election of young Iulius Naso (*si quando nunc* **praecipue cuperem esse** *te Romae*, 'Now, if ever, I could wish you were in Rome', 6.6.1). In 6.10 it is Verginius Rufus, dead ten years now, who provokes desire for reunion in Pliny (*ipse mihi locus optimi illius et maximi uiri* **desiderium** *non sine dolore renouauit . . . illum animus illum oculi* **requirebant**, 'the sight of the place itself painfully renewed my longing for that great and noble man . . . my

---

[68] Cf. Trapp (2003) 1.

soul, my eyes looked for *him*', 6.10.1–2).[69] Significantly, however, the only person in Book 6 whose absence from Rome (6.13.2) is followed by a recorded arrival (6.22) is the leading citizen himself, Trajan. The emperor's exceptional status is subtly underlined.

If 6.1 and 6.2 share the theme of missing the 'absent', they also present a contrast. Pliny misses Tiro as an intimate friend, but he can hardly miss his dead rival Regulus in quite the same way: the difference is marked in the phrases *nolo enim dicere desiderare* (6.2.1) versus *desiderium absentium* (6.1.1). The second letter, which will be dealt with towards the end of the chapter as part of a cycle particular to Book 6, introduces themes which will undergo development in the book: the good government of Trajan (6.2.4), the pre-eminence of Pliny in the Centumviral courts (now that Regulus is gone forever), and the responsibilities of orators and judges (6.2.5–8).[70] It ends on an enigmatic note: 'Now, let us cast a glance at our households. Is all well in yours? In mine there is nothing new. For me, the blessings [*bona*] I enjoy are rendered more grateful by their continuance, while inconveniences [*incommoda*] are lightened by habit' (6.2.10). What are these 'blessings' and persisting 'inconveniences' in Pliny's life? This (characteristic) piece of imprecision from Pliny invites the reader to be on the lookout for domestic blessings and troubles in the letters to follow. The first candidate for Pliny's troubles in fact appears immediately in 6.3, where he writes to an unidentified Verus about the falling revenue and value of a farm donated by Pliny to his nurse. Another follows in 6.4, where Pliny writes to his young wife Calpurnia, recuperating in Campania from an unspecified illness, and laments that his *occupationes* in Rome do not allow him to join her.

If letter 6.2, as suggested above, belongs to a sequence which achieves special meaning within the context of Book 6, then letter 6.4 lies at the heart of a rather more complex set of interrelations which spread both forwards and backwards in the collection as a whole. The letter has a sequel within Book 6, where letter 6.7 is also addressed in tones of solicitude to the absent Calpurnia. In this way the two letters contribute to a special feature of Book 6, namely its remarkable number of internal sequels.[71] Letters 6.4 and 6.7,

---

[69] Such desire for the presence of the absent is not an obvious feature of Book 5, by contrast, although it does recur in more muted fashion at the beginning of Book 7, where Pliny again writes to Calpurnia (*desiderio tui tenear*, 'a longing for you possesses me', 7.5.1) and requests the company of Bruttius Praesens (7.3).

[70] On 6.2, see also Lefèvre (2009) 106–9.

[71] Cf. 6.5 and 6.13 (senatorial skirmishes over the prosecution of Varenus Rufus: both addressed to Cornelius Ursus), 6.6 and 6.9 (the candidature of Iulius Naso), 6.11 and 6.26 (the first appearance

nevertheless, belong to a larger cycle of letters which asks also to be read across a series of books as a valid entity in its own right.[72] This cycle consists of one letter to Calpurnia's aunt (4.19) and three to Calpurnia herself (6.4, 6.7, 7.5), where the first emphasizes Calpurnia's feelings for Pliny and her dedication to him, and the last provides a mirror-image reversal by concentrating on the feelings of a Pliny who pines for Calpurnia. As de Pretis (2003) 144 points out, we are licensed to read these four letters together by the presence of strong lexical similarities between them, and 'once we notice this, we also realize that 4.19 precedes 6.4 by thirty-five letters, a number which appears surprisingly similar to the thirty-one that separate 6.7 and 7.5'. In other words the four letters comprise a kind of unit, with the two letters in Book 6 roughly in the middle between the extremes at 4.19 and 7.5. And lest we query the ability of ancient readers to appreciate effects of this kind, the late-antique indices mentioned earlier may be thought of as facilitators of, and potential evidence for, interest in placement of related letters.[73]

Of course, Calpurnia appears (named or unnamed) in rather more letters than these four,[74] and other cycles might be created by the addition and subtraction of not only these but other letters relating to her grandfather Calpurnius Fabatus.[75] Indeed, as we shall suggest later in this chapter, a number of letters within Book 6 combine to give a weakly suggested narrative of a journey by Pliny into Campania to join the convalescing Calpurnia. As such, we ought to recognize that the openness of Pliny's individual letters to being read as members of different cycles and combinations – whether within or across books – constitutes one of their greatest literary interests and virtues.

However, for all that, we ask now a question rarely posed: what happens when the Calpurnia letters are read not in isolation or in relation to one another (in whatever combination), but rather within their immediate

---

of Fuscus Salinator followed by the report of his betrothal), and 6.16 and 6.20 (the two Plinii at Vesuvius: both addressed to Tacitus). Other, less strongly realized pairs include letters addressed to the same addressee on different subjects, i.e. those to Calestrius Tiro (6.1, 6.22), Calpurnius Fabatus (6.12, 6.30) and Voconius Romanus (6.15, 6.33).

[72] We follow here the persuasive analysis of de Pretis (2003). On the Calpurnia letters, see also Carlon (2009) 157–75, and Appendix 3.

[73] For evidence in Sidonius Apollinaris of appreciation of Pliny's games in this respect, see Gibson (forthcoming a).

[74] Cf. 4.1, 5.14.8, 8.10, 8.11, 8.19.1, 10.120.2, 10.121.

[75] See further Chapter 5, where cycles of letters can be variously constructed according to addressee or mentions of their name. Cf. Lorenz (2004) 257 on critical debates within studies of Martial on the nature and membership of cycles of poems; also Fitzgerald (2007b) 88, 107ff. for a practical demonstration of the effects of trying to read Martial by sequence or cycle.

context? For if 6.4 is read within the context of Book 6, then it appears that this letter has strong links with the opening letter of the book. First, the two letters present a reverse image of one another: in 6.1 Pliny is in Rome impatiently waiting Tiro's return, while in 6.4 he is kept in Rome against his will longing to be with the addressee who is outside the city. Secondly, just as a letter to Calestrius Tiro on the author's urgent desire to be re-united in Rome with the addressee recalled various letters in Cicero's book addressed to *his* Tiro (*Fam.* 16), so this letter to an ill wife showing solicitude for her health alludes to letters addressed by Cicero to Terentia (e.g. *Fam.* 14.2–4).[76] Guillemin (1929) 138ff. rightly notes the combination of this Ciceronian strain with various reminiscences of the language in which Ovid addresses his wife from exile, and other scholars have mined this seam by uncovering further possible resonances with elegiac texts here and elsewhere in the Calpurnia sequence.[77] And we may add that letter 6.4 is the first payment on the promise effectively made by the striking allusions to Cicero which open and close Book 6, namely that the Ciceronian model will be significant in this suite of letters.[78]

If we now concentrate on the verbal links between 6.1 and 6.4, then a resonance between their language begins to emerge. Compare the register of 6.4.2–5

praecipue simul esse cupiebam . . . etiam fortem te non sine cura desiderarem; est enim suspensum et anxium de eo quem ardentissime diligas interdum nihil scire. nunc vero me cum absentiae tum infirmitatis tuae ratio incerta et uaria sollicitudine exterret. uereor omnia, imaginor omnia . . . impensius rogo . . .

I particularly desired to be with you . . . even if you were quite strong, my longing after you would not be unmixed with worry; for to be sometimes without news of an ardently loved person is fraught with suspense and uneasiness. Now, however, the consideration of your delicate health, as well as your absence, torments me with vague anxieties of various kinds. I fear everything, imagine everything . . . more urgently I beg . . .

with the scarcely less impassioned language of 6.1, addressed to Tiro (quoted above p. 42). Letter 6.1 emphasizes sharpness of desire and torment (not unlike Catullus in his famous poem 50 on temporary separation from

---

76 For the suggestion that 6.4 also echoes Cicero's letters to the ill Tiro in *Fam.* 16, see Carlon (2009) 166–7 (cf. 169–79 on letter 7.5). For a detailed reading of Cicero's letters to Terentia (in *Fam.* 14) and those to Tiro (in *Fam.* 16), see Gunderson (2007).

77 See Shelton (1990) 166, 170–1, also Gunderson (1997). The passionate language directed towards Tiro in 6.1 could also be explained by the adherence of the addressee to the Epicurean sect (as also for Bruttius Praesens in 7.3); see Syme, *RP* 2.784 [= (1969a) 361], *RP* 7.565.

78 For the significance of this correlation between frame and developing themes, and its assurance that this is an authorially constructed book unit, cf. Gutzwiller (2005a) 289 (quoted above).

Licinius Calvus), while 6.4 focuses more on fear and anxiety; but both are in essentially the same register.[79] Alongside viewing these Calpurnia letters as part of a project to break new epistolary ground with love letters to one's wife, we should also see that Pliny is inviting us to read 6.4 in tandem with 6.1: Pliny can 'replicate' the intensity of Cicero to both Tiro and Terentia.[80]

Letter 6.5, like its predecessor, is part of a sequence of letters which stretches across several books. However, unlike the Calpurnia sequence, this cycle demonstrates strong narrative progression rather than simply lexical repetition and thematic elaboration or variation. Such cycles narrating an unfolding series of events in chronological order are most common, as Sherwin-White (1966) 48 notes, across Books 4–7. The particular example here involves the ongoing saga of the troubles of the Bithynians with their governors, where Pliny first defends Iulius Bassus on charges of corruption and then relates his own role in the lengthy defense of Varenus Rufus. Both delinquents, by the standards of earlier times, were relatively trivial; but the trials themselves took place in Rome's highest court, the senate. As such the letters lie, in some sense, at the very heart of Pliny's epistolary project, since they put him before us in the role with which he most fully identified (as suggested earlier), namely that of leading consular orator. As a sequence there are signs of conscious design, since the first four members (4.9, 5.20, 6.5, 6.13; cf. 6.29.11) are united by their address to a single correspondent, Cornelius Ursus, and the final pair by their address to Caecilius Macrinus (7.6 and 7.10). Further unity is provided by a complex series of epistolary references both backwards and forwards in time as events unfold.[81] As a cycle the letters give the troublesome province of Bithynia extraordinary prominence across the central books of the collection, and for the reader moving towards Book 10 form a very effective thematic 'prequel' for Pliny's gubernatorial mission to the province.[82]

Looking more closely at the cycle itself, we see that 5.20 had reported Pliny's involvement in the defence of Varenus against his Bithynian prosecutors, while the new letter in Book 6, with a specified context 'at the next meeting of the senate' (6.5.1), invites an especially attentive reader to

---

[79] Note also the parallel between the *eripe me huic tormento* of 6.1.2 (quoted more fully above, p. 42) and 7.5.1 (of separation from Calpurnia) *unum tempus his tormentis caret* (quoted more fully below, p. 59).

[80] Pliny recombines Tiro and Calpurnia in Book 7; see Chapter 3.

[81] E.g. 5.20.1, 6.5.1, 6.13.6, 7.10.1. The sequence also preserves documentary realism inasmuch as the letters devoted to this single topic decrease in length over time (only 7.6 disrupts the tendency to greater economy).

[82] On the role of Book 10 here in giving retrospective prominence to the 'Bithynian' letters found earlier in the collection, see Chapter 8. For a bold suggestion of conscious design in the Regulus cycle, see Murgia (1985).

infer the elapse of just two weeks after the events described in Book 5. This bolsters Pliny's initial claim to have arranged his letters 'without preserving the order of dates' (1.1.1), since overall chronological order is disturbed, for example by placing a return from distant Comum (6.1) in the middle of two letters set in Rome just two weeks apart. On the other hand, we may now admire Pliny's skill in weaving a good story out of his disordered letters, since the Bithynians of 6.5 – whatever the actual chronology of the surrounding letters[83] – provide an example of one of those sorts of *occupationes* mentioned in 6.4.1 which prevent Pliny from following the ill Calpurnia into Campania. The impassioned register of 6.4 also presents an obvious contrast with the dry (but engaged) tone of 6.5. For here Pliny describes a 'disgraceful' scene in the senate where two praetorian senators lead, and others stoke, an ongoing altercation over whether Varenus should be allowed to summon witnesses in his defence.

Such a juxtaposition of uxorious solicitude and senatorial business was perhaps startlingly novel, at least for the reader who comes to Pliny's correspondence straight from that of Cicero.[84] For the editors of Cicero's correspondence had collected his letters to Terentia (in *Fam.* 14) separately from his more 'senatorial' books and letters (e.g. the report of the altercation between consul and tribune in *Fam.* 1.2), although it is true that the letters to his wife are not devoid of political news relevant to them both (unlike Pliny's). Nevertheless, in his next letter to Calpurnia – in Book 7 – we appear to encounter a retrospective comment on this juxtaposition in Book 6:

unum tempus his tormentis caret, quo in foro et amicorum litibus conteror. aestima tu, quae uita mea sit, cui requies in labore, in miseria curisque solacium. (7.5.1–2)

One time alone is free from these torments: when I am worn out in the forum by the law-suits of my friends. It is for you to judge what my life must be when it finds its rest in labour, its solace in misery and cares.

The only time that Pliny is free from the emotional torture of being separated from Calpurnia is when he is involved in the legal affairs of friends and in the forum. The strong nudge to apply this sentiment retrospectively to 6.4 and 6.5 is provided by the fact that the Calpurnia letter in Book 7

---

[83] If we accept, for the sake of argument, Sherwin-White's provisional dates for each letter – 6.4 (early summer 107), 6.5 (late 106 or early 107), 6.6 (autumn 106), 6.7 (early summer 107) – then it becomes clear how Pliny has rearranged the letters in a series which disturbs strict chronology but which, in thematic terms, tells a good story.

[84] For our own 'Ciceronian' approach to Pliny's letters, see Chapter 5.

is itself juxtaposed to the next letter in the 'Bithynia' sequence, i.e. 7.6, where Pliny informs Macrinus of the latest twist in the prosecution of Varenus. Under Pliny's guidance we may infer that the dry legalities of letter 6.5 provide some much needed relief from the personal torments of letter 6.4 (although, with satisfying circularity, Pliny's legal duties are the very things which torment him with separation from Calpurnia in the first place).[85]

Letter 6.6 brings on the book's first distinguished addressee, Minicius Fundanus, whose suffect consulship in 107 possibly occurred within the dates of Book 6.[86] The letter opens with the now familiar theme of desire for the absent, although this is *desiderium absentium* in a less purely sentimental sense. For Pliny desires the addressee's presence alongside him in the same world of senate and duty evoked in letter 6.5, and Fundanus is asked that he return to Rome immediately to support the candidature of the young Iulius Naso. The reader may again infer that this is another one of the sorts of tasks keeping Pliny away from Calpurnia. Letters 6.5 and 6.6 are further linked by strong connections with the two closing letters of Book 5.[87]

Senatorial business is brought to an end, for now, with a second appearance for Calpurnia in 6.7. As suggested earlier, the return in 6.1 from Comum midway between two letters apparently written at Rome within two weeks of one another (5.20, 6.5) had bolstered Pliny's claim to order his letters without regard to (strict) chronology. Here, by contrast, Pliny engineers a nicely judged 'reality effect'. For, in the words of de Pretis (2003) 144, noting that the first letter to Calpurnia is followed by letters to two other addressees, 'when . . . 6.7 opens by quoting Calpurnia's letter . . . the two intercalary epistles become a symbol of the time that has passed between Pliny's sending his first letter, receiving an answer and finally replying with the second letter'.[88] Capping a series of earlier letters in which Pliny has proclaimed his desire to see various addressees in person

---

[85] Of course, the lessons of 7.5 apply also to the reading of the dry legalities of 7.6; see further Chapter 6, where the lessons for the Praesens of letter 7.3 (who stays with his wife in Campania and never comes to Rome) are also discussed.

[86] See Sherwin-White (1966) 361. For Fundanus' career, see Syme, *RP* 7.603–19.

[87] If 6.5 looks back to 5.20, then 6.6 looks back to 5.21. For it is revealed at 6.6.6–7 that Naso has recently lost his brother, who accompanied Naso as they both attached themselves to Pliny. The deceased brother is almost certainly Iulius Avitus (Syme, *RP* 7.605, Jones (1968a) 281), whose death as he returned from a quaestorship – the post Naso is apparently now seeking – is lamented prominently in 5.21. Since it is also stated that Naso chose Pliny as his model as soon as judgement allowed (6.6.5), these brothers appear, in the context of Book 6, to be forerunners of Ummidius Quadratus and Fuscus Salinator, who look to Pliny as their exemplar (6.11.2–3). On Pliny as exemplar, see also Chapter 4.

[88] For further links between 6.4 and 6.7 in service of this 'reality effect', see de Pretis (2003) 144.

(6.1, 6.4, 6.6), in 6.7 it is Pliny's turn to be missed in his absence: *scribis te **absentia mea** non mediocriter adfici*, 'You write that you are not a little affected by my absence' (6.7.1). For Pliny, Calpurnia's letters are a source of renewed ardour (*eo magis ad **desiderium tui** accendor*, 'all the more am I inflamed with a longing for you', 6.7.3), and he asks her to write more often even though her letters bring pleasure *and* pain (*licet hoc ita me delectet ut **torqueat***, 'though your doing so delights me in such a way as to torment me at the same time', 6.7.3).[89] Again, this is essentially the same language as that used to Calestrius Tiro in 6.1 (quoted above p. 42), although the near request that the torture continue marks an increase in temperature that is nearly Ovidian.

Letter 6.8 introduces a quite new topic: the obligations of *amicitia* in the upper classes of Roman society. Pliny, writing in notably firm but polite tones, seeks the recovery of a debt on behalf of a close friend. The letter places great emphasis on the ardour of the affection between Pliny and this friend, Atilius Crescens: *ipsi amare inuicem, qui est flagrantissimus amor, adulescentuli coepimus*, 'Our love for each other began – and this is the most fervent kind of love – when we were very young men' (6.8.2).[90] Once more, the language used to Calpurnia appears less exceptional when viewed in the context of the book as a whole. The following letter marks the first appearance of Tacitus in the book, and is also the second 'sequel' of the book after the Calpurnia letters. For here Pliny writes again on the candidature of Iulius Naso, this time to Tacitus, who is yet another of the absentees from Rome in this opening suite of letters (6.9.1).[91] Furthermore a motif from the Calpurnia letters (*uaria **sollicitudine**... uereor **omnia**, imaginor **omnia***, 'disquietudes of various kinds... I fear everything, imagine everything', 6.4.4) now finds its way into the Tacitus epistle (*habet hoc **sollicitudo**, quod **omnia** necessaria putat*, 'there is this about anxiety, that it thinks everything necessary', 6.9.2). For both Pliny and Tacitus, worry and concern turn out to have a deluded but all-embracing reach in both their lives.

In an emotional variation on the motif of desire for those absent from the city, 6.10 begins with the scenario of Pliny, now himself absent from Rome, nevertheless experiencing desire for the absent, although here the absence is one caused by death: 'On arrival at my mother-in-law's house

---

[89] For Pliny's beloved pleasure/pain polarity, and its frequent collapse (as here), see Chapter 7.

[90] For this friend, and his strange failure to receive a letter from Pliny in the collection, see Chapter 5.

[91] Tacitus has his own connection with Iulius Naso, since the latter's probable father, Iulius Secundus, appears as a character in the *Dialogus* (and is mentioned by Pliny at 6.6.6 just after another personage from the *Dialogus*, Nicetes Sacerdos); see further Jones (1968a) 281ff., and above p. 40 n. 11 for Pliny and the *Dialogus*.

near Alsium, which was once the property of Rufus Verginius, the sight of
the place itself painfully renewed my longing for that great and noble man
[*maximi uiri desiderium*] . . . my soul, my eyes looked for *him* [*illum oculi
requirebant*]' (6.10.1). Pliny's first trip out of Rome in the linear sequence
of Book 6 is not to see Calpurnia in Campania, but rather to stay at the
house of the mother of his (dead) former wife. What is Pliny doing here
at Alsium, on the coast not far north of Rome? On reaching letter 6.31
towards the end of the book, where Pliny tells the story of his role on the
imperial *consilium* at Centum Cellae (a little further up the same stretch
of coast), the reader might conclude that Pliny has stopped at Alsium on
the way there. But if we turn our gaze from reader to writer, it will be
noted that Pliny himself makes no particular or marked effort to connect
the two, and has evidently preferred that 6.10 be used primarily to cap a
sequence of letters on desire for the absent. We perhaps see here an actual
instance of a theoretical possibility noted earlier, namely the positioning
of letters stripped of strong chronological markers according to primarily
artistic demands.

Finally, 6.10 also displays strong links with 6.6. There Pliny had lamented
the speed with which members of the senate had forgotten the father of
Iulius Naso: 'But now there are many in the senate to whom he was
unknown, and though there are many to whom he *was* known, yet these
honour none but the living' (6.6.4). Iulius Secundus was an orator of
repute, praised by Quintilian, and according to Pliny a lover of *studia* and
the *studiosi* (6.6.3). He provides the civil half of a pairing with Verginius
Rufus, the great military man, who is also forgotten only ten years after his
death: 'so easy is it to forget the dead [*tam parata obliuio mortuorum*], that
we ought even to raise our own monuments and anticipate all the duties
of our heirs' (6.10.5–6).[92] Both orators and generals, it appears, may soon
be forgotten: a sobering thought which ought to redouble one's efforts to
secure one's immortality while still alive.

Letter 6.11 returns the reader immediately to Rome and to the young
aristocratic advocates Ummidius Quadratus and Fuscus Salinator, who, we
learn, look to Pliny as *rector*, *magister* and *exemplar*, 'guide', 'teacher' and
'model' (6.11.2, 3). Verginius Rufus, the subject of the previous letter, had
been hailed by Pliny at the time of his death as *exemplar aeui prioris*, 'model
of a bygone age' (2.1.7) and praised for his affectionate solicitude towards
the teenage Pliny in his role of guardian. One function of the placement of

---

[92] On Verginius Rufus, see further Chapter 4. On letter 6.10 and its pair at 9.19, see Marchesi (2008)
157–60. Letter 6.10 also demonstrates links with its immediate predecessor, since it is addressed to
the man who delivered the oration at Verginius' state funeral (2.1.6).

letter 6.11 immediately after a letter on Verginius Rufus – as will be argued later in Chapter 4 – is to suggest how Pliny has stepped into the role of one of his admired elders as patron to the younger generation. However this function, as so often, becomes apparent only when the letters are read in relation to one another, rather than in isolation.

Letter 6.12 then introduces a figure emphatically not to be counted among Pliny's exemplary elders (as will be noted again in Chapter 4). This is Calpurnius Fabatus, grandfather of Pliny's current wife and memorable within the correspondence chiefly for his consistently irritable attitude towards the ingenuous consular orator. The context is a request that Pliny render aid to a certain Bittius Priscus in the Centumviral court, and it appears that the old man has now thought (almost) to apologize for the tone of his earlier letters on the subject: 'you bid me forget those letters which you wrote me, as you term it, with your heart laid open [*aperto pectore*]. But there are no letters which I desire to bear in mind more' (6.12.3). Pliny praises Fabatus for his commendable *simplicitas*, but surrounding letters in Book 6 pointedly underline the gracelessness of his behaviour. For Pliny has already shown – in letter 6.6 on Iulius Naso – how a proper letter requesting the support of another for a needy third party ought to be written.[93] Furthermore letter 6.8 on the recovery of a debt demonstrates how a letter may be written *aperto pectore* without causing regret to the author. Calpurnius Fabatus will not be allowed to forget the lesson, as fitting replies to polite requests for legal representation in the courts are found soon after at 6.18 and 6.23.

Letter 6.13 introduces the third internal 'sequel' of Book 6, with Pliny's update on the progress of the Bithynian affair. After the disgraceful scenes described in 6.5, the news is better: *senatus ipse mirificus*, 'The senate itself was admirable' (6.13.3). For the senate has now agreed that an original motion to allow Varenus to summon witnesses should be made to stand. Letter 6.14 returns to a more personal and domestic note, and again takes the reader outside Rome as Pliny writes to arrange a stay with the Stoic Iunius Mauricus in Formiae on the coast in Latium, on condition that the (now elderly) addressee make no special arrangements. A holiday atmosphere of *otium* is introduced, providing some much needed relief after the heavy-duty letters on sentorial, court and other business that have dominated the book so far: 'For it is not the sea and the seaside that I am going after, but leisure, liberty [*libertatem*], and *you*' (6.14.1). The letter

---

[93] At first sight that lesson might appear to be reinforced in the equally gracious 6.9; but for a suspicious reading of this letter as a rather prickly one in which Pliny firmly reassures Tacitus that his friendly request for support of Iulius Naso is superfluous, see Chapter 5.

ends on a firm note emphasizing Pliny's intention to stick to the conditions of his visit: *oportet enim omnia aut **ad alienum arbitrium aut ad suum** facere. mei certe stomachi haec natura est, ut nihil nisi totum et merum uelit,* 'One's actions should be entirely dependent on the will of others, or else on one's own. The nature of *my* taste is certainly such that it will have nothing but what is complete in itself and free from admixture' (6.14.2). A frank statement of intent, showing once more how writing 'with heart laid open' is best done. The vocabulary highlighted above also carries with it a strong whiff of debate about imperial rule that is not inappropriate when addressed to a man whose name we first heard in the context of his exile by Domitian and Pliny's deliberate wait for his return before settling dealings with Regulus (1.5.9–10). The freedom with which Pliny expresses his mind on personal matters is another marker of how far we have come since the bad old days of Domitian – a liberty to be set alongside the book's second letter on the death of Regulus himself.

Formiae would make a good stopover for Pliny travelling to join the convalescing Calpurnia. We saw earlier that Pliny provided little encouragement to connect his two letters on visits to locations on the coast north of Rome (6.10, 6.31). But in the present case there is some evidence that a species of (weak) narrative is offered to readers who attempt to join the initial dots between Calpurnia in Campania (6.4) and a proposed visit to Formiae (6.14). For if we leap to the second half of the book, we discover Pliny now actually in Campania (6.28) visiting a friend there (only to discover the latter is absent). Finally, in letter 6.30 we learn that Pliny has been inspecting a property in Campania owned by Calpurnius Fabatus, and he now writes to report on its current state of preservation. Is Calpurnia convalescing at this family estate, and is this the end of Pliny's journey in Book 6 southward through Latium and Campania? The letters might in fact be unrelated in terms of an actual sequence of events in Pliny's life, but in a book which contains multiple ongoing narratives of varying formality it is tempting to connect these letters, even if only to produce thematic rather than documentary evolution. Nevertheless, readers inclined to finish the 'Calpurnia in Campania' narrative may well detect her lurking inside the first-person plurals which frame the birthday greeting to Fabatus which opens the final letter in the sequence: *Debemus mehercule natales tuos perinde ac nostros celebrare, cum laetitia nostrorum ex tuis pendeat, cuius diligentia et cura hic hilares istic securi sumus,* 'We are bound, by Hercules, to celebrate your birthdays like our own, since the joy of ours depends on yours, and through your diligence and care we are happy here, and at our ease when with you' (6.30.1). The plurals here might simply be a 'royal' we;

but Pliny does later lapse into the first-person singular when unmistakably talking about himself alone (*ego uideor habere multos amicos*, 'I seem to have many friends', 6.30.3).[94]

Letter 6.15 continues the theme of *otium*,[95] but introduces a favourite subject whose absence has been conspicuous in Book 6 so far: literature and its public recitation.[96] The letter contains the well-known anecdote of the humiliation of the elegist Passenus Paulus by Priscus. The latter, on hearing the poet's honorific phrase of dedication (*Prisce, iubes*, 'Priscus, you bid me'), shatters the artistic illusion and offered compliment by interjecting *ego uero non iubeo*, 'I don't bid you, however.'[97] Priscus' wit at the expense of the poet is heartlessly comic – and perhaps one of the funniest anecdotes in Latin literature, memorable above all for its 'Catullan' irreverence.[98] But Pliny will have none of this. Where the *simplicitas* of Calpurnius Fabatus may be indirectly exposed as merely graceless (6.12), and poor behaviour in the senate be reported with the heat carefully taken out (6.5), more forthright condemnation is required for the public actions of a man who threatens to bring down the whole system of reciprocity and the circulation of literary favours: 'To be sure, Priscus is of doubtful sanity [*dubiae sanitatis*] . . . which makes this action of his all the more ridiculous and remarkable . . . People should take particular care beforehand, when they are going to recite, not only to be sane themselves, but also to invite a sane audience' (6.15.3–4). Some personal animus against Priscus may be detected;[99] Regulus is not the only character in Book 6 to elicit uncharacteristically negative emotions from the polished epistolographer.

The next letter to follow in Book 6 is the anthologist's favourite, namely 6.16 on the death of the Elder Pliny nearly thirty years previously. This

---

94 Letter 4.1, also addressed to Calpurnius Fabatus, provides plenty of parallel sentiments in the first person plural where the implied speakers are more clearly Pliny and Calpurnia together, e.g. 4.1.1–3.

95 The opening of the letter also allows the inference that Pliny is away from Rome, thus creating dramatic continuity with 6.14.

96 For the great importance of the *recitatio* to Pliny, and the protocols he attempts to establish for it in the *Letters*, see Johnson (2010) 42–62.

97 For the honorific use of *iubere* in the context of literary requests, see White (1993) 266–8. In fact, the point of Priscus' intervention remains controversial; see Courtney (1993) 371, Schröder (2001).

98 Cf. Pliny's forthright disapproval in 4.25 of the despoiling of senatorial ballot papers with witty obscenities by some *dicax et urbanus et bellus* ('witty, elegant and smart fellow'); see further Roller (1998) 287. Pliny had already shown in Book 5 the 'proper' way to appreciate an elegist, with his letter in praise of the young Calpurnius Piso (5.17).

99 If the Iavolenus Priscus of this letter is the Priscus of 2.13 (Syme, *RP* 2.481 [= (1960) 366], 5.488 [= (1985b) 184]), then the addressee of 6.15, Voconius Romanus, might be especially interested to hear further evidence of Priscus' lack of judgement, since the Priscus of 2.13 appears to have turned down Pliny's request that he offer a military post to Voconius Romanus. The open condemnation of a living person may be uncharacteristic of Pliny as a whole; see Sherwin-White (1966) 371.

letter and its sequel in 6.20 stand out from the rest of Book 6 – like the
ancient peak of Vesuvius itself towering over the bay of Naples – in terms
of their marked length,[100] rather elevated style and notably heroic themes.
And this distinctiveness is part of their point. The petty squabbles and
varying forms of poor behaviour prevalent among Rome's elite, all too
evident in the book so far (with more to come at 6.17, 6.19, 6.22 etc.) are
emphatically overshadowed by the heroism of the Elder's death during the
spectacular catastrophe of the Vesuvius eruption of AD 79. The deliberate
elevation of the Elder in this way becomes clear only when the two letters
are read within their context in Book 6.

A fuller treatment of 6.16 and 6.20 in Chapter 4 makes it clear that these
letters ask to be read in dialogue with various letters devoted to exemplary
elders and their competing lifestyles in Book 3. This dialogue with letters
outside Book 6, allied to the distinctiveness of the pair within the book, in
some sense explains the ease with which anthologists have detached 6.16
and 6.20 from their original context and scholars have produced successful
readings of the pair without strong reference to that context. (As suggested
earlier in this chapter, the ancient indices to Pliny certainly seem to cater
to the eyes and instincts of the anthologist.) Yet, for all that, it is clear
Pliny has made an effort to integrate them within the book. As argued
earlier, Book 6 is distinguished by the attention given to regions in central
and southern Italy, particularly Campania. The narrative of the Elder's
death on the Campanian coastline (6.16.2) participates in this distinctive
geographical focus within Book 6. Indeed, given the prominence of the
Vesuvius letters within the book, one wonders whether Pliny has allowed
an emphasis on Campania and surrounding regions to emerge as a means
of providing a sympathetic context for the pair.

More obviously – if little remarked – the beginning of letter 6.16 creates
a strong contrast with the anecdote told in the preceding letter. Letter 6.15
had told of a literary request gone wrong: '*Prisce, iubes...*' (6.15.2). The
beginning of 6.16, by contrast, shows how it should be done: *Petis ut tibi
auunculi mei exitum scribam, quo uerius tradere posteris possis. gratias ago;
nam...*, 'You ask me to write to you an account of my uncle's end, so
that you may be able to transmit it to posterity the more faithfully. I thank
you, as...' (6.16.1). Tacitus is the recipient of a literary piece for which,
according to its author, his friend has asked. And, in the sequel, Tacitus
comes back to ask for more: *Ais te adductum litteris quas exigenti tibi de*

---

[100] For the exceptional length of a piece as a critical factor to be taken into account when studying a
book, see Scherf (2008) on the *epigramma longum* of Martial.

morte auunculi mei scripsi, cupere cognoscere, quos ego..., 'You say that the letter I wrote you, at your request, on my uncle's death has made you wish to know what I myself...' (6.20.1). Pliny and Tacitus demonstrate the proper courtesy and reciprocity in literature which is shown to be so severely lacking in the anecdote about Iavolenus Priscus and the poet he regarded as his close friend (6.15.2).[101]

Finally, in terms of integration with the rest of the book, letter 6.16, with its concern for the memorialization of the dead, also looks back to 6.10. There Pliny laments the fate of the northern Italian friend of the Elder Pliny, and the fact his ashes lie without a memorial ten years after his death. In 6.16 literature is confirmed as the best memorial, as the Elder's own works and Tacitus' histories – joined now by Pliny's own letters – are explicitly said (6.16.2–3) to grant the Elder the immortality which appears to be threatened in the case of Verginius Rufus in 6.10. The pessimistic sentiments of that letter undergo emphatic redemption in the Vesuvius letters.

In 6.17 Pliny denounces those who attend literary recitations but show no appreciation. The subject in 6.17 is a partial reverse of that in 6.15: unresponsiveness as opposed to (inappropriate) responsiveness. But, as Pliny shows, the effect is the same: the *amentia*, 'madness' (6.17.3) of these literary deaf mutes matches the 'doubtful sanity' of Iavolenus Priscus, and the offence given to friends is no different (*inimicum relinquas ad quem tamquam amicissimum ueneris*, 'you leave as an enemy the man to whose house you have come as a particular friend', 6.17.3; cf. *Iauolenus Priscus (aderat enim ut Paulo amicissimus)*, 'Javolenus Priscus (who was present as a particular friend of Paulus)', 6.15.2). Pliny ends the letter with the insistence that one should praise equally literary peers, inferiors and superiors. And for good reason, since one will not be praised if one's superiors are not praised, and praise of equals or inferiors will make one's own literary glory appear all the greater. Readers of these sentiments may have cause to think back to the beginning of the preceding letter where Pliny, with fine gradation, praises Tacitus' immortal works (*scriptorum tuorum aeternitas*, 'the immortality of your writings', 6.16.2) and the nearly immortal works of the Elder Pliny (*plurima opera et mansura*, 'many and enduring works'). That is to say, the opening of 6.16 provides a demonstration of what 6.17 discusses in theory.

Our linear reading of the first half of Book 6 ends here. Yet we may glance forward to letter 6.18 to discover further evidence of Pliny's concern

---

[101] Letter 6.15 may also be linked to 6.20 by shared allusion to the narrative frame of Verg. *Aen.* 2; see Berry (2008) 302–3. For the technique of connecting thematically diverse letters in this fashion, found also in Martial, see above p. 37 n. 4.

with the formal architecture of his books. If the frames to Book 6 revealed a notable example of symmetrical arrangement in the disposition of 6.1–3 in relation to 6.32–4, then it perhaps will not be too much to expect Pliny to mark the beginning of the second half of the book in some way. And 6.1, it will be noted, started with the revelation that Calestrius Tiro lingered in Picenum; while 6.18 opens with Pliny's agreement to represent in court one of the leading towns of the same region, namely Firmum. The same geographical region opens both halves of the book.

READING BY CYCLE: REGULUS AND PLINY'S LEGAL CAREER

The preceding pages aimed to establish the difference between reading letters in isolation and reading letters as part of a linear sequence, and to give some indication of the critical riches unlocked by taking Pliny's books seriously as artistic entities. Short, heterogeneous and often apparently insignificant 'filler' items take on new meanings or resonances when read – and above all re-read on the basis of newly acquired knowledge – for their interrelations with surrounding pieces. In the course of reading those letters as part of a sequence, we had frequent opportunity to mention other reading methods, above all the alternative option of reading a number of those same letters as members of a larger thematic cycle, whether within Book 6 or across several books. We end the chapter by providing a more detailed reading of a number of letters from both halves of Book 6 as part of an informal cycle which takes on great significance within the book. Here the focus will be on different but complementary meanings of letters when read as part of a cycle (rather than strictly for relations with near neighbours).

The chosen cycle is an informal one, which works by reinforcement of a theme without narrative development or thematic crescendo. Furthermore, it embraces a heterogeneous set of letters, pulling in whole epistles here and paragraphs or even single sentences there. In this sense the cycle of letters involving the death of Regulus and Pliny's legal career is to be distinguished from the more strongly realized cycles for Calpurnia and the progress of Bithynian prosecutions of provincial governors. Like them, however, the 'Regulus cycle' (for short) is itself part of a much more extensive cycle which stretches across the central books of the collection. It will nevertheless become evident that those letters which make up the Regulus cycle in Book 6 have a particular point to make within this book.

As noted earlier, Book 6 contains a sequence of letters which reflects the return of Trajan from Dacia to Rome. The city to which Trajan is making his way hums with the operation of the city's courts, and the emperor must deal, even in his absence, with the prosecution of Varenus (6.5, 6.13). After his return the emperor is pictured forming imperial *consilia* to hear various trials (6.22, 6.31). Around these letters cluster others which have at their centre Pliny and his involvement in the full range of Rome's courts. This sequence includes 6.2 (on the death of Regulus), 6.11 (on Pliny's role in the court of the City Prefect), 6.12 (Pliny agrees to appear on behalf of his grandfather-in-law's associate in the Centumviral court), 6.18 (on Pliny's readiness to appear as advocate for the town of Firmum in court), 6.23 (Pliny accepts a private case in the Centumviral court), 6.29 (a review of Pliny's most important senatorial cases to date) and 6.33 (Pliny on his greatest ever speech in the Centumviral court). Such distinctive emphasis within a book which also puts Trajan on show further reinforces a point already made: the world to which Trajan returns – and into which he is shown fitting himself – is decidedly one where civil rather than military accomplishments are prerequisite.

Book 5 is also filled with reports of legal business, but Pliny's own appearances in court there are confined to his speech in the senate on behalf of Varenus (5.20) and to the report of a postponed appearance in the Centumviral court (5.9). Book 6, by contrast, displays Pliny as an active participant 'on stage' in Rome's courts. And this is crucial to understanding the point of the Regulus cycle: Pliny flourishes as a practising lawyer in a Rome now definitively free of that egregious performer. In particular, as we argue below, Pliny flourishes in a Centumviral court revivified after the passing of Regulus. Nevertheless, in order to appreciate the impact of this courtroom theme in Book 6 a return must be made to Book 4. In the earlier book Pliny can only express disgust at the high reputation of Regulus, criticizing his delivery and powers of memory and highlighting only his 'insanity' as a gift (4.7.4–5; cf. 1.20.14–16). Not unconnected with this outburst is Pliny's insinuation later in the book that he himself is the greatest speaker currently operating in the Centumviral courts. In 4.24, having just finished a speech at an extremely rare four-panel session of the Centumviral courts, he looks back to a speech which he had given at a similar session while only a young man.[102] Thinking over those who were involved in both the first case and the most recent, he comes to the

---

[102] A *iudicium quadruplex* sits with the four panels of 180 jurors (in total) together and represents a special event in the context of the Centumviral court; see Sherwin-White (1966) 399, and on the more normal procedures of the court, 183, 336; also Bablitz (2007) 61–70. 'Centumviral' refers to the fact that the original panels of jurors totalled 100 men, although this had now been increased to 180; see Sherwin-White (1966) 336.

realization that he is the only one who has spoken at both, since the others are either dead, exiled, retired or in imperial service (4.24.2–3). One of the retired men is to be understood as Regulus, who appears elsewhere in Book 4 described as a *senex* (4.2.7) and debilitated by grief for his dead son (4.2, 4.7).[103] With his main Centumviral competition retired from the field (but not yet dead), Pliny can begin to put out claims to pre-eminence. That pre-eminence is finally established beyond any doubt (to Pliny's satisfaction at least) in the second letter of Book 6, where the death of Regulus is announced. Later in Book 6, Pliny in fact refers to the Centumviral court as virtually 'my turf':

itaque Bittio Prisco quantum plurimum potuero praestabo, praesertim **in harena mea**, hoc est apud centumuiros. (6.12.2)

Consequently I will do all in my power for Bittius Priscus, particularly in my own arena – that is, in the Centumviral court.

This claim carries particular point and force now in the context of the obituary letter for his former rival.

Letter 6.11 further develops the theme in a notably subtle way. Here Pliny is found acting as assessor in the court of the City Prefect,[104] where the representatives of the opposing sides are the young Ummidius Quadratus and Fuscus Salinator. Pliny praises their talents in terms which directly reverse the censure loaded on Regulus in Book 4.[105] For the rhetorical skills attributed to the pair (*os Latinum, uox uirilis, tenax memoria, magnum ingenium*, 'pure Latin, manly voice, tenacious memory, great natural capacity', 6.11.2) are precisely those lacked by the older man (*os confusum, haesitans lingua, tardissima inuentio, memoria nulla, nihil denique praeter ingenium insanum*, 'confused language, a faltering delivery, the slowest faculty of imagination, no memory at all; nothing, in short, beyond his wild capacity', 4.7.4). When this observation is added to the revelation (recorded above) that Ummidius Quadratus and Fuscus Salinator look up to Pliny as 'guide', 'teacher' and 'model' (6.11.2–3), we are invited to feel there is now hope for Roman oratory when Pliny's exemplarity leads in the opposite stylistic direction from that of Regulus.

Further reasons for optimism about the future of oratory emerge in letter 6.23. Here Pliny agrees to represent the addressee in a forthcoming case,

---

[103] See Sherwin-White (1966) 303 on 4.24.3.

[104] On this court, see Sherwin-White (1966) 367, also Bablitz (2007) 39–40, 91–2, 179.

[105] The parallel is also noted by Sherwin-White ad loc., but without comment (or reference to Regulus). For Pliny's views on oratory, see Appendix 3.

but only if the young Cremutius Ruso be allowed to act with him. He explains his reasons for this stipulation:

solitum hoc mihi et iam in pluribus claris adulescentibus factitatum; nam mire concupisco bonos iuuenes ostendere foro, adsignare famae. (6.23.2)

This is a practice of mine, and one which I have frequently followed before now in the case of several young men of distinction. For I am excessively anxious to exhibit young men of promise to the forum, and to introduce them to fame.

There is a reference here back to 2.14, in which Pliny complained at some length about declining standards and the appearance of 'almost unknown youths' in the Centumviral court. This court, to Pliny's mind in Book 2, is the hardest place to start, and, in former times, such was the reputation of the place that not even 'the most high born young men' were admitted as pleaders unless introduced by a man of consular rank.[106] Letter 6.23 is in effect a redemption of the pessimistic assessment in 2.14 of the lowered prestige of the Centumviral court. For in Book 6 proper order has been restored: a 'young man of distinction' is being introduced by a man of consular rank to the Centumviral court.[107] With Regulus dead and Pliny its greatest living advocate, now is the time for the pessimistic judgements of 2.14 to be firmly erased and for the flourishing of oratory (and the Centumviral court) to be celebrated.[108]

Further erasure of those sentiments takes place in the penultimate letter of the book, where, as we have already seen, Pliny announces the publication of his finest speech to date:

accipe orationem meam . . . re uera ut inter meas pulchram; nam mihi satis est certare mecum. est haec pro Attia Viriola, et dignitate **personae** et exempli **raritate et iudicii magnitudine insignis**. nam femina splendide nata, nupta praetorio uiro, exheredata ab octogenario patre intra undecim dies quam illi nouercam amore captus induxerat, quadruplici iudicio bona paterna repetebat. sedebant centum et octoginta iudices (tot enim quattuor consiliis colliguntur) ingens utrimque aduocatio. (6.33.1–3)

Take in hand *my* speech . . . well, in sober truth, an excellent one for a production of mine, and it is enough for me to compete with myself. This speech is on behalf of Attia Viriola, and remarkable for the station of the individual, the singularity of the

---

[106] 2.14.2–4; cf. Quintilian on introducing young men at a none-too-early age, at *Inst.* 12.6.2.

[107] For *forum* (6.23.2) referring to the Centumviral court, cf. the cross-reference in 5.8.8 to 1.18.3. The Centumviral court assembled in the Basilica Iulia (5.9.1, 6.33.4) in a prominent position in the Forum Romanum.

[108] In the context of Book 2, letter 2.14 is itself connected – in tone at least – with the book's only other 'pessimistic' letter, namely the final letter on the disgraceful legacy-hunting of none other than Regulus himself (2.20).

case and the importance of the decision. For this lady, of lofty birth, married to a man of praetorian rank, and disinherited by her octogenarian father, within eleven days of the time when, smitten with love, he had brought home a stepmother for her, sought to recover her paternal property by a process instituted before the four courts. One hundred and eighty judges sat (for so many are brought together in the four chambers); there was a vast crowd of assistants on either side.

These sentiments (again) offer a strong contrast with Pliny's lament in 2.14 on the kinds of cases currently being conducted in the Centumviral court:

distringor centumuiralibus causis, quae me exercent magis quam delectant. sunt enim pleraeque paruae et exiles; **raro** incidit uel **personarum claritate** uel **negotii magnitudine insignis** (2.14.1)

I am distracted by my cases in the Centumviral court, which are work for me rather than pleasure. For most of them are small and insignificant; rarely does one occur that is remarkable for the position of the parties or the importance of the issue.

Through a combination of similar vocabulary, sentence structure and syllabic symmetry, Pliny directs readers of 6.33 back to the gloomy judgements of 2.14. The sentiments expressed are not essentially in disagreement: both acknowledge the rarity of 'big' cases in the Centumviral court. But whereas 2.14 is locked into uncharacteristic pessimism on the subject, 6.33 celebrates the arrival of one of these rare 'big' cases. And that it does so, we suggest, is closely connected with the death of Regulus in the letter which occupies second position in the book (just as 6.33 is placed in penultimate position in the same book). The death of Pliny's great rival in the Centumviral court provides the opening for the delivery of Pliny's finest speech in Regulus' old stamping ground. In this context, the statement that 'it is enough for me to compete with myself' is somewhat loaded.

Furthermore, just as in 4.24 the occasion of a speech at a rare combined four-panel session of the Centumviral court provided a chance to reflect on Regulus' retirement and Pliny's pre-eminence there, so now in 6.33 Pliny takes care to emphasize the very same context for his greatest speech. For he explains the four-panel arrangement for the benefit of Voconius Romanus (6.33.3, quoted above), despite the fact that his boyhood friend will not have needed it,[109] and the fact that no similar explanation has been offered on either of the two previous occasions on which Pliny addressed the same court (1.18.3–4, 4.24). If we follow the prompt to look back at Book 4, we will discover that the letter celebrating the red-letter day of this appearance

---

[109] For the significance of Voconius Romanus in the collection, see Chapter 5.

in court is found seven letters from the end of the thirty-letter book, while the earlier letter which prominently attacks Regulus' rhetorical style (4.7.3–5) is found seven letters from the book's beginning. In arranging Book 6 Pliny evidently had one eye on this earlier (and less visible) symmetry, and took care to place in second position from either end the letters on the death of Regulus and his own triumph before a special session of a court that Regulus no doubt once claimed as 'my turf'.

In sum, the Regulus cycle, while necessarily informal, and one which requires to be read in connection with letters from earlier books, is clearly designed to achieve a particular impact within Book 6.

CHAPTER 3

Epistolary models
Cicero and Seneca

A careful reading of the Regulus cycle, as shown in Chapter 2, can help us track the 'narrative' of Pliny's growing professional dominance in comparison with a contemporary rival. However, it is the comparable programme of intellectual and professional self-positioning built into Pliny's competitive engagement with his most eminent predecessor, Cicero, which readers might expect to find most prominently highlighted in the collection. In examining this programme, we continue the process of reading by cycle with which we concluded Chapter 2, this time focusing on the set of letters (scattered across the collection) in which Pliny explicitly acknowledges the relationship between his own work and that of Cicero. Cicero's name occurs eleven times in the collection (while other passages clearly refer to Cicero without naming him) and Pliny's wish to emulate him is advertised almost from the very beginning. The cycle records – in letters which appear to the sequential reader to have been loosely grouped by selected aspects of the Ciceronian model (almost under 'headings' within the cycle, one might say) – Pliny's 'Ciceronian' work as an orator and lawyer (1.2, 1.5, 1.20, 3.21, 9.26),[1] his generosity as a patron of poets (3.15, 3.21), the overall shape of his public career by comparison with that of Cicero (4.8), his 'Ciceronian' versifying (5.3, 7.4), his painstaking revision of literary work (5.3, 7.17) and finally – unexpectedly late in the collection – his ostensibly frustrated ambition to emulate Cicero as a letter-writer (9.2).[2]

Given the traditional dominance of the Ciceronian epistolary voice, and the close proximity of genre and persona (prose letters of a lawyer

---

[1] The relative dominance of letters about Cicero as orator naturally reflects Pliny's wish to highlight his own image as consular orator (see Chapter 2). It is striking, however, that no letter in Book 6 (the book of Pliny's *negotium*) mentions Cicero by name; the Ciceronian background is conveyed instead only by the subtle structuring allusions we have discussed in the previous chapter.

[2] For a comparable shaping of books of letters by reference to the different types of Pliny's literary works to which he wishes to draw the reader's attention, cf. our remarks in Chapter 1, above, on the importance of the *de Heluidi ultione* and *Panegyricus* as contexts for Books 1 and 3 respectively; on Pliny's decision to follow Cicero in avoiding work on historiography, see Chapter 4.

consul) between Pliny's epistles and the Ciceronian epistolary corpus, we would naturally expect the colour of the letters themselves to be strongly and explicitly Ciceronian. The differences, however, between the letters of Cicero and those of Pliny raise important questions about what it might mean for a letter-writer to adapt a model.[3] Although Cicero is, as Marchesi observes, 'background music' in the collection, Pliny is highly selective in his choice of Ciceronian motifs for imitation and reworking; he is also very subtle, of course, to the degree that it is often difficult to pin down the Ciceronian inheritance, and one often wonders if we are simply looking either at shared cultural and generic expectations (i.e. these are just the kinds of things people wrote letters about) or coincidental similarities.[4]

Our own particular interest in the more 'architectural' features of the collection as a whole has kept our attention thus far upon Pliny's subtlety and sophistication in framing a whole book (in this case Book 6) within embedded allusions to Cicero at beginning and end (see Chapter 2).[5] At the level of the individual letters, Pliny's epistolary programme of allusion to Cicero's works is rich and complex, and embraces not only the letters[6] but also, as we shall see, the larger Ciceronian oeuvre. Nevertheless, as we noted in Chapter 2, Pliny tends to keep his Ciceronian allusions quite understated, relying upon the reader's own detailed knowledge of the Ciceronian corpus (and upon his willingness to re-read earlier letters in the light of later more strongly marked allusions). Similarly he seems willing to tantalize and frustrate a reader who looks for any obvious reference to Cicero as epistolographer early in the collection; meanwhile, readers who look instead for acknowledged affinities with the most eminent epistolographer of the previous generation, Seneca the Younger, will seem to draw a complete

[3] The whole notion of following earlier letters as models is a difficult one; it raises issues of literary inheritance which are markedly different from those we face when discussing most other literary genres. Sherwin-White (1966) 477, for example, identifies *Q. fr.* 1.1 as the 'prototype' for Pliny's letter of advice to a governor of Achaia (8.24) but the two letters are quite different in content and approach, although they both belong to a loose and varied genre of letters of professional advice.

[4] On 'hyper-ciceronianizing' readings of Pliny's letters, see Marchesi (2008) 214–18, who reminds us that Pliny's letters are fully literary in that they will simultaneously allude to a broad range of models – including Cicero, certainly, but also deeply engaged with Horace, Catullus and other poetic predecessors.

[5] Readers seeking dedicated analysis of Pliny's allusive linguistic and thematic interaction with Cicero will find an invaluable starting point in Marchesi's chapter on the subject, together with her appendix listing the references and echoes of Ciceronian texts which have attracted critical interest: Marchesi (2008) 207–40, 252–7. On the subtlety with which Pliny is 'testing knowledgeable readers' by keeping his Ciceronian allusions understated, see Woodman (forthcoming). For further bibliography, see Appendix 3.

[6] For Pliny's marked allusions to the Ciceronian letters to Tiro and Terentia, for example, see the discussion in Chapter 2. For the prominence of the *de Legibus* and the *de Officiis* in Pliny's thinking about respected elders, too, see Chapter 4.

blank, as Seneca is mentioned only once in the collection (as a writer of verse, rather than epistles), and the *Letters to Lucilius* have been thought to belong to an entirely different kind of epistolographical tradition.[7]

In this chapter, then, we move on to examine the way in which Pliny builds his professional and epistolary persona upon Ciceronian foundations. We begin with a brief sketch of the ancient perceptions of the 'Ciceronian' letter which prompted Cicero's successors – including Seneca and Pliny – to adapt or reject key features of the tradition; we move on to examine the increasing value placed on the crafted letter, written with care as a literary composition, which is Pliny's characteristic product, and which itself reflects the fusion of prosaic and poetic traditions in Pliny's collection. The remainder of the chapter is devoted to a reading of the Cicero cycle, highlighting, in particular, Pliny's seemingly idiosyncratic selection of activities in which to emulate Cicero (Cicero as the inspiration for Pliny's attempts at erotic verse, for example, might surprise, especially given well-known ancient criticism of Cicero's poetic talents) and his tendency to attribute comparisons between himself and Cicero to addressees or third parties (with a concomitant insistence upon his own thoroughgoing engagement with modernity and the contemporary world). Above all, we note that Pliny makes his reader wait until Book 9 before he engages with Cicero as a specifically *epistolary* model, advertising instead the Ciceronianism of his oratory (particularly at beginning and end of the collection), his verse, his literary friendships and his career. Finally, we explore two instances in which Pliny's arrangement of contrasting pairs of letters signals his engagement not only with Cicero but also with other models, poetic and prosaic, and with the other great epistolary predecessor who is kept in the shadows of the collection, but whose influence nevertheless colours Pliny's new epistolary project: Seneca.[8] Unlike Pliny, however, we begin with Cicero in his role as the obvious epistolary archetype for all prose epistolographers.

CICERO AND THE EPISTOLARY TRADITION

Letters make up an astonishingly varied genre in themselves, one which (unlike, say, historiography or epic) lacks a named founder/inventor figure.[9]

---

[7] Sherwin-White (1966) 2.

[8] For Pliny's engagement with Seneca, see also Chapter 6 and Appendix 3.

[9] Marchesi (2008) 7. It is notoriously difficult to systematize and theorize letters, given the plethora of epistolary topics, styles and linguistic features. For a useful survey of letter-types (both documentary and literary) and canonical letter collections of classical antiquity, see Trapp (2003) 1–47. For ancient

However, by Pliny's day, Cicero had become the great Latin archetype, in epistolary as in oratorical prose. The date and manner of publication of Cicero's own letter collections is likely to remain mysterious; some letters were probably well known from an early date, but plans to publish a relatively small selection appear to have come to nothing during Cicero's lifetime, and the transmitted collections are usually thought to have been assembled and published later by an unknown editor or editors.[10]

Nevertheless, their distinctiveness soon gave them canonical status. Cornelius Nepos, in a context already mentioned in Chapter 1, notes their comprehensiveness (*nihil in his non appareat*, 'nothing does not appear in them'), the public importance of their subject matter, and their remarkable prescience about future developments (*cecinit ut uates*, 'he sang like a prophet,' *Att.* 16.4).[11] By the younger Seneca's time, an epistolographer – even one with the separate traditions of the letters of Epicurus at his disposal – needed to position himself carefully vis-à-vis the Ciceronian collections.[12] Seneca's response was to reject the journalistic qualities of Ciceronian letters in order to reassert the primacy of philosophical content, and to re-situate Latin epistolography in the landscape of philosophic *otium* and in the tradition of the didactic philosophical letter:

nec faciam quod Cicero, uir disertissimus, facere Atticum iubet, ut etiam si rem nullam habebit, quod in buccam uenerit, scribat. numquam potest deesse quod scribam, ut omnia illa quae Ciceronis implent epistulas transeam: quis candidatus laboret; quis alienis, quis suis uiribus pugnet; quis consulatum fiducia Caesaris, quis Pompei, quis arcae petat; quam durus sit faenerator Caecilius a quo minoris centesimis propinqui nummum mouere non possint. (Sen. *Ep.* 118.1–2)

I shall not do what Cicero, the most fluent of men, tells Atticus to do, that is to write even if he has nothing in his mind he wants to say. In writing to you I never run out of ideas even though I bypass all the things with which Cicero fills his letters: which candidate is in trouble; who is contesting on borrowed funds, who on his own resources; who, in his bid for the consulship, is depending on Caesar, who on Pompey or his own cashbox; what a cruel usurer is Caecilius who won't lend even to his relatives at less than 12% interest! (trans. M. Wilson)

---

epistolary theory, see Malherbe (1988), and Poster (2007) with references to earlier literature; more generally, Appendix 3 (on letters/epistolography).

[10] On the editorial principles and publication of the Ciceronian collections, see White (2010) 31–61, Beard (2002), Nicholson (1998), Cugusi (1983) 168–73, Shackleton Bailey (1965–70) 1: 59–76. On the contemporary fame of *Fam.* 5.12, for example, see Woodman (1988) 151 n. 55.

[11] However, on the unexpectedly small number of narratives of political events which are actually preserved in the transmitted Ciceronian collections, see White (2010) 17.

[12] Inwood (2007) 133–48.

Seneca builds his *recusatio* upon the model of a single Ciceronian letter, *Att.* 1.12, which exemplifies 'typical' Ciceronian material.[13] In this letter Cicero says that he wants to hear from Atticus just for affection's sake, and that he does not expect his addressee to be able to match the profusion of news and gossip which fills his own letters. Seneca, on the other hand, is not dependent upon 'news' or upon external circumstances of any kind, as his subject matter is the examination and improvement of the soul, about which there is always something fresh to say (*integram . . . materiam,* *Ep.* 118.5).[14]

Pliny also recognized the contrast between the newsworthiness (and therefore 'letterworthiness') of Cicero's material and the topics which he himself covered in his letters (9.2.2), but he seems to reject not only the mundane specificities of Cicero's letters which Seneca's *Ep.* 118 implicitly criticizes, but also the purely philosophical epistolary programme which Seneca supplied in their place.[15] Ciceronian letters were often quite long and many separate topics might appear within the confines of a single letter. Gossip about scandal, requests for support, thanks for favours received, reports of the writer's recent activities and preoccupations, and greetings sent to a correspondent's family might all sit next to one another in jumbled, busy letters. 'Single theme' letters (e.g. the famous *Fam.* 5.12, to Lucceius, asking him to write about Cicero's consulship) are generally in a minority in the Ciceronian collections. Pliny's letters, as we noted in our Introduction, usually reflect upon a single main topic (although a surprising number of subthemes can emerge as we re-read the collection and find ourselves re-situating any given letter within its immediate context in a book or within the 'cycles' which cross book boundaries).

Pliny also tends, as we noted in Chapters 1 and 2, to strip out details such as dates, times, places or specifics of situation – both his own and that of his addressee – leaving the reader in doubt, for example, about where (or even whether) a military addressee is serving on campaign, or

---

[13] On this letter, and the 'nothing to say' motif in general, see Morello (2003).

[14] Seneca also converts conventional epistolary motifs (including some not necessarily distinctively or exclusively Ciceronian ones) into 'hooks' for philosophical discussion. *Ep.* 15, for example, opens a discussion of philosophical and intellectual health with a meditation on the traditional epistolary formula *si uales bene est. ego ualeo* ('if you are well, that's good. I am well'); here the conventions of epistolary engagement, together with an acknowledgement that the health of addressee and writer is one of the most traditional epistolary topics, become the foundation for closer instruction in the maintenance of the mind's health.

[15] However, for Pliny's adaptation in 1.10 (in 'miniaturized' form) of the distinctively Senecan philosophical epistolary programme, see Chapter 6.

about which of his own speeches he is currently polishing for publication. This fosters a certain timelessness which makes the correspondence easier to read for the general reader (even if this ultimately creates other challenges and frustations, such as those mentioned earlier), as well as easier to imitate. Indeed, his procedure might usefully be understood in the terms Aristotle applied to a contrast between poetry and history in *Poetics* 9:

the one [history] relates actual events, the other [poetry] the kinds of thing that might occur. Consequently, poetry is more philosophical and more elevated than history, since poetry relates more of the universal, while history relates particulars. 'Universal' means the kinds of things which it suits a certain kind of person to say or to do, in terms of probability or necessity: poetry aims for this, even though attaching names to the agents. A 'particular' means, say, what Alcibiades did or experienced. (trans. S. Halliwell)

Pliny's letters clearly do aim beyond history and the mere particulars of 'what Alcibiades did' towards what his elite contemporaries will have experienced as closer to the 'universals' of their place and time.[16] His crafted letters of polite communication must have seemed culturally accessible in late antiquity in a way that the context-dependent late-republican correspondence of Cicero could not; indeed, later letter-writers such as Ambrose, Symmachus and Sidonius might all praise Cicero; but the model they (or their editors) adopted was the nine or ten books of letters by the rather less prestigious Pliny.[17]

Moreover, critics have observed that Pliny 'miniaturizes' other genres in his collection (Ash, for example, sees Pliny's 'historical' letters as 'miniaturizations' of popular historical modes such as accounts of the deaths of great men, while Freudenburg describes the letters about martyrs of tyranny as 'miniature epics'), but the point might usefully be made more generally: by concentrating his attention Pliny in some sense 'miniaturizes' and refines even the letter genre itself.[18] So, for example, he might produce an epigrammatic piece on the perfections of an addressee's letters (7.13), or full and lengthy discussion of a single event or issue, such as the account of his uncle's death after Vesuvius' eruption (6.16) or the showpiece on ghosts addressed to Licinius Sura (7.27).

---

[16] We might usefully compare Seneca's practice of mentioning no dates in his letters (see Chapter 1).

[17] See Gibson (2012). It is also worth pondering Asconius' neglect of Cicero's letters in his first-century commentary on the speeches (although this may be to do with the unavailability of the letters in his day), and Plutarch's preference for the speeches as a source for his biography of Cicero. For the former, see Shackleton Bailey (1965–70) I: 68, Beard (2002) 118 n. 47; for the latter, see Trapp (2007) 335–8.

[18] Ash (2003) 224, Freudenburg (2001) 216.

PLINY AND THE EPISTOLARY CRAFT

This very emphasis on 'miniaturized', restrained elegance reflects an increasing cultural interest in letters which displayed a high degree of craft and finesse. For Statius, for example, a showpiece letter, written with special *cura*, crowns Manilius Vopiscus' literary work in the sumptuous peace of his Tibur villa:[19]

> hic tua Tiburtes Faunos chelys et iuuat ipsum
> Alciden dictumque lyra maiore Catillum,
> seu tibi Pindaricis animus contendere plectris
> siue chelyn tollas heroa ad robora siue
> liuentem satiram nigra rubigine turbes
> seu tua non alia splendescat epistola cura.
>
> (Stat. *Silu.* 1.3.99–104)

Here your lyre delights the Fauns of Tibur and Alcides himself and Catillus, sung of by a mightier harp, whether you have a mind to compete with the Pindaric quill, or raise your lyre to the height of heroic deeds or stir up the black venom of bitter satire, or whether your letters are resplendent with no less skill.

Here the radiance of Vopiscus' letters (*splendescat epistola*) matches that of his house (*splendor*, 1.3.53). They are presented without apparent incongruity as part of a varied output of elegy, epic, Pindaric compositions or satire; presumably, indeed, they are themselves verse epistles, as tightly structured and conceptually sophisticated as any (other) poems, their language, style and content chosen with equal care (*non alia... cura*). Vopiscus' letters, with their poetic affinities (and perhaps also poetic form), appear to belong in a very different category from the Ciceronian collections, and also, one would think, from Pliny's letters.

Nevertheless, Pliny, too, signals in his opening dedication the care which he has lavished on the letters of his published collection (*curatius*, 1.1.1); further, the special qualities to be achieved in a beautifully written epistle receive some attention also in at least two letters about his friends' epistolary output. One should note that such a crafted letter may treat a range of apparently mundane topics. In 9.28, for example, Pliny reports that Voconius has sent him three letters (mostly on ordinary, everyday topics), with a promise of yet another which has been written with special stylistic attention (*curiosius scriptas*, 9.28.5).[20] The distinction is a relatively fine one: Voconius' specially crafted letter has apparently been sent

---

[19] For Statius and Pliny, see Appendix 3.   [20] For more extended discussion of 9.28, see Chapter 5.

in just the same way as more workaday epistles about the grape harvest, while the topics of even those letters which have arrived (themselves *elegantissimas*, 9.28.1, but nevertheless differentiated from the finer one by Voconius himself) are strongly reminiscent of Pliny's own letters in the collection – all of which, according to the manifesto of 1.1, are *curatius scriptae*.

For Pliny, as for Statius' Vopiscus, the composition of letters belongs in a varied (and consciously designed) literary programme for the educated man who is enjoying some period of *otium*; in his case, the programme embraces work in both prose and poetry, and is designed with a single aim in mind, namely the refinement of rhetorical skill. This is most explicitly acknowledged in 7.9, in which we hear that Fuscus has asked him to define an agenda for literary training in *otium*: *quaeris quemadmodum in secessu, quo iam diu frueris, putem te studere oportere*, 'you ask me after what manner I think you ought to pursue your studies in the retirement which you have now for some time enjoyed' (7.9.1). Pliny's 'Quintilianic' answer prescribes a programme of compositional exercises, to include translation to and from Greek and Latin, competitive emulation (in private) of the greatest models, and painstaking revision of one's own work.[21] The focus is principally upon oratory, rather than poetry, in keeping with their shared professional interests; indeed, sections 1–6 of the letter are entirely devoted to that one art.

However, Pliny also recommends that such work be supported by a variety of shorter efforts in other genres, to refresh the mind and give practice in varying styles. These other genres include poetic ones, but Fuscus, unlike Manilius Vopiscus, is expected to eschew longer stints of poetic labour; epic, for example, would require real *otium*, and although Fuscus is enjoying a moderately extended period of leisure, it clearly cannot encompass poetic composition in the grand style:

fas est et carmine remitti, non dico continuo et longo – id enim perfici nisi in otio non potest – , sed hoc arguto et breui, quod apte quantas libet occupationes curasque distinguit. (7.9.9)[22]

Even poetry is a fitting relaxation. I don't say long and sustained poems (for such as these can only be elaborated with full leisure) but of that lively and short kind which form a suitable interruption to occupations and business, however important.

---

[21] A Ciceronian version of this study programme may be found at *De or.* 1.154–5.

[22] We are indebted to Tony Woodman for pointing out the allusion here to Cic. *Leg.* 1.9, the *recusatio* in which Cicero characterizes history as a genre requiring extended *otium*.

This category of supporting exercises designed for short periods of *otium*, and for refreshment of the mind and refinement of stylistic versatility between more extended work on oratory, also includes two prose genres: history and epistles, the latter particularly to be valued as an exercise in clean stylistics:

uolo interdum aliquem ex historia locum adprendas, uolo epistulam diligentius scribas. nam saepe in oratione quoque non historica modo sed prope poetica descriptionum necessitas incidit, et pressus sermo purusque ex epistulis petitur. (7.9.8)

I should wish you occasionally to take up some historical topic. I should also wish you to write a letter with especial pains. For oftentimes even in an oration, a necessity occurs, not only for historical, but almost for poetical treatment, and a concise and pure style is acquired by letter-writing.

The intermediate stage between composition of speeches and of verse is occupied by snippets of history (again, *extended* work on history is not what is being recommended) and by letters, two exercises which bring good training in quasi-poetic prose on the one hand and purity of expression on the other.[23]

Indeed, it is this middle ground which letters occupy between prose and poetry which Pliny's work colonizes, as he creatively enriches a (now) Ciceronian genre with a programme of allusion to other genres such as elegy, epigram and historiography to a much greater extent than Cicero's letters did.[24] His books present an innovative fusion of the traditions of both poetry and prose at the level both of the single letter and of the collection more broadly considered; many individual letters are built around poetic or quasi-poetic motifs or themes, such as the 'dinner party invitation' or the 'lament of the *exclusus amator*'. In 1.15, to take just one example, a spurned dinner invitation has inspired Pliny to an epistolographic version of 'dinner' poems – familiar from Horace, Catullus and elsewhere – which yet retains something of the flavour of Cicero's correspondence too. Pliny then makes the new hybrid distinctively his own by building his version around a reworking of the legal metaphor at the end of Catullus 50 which casts his addressee in the role of defendant and Pliny as an aggrieved plaintiff.[25] Pliny's collection innovates, then, by successfully combining

---

[23] Such peculiarities of epistolary style may help to illuminate Pliny's slightly puzzling characterization of well-written letters as 'Plautus or Terence in prose' (1.16.6).

[24] On Pliny's allusions to Cicero, Ovid and Seneca in 8.14, for example, see Whitton (2010).

[25] On 1.15 and its simultaneous and composite allusions to *Fam.* 7.22 and Catull. 50, see Morello (2007) 187–6. For the combination of a Ciceronian strain of epistolary allusion with an Ovidian strain, see Chapter 2.

the influences of multiple models, some epistolary but many not, to the degree that it would be impossible to attempt a thorough discussion of the literary history of the work without discussing not only Cicero but also Horace, Martial, Statius, Seneca and the remains of the great Roman historiographers. The result is a collection of letters in which style and craft are elevated.

PLINY'S EMULATION OF CICERO: THE CICERO 'CYCLE'

Pliny's emphasis on such craftsmanship in his letters complements the sustained engagement with Cicero which not only adds a distinctive colour to his letters but also serves to underpin the quasi-autobiographical construction of his own persona. By Pliny's day, Cicero had become a cultural cliché, 'an icon more important as an abstract representation than the historical reality of the man and the sensible reality of his words'.[26] For the elder Seneca he was already the embodiment of *ingenium*, and he is a sentimentalized, quasi-heroic figure for the schoolmen of the *Controuersiae* and the *Suasoriae*, who were fascinated by the rhetorical problems which could be generated from the stories of his death and of his enmity with Antony.

Allusion to or quotation from his published works, however, could be problematic. For the younger Seneca, for example, Cicero was a crucial *exemplum* and a validating voice to confirm Seneca's own positions, where appropriate, but nevertheless we can occasionally hear a note of defensiveness. In *Ep.* 58.5, for example, Seneca anticipates that an example or quotation from Cicero's philosophical writing might seem a little outdated, and that a reader might want it to be supported by more contemporary authorities (*Ciceronem auctorem huius uerbi habeo, puto locupletem; si recentiorem quaeris, Fabianum*, 'I have Cicero as authority for the use of this word, and I regard him as a powerful authority. If you desire testimony of a later date, I shall cite Fabianus'). Both the defensiveness and the sentimentalized hero-worship of Cicero as the pure embodiment of *ingenium* manifest themselves in Pliny's collection, and these positions (and their ramifications) shape several of the letters in which Pliny mentions Cicero by name.

In his dedication to Septicius Clarus, Pliny appears to define his letters partly in opposition to the more or less chronologically arranged Ciceronian *ad Atticum* collection which Nepos had seen as a quasi-history (*neque*

---

[26] Kaster (1998) 254.

enim historiam componebam, 'since it was not a history I was compiling,'
1.1.1). Indeed, marked differences in organizational strategies between the
two epistolary corpora do make Pliny's collection look unlike any version
of Cicero's letter books, and, as we have already noted, one can look
more fruitfully for the inspirations for Pliny's collection design to Martial's
epigram books, to Horace's *Epistles*, or even (as we do in Chapter 8) to
Ovid's *Tristia* or *Epistulae ex Ponto*. Nevertheless, Pliny names Cicero as
his model for the first time in 1.2; it is important and perhaps unexpected,
however, that Cicero first appears not as an epistolographer, but as an orator
with a distinctive gift for 'decorative' artistry:

temptaui enim imitari Demosthenen semper tuum, Caluum nuper meum, dumtaxat figuris orationis; nam **uim** tantorum uirorum, 'pauci quos aequus ...'
assequi possunt. nec materia ipsa huic – uereor ne improbe dicam – aemulationi
repugnauit: erat enim prope tota in contentione dicendi, quod me longae desidiae
indormientem excitauit, si modo is sum ego qui **excitari** possim. non tamen
omnino Marci nostri ληκύθους fugimus, quotiens paulum itinere decedere non
intempestiuis amoenitatibus admonebamur: acres enim esse non tristes uolebamus
(1.2.2–4).

For I have attempted to imitate Demosthenes, always your model, and Calvus,
who has lately become mine, at least in their rhetorical turns; the **power** of such
mighty men is indeed only to be attained by 'the few whom the Gods favour'.
The subject matter, too, lent itself to this kind of emulation (if the word be not
too presumptuous), being almost entirely in the line of vigorous expression, such
as to rouse me from the lethargy of my long sloth, provided only I was capable of
being **roused**. Yet I have not altogether avoided the 'touches of colour' of Cicero,
whenever a pleasant topic, not unseasonably introduced, suggested to me a slight
divergence from the beaten road: since it was my aim to be spirited rather than
solemn.

The letter distinguishes the tastes of writer and addressee in the models adduced for the speech it accompanies: Demosthenes, Pliny says, is
Arrianus' longstanding favourite (*semper tuum*), while Pliny has brought a
recent liking of his own for Calvus (*nuper meum*) into play. The imitation
is modestly restricted to their figures of speech, and the tone is almost
excessively tentative (*temptaui, dumtaxat, uereor ne improbe dicam, si modo
is sum*). A self-conscious Vergilian quotation economically suggests both
the excessive ambition inherent in any greater emulation of their *vis*, and
the immense *labor* required even in the attempt.[27]

---

[27] Verg. *Aen.* 6.129–31; see Marchesi (2008) 27–30. For failure to match Demosthenes, cf. Cicero's own
modesty at *Brut.* 289.

Cicero is their shared taste (*Marci nostri*), but his influence differs from
that of the two primary models for the speech. Pliny abandons his tentative
stance once Cicero is in the picture: to balance out the labour of oratorical
achievement in the more austere style, and thereby to suggest that he is also
a gentler, more pleasure-loving soul, he relaxes into the Ciceronian mode
for his digressions.[28] A Ciceronian passage is, Pliny suggests, a different kind
of creation, one which – unlike the sterner Demosthenic/Calvan efforts of
the main body of the speech – brings ease and creative pleasure to reader
and writer.[29] However, Cicero's epistles are also part of the allusive scenery,
since Pliny takes the image of Cicero's 'colours' from a famous letter to
Atticus in which Cicero describes Crassus' emulation of Ciceronian style:

totum hunc locum, quem ego uarie meis orationibus, quarum tu Aristarchus es,
soleo pingere, de flamma, de ferro (nosti illas ληκύθους) ualde grauiter pertexuit
(*Att.* 1.14.3)

He worked up the whole theme which I am in the habit of embroidering in my
speeches one way and another, all about fire, sword, etc. (you are their Aristarchus
and know my colour-box) really most impressively.

Pliny's self-conscious allusion, in a letter about his own attempts to imitate
Ciceronian oratory, to a letter from Cicero about a similar attempt mounted
in his very presence, suggests the dominance of Cicero as an epistolary
model, but its subtlety requires the reader to do the work of picking
up and interpreting the allusion; Cicero the epistolographer will remain
otherwise virtually unacknowledged until the final book of the nine-book
collection.

---

[28] The tension between utility and pleasure which is familiar to readers of historiographical openings,
for example, is played out quite differently in this author. Early in the collection Pliny allies
himself with pleasure-lovers, partly by depicting himself as a lazy man, and partly by collapsing
the boundaries between *otium* and *negotium* (1.3.3). We shall find later that the revision of old
material (such as that referred to in 1.2) is an unappealing labour, but for the time being, a variety of
pleasures (writing in a decorated style, receiving the compliments of the booksellers, enjoying the
loci amoeni at Comum or the baths at his mother-in-law's house (1.4)) seem to dominate, and utility
is served by the (pleasing) convenience of publishing things which are already in draft (1.2) or by
the assurance that writing and publication give one an inalienable possession, not to be bought or
inherited by anyone else (1.4). On the antithesis between *uoluptates* and productive literary work,
see Leach (2003) 147–8.

[29] The contrast between Cicero's richer, more poetic style and the usual (though not unbroken)
austerity of Demosthenes sets the tone here for Pliny's own oratorical tastes, and will recur in the
very last named reference to Cicero of the collection at 9.26.8 which gives the closing summary of
Pliny's approach to Cicero: *at enim alia condicio oratorum, alia poetarum. Quasi uero M. Tullius
minus audeat!* 'but it will be said that the conditions of oratory are one thing and those of poetry
another. Just as if M. Tullius were less daring!'. For Pliny's views on rhetoric more generally, see
Appendix 3.

Pliny may also be picking up on *Fam.* 15.21.4, in which Cicero describes to Trebonius a letter in which he sought to rouse Calvus (*excitando*) to improve his style, which he thought lacked force (*uis*).[30] Not only is *uis* the very quality in Calvus which Pliny has doubts of matching (1.2.2), but he starts early in this letter to establish his own persona as a man who needs to be roused to effort, just as Cicero had attempted to rouse Calvus to add vigour and body to his speaking.[31] That Pliny cites Calvus as the model of his own selecting (a model whom Pliny's contemporary, Tacitus, had criticized for want of intellectual power, and who was clearly the focus of considerable disagreement among critics)[32] subtly lays the foundations for the modest persona Pliny will develop over the course of the Cicero cycle: that of a man earnestly selecting the best models he could find, but lacking the *ingenium* of a Cicero, and perhaps working almost too hard at the revision and polishing of his own work.

At all events, as a man of natural *desidia* who tends to give way to pleasure even in his work,[33] Pliny anticipates his addressee's disapproval not that he emulates Calvus, but that he abandons Attic restraint in his digressions (*nec est quod putes me sub hac exceptione ueniam postulare*, 'now don't suppose that these are reservations under which your indulgence is solicited,' 1.2.5). This is the first instance of a striking phenomenon in the letters: all three references to Cicero in Book 1, indeed, are coloured by some degree of (more or less artificially constructed) defensiveness on Pliny's part, and Pliny (even more than Seneca) frequently depicts Ciceronianism as the focus of disagreement, invented or otherwise, between writer and addressee. In the next letter in the cycle, for example, Pliny counters Regulus' attack upon his Ciceronianism:

ait timere se ne animo meo penitus haereret, quod in centumuirali iudicio aliquando dixisset, cum responderet mihi et Satrio Rufo: 'Satrius Rufus, cui non est cum Cicerone aemulatio et qui contentus est eloquentia saeculi nostri.' respondi nunc me intellegere maligne dictum quia ipse confiteretur, ceterum potuisse honorificum existimari. 'est enim' inquam 'mihi cum Cicerone aemulatio, nec sum

---

[30] Cf. Cic. *Brut.* 283. On stylistic disagreements between Cicero and Calvus, cf. also Quint. *Inst.* 12.1.22.

[31] For a contradictory report of Calvus as an unusually violent and passionate speaker in the prosecution of Vatinius, see Sen. *Controu.* 7.4.7–8. Cf. Quint. *Inst.* 10.1.115 (a passage which confirms that Cicero's criticism of Calvus' style was well known, but also that Calvus retained many admirers).

[32] Tac. *Dial.* 21.2: *ingenium ac uires defuisse.*

[33] We shall see, too, that Pliny favours in his oratory fullness and comprehensiveness rather than the leanness of the Atticist (see Chapter 8).

contentus eloquentia saeculi nostri; nam stultissimum credo ad imitandum non optima quaeque proponere.' (1.5.11–13).

He was afraid, he said, that I harboured a recollection of an observation once made by him in the course of a trial before the Centumviri, when replying to Satrius Rufus and myself: 'Satrius Rufus, who does *not* try to emulate Cicero, and who *is* satisfied with the eloquence of our epoch.' I answered that I understood now, upon his own confession, that this was said ill-naturedly, otherwise it might have been taken in a complimentary sense. 'I do, indeed,' said I, 'try to emulate Cicero, nor am I satisfied with the eloquence of our epoch. For I look on it as the height of folly not to propose to one's self in every case the best models for imitation.'

Regulus has misrepresented Pliny by suggesting that his admiration for Cicero goes alongside a hostility to contemporary oratory, but it turns out that this manufactured dispute over Pliny's greatest literary model is merely a foil in the letter for a considerably more dangerous and more exclusively modern issue, namely Regulus' attempt to trap Pliny into a compromising declaration about the Domitianic exile, Mettius Modestus (1.5.13). Regulus' judgement is so poor, it seems, that he turns a relatively 'safe' issue into grounds for disagreement, failing all the while to perceive a more pressing source of ill feeling between the two men. It is Regulus, rather than Pliny, who has made an erroneous choice between ancients and moderns in recalling an occasion on which he baited Pliny over Cicero and forgetting their clash over Mettius Modestus; and it is Pliny who comes out on top and discomfits the enemy who had tried to manoeuvre him into danger.[34] Furthermore, Regulus' mistake in accusing Pliny of contempt for modern eloquence is highlighted by the letter's context in Book 1, which celebrates a literary 'renaissance' which began (like Regulus' fearfulness) after Domitian's death.[35]

Even in 1.20, where Pliny does himself adduce Cicero (as author of *Philippics* 2) as the prime exponent of the rhetorical expansiveness which suits his own taste, the context is a heated debate with an unnamed opponent on the merits of length over brevity in oratory:

ego Lysiae Demosthenen Aeschinen Hyperiden multosque praeterea, Gracchis et Catoni Pollionem Caesarem Caelium, in primis M. Tullium oppono, cuius oratio optima fertur esse quae maxima. (1.20.4)

To Lysias I oppose Demosthenes, Aeschines, Hyperides and many others: to the Gracchi and Cato, Pollio, Caesar, Caelius, Marcus Tullius especially, the best of whose speeches is said to be the one which is the longest.

[34] For Cicero's own engagement in the battles of his day between admirers of ancients and moderns in oratory (and his attachment to the moderns), see Tac. *Dial.* 22.1.

[35] See 1.10.1, with Chapter 1, above; see also 6.2 and the discussion in Chapter 2.

Where Cicero features as part of an ongoing conversation, then, he is the focus of contention, and is more often than not introduced by someone other than Pliny. In 1.5 the interlocutor was an enemy, but later books offer more friendly instances of this phenomenon. In 3.15, for example, Silius Proculus cites a different Cicero as an *exemplum* for Pliny – Cicero the literary patron:

petis ut libellos tuos in secessu legam examinem, an editione sint digni; adhibes preces, allegas exemplum: rogas enim, ut aliquid subsiciui temporis studiis meis subtraham, impertiam tuis, adicis M. Tullium mira benignitate poetarum ingenia fouisse. (3.15.1)

You ask me to read your short productions in the retirement of the country, and to examine whether they are worth publishing. You employ prayers and you allege an authority; for while you beg me to subtract some odd hours from my literary pursuits and bestow them on yours, you add that M. Tullius was wonderfully kind in encouraging poetic dispositions.

This appeal to Cicero is an unnecessary persuasive manoeuvre, since Pliny would have read Silius' work with care and pleasure anyway, but it preserves him from the immodesty of an overambitious attempt to depict himself as a Cicero for his own age, while also broadening the scope for Pliny's emulation of a model whose *studia* are primarily non-poetic and for whom poetry occupies only small bits of spare time (*aliquid subsiciui temporis*).[36]

Pliny elegantly illustrates the balance between 'Ciceronian' poetic activities (both the interest in poetry and the support of the poets themselves[37]) and 'Ciceronian' prose/professional activities later in the same book. In the final letter of Book 3, Pliny laments the death of Martial, and quotes the second half of Martial 10.20 in grateful tribute.[38] Martial's poem distinguishes between Pliny's evenings of relaxation (when a poem from Martial might properly receive attention), and his daytime labours, when he works up speeches for the Centumviral court 'which this and the coming age may venture to match with Arpinum's page' (*quod saecula posterique possint | Arpinis quoque comparare chartis*, 3.21.5 = Mart. 10.20.20–1). Once again, the parallel between Cicero and Pliny is voiced by someone other than

---

[36] Cf. Cic. *Leg.* 1.9, 1.13; Pliny, *HN praef.* 18; Quint. *Inst.* 1.12.14.

[37] For Cicero's interest in contemporary poets, see not only the *Pro Archia* but also the favourable view of Lucretius in *Q. fr.* 2.10.3 (and the famous report – admittedly suspect – in Jerome that Cicero edited the *de Rerum Natura* after Lucretius' death, *Chron.* (Helm) p. 149). For Pliny's commitment to the literary encouragement of his friends, see Chapter 2.

[38] On this letter, see Fitzgerald (2007b) 153 and Chapters 7 and 8 of this volume. The inclusion of the tribute to Martial is especially appropriate at the end of this book, given that only a few letters earlier (3.16) Pliny meditates upon the tale of Arria's courage which is also the subject of Mart. 1.13. For Martial and Pliny, see further Appendix 3.

Pliny himself – not just Martial, in this case, but also those imagined future generations (*posteri*) who will compare Pliny's oratory with Cicero's. Poetic and oratorical activities are safely demarcated from one another, but the letter as a whole confirms Pliny's own support of poets, a patronage defined as peculiarly Ciceronian only six letters previously and now broken down into specific parts: quotation of the poetic friend's work in his own work, advertised ownership of the whole volume of poems from which this one has been excerpted, and finally the account of financial assistance given to Martial as due return for these flattering lines in 10.20.

The next letter about Cicero, namely 4.8 (also, like 1.2, addressed to Maturus Arrianus) similarly deploys Cicero as a conversational gambit and a bond between writer and addressee.[39] This time no specific literary genre is under discussion; rather, the shade of Cicero the public and professional man is invoked for synkrisis with Pliny.[40] Maturus has congratulated Pliny on following in Cicero's footsteps (already his model in his literary work) by winning appointment to the augural college:

te quidem, ut scribis, ob hoc maxime delectat auguratus meus, quod M. Tullius augur fuit. laetaris enim quod honoribus eius insistam, quem aemulari in studiis cupio. (4.8.4)

You, however, as you write, are chiefly delighted at my being augur because M. Tullius was one. You are rejoiced, that is, at my stepping into the honours of one whom I long to emulate in my intellectual pursuits.

There are two points of view in this letter – those of Pliny and of Arrianus – and each of the two 'voices' offers a different list of causes for congratulation; once again, the interlocutor (here the addressee) focuses more upon the past, while Pliny remains resolutely attached to the contemporary context. The letter opens with a bald statement of the topic: *gratularis mihi quod acceperim auguratum* ('you congratulate me on my having been invested with the augurship'). Pliny then 'interrupts' the report of Arrianus' letter to give three reasons why he himself is proud of his achievement, all drawn not from Ciceronian tradition, but from the contemporary world:

a) it is a fine thing to be honoured by the emperor;
b) the augurate's hallowed status is attested by the fact that it is held for life;
c) the item most important to Pliny – Pliny is the successor as augur to his friend and patron Julius Frontinus, who proposed Pliny as a suitable

---

[39] This letter itself falls between two letters about oratory and legal practice (4.7, a study of Regulus as bad orator, and 4.9 on the Bassus case).

[40] For more on Pliny's personal models for the conduct of life as a public servant, see Chapter 4.

candidate for the post. The notice of his predecessor's support suggests
that Pliny has now reached his natural and predestined place in life.
It is only once the personal *exemplum* of Frontinus completes Pliny's list of
grounds for celebration that we find Cicero brought into the issue – once
again at the instigation of the addressee. Cicero's introduction changes
the direction of Pliny's letter, and triggers not only an account of Pliny's
achievements but also a confession of unfulfilled wishes:

sed utinam ut sacerdotium idem, ut consulatum multo etiam iuuenior quam ille
sum consecutus, ita senex saltem ingenium eius aliqua ex parte adsequi possim!
sed nimirum quae sunt in manu hominum et mihi et multis contigerunt; illud
uero ut adipisci arduum sic etiam sperare nimium est, quod dari non nisi a dis
potest. (4.8.5–6)

But oh that, as like him I have obtained the priestly office and the consulship,
and indeed at a much earlier time of life than his, so also, in old age at any rate,
I might attain to some share of his mental powers! Yet, to be sure, what is in the
power of man falls to my lot as well as to that of many others. But in proportion
as it is difficult to acquire, so is it too much even to hope for gifts which lie in the
hands of the gods alone.

Pliny's response to Arrianus' compliment is a masterpiece of modest one-
upmanship: not only does he note that he reached both augurate and
consulship at an earlier age than Cicero, but he declares an ambition
to engage in the more testing literary/intellectual competition with his
predecessor, even if his success in this arena must be delayed until later in
life than Cicero achieved it.[41] He has beaten the great man's record in the
early heats, one might say, but still has to come good in the final, and,
like the *otium* he longs for (see Chapter 6), a reputation for 'Ciceronian'
ingenium must wait for Pliny's old age.

The one-upmanship extends to his engagement with his addressee's
letter of congratulations; Pliny has his own modern reasons for delight
at his own advancement, reasons rooted not only in the august nature
of the office itself, but also in his relationship with the emperor and
with one of his great mentors. Arrianus, however, has erroneously located
Pliny's competition with Cicero primarily in the professional arena; 4.8
gently corrects the mistake, redefining Cicero for the collection as the
embodiment of *ingenium*, while once more emphasizing the dominance of
the modern world in Pliny's thinking. In 4.8, as in 1.5, it is Pliny who once

---

[41] The extraordinarily competitive quality of Pliny's assertion that he achieved the offices of augur and
consul earlier in life than Cicero had is all the clearer when one recalls Cicero's own lifelong pride
in having achieved his consulship *suo anno* (see e.g. *Cat.* 1.28.4, *Brut.* 323). Thanks are due to John
Briscoe for reminding us of this.

again emphasizes the contemporary world and an interlocutor who raises the issue of emulation of the past.[42]

That there is a contemporary agenda at work here is suggested too by the placement of this letter in Book 4, between the famously negative review of Regulus' talents (4.7), and the lengthy 4.9, on the Bassus case, one of Pliny's most important court appearances. This is a point at which the Cicero cycle implicitly intersects with the Regulus cycle which we examined in Chapter 2, as Regulus is made to look absurd for his excessive grief for his deceased son, as well as for his limited natural gifts as an orator, while Pliny openly declares, by contrast, that Cicero can be seen as a suitable paradigm for his own career – immediately before he gives an account of one of his own greatest legal triumphs. The echoes in the Regulus letters of Book 4 (especially 4.2 and 4.7) of Cicero's famously extreme grief for his daughter add a further reminder to the reader that we are expected here to think of the great man, and to call Regulus, Cicero and Pliny to mind for comparison in both the moral and the professional spheres. 4.8 is, then, a nodal letter in the cycle, one which encourages the reader to step back once again and take a wider view of the whole issue of Cicero as the appropriate model for Pliny.[43]

Pliny next returns to consideration of his relationship with Cicero in a letter which picks up the interest in Cicero as an aficionado of verse which we saw in 3.15 and now turns our attention to Cicero as himself a *poet* who provides a model for Pliny's own poetic work. Once again, when Pliny responds to criticism of his verse, his chosen gambit is a defensive invocation of Cicero as precedent and validating model. Cicero's influence is not advertised in the first letter about Pliny's poetry, 4.14, where Pliny alludes rather to Catullus 5 (and quotes Catullus 16) as the archetype for his playful persona in his verse.[44] Indeed, in substituting a volume of hendecasyllables (his *lusus*) for the speech his addressee has been expecting, he is ostensibly moving away from Ciceronian activities (*tu fortasse orationem, ut soles, et flagitas et exspectas; at ego . . . lusus meos tibi prodo*, 'you, perhaps, as your way is, are calling for, and indeed expecting an oration from me; but I . . . produce for you my poetical recreations,' 4.14.1). His playfulness, however, stops short of the frank expressions and explicit language employed by his models:

---

[42] For Pliny's general avoidance of traditional *exempla* in his letters, in favour of figures drawn from recent generations (especially from the generation still alive in his own youth), see Chapter 4.

[43] We might also note that this is the first letter in the Cicero cycle after Book 3, in which Pliny's achievement of the consulship is delicately highlighted (see Chapter 1).

[44] For an indispensable reading of 4.14, see Marchesi (2008) 71–8.

erit eruditionis tuae cogitare summos illos et grauissimos uiros qui talia scripserunt
non modo lasciuia rerum, sed ne uerbis quidem nudis abstinuisse; quae nos
refugimus, non quia seueriores (unde enim?), sed quia timidiores sumus. (4.14.4)

It will become one of your learning to reflect that those men of great position
and high dignity who have written this kind of thing, have not abstained – to say
nothing of frolicsome themes – from the most naked expressions. These last I have
avoided, not from my being more austere (how indeed could that be?) but from
my being more timid than they.

We have not entirely left the world of Cicero's letters – *Fam.* 9.22, after all,
is about the proper use of risqué language where appropriate – and that an
appeal in a letter about poetry to the *grauissimi uiri* of previous generations
should call Cicero to the reader's mind (as a letter about oratorical style
already had in Book 1) is confirmed by Cicero's next appearance in the
collection, at 5.3.5, where his name leads the list of the great men who
allowed themselves to relax in verse:

an ego uerear – neminem uiuentium, ne quam in speciem adulationis incidam,
nominabo – , sed ego uerear ne me non satis deceat, quod decuit M. Tullium,
C. Caluum, Asinium Pollionem, M. Messalam, Q. Hortensium, M. Brutum, L.
Sullam, Q. Catulum, Q. Scaeuolam, Seruium Sulpicium, Varronem, Torquatum,
immo Torquatos, C. Memmium, Lentulum Gaetulicum, Annaeum Senecam et
proxime Verginium Rufum et, si non sufficiunt exempla priuata, Diuum Iulium,
Diuum Augustum, Diuum Neruam, Tiberium Caesarem?

Shall I be afraid (I won't name any living person, for fear of exposing myself to any
appearance of flattery), but shall I be afraid that that is not quite becoming to me
which became M. Tullius, C. Calvus, Asinius Pollio, M. Messala, Q. Hortensius,
M. Brutus, L. Sulla,. Q. Catulus, Q. Scaevola, Ser. Sulpicius, Varro, Torquatus,
nay the Torquati, C. Memmius, Lentulus Gaetulicus, Annaeus Seneca and recently
Verginius Rufus; or if examples short of imperial do not suffice, the Emperor Julius,
the Emperor Augustus, the Emperor Nerva, Tiberius Caesar?

Again, Pliny is defensive, and almost excessively modest. Since he has been
criticized for writing *and reciting* light verse, his appeal to Cicero (and
others) situates Pliny in respectable traditions in which a great man's verse
may win fame but remain safely classified as a second string.[45] In this
letter, however, he presents himself as falling short of his model; just as
he had been too shy in 4.14.4 to write in the blunt language of his poetic
predecessors, here Pliny portrays himself as unable to trust in his own

---

[45] We should note that the first two names in the list are those of the Latin models to whom he looks
for oratorical inspiration in 1.2. This list also contains the only instance in which Seneca is named in
the entire collection; this epistolary predecessor, at least, is to be found only by the knowledgeable
and alert reader.

talent and needing critical assistance from his recitation audiences in order to produce worthwhile work:

recito tamen, quod illi an fecerint nescio. etiam: sed illi iudicio suo poterant esse contenti, mihi modestior constantia est quam ut satis absolutum putem, quod a me probetur. (5.3.7)

However, I recite too; and I do not know whether those who have been named did this or not. Very good. But *they* might well be content with their own judgement, while my self-consciousness is too modest for me to think a thing sufficiently perfect because it is approved by myself.

What Pliny has not yet made explicit, however, is the kind of Ciceronian poetry we are expected to be thinking of, although given the contexts in 4.14 and 5.3, in which Pliny is clearly talking about short, light verse, we are not being steered towards the translations of Aratus or the epic upon Cicero's own consulship. Pliny focuses rather upon Cicero's varied, 'Alexandrian' early work (*Halcyones, Pontius Glaucus, Uxorius, Nilus*) which showed Cicero as 'an experimental precursor of the Neoterics'.[46]

However, the next letter to mention Cicero, 7.4, expands upon both Cicero's inspirational role for Pliny and the nature of Pliny's own versifying. Like so many others in the collection, the letter is about Pliny's commitment to variety: he tells his addressee, Pontius, that his poetic output began with an unnamed *tragoedia*, continued in Icaria on Pliny's journey home from military service with some elegies inspired by the island, and even included a little epic (subject matter unspecified). It picks up 3.15 in the declaration of Pliny's long-standing poetic interests (*numquam a poetice... alienus fui*, 'I was at no time... averse from the poetic art,' 7.4.2) and also recalls 4.14 as it purports to offer a 'career history' of Pliny's poetic composition in *otium*, culminating in the hendecasyllables which Pliny had also sent to Plinius Paternus.[47] At 7.4.6, however, he sends Pontius the verses he wrote upon finding Cicero's poem to Tiro in Asinius Gallus' synkrisis between Cicero and Asinius' own father.

---

[46] Wilkinson (1982) 247. Cf. Gee (2001) 522–3. Plutarch's report (*Cic.* 2.3) of Cicero's early productivity is strongly reminiscent of Pliny's claim to a youthful interest in poetry. The echo of the title of Cicero's earliest work, *Pontius Glaucus*, in the name of the addressee of 7.4, Pontius, may be coincidental, although we remark elsewhere upon Pliny's habit of playing upon addressees' names.

[47] This account of a compositional history should be contrasted with Pliny's index to his uncle's output in 3.5; each genre is presented in sequence, and the first two, at least, are tied to particular phases of the young Pliny's life. Moreover, these compositions are the fruit of snatches of *otium* (on journeys, and on sleepless afternoons when Pliny is trying to rest), as the elder Pliny's were of the extra time he squeezed out of a busy professional day. The surprise, if one thinks of the traditional 'hierarchy' of poetic genres, is that Pliny makes his hendecasyllables, not his hexameters, into the crowning element of his poetic 'career'. See further Gibson and Steel (2010) 125–37.

legebantur in Laurentino mihi libri Asini Galli de comparatione patris et Ciceronis. Incidit epigramma Ciceronis in Tironem suum. dein cum meridie (erat enim aestas) dormiturus me recepissem, nec obreperet somnus, coepi reputare maximos oratores hoc studii genus et in oblectationibus habuisse et in laude posuisse. intendi animum contraque opinionem meam post longam desuetudinem perquam exiguo temporis momento id ipsum, quod me ad scribendum sollicitauerat, his uersibus exaraui. (7.4.3–5)

The chapters of Asinius Gallus on the comparison between his father and Cicero were being read to me at my house at Laurentum, when an epigram of Cicero on his favourite Tiro occurred. Afterwards, on retiring for a midday siesta (for it was summer time) when sleep failed to steal over me, I began to ponder how the greatest orators not only esteemed this kind of literary effort as a recreation, but also took credit for it. I applied my mind, and, contrary to my expectation, after such long disuse, in a remarkably short space of time scribbled the following verses on the very subject which had induced me to write.

Once again, Cicero is introduced by a hostile source who (as the opening lines of Pliny's poem emphasize) judged his own father's work to be superior to that of Cicero; the love poem about Tiro which has caught Pliny's imagination was almost certainly included to mock Cicero's poetic style.

It is Pliny's construction of his relationship with this (undeniably peculiar) poetic model, and what he does with it in his own poetry, which is at issue here. The reader is invited here to think of a very mixed background indeed (one which is, paradoxically, not entirely or even primarily Ciceronian), and Pliny's commitment to variety is instantiated here in the very form and language of the letter's narrative and the enclosed poem. The story of Pliny's inspiration begins in the world of prose during Pliny's normal studies at his villa (*in Laurentino*), but Pliny seizes upon a (probably pseudepigraphic) erotic epigram quoted in Asinius' work, and then casts the next part of the story in the language of erotic poetry. Instead of an Ovidian afternoon with a girl while sleep eludes him,[48] Pliny expresses poetic eroticism by constructing a kind of 'meeting with a mentor' moment (in the style of Callimachus' dream of Hesiod, for example) which gives rise to an almost bucolic competition in love songs (*his ego lectis | 'cur post haec' inquam 'nostros celamus amores'*, 'when I had read these verses, I asked, "why should I conceal my loves after this?"' 7.4.6).

There is a kind of metaliterary voyeurism here, by comparison with *Amores* 1.5 (or, indeed, with Catullus 50), since Pliny is a third party,

---

[48] Cf. Ov. *Am*.1.5.1–2. 7.4.4 is also particularly reminiscent of Catull. 50.10–13. For the motif of literary composition during a bout of insomnia, see Gibson, B. (2006) 381. For Pliny's replication of the intensity of Catull. 50 in 6.1, see Chapter 2. For Pliny as a poet, see Appendix 3.

a watchful/watching reader of Cicero's erotic epigram which gives him licence to attempt something of his own in this line. The key elements in Pliny's description of his work here, however, are his speed of composition (7.4.5)[49] and the gaps of time between the separate phases of his poetic career.[50] This is entirely unlike his usual laborious, time-consuming writing process (described in 9.36, also in a slightly Ovidian setting of closed shutters and half-light). Once again, then, a Ciceronian work is associated with pleasure and creative ease.

It is important to recognize that Pliny's allegiance to a Ciceronian model (even a creatively enriched one) for his poetic efforts represents a contentious and self-conscious choice; to set oneself in the tradition of a statesman-poet who became synonymous with limited poetic talent suggests the playful self-awareness of the man who knows that verse is not the foundation of his career but who knows, too, that the quality of Cicero's verse was a topic of great interest among his contemporaries and the *littérateurs* of the previous generation; moreover, his process of matching himself against Cicero in almost every genre only highlights yet again the long delay before this 'Ciceronian' epistolographer gets round to matching his own *letters* (as opposed to his oratory or his verse) against those of his model.[51]

Even while Pliny delays direct engagement with Cicero's letters, however, they remain in the allusive infrastructure of the collection. That the Ciceronian epigram of 7.4.3 should be addressed to Tiro, for example, is suggestive: Tiro is certainly best known from Cicero's own letters, and Pliny may here be playing upon the potential for surprises in a relationship between epistolographer and addressee; at all events, there is a confusion of several genres in this letter. In the erotic half-light of the afternoon siesta Pliny realizes (once again?) that an orator and epistolographer may also be a poet (here with a special passion for an addressee named Tiro).

Pliny further delays explicit acknowledgement of Cicero as an *epistolary* model, and returns to defence of his oratorical recitations in 7.17, with a creative reworking of one or perhaps two Ciceronian passages. At the heart of the letter, Pliny's account of the laborious and multi-stage process of revising his work (*nullum emendandi genus omitto*, 'I neglect no means of

---

[49] Cf. 7.4.7. For Cicero's speed and facility in poetic composition, see Plut. *Cic.* 40.3. For Pliny's more habitual earnest and effortful revision of his (non-poetic) work, cf. 5.8.6.

[50] Cf. 3.15.1.

[51] 4.14.10. For criticism of Cicero's poetic talents, see Sen. *Controu.* 3 *praef.* 8; Quint. *Inst.* 11.1.24; Tac. *Dial.* 21.6; Mart. 2.89.3–4; Juv. 10.122–6. Plut. *Cic.* 2.4–5 records Cicero's stellar reputation as a poet in his later years, but also the increasingly critical response of later generations.

improvement', 7.17.7) recalls Crassus' strictures in the *de Oratore* about the importance of care in composition, where diligent preparation is prized above impromptu facility, and polish in writing above both. Crassus recommends that one write as much as possible, since 'the pen is the best and most eminent author and teacher of speaking' (*stilus optimus et praestantissimus dicendi effector ac magister*, Cic. *De or.* 1.150). *Fam.* 7.25 offers similar advice to Gallus, as part of a paragraph praising the style of a passage in the letter to which Cicero is here replying:

urge igitur nec transuersum unguem, quod aiunt, a stilo; **is enim est dicendi opifex**; atque equidem aliquantum iam etiam noctis assumo. (*Fam.* 7.25.2)

So press on and don't budge a nail's breadth, as they say, from your pen. The pen makes the author! For my part I work o'nights now as well as in the daytime.

However, Pliny adapts Crassus' advice from the *de Oratore*, adding to the list of exercises (translation, copious writing, vocal exercises, and memory training) Pliny's own favoured practice of recitation and emendation on the basis of audience feedback. The spur to perfecting written work, he says, is fear of adverse reactions from his public: *quod M. Cicero de stilo, ego de metu sentio: timor est, timor emendator asperrimus*, 'For M. Cicero's opinion about the pen I hold with regard to fear. Apprehension is the sharpest corrector' (7.17.13).[52] Pliny's reworking of Cicero's passage supplies, by implication, something he claimed to lack in 5.3: a (quasi-)Ciceronian justification for his habit of recitation.[53] At the same time, it reinforces Pliny's persona as a cautious writer, lacking in confidence in his own talent, and reliant rather upon diligent revision and polishing of the work on which his best chance of lasting fame depends.[54]

So far, then, Cicero as letter-writer has been the target of allusion but not explicitly named in Pliny's collection as a model for letters, as Pliny has focused rather on the orator, poet, literary patron and public man. The only time we have come close to an open acknowledgement of the Ciceronian model is in 3.20.10. Here Pliny closes a letter to Maesius Maximus on the dangers of the *lex tabellaria* with an invitation to the reader to remember

---

[52] His disdain for the *sermunculi* of those who criticize his recitations may also allude to another pair of Ciceronian texts (*Deiot.* 33, *Att.* 13.10.3); see Ussani (1974–5) 182.

[53] For Pliny's habit of planting an idea to which he will return in a later letter, one might compare the increase in specificity and development of thought between 4.14.4 (where Cicero is similarly unnamed) and 5.3.5 (which does name Cicero), as well as that between 5.3.7–8 and 7.17.13 (all discussed above). For at least one instance in which Cicero himself did read his work to others, see *Q. fr.* 3.5.1–2 (on changes made to the *de Re Publica* at the instigation of his friend Sallustius, after a reading of an early draft).

[54] 5.8.6.

the *ueteres* who were the great archetypes in letter-writing, and who were blessed with an abundance of important subjects:

haec tibi scripsi, primum ut aliquid noui scriberem, deinde ut non numquam de re publica loquerer, cuius materiae nobis quanto rarior quam ueteribus occasio, tanto minus omittenda est.[55]

I have written this to you, first, in order to write of something new; next that I may occasionally speak of public affairs the occasions for which, as they are rarer for us than for our ancestors, so they are the less to be neglected.

The reader's natural assumption that these *ueteres* are Cicero and his correspondents is reinforced by the letter's strongly Ciceronian allusions: Pliny begins by recalling other texts about the same issue (*meministine te saepe legisse*, 'do you not remember often reading . . . ?'), and clearly draws upon Cicero's discussion of the risks and benefits of secret ballots at *Leg.* 3.34.[56] Here the distinction between Cicero's generation of letter-writers and Pliny's rests solely upon the availability of *materia*, and Pliny asserts a wish for his collection to carry at least some of the flavour of the letters of earlier generations (*habeant **nostrae quoque litterae** aliquid non humile nec sordidum*, 'I would have *our letters, too*, be of those which contain something out of the common and the paltry').

In a pattern which should now be familiar to the reader, then, it is only at the beginning of Book 9 that Pliny first mentions Cicero by name as the great predecessor in epistolography, as he returns in 9.2 to the disparity between his *ingenium* and that of Cicero.[57] Once again, comparison between Pliny and Cicero is ascribed to the addressee, while Pliny himself demurs:

praeterea nec materia plura scribendi dabatur. neque enim eadem nostra condicio quae M. Tulli, ad cuius exemplum nos uocas. illi enim et copiosissimum ingenium, et par ingenio qua uarietas rerum qua magnitudo largissime suppetebat; nos quam angustis terminis claudamur etiam tacente me perspicis, nisi forte uolumus scholasticas tibi atque, ut ita dicam, umbraticas litteras mittere. (9.2.2–3)

Besides, I had no materials for writing more. Nor, indeed, is my situation the same as that of M. Tullius, whose example you invite me to follow. For not merely was he gifted with a most prolific genius, but events in great variety and of great

---

[55] One might note here the contrast with 1.2 in the pattern of allusion: Pliny here claims to be harking back to the letters of earlier generations, but gestures rather towards a Ciceronian treatise, whereas 1.2 (ostensibly about oratorical composition) alludes to a Ciceronian *letter* on the subject of imitating Ciceronian style.

[56] For discussion, see Morello (2003) 189–91.

[57] For more on the interplay between 3.20 and 9.2, considered in the light of the collection as a whole, see Chapter 8.

importance supplied that genius with abundant material. How narrow are the limits in which *I* am enclosed, you well know, without my telling you, unless haply I should wish to send you letters of the school-exercise kind, and from the shade of the closet, if I may so express it.

Pliny obliquely acknowledges the risks inherent in selecting one's letters for publication on the basis of *cura* alone, and recognizes a reader's expectations that the letters of a lawyer consul might be both numerous and lengthy. Indeed, he seemingly acknowledges his distance from Cicero as epistolographer at the very moment he first acknowledges Cicero's letters as the model with whom all Pliny's readers would have been comparing his work so far. 9.2 also seems to advertise the character and design of the final book, in which a greater proportion of the letters are indeed to be rather shorter in length than has been the norm in Books 1–8.[58]

   This belated placement of the only explicit reference to Cicero's letters, right at the beginning of the ninth book of the collection, finally acknowledges the reader's natural tendency to think of literary predecessors in the same genre. Moreover, given that a reader's interest in letters is often quite naturally stimulated by the fame of the letter-writer himself, it seems appropriate that Pliny delays the most explicit and self-conscious acknowledgement of Cicero as an *epistolary* model until Book 9, when the success both of his public career and of his literary output has been most fully established and documented. As Marchesi notes, this letter, although seemingly modest about Pliny's epistolary standing, actually trumps Cicero by alluding to one of Pliny's own earlier letters, in which Pliny himself writes to Paulinus to ask for more, and longer letters:[59]

grauiter irascor, quod a te tam diu litterae nullae. exorare me potes uno modo, si nunc saltem plurimas et longissimas miseris. (2.2.1)

I am grievously angry with you for not having sent me any letter for such a long time. There is only one way in which you can obtain my forgiveness, and that is by now at all events writing to me frequently and at great length.

   Echoes of 2.2 in 9.2 suggest that Sabinus (the addressee of 9.2) is expected to have read the published version of 2.2 and to have treated its motifs as a 'vehicle of new allusions'.[60] Pliny is, therefore, demonstrating, in a letter about the relative weakness of his *ingenium* and the paucity of his material, just how popular his letters have actually become – so popular, indeed,

---

[58] One should note also that Pliny elsewhere feels the need to apologize for long letters, even in letters which are shorter than the Ciceronian average (see e.g. 2.5.13).
[59] Marchesi (2008) 230–3.   [60] Marchesi (2008) 233.

that he has himself provided an epistolary model for the addressees of his later letters. This approach is very attractive: Book 9 as a whole is full of suggestions that Pliny's addressees have been reading his work, and at 9.19 we find another instance of an addressee apparently having read a letter addressed to another individual (and published as 6.10); such 'advertisement' serves as a neat (and relatively modest) counterweight to the apparently anxious self-deprecation of 9.2.

Finally, however, as we shall see in Chapter 8, it is in the letters of Book 10 that Pliny's mastery of Ciceronian letters comes to fruition, as he develops a new way of writing about public service in an eastern province (an obviously Ciceronian topic) in a plethora of most un-Ciceronian short letters which seem at first sight to match the description of the *inlitteratissimas litteras* that Pliny bemoans in 1.10.9.

PLINY'S 'ENRICHMENT' OF THE CICERONIAN EPISTOLARY MODEL

Pliny, then, situates himself in a 'Ciceronian' tradition, defending his current literary and professional practices by reference to the illustrious model his readers and contemporaries are expecting him to emulate. His allusions to Cicero are multiple and varied, even within a single letter: so, as we have observed above, a letter such as 1.2, which reflects upon Cicero as an oratorical model, alludes to a Ciceronian letter about a contemporary orator's flattering attempts to emulate him, while, conversely, the meditation upon the gap between Pliny and the *ueteres* in letter-writing crowns 3.20, itself reminiscent of a non-epistolary Ciceronian work, the *de Legibus*.

Ultimately, however, if we wish to understand how Pliny presents himself in relation to his predecessors, we need to read not just individual letters, nor even solely the 'Cicero cycle' which we have discussed in this chapter. We must also read each letter in the Cicero cycle in relation to its immediate context within its book. Limitations of space preclude a full study of each letter in this regard, but in at least two cases we see Pliny exploiting the interpretative possibilities of letter pairings to invite readers to consider the broader spectrum of his models: both 7.4 and 9.2 are followed by letters which are thematically linked to them but call to mind alternative (unnamed) models for Pliny's work.

In 7.4, as we have seen, Pliny showcases his own verses about the erotic epigram to Tiro which he discovered in a passage of Asinius Gallus. After the passage's reading, Pliny says, he withdrew to his room for a siesta but, as sleep proved elusive, he began to think about his Ciceronian model and wonder if he could not also produce the same sort of work. The poem is unusually specific for Pliny, as he gives the names of his subjects, Cicero and Tiro, and spells out his own compositional motivations. A Ciceronian inspiration for a poem about the writing of erotic verse is surprising enough, and we have already noted the faintly Ovidian quality Pliny confers upon the situation he depicts: where the Ovid of *Amores* 1.5 would have spent a sleepless afternoon in the half-light of his room making love to his girl, Pliny builds upon his alternative model of Catullus 50 (a passionate account of competitive banter with Calvus) and uses the time of insomnia to compete with Cicero in yet another genre.[61] However, Pliny compounds the surprise – and the unexpected mixing of genres – by positioning next in the book a prose love letter to his wife, Calpurnia, in which he depicts himself as an *exclusus amator*:

incredibile est quanto desiderio tui tenear. in causa amor primum, deinde quod non consueuimus abesse. inde est quod magnam noctium partem in imagine tua uigil exigo; inde quod interdiu, quibus horis te uisere solebam, ad diaetam tuam ipsi me, ut uerissime dicitur, pedes ducunt; quod denique aeger et maestus ac similis excluso a uacuo limine recedo. unum tempus his tormentis caret, quo in foro et amicorum litibus conteror. aestima tu, quae uita mea sit, cui requies in labore, in miseria curisque solacium. (7.5)

It is incredible what a yearning for you possesses me. The reason of this is first of all my love for you, and next that we have not been accustomed to be separated. Hence it is that I spend a great part of my nights wakeful over your image; hence in the day, at the times when I was in the habit of looking in on you, my feet of their own accord take me – as the phrase runs most truly – to your apartment; hence in the end, sick at heart and sad, as one who has been denied admittance, I retire from the deserted threshold. One time alone is free from those torments, that in which I am worn out in the Forum by the lawsuits of my friends. It is for you to judge what my life must be when it finds its repose in labour, its solace in miseries and cares!

In 7.5 Pliny picks up the erotic tone of 7.4 in what is effectively a prose version of amatory elegy, thereby neatly illustrating not only his mastery of the elegiac topos but also his distance from the elegiac persona: where an elegist might be expected to talk about how the author has rejected the respectable world of political and professional life in the Forum for the sake of *militia amoris*, here, by contrast, the lover writes his 'poem' in prose, and comforts himself with precisely that 'wearing' professional activity (*litibus conteror*) which is the subject of so many other letters in his collection. We are 'seeing double', as it were: Pliny competes both with Cicero and (by

---

[61] For Pliny's interest in Catull. 50 (a model also for 1.15), see Morello (2007) 187–8.

the subtlest of implications) with Ovid or any other elegist, but ultimately reaffirms his persona as the man of *labor*.

We are, however, invited to 'see double' in another respect, too. We have already noted (Chapter 2) a programme of witty allusion to the Ciceronian Tiro in Pliny's passionate treatment of his own friend, Calestrius Tiro, and, further, a remarkable concinnity of language in Pliny's letters to Tiro and to Calpurnia, as well as a subtle interlinking of 6.1, to Tiro, and 6.4, another letter in which Pliny is missing Calpurnia. In Book 7 the pairing of Pliny's Tiro first with Cicero's freedman and then with Calpurnia recurs, as Pliny 'reports' and reworks Cicero's complaints of amatory frustration to compose equally passionate verse about his own emotions (and his own Tiro), and then shifts quickly to a different sort of amatory address, returning to prose and to his relationship with his absent wife.[62] The linkage between 7.4 and 7.5 and the simultaneous presence of the two Tiros (Ciceronian/ancient and Plinian/modern) seem all the more strongly marked in the light of the Calpurnia–Tiro nexus which had been established more subtly in the previous book.[63] An instance, then, of Pliny mixing genres and literary models in surprising ways is to be found in these paired and contrasted letters.

Another allusive linkage via twin models for the letters may be observed between 9.2 and 9.3. The former, as we saw above, situates Pliny as a letter-writer in relation to Cicero, and defensively rejects a Ciceronian epistolary style as being out of reach in Pliny's day, while simultaneously (and allusively) highlighting Pliny's position as an epistolographical model in his own right. The letter also, however, offers (and once again rejects as inappropriate to the addressee's circumstances) an alternative epistolary model: the scholastic and philosophical letter ('letters of the school-exercise kind, and from the shade of the closet, if I may so express it', 9.2.3). A reader might well think of Seneca at this point; the letters to Lucilius are never explicitly mentioned in Pliny, but it would be misguided to think that Seneca's works – letters and treatises alike – are not also part of the allusive infrastructure of Pliny's work. Here the reader who thinks of Seneca in 9.2.3

---

[62] We might further compare with Pliny's paired letters (which end in the rejection of *otium* in favour of professional distractions) the juxtaposition of Catullus' poem 50, the poem of passionate affection for Calvus (felt and expressed in *otium: otiosi*, Catull. 50.1) and poem 51, his reaction to the sight of Lesbia unattainable and in company with another man, which ends with the famous meditation upon the dangers of *otium* (Catull. 51.13–16). On this pairing, see Finamore (1984) 12.

[63] For a similar intertextual game in which Pliny plays upon the coincidence of names, see Marchesi (2008) 232–3 on the allusion in 9.2 (addressed to Sabinus) to the Sabinus of Ovid's *Am.* 2.18.27–32 and *Pont.* 4.13–16; cf. further Marchesi (2008) 234–5 on the (not accidental) coincidence in the name (Paulinus) of the addressees of 9.3 and Seneca's *de Breuitate Vitae*.

will find Pliny returning – once again in competitive mode – to a concise survey of Senecan themes in the immediately following letter: 9.3, a pithy assessment of the criteria for a good life, recalls within its short compass three Senecan works, the *de Beata Vita*, the *de Otio* and the *de Breuitate Vitae*, and simultaneously makes multiple allusions to another prose model whose importance for Pliny has been too rarely explored, namely Sallust's proem to the *Bellum Catilinae*:

alius aliud: ego beatissimum existimo, qui bonae mansuraeque famae praesumptione perfruitur, certusque posteritatis cum futura gloria uiuit. ac mihi nisi praemium aeternitatis ante oculos, pingue illud altumque otium placeat. etenim omnes homines arbitror oportere aut immortalitatem suam aut mortalitatem cogitare, et illos quidem contendere eniti, hos quiescere remitti, nec breuem uitam caducis laboribus fatigare, ut uideo multos misera simul et ingrata imagine industriae ad uilitatem sui peruenire. haec ego tecum quae cotidie mecum, ut desinam mecum, si dissentis tu; quamquam non dissentis, ut qui semper clarum aliquid et immortale mediterere. uale.[64]

Different men have different ideas on the subject, but I for my part deem that individual the most fortunate who enjoys to the full the foretaste of a noble and enduring fame, and, assured of posthumous reputation, lives in the company of his future glory. And for me indeed, if the prize of immortality were not before my eyes, the usual comfortable and sound repose would be my choice. For I suppose it is the duty of all men to think of themselves as either immortal or mortal; in the former case, certainly, to contend and to exert themselves; in the latter, to keep quiet, to repose themselves, and not to fatigue their short existence by fleeting efforts; as I see many do, who, by a wretched and at the same time thankless appearance of activity, only attain in the end to a contempt for themselves. All this, which I say daily to myself, I now say to you, that I may leave off saying it to myself, if you dissent; though to be sure you, in your character of one who is always meditating some great and immortal work, will not dissent.

Here Pliny caps 9.2, in which he seemed to reject Ciceronian and Senecan epistolography alike, with a short letter in which (in an extreme instance of the process of 'miniaturization' we have mentioned) two pre-eminently Senecan topics – the principled choice of *otium* and the proper use of one's *uita breuis* – are further coloured by Sallust's insistence at the beginning of the *Bellum Catilinae* that man must strive to leave a record of himself (an obsession which has already emerged as one of the dominant motifs in Pliny's own collection, and which is therefore all the more appropriately

---

[64] *Alius aliud* ~ Sall. *Cat.* 2.9, 3.1; *omnes homines arbitror oportere aut immortalitatem suam aut mortalitatem cogitare et illos quidem contendere eniti* ~ *Cat.* 1.1; *breuem uitam* ~ *Cat.* 1.1. For Seneca's letters as models for Pliny's, see Marchesi (2008) 15; for 9.3 in particular as a 'miniaturised response' to Seneca's *de Breuitate Vitae*, see Marchesi (2008) 235.

revisited at the beginning of the final book).[65] That Pliny's Sallustianism is here so markedly based on Sallust's monograph about the events of Cicero's consulship is serendipitous, to say the least. Once again, Pliny's readers are invited to see (at least) double: Pliny rejects both Cicero and Seneca, but manages then to compete with both, and with others as well. Pliny's relationship with his models, then, is complex and multi-faceted, and his relationship with Cicero, in particular, is always set in the context of alternative and competing models, some of very different kinds.

We move on now from a study of Pliny's literary models from the late republic and early empire to consideration in Chapter 4 of his personal models from the more recent past, but we close this chapter with a suggestion that will be further explored in Chapter 8. Pliny differentiates between the subject matter of Cicero's letters and his own by contrasting the different levels of *uarietas rerum* available to Cicero and to himself – a motif which, as we have indicated, became commonplace among Cicero's successors, but which was also founded upon Cicero's own awareness of the richness of the contemporary narrative.[66] Individual letters of Pliny, to be sure, tended (ostensibly, at least) to focus upon restricted material. Nevertheless, if we look at pairings and juxtapositions of letters, and at the design of the collection as a whole, the wider perspective reveals the multiplicity and competitiveness of Pliny's allusions and the sophistication of his reworkings of an astonishingly broad range of models. If *uarietas* is to be regarded as especially and typically Ciceronian, and Pliny can offer no variety of contemporary political material, nevertheless his letters will in their totality embody *uarietas*, and become in themselves a part of the literary *uarietas* which he enjoins upon Fuscus in 7.9 and for which he finds justification for himself in the variety of literary output – oratorical, poetic and epistolographic – which he ascribes to Cicero in the Cicero 'cycle'.

---

[65] Cf. 5.5.4.   [66] E.g. *Fam.* 6.6: *temporum nostrorum uarietatem.*

Pliny's elders and betters
The Elder Pliny, Vestricius Spurinna, Corellius Rufus, Verginius Rufus (and Silius Italicus)

As noted in the Introduction to the present book, this chapter and the three which follow it form a loose quartet. Moving away from sustained exploration of methods of reading the collection – and from study of the literary context of the *Letters* – these four chapters focus more intensely on subjects thrown up by the collection or on themes evident within it. They divide into two loose pairs, where the first pair joins a study of Pliny's relationship with the older (and eventually younger) generations (Chapter 4) to a study of Pliny and his equals and peers (Chapter 5). Even here, however, we will continue to raise questions about methods of reading the collection, since in both chapters we shall be reading Pliny for cycles of letters connected by recurring individuals. As will become clear, these cycles display a formal difference from one another: where the (elderly) individuals of Chapter 4 are largely the subject of obituary or 'commemorative' letters, the equals and peers of Chapter 5 often feature instead as addressees of Pliny.

In terms of subjects and themes within the collection, the present chapter focuses particularly on Pliny's awareness both of the example set by his 'elders and betters', and of the need to use one's time and manage one's day (and even career) effectively. The management of time, in fact, is never very far from Pliny's mind within the correspondence. This may surprise modern readers, but time (and its use) is the main topic of discussion in Seneca's very first letter.[1] Its prominence also in Pliny's *Letters* is reflected in the second pairing of chapters to follow Chapters 4 and 5. Chapter 6 will include a closer look at those parts of the day devoted specifically to literary study (and will give especial prominence to the model of Seneca), while Chapter 7 will include study of a particular context for time management, that is Pliny's country villas.

---

[1] For Seneca's concern with time as a concept of moral importance throughout the letters, see Richardson-Hay (2006) 131. Cf. Henderson (2002a) 83–5 for the influence of Seneca's first letter on Pliny 3.1 and 3.5 (both analysed below), and 118–24 for Seneca's importance in Book 3 generally.

THE ELDER PLINY, SPURINNA, CORELLIUS, VERGINIUS

The insistence that we have important lessons to learn from the example set by national ancestors or family elders is a familiar Roman way of investing the past with value.[2] Pliny's participation in this tradition of respect for such 'exemplarity' is evident throughout the corpus, for example with regard to members of the 'Stoic opposition',[3] and – even more emphatically – to men of an older generation who are either members of Pliny's family or closely connected to it.[4] In this chapter we concentrate on the latter group, focusing above all on his uncle and adoptive father (the Elder Pliny) and on Vestricius Spurinna; but including also Corellius Rufus and Verginius Rufus. The collective prominence of these four men is a notable feature of the *Letters*, and Pliny devotes much energy to working through the implications for his own behaviour of the examples they have set. The present chapter begins with the final appearance of the Elder Pliny in the collection in Book 6, where the Younger Pliny reflects on the closeness with which he modelled himself in his adolescence on the Elder. We then work our way back through the collection towards Book 3, where Pliny engages with the limitations of the Elder Pliny as a potential model for his more mature self, and with the greater attractions of the twice-consul Vestricius Spurinna.[5] Even the latter will turn out to be a not entirely appropriate model for the Younger Pliny. Nevertheless, as we shall see, Book 3 also features Silius Italicus in the significant role of thoroughly negative example. The chapter will conclude with a look at the limitations for Pliny of such other models as Corellius and Verginius amidst Pliny's growing insistence on his own exemplarity for Rome's younger generation.

   In order to provide some context for our study of Pliny and his elders, we revive the reading habits of Chapter 1 (where the *Letters* were read for a narrative of Pliny's life), and attempt to reconstruct the particular story of Pliny's evolving relationships with his seniors. In handling the fragments of this story – scattered over Books 1–9 of the *Letters* (and the epistolary

---

[2] See esp. Roller (2004) and T. Morgan (2007) 122–59 for the broader Greco-Roman context; more briefly Mayer (1991) 143–8. For Pliny's rhetoric of exemplarity in general, see Gazich (2003).

[3] For the language of exemplarity applied particularly to Arria and Fannia, cf. 4.16.1, 7.19.7, also 6.24.4–5. Pliny does not hesitate to apply such language to women in the correspondence in general; cf. e.g. 1.14.6, 3.1.5, 4.19.1, 8.5.1.

[4] For a Roman tendency to seek models particularly from within one's own family, see Roller (2004) 24–5, and cf. esp. 8.13.1.

[5] Compare the broadly complementary conclusions of Cova (2001), who includes several letters not considered here, including 7.9, 8.20 and 9.33. See also Méthy (2007) 424–39. For literature on the Younger Pliny in relation to the Elder, see Appendix 3.

preface to the Elder's *Natural History*) – we will offer even less resistance than in Chapter 1 to the temptation to supply gaps in the narrative.

Vestricius Spurinna, Corellius Rufus and Verginius Rufus are almost certainly connections inherited by Pliny directly from the Elder,[6] and all three may originally have been residents of 'Pliny country',[7] i.e. the regions bordering Pliny's home town of Comum in Northern Italy.[8] Indeed, an especially determined reader could come to the conclusion, based on various hints in the *Letters*, that Pliny was related in some way to the families of Corellius[9] and Spurinna.[10] For his part Verginius achieved a closeness of connection to the Younger through being appointed his legal guardian (2.1.8 *tutor*).[11] Since only those under fourteen were assigned a guardian, Pliny must have lost his natural father while still relatively young. At any rate Verginius, as guardian, 'showed towards me the affection of a parent', according to Pliny (2.1.8). Pliny nevertheless appears to have spent a large amount of time in the company of his maternal uncle (3.5, 6.16), who would later adopt him (5.8.5). However, the death of the Elder in Pliny's eighteenth year (6.20.5) apparently left the Younger without a close family member to guide him at the very outset of his civilian career during the last months of the reign of Titus and the start of the reign of Domitian. The loss may have appeared particularly acute at the time, since, as Pliny himself tells us, the Elder had been in some favour with the father of Titus and Domitian (3.5.9), not to mention the fact that he had dedicated the *Natural History* to Titus before the latter's elevation and recorded there explicit instructions that his history of the Flavian dynasty be published by the Younger after his death (*HN* praef. 1, 20). Corellius and Verginius stepped into the breach. For in 4.17 Pliny reveals how, seeking office as a

---

[6] Syme, *RP* 7.50–89.

[7] For the classic definition of 'Pliny country' in the Transpadane areas stretching across the Augustan *regiones* from Vercellae in the west to Verona and beyond in the east, see Syme, *RP* 2.694–8 [= (1968) 135–7], 5.460 [= (1985a) 343].

[8] Pliny explicitly vouches for an origin shared with Verginius at 2.1.8, while the reader may infer the same for Corellius from the late-revealed closeness in 7.11 between Corellius' sister and Pliny's mother. Epigraphical evidence suggests that Verginius came from Mediolanum (*ILS* 982), thirty miles south of Comum, while Corellius appears to have his origin in Laus Pompeia, a town near Mediolanum; see Syme, *RP* 2.714–15 [= (1968) 146–7], 7.508–9, 640–1; also Birley (2000a) 51–2. For hints in Pliny's letters of an origin for Spurinna in 'Pliny country', see Syme, *RP* 7.542–3, also Syme (1958) 616.

[9] Syme, *RP* 5.465 [= (1985a) 347] (cf. 7.509) infers from 1.12.9 that a sister-in-law of Corellius stood as grandmother to Calpurnia (Pliny's wife). For Pliny and the Corellii, see Carlon (2009) 68–99.

[10] The assumption of some relation to Spurinna is based on the fact that Vestricius' wife Cottia is the joint addressee of 3.10: 'in the whole collection the only women who receive letters are related in some way to the author, even if remotely' (Syme, *RP* 7.542; cf. 7.511, 5.468 [= (1985a) 350]).

[11] On the reasons for the preference for Verginius over the Elder in this role, cf. Syme, *RP* 7.508 on the attractions of the childless Verginius and the probable absence abroad of the Elder in AD 70–6.

young man, Corellius was his *suffragator et testis*, 'supporter and backer', as he began office his *deductor et comes*, 'escort and attendant', and as he performed office his *consiliator et rector*, 'adviser and guide' (4.17.6). While Verginius, we learn, supported Pliny's candidature for office, came out of retirement to attend all his inaugurations and repeatedly nominated him for a priesthood (2.1.8). To judge from the affection shown Spurinna in 3.1 (and the closeness of connection evident elsewhere),[12] he too may have had some role to play in these formative years for the young Pliny.[13]

While it takes three people to fill the shoes of the Elder, this triad of men from 'Pliny country' is also a sharp reminder of one fundamental sense in which the Elder could not be fully exemplary to the Younger, particularly in his ascent of the *cursus honorum*. Unlike the Elder Pliny, who held a series of equestrian posts (3.5.3–4, 17; 6.16.4), these men were distinguished senators and each achieved the consulship during the Elder's lifetime. Corellius had been consul in the year before the eruption of Vesuvius in 78, Spurinna became consul for the second time in 98, while Verginius achieved the honour three times (63, 69 and 97).[14] Indeed Verginius, in the course of playing an ambiguous role in the revolt against Nero and accession of Galba in 68, had been proclaimed emperor by his own troops (Tac. *Hist.* 1.8.2, 1.52.4).[15] Pliny loyally defends Verginius' record in the *Letters*, and highlights his refusal of the supreme office.[16] At any rate all three, having lived quietly under Domitian and untainted by association with him, regained prominence under Nerva and served the new emperor in various capacities as part of his notorious 'gerontocracy' (mentioned already in Chapter 1).[17] As remarked also in Chapter 1, both Corellius and

---

[12] Cf. 1.5.8–10, 2.7, 3.10, 4.27.5, 5.17.

[13] However, as the example of Pliny's grumpy grandfather-in-law Calpurnius Fabatus suggests, to join this circle of admired elders it was not enough simply to be old, related to Pliny, and from near the Comum area; see Chapter 2 for Pliny's gentle correction of his non-exemplary behaviour in Book 6.

[14] The date for Spurinna's first consulship is uncertain (but is probably Vespasianic). For the epigraphical evidence against the old assumption of a third consulship for Spurinna, see Syme, *RP* 7.546. On the full careers of Spurinna and Verginius, see in more detail Syme, *RP* 7.512–20, 541–50. For Corellius, see McDermott (1971) 86–8.

[15] See Syme, *RP* 7.513ff., Shotter (2001). The Elder Pliny must have covered these events in his annalistic continuation of the history of Aufidius Bassus (3.5.6); see Syme (1958) 180 for speculation on the Elder as a source for Tacitus.

[16] Pliny defends the behaviour of Verginius Rufus in 68–9 at 9.19; the issue remains clearly visible in the background in 2.1 and 6.10. But for Tacitus' unenthusiastic attitude towards Verginius in the *Histories*, see Shotter (1967), Syme, *RP* 7.517, Whitton (2012).

[17] Spurinna appears to have been governor of Germania Inferior in 97 (2.7.1–2, 3.1.12); Corellius served on a land commission for Nerva (7.31.4); while Verginius, in addition to his third consulship, seems to have been marked down for service on a senatorial board (2.1.9). For all three men under Nerva, see Syme, *RP* 7.543–50.

Verginius would die during Nerva's reign, and Pliny carefully allots their obituary letters separate space in Books 1 and 2 (1.12, 2.1).

THE YOUTHFUL PLINY AND THE EXAMPLE OF THE ELDER AT VESUVIUS

For all the glamour and attractiveness of this consular triad, the Younger's relationship with the Elder is essential to Pliny's identity within the *Letters*. As such the Younger makes sustained efforts to come to terms with the implications of that relationship, particularly in the first six books of the correspondence. To help grasp the fundamental importance of the connection with the Elder, we begin with the text of a somewhat damaged inscription found in the late nineteenth century inside Roman Comum:[18]

[Caeci]liae f(iliae) suae nomin[e] L(ucius) Ca[eciliu]s C(ai) f(ilius) Ouf(entina tribu) Secundus praef(ectus) [fabr(um)] a co(n)s(ule) (quattuor)uir i(ure) d(icundo) pontif(ex) tem[plum] Aeternitati Romae et Augu[stor(um) c]um porticibus et ornamentis incohauit

[– Caeci]lius Secundus f(ilius) dedic[auit]

In the name of his daughter Caecilia, Lucius Caecilius Secundus, son of Gaius, of the tribe Oufentina, *praefectus fabrum* on the nomination of the consul, *quattuoruir* for the administration of justice, *pontifex*, began a temple to the Eternity of Rome and the Augusti with porticoes and decorations.

... Caecilius Secundus, his son, dedicated it.

The inscription apparently commemorates the establishment of a substantial temple of the imperial cult in Comum by Pliny's natural father L. Caecilius Secundus, and the eventual dedication of the temple by Pliny himself.[19] As the text of the dedication indicates, Pliny's father was of equestrian status (so *praefectus fabrum* suggests), a local magistrate of considerable importance in Comum, and clearly very wealthy. The foundation of the temple in the name of his daughter Caecilia vouchsafes to us the knowledge that Pliny had a sister. She is unmentioned in the correspondence and was presumably deceased.

---

[18] *CIL* 5, Add. 745 = *AE* (1983) 443 = Alföldy (1983) = Alföldy (1999a) 211–19 (with extended commentary on the inscription in the contributions of Alföldy). The text here is reprinted from Krieckhaus (2006) 215; for the place of discovery, see Krieckhaus (2006) 40 with n. 41. The second half of the inscription reappears in more lacunose form as *CIL* 5, Add. 746 (discovered in the same location as 745, and reproduced at Krieckhaus (2006) 215).

[19] A rival candidate for Pliny's father appears in *CIL* 5.5279 (L. Caecilius Cilo), although this man – another municipal magistrate at Comum – is more likely from an earlier period and perhaps a collateral relation; see Vidman *PIR*² P 490, Sherwin-White (1966) 70.

What is particularly significant about this inscription from the viewpoint of the present chapter is that it catches Pliny at a moment and in a guise in which he never appears in the letters: as Caecilius Secundus son of L. Caecilius Secundus, prior to his adoption by his maternal uncle.[20] In the *Letters* Pliny mentions his natural father only very indirectly, e.g. when referring to the designation of Verginius Rufus as legal guardian (2.1.8), or when mentioning sentimental attachment to estates near Comum which had belonged to his parents (*ex praediis meis . . . exceptis maternis paternisque*, 'out of my estates . . . excepting what had come to me from my mother and father', 7.11.5). By contrast, the memory of the Elder Pliny is perforce evident on every page of the correspondence. The full name of the Elder is C. Plinius Secundus, and his *nomen* is reflected prominently in the nomenclature of the Younger, after the latter is adopted. For in private inscriptions the Younger now appears regularly as C. **Plinius** L.f. [Ouf.] Caecilius Secundus,[21] while in the public *Fasti Ostienses* (Vidman (1980) 45) his name is shortened to C. Plinius Secundus. Significantly, the Younger Pliny would have been entitled to use his natural father's *nomen* and see his name inscribed there rather as **Caecilius** Secundus.[22] In the headings to his letters – if we can trust the evidence of the manuscripts[23] – he chooses to identify himself even more simply as C. Plinius.[24] This reduced nomenclature links the Younger quite unambiguously on every page to his well-known literary uncle and adopted father. The names used to address Pliny in elite social intercourse tend to reinforce the point. For the evidence provided by his own letters shows that he was known as both Plinius and Secundus – never as Caecilius – to contemporaries.[25] In broad terms, while individuals appear to have addressed him in conversation as 'Secunde', Plinius appears to have been the name by which he was referred to and

---

[20] Pliny's *praenomen* prior to adoption is unknown, but was presumably either Gaius or Lucius; see Sherwin-White (1966) 70.

[21] E.g. in the great Comum inscription *CIL* 5.5262 (printed in Appendix 1), also *CIL* 5.5263, 5.5264, 5.5667, *AE* (1972) 212; cf. the initials CPCS found as brick stamps at the site of the 'Tuscan' villa (documented in Chapter 7). For inscriptions relating to Pliny, see further Appendix 1.

[22] See Syme, *RP* 7.551.

[23] For the rather different situation in Cicero's *ad Familiares*, where the letter headings display a rich variety in the nomenclature of both sender and recipient, see White (2010) 67–73. For the likely provision of only two names for each recipient in Pliny, see Appendix 2.

[24] Cf. Dickey (2002) 60 on a special category of address or reference where literary figures can be identified by a well-known *gentilicium* alone (rather than the more normal *cognomen*); the example of letter 9.23.3 is cited at Dickey (2002) 60 n. 39.

[25] Cf. Syme, *RP* 5.644 [= (1985c) 195], 'In this instance, the *nomen* of the mother's brother prevailed, universally. "Caecilius" was common to excess.' In fact, the matter is perhaps more complicated; see Salomies (1992) 27–8, 59–60 with 59 n. 10.

popularly known.[26] By contrast, many inscriptions tell a visibly different story about the Younger, since there he is identified as (also) a Caecilius and the link of filiation to his natural father (Lucii filius) is retained.

If every page of the *Letters* bears witness to the memory of the elder Plinius Secundus as adoptive father, two epistles in particular possess significance as markers of the moment at which Caecilius Secundus became the younger Plinius Secundus. If the Younger's adoption was formalized, as is virtually certain, only after the death of his uncle,[27] then the Elder's death during the eruption of Vesuvius in AD 79 takes on added personal significance. The intense focus of the Vesuvius letters in Book 6 on the catastrophic events surrounding the eruption allows no mention of an adoption. But Pliny does offer, significantly, some intense reflection on the Elder as personal model at this stage of his life. Here, as promised in the introduction to this chapter, we tackle the key subject of the effective management of one's time.

As is well known, letter 6.16 narrates, for the benefit of Tacitus,[28] the eruption of the volcano and the heroic mission of the Elder to the scene, while letter 6.20 supplies details on the sequence of events endured by Pliny and his mother – left behind in safety at Misenum on the opposite side of the bay of Naples – during the same day and following night.[29] By the standards of Pliny's letters the two accounts are remarkably precise in terms of facts and figures. We learn, for example, that Pliny was in his eighteenth year at the time (6.20.5) – a circumstance not irrelevant for understanding Pliny's representation of his behaviour as modelled on that of the Elder. We also learn that the Vesuvian 'cloud' made its appearance around the seventh hour (i.e. in the early afternoon) of the 24th of August, and so finds the Elder at a very precise point in his daily routine:[30]

---

[26] See the evidence presented by Birley (2000a) 79 s.v. Plinius Secundus. For the lack of necessary correlation between forms of salutation in a letter address and the names by which people were addressed in ordinary conversation, see Dickey (2002) 37 with n. 32.

[27] See e.g. Salomies (1992) 6 on the classic study of Mommsen, also Sherwin-White (1966) 70.

[28] For Pliny's relationship with the exemplary Tacitus, see (briefly) the end of this chapter and (in more detail) Chapter 5.

[29] For recent contributions to the vast bibliography on these letters, which survey many of the standard issues not covered here – vulcanology, historiography, Vergilian allusion etc. – and associated secondary literature, see Berry (2008) and the sophisticated analysis of Marchesi (2008) 171–89, plus Lefèvre (2009) 126–41 [= (1996a)], and the relevant bibliography cited in Appendix 3. For a series of links between Pliny's Vesuvius letters and the epistolary poems of Statius which touch on the same eruption (*Silu.* 3.5 and 4.4), see Newlands (2010).

[30] For a clear and accessible account of the mechanics of the Vesuvian eruption, see Scarth (2009) 39–85; for a more technical account, see Sigurdsson and Carey (2002), with references to earlier literature; also Marturano and Varone (2005). For doubts about the August date of the eruption of Vesuvius (and a preference for a date in the autumn), see Beard (2008) 17–18, 319.

nonum kal. Septembres hora fere septima mater mea indicat ei adparere nubem inusitata et magnitudine et specie. usus ille **sole**, mox **frigida**, **gustauerat** iacens **studebatque** . . . (6.16.4–5)

The ninth day before the Kalends of September, at about the seventh hour, my mother indicated to him the appearance of a cloud of unusual size and shape. He had sunned himself, and next gone to his cold bath; and after a light meal, which he took reposing, was engaged in study . . .

The point at which the Elder has sunbathed, taken a cold bath, lunched, and started on his studies, while on duty at Misenum, corresponds closely to the early afternoon part of his normal routine while in Rome, after finishing official business.[31] This routine had already been laid out before the reader in a key letter in Book 3 – to which we return in rather more detail below:

reuersus domum quod reliquum temporis studiis reddebat. post cibum saepe . . . aestate si quid otii iacebat in **sole**, liber legebatur, adnotabat excerpebatque. . . . post **solem** plerumque **frigida** lauabatur, deinde **gustabat** dormiebatque minimum; mox quasi alio die **studebat** in cenae tempus. super hanc liber legebatur . . . (3.5.9–11)

On his return home, he gave the rest of his time to study. After some food, often . . . in summer if he had any spare time he would lie in the sun, when a book was read to him, of which he made notes and extracts . . . After his sunning he commonly took a cold bath; then he ate something and went to sleep for a short time. Shortly afterwards, as though he were beginning a fresh day, he studied on till dinner-time. At this meal a book was read out . . .

The account in 6.16 is necessarily more compressed than that in 3.5, but the key shared element is that after sunbathing etc. the rest of the day until the evening meal is normally devoted to *studia*. 24 August AD 79 is no normal day, of course, and not just because of the eruption of Vesuvius.[32] For this is the first full day of the Elder's annual shift in routine, after the Vulcanalia of 23 August, as recorded also in the important earlier letter in Book 3:

lucubrare Vulcanalibus incipiebat non auspicandi causa sed studendi statim a nocte multa, hieme uero ab hora septima uel cum tardissime octaua, saepe sexta. (3.5.8)

He began to work by candlelight at the feast of Vulcan, not with the view of seizing an auspicious occasion, but for the purpose of study immediately after midnight;

---

[31] See Sherwin-White (1966) 224 on 3.5.9.

[32] Note that Pliny, in line with the rationalistic perspective of both himself and his uncle, makes no connection between the proximity of the feast of Vulcan and the eruption of one of the god's volcanoes.

in winter, indeed, at one o'clock in the morning, or at the latest at two, often at midnight.

Given the rarity of dates in the correspondence,[33] the temptation to link the two letters around 23 and 24 August is overwhelmingly strong. The Vulcanalia was the Elder's annual signal to get out of bed early and start working by candlelight.[34] A man of fixed purpose who has just entered upon a new phase of his routine will clearly not be derailed by the appearance of an unusual cloud. And so it transpires: the rest of his day until dinner (*cena*) will be occupied, as normal, by *studia*. For the Elder decides that he must take a closer look, as a man of learning (6.16.7, quoted below), and initially takes up his task as a matter of scholarly interest: *quod* **studioso** *animo incohauerat obit maximo*, 'having started on his enterprise as a scholar, he proceeded to carry it out in the spirit of a hero' (6.16.9). The journey across the bay of Naples is no excuse for stopping the practice of making notes (as similarly, so we shall see, the eruption was no grounds for the Younger Pliny to interrupt the excerption of Livy). A man who saw travelling as the perfect opportunity for concentrating entirely on work, and kept a secretary with him for that purpose (and disapproved of walking as wasted time) – as we learn also in Book 3[35] – will find a way to put a short sea journey to good use:

rectumque cursum . . . tenet adeo solutus metu, ut omnes illius mali motus omnes figuras ut deprenderat oculis dictaret enotaretque. (6.16.10)

. . . holds a direct course . . . so free from fear that he dictated and caused to be noted down, as fast as he seized them with his eyes, all the shiftings and shapes of the dreadful prodigy.

Some slave or crew-member has evidently been recruited for the role of 'secretary at his side with . . . tablets' (3.5.15), and writes down the Elder's notes on the phases of the disastrous phenomenon. (The precision of the Younger's own description of the phenomenon is of course substitute for, or tribute to, the Elder's own sharp-eyed reporting.[36]) In this way the afternoon is devoted in the normal manner to *studia*.

---

[33] See Riggsby (2003) 180.
[34] For the 'culture of *lucubratio*' or writing by night in Rome, and its significance in the preface of the Elder's *Natural History* (itself described as a product of the night), see Ker (2004), esp. 232–6.
[35] 3.5.15–16.
[36] Cf. Sherwin-White (1966) 373. For 6.16 and particularly 6.20 as deliberately historiographical in nature – and a challenge to their addressee, the historian Tacitus – see Marchesi (2008) 171–89. Cf. similarly Augoustakis (2005) on Tacitus, and the tribute implicit in these letters to the Elder as historian (for which see below). For literature on Pliny's engagement with historiography, see Appendix 3.

A reading of the same Vesuvius letter will reveal with what close attention the Younger has been following the example of the Elder, above all by displaying a similar devotion to the maintenance of routine and fostering of *studia*. In 6.16, the Younger appears first at the moment the Elder is about to set off to investigate the phenomenon:

magnum propiusque noscendum ut eruditissimo uiro uisum. iubet liburnicam aptari; mihi si uenire una uellem facit copiam; respondi **studere** me malle, et forte ipse quod scriberem dederat. (6.16.7)

To [my uncle], a most learned man, it seemed a remarkable phenomenon, and one to be observed from a nearer point of view. He ordered his fast-sailing cutter to be got ready, and, in case I wished to accompany him, gave me leave to do so. I replied that I preferred to go on with my studies, and it so happened that he had himself given me something to write out.

The Younger's decline of the offer of adventure has provided critics largely with a (not undeserved) opportunity for hilarity at his expense; but this is to neglect its significance. For the Younger may lack the scientific curiosity of the Elder, but at this early stage in his life he shares the utter devotion to *studia* already shown to be central to the Elder in the letter from Book 3.[37] For if the Elder was (characteristically) able to convert his travel time across the bay of Naples into learned notes, then the Younger has made a choice which allows his afternoon to be successfully devoted to *his* task in hand. As we learn at 6.20.5, that task is to produce excerpts from Livy. This is clearly not a form of *studium* which might be successfully pursued on board a ship making straight for the scene of a volcanic eruption. Both the Younger and the author of the *Natural History* have chosen activities which allow a successful afternoon's devotion to learning.

In the sequel letter which records events at Misenum, we (and Tacitus) find that the Younger's day progressed exactly as it should have done on a normal day at the house of the Elder, with an afternoon devoted entirely to *studia*:

profecto auunculo ipse **reliquum tempus studiis** (ideo enim remanseram) impendi; mox balineum cena somnus inquietus et breuis. (6.20.2)

After the departure of my uncle I devoted what time was left to study (it was for that purpose that I remained behind); the bath shortly followed, then dinner, then a short and troubled sleep.

---

[37] Nevertheless, for the Younger's mature rejection of natural science – alongside (Senecan) ethical philosophy – as the best form of study for a man's *otium*, see Chapter 6 and cf. Cova (2001) 58–63.

As readers will know once more from letter 3.5, this was the part of the day in which the Elder *quod **reliquum temporis studiis** reddebat,* 'gave the rest of his time to study' (3.5.9); in which, after lunch, he normally 'studied on till dinner time' (3.5.11). The verbal similarity between 6.20 and 3.5 underlines the extent to which the Younger has been modelling himself on the Elder. The Younger indeed follows the Elder's normal routine of *studia, cena* and bed with only one minor variation: he has a bath before dinner (as in later life, 9.36) rather than in the middle of the day. In context, however, this only serves to increase the parallelism with the Elder, who, under Vesuvius, is breaking his normal routine (3.5.11) by having a bath before dinner in order to reassure those around him (6.16.12). Yet here a difference also asserts itself: the Elder's sleep at Vesuvius is apparently profound (6.16.13), while the worried Younger's is fitful. This is an implicit tribute to the fearlessness and resolve of the Elder.[38]

Parallel lives reassert themselves almost immediately: the Younger's mother bursts into the bedroom to rouse him so that the pair can take safety in the open (6.20.4), just as the Elder is woken to join Pomponianus in his eventual exit to the open air (6.16.14–15). The Elder's routine is tragically broken at this point, but the Younger carries on in a manner appropriate to the house of the Elder Pliny:

dubito, constantiam uocare an imprudentiam debeam (agebam enim duodeuicensimum annum): posco librum Titi Liui, et quasi per otium lego atque etiam ut coeperam excerpo. (6.20.5)

I do not know whether to call it perseverance or imprudence on my part (seeing that I was only in my eighteenth year); however I called for a volume of Livy, and read it as though quite at my ease, and even made extracts from it, as I had begun to do.

Again, this detail has given rise to understandable mirth at Pliny's expense.[39] But it also has a serious purpose, namely to act as a decidedly youthful

---

[38] A reader might, however, choose to interpret the Elder's sleep in a different way. See Eco (1994), where it is persuasively argued that the underlying story of the Vesuvius letters suggests that the Elder Pliny was completely unable to cope with the situation, but that through his skill as narrator Pliny the Younger persuades reader to understand the events rather differently. The germ of the idea is found in Haywood (1952–3); cf. Cova (2001) 55–8.

[39] Beginning with Bulwer-Lytton's notorious (and frequently filmed) 1834 novel, *The Last Days of Pompeii,* Book 1, Chapter 2 (clearly inspired by this passage): 'His nephew (oh! whip me such philosophical coxcombs!) was reading Thucydides' description of the plague, and nodding his conceited little head in time to the music, while his lips were repeating all the loathsome details of that terrible delineation. The puppy saw nothing incongruous in learning at the same time a ditty of love and a description of the plague', etc. (For the reception of Pliny, see above p. 18 n. 38 and Appendix 3.) Nevertheless, in structural terms the detail of concentrating on one's books in a climate of fear has much in common with Athenodorus bravely ignoring the ghost at 7.27.8–9.

tribute to the example set by the Elder Pliny. Rising before dawn (6.20.6) soon after the Vulcanalia can only mean one thing in the Elder Pliny's house: the undertaking of *studia* (3.5.8). And so the Younger, who now finds himself unemployed at this early hour, asks to continue with his own *studia*.[40] The Younger allows criticism of his own behaviour as folly and foolhardiness (as later at 6.20.10–11, 12, 17). Yet the behaviour he describes is also a youthful homage to the Elder. Like his uncle, Pliny strives to maintain a routine and devote himself to *studia* at every opportunity (including the lucubrations so characteristic of the Elder). Yet, as we shall see next, readers of Book 6 will grasp from their reading of Book 3 that Pliny's behaviour in AD 79 was ultimately that of an inexperienced adolescent.[41] The consular orator of the earlier book has already made clear how his mature life rejects a monomaniacal focus on *studia*, and seeks other models for conducting an active life. Slavish imitation of one's elders is only for the very young.

VESTRICIUS SPURINNA AND THE ELDER PLINY AS EXEMPLARS IN BOOK 3

As we make our way back from Book 6 towards Book 3 we will encounter a letter in Book 5 which explicitly raises the question of the Elder Pliny as *exemplum* for imitation by the now mature nephew.[42] For in letter 5.8 the Younger Pliny contemplates following in his uncle's generic footsteps and writing historical works. Again letter 3.5 provides context for this piece, since there the Younger had listed the entire literary output of the Elder in order of composition (3.5.3–6). Two of the longest works took the form of imperial history: an early work in twenty books on Roman wars in Germany, and a later work of Flavian history in thirty-one books. It is against this background that Pliny ponders his own literary future:[43]

me uero ad hoc studium impellit **domesticum quoque exemplum**. auunculus meus **idemque per adoptionem pater** historias et quidem religiosissime scripsit.

---

[40] For the significance within the economy of the letter of the fact that the object of study is Livy, see Schönberger (1990) 535–9, who emphasizes the reputation of the historian as repository of *exempla uirtutis* in a context where the Younger is striving to live up to the example of the *constantia* of the Elder. Marchesi (2008) 186–8 points out that reading Livy in the context of 6.20 is consonant with the many echoes of Livy's text which Pliny incorporates; cf. Görler (1979) 430 for the Livian parallel of reading a book amidst a major calamity (25.31.9, the sack of Syracuse).

[41] For a different but complementary point, namely that throughout 6.20 the Younger strives in a variety of ways to underline his failure to live up to the example set by the Elder, see Jones (2001).

[42] The debt of this section to Henderson (2002a) is warmly acknowledged. For a catalogue of addressees and letter contents in Book 3, see Appendix 2.

[43] For an analysis of the complex theories of historiography raised by this letter and – to travel in the opposite direction from this chapter – the suggestion that it is designed to act as a forerunner to the historiographical essays in 6.16 and 6.20, see Marchesi (2008) 149–71.

inuenio autem apud sapientes **honestissimum** esse maiorum uestigia sequi, si modo recto itinere praecesserint. (5.8.4–5)

In my case, I am further impelled to this pursuit by an example in my own family. My maternal uncle, who was also my father by adoption, wrote histories, and with very great scruples. Now, I find it stated by the sages that it is a most noble thing to follow in the footsteps of one's ancestors, provided only the way they have gone before was the right one.

Running through this passage and indeed the whole of this letter is a dialogue with Cicero, particularly the *de Legibus* – in whose opening paragraphs (1.5–9) Atticus tries to convince a similarly reluctant Cicero to take up historiography[44] – and the *de Officiis*, where Cicero discusses the propriety of following in the footsteps of one's father (or ancestors) in choice of career.[45] That the *de Officiis* is weighing on Pliny here is confirmed not only by an allusion to the main subject of its first book (the *honestum*),[46] but also by the fact that in this passage alone is the Elder referred to as Pliny's father. In every other instance in the correspondence he is designated *auunculus*. The specific reference to the Elder as adoptive father suggests a deliberate allusion to the Ciceronian passage on choosing one's father as an exemplar. Like Cicero, Pliny never does write a straightforward historiographical work, and, after the *de Legibus* has been played off against the *de Officiis* here in Book 5, the remaining books of the correspondence show him taking the (Ciceronian) path of revising and publishing speeches, and writing letters. The model of the Elder Pliny is thus implicitly rejected – albeit with clear pride.

Readers will once more have been prepared for this rejection, in some sense, by their experience of Book 3, and it is to this key unit we now turn attention at last. The first letter of Book 3 explicitly introduces Vestricius Spurinna as an exemplary figure for imitation by Pliny: 'there is no one whom I would sooner take for my model in old age' (3.1.1, quoted more fully below); 'Spurinna is at once my solace and example' (3.1.11, quoted more

---

[44] See Leeman (1963) 334 (adding the parallel between 5.8.5 *pater historias* and Cic. *Leg.* 1.5 *pater historiae*); and on letter 5.8 as a whole, see Gamberini (1983) 58–79, Morello (2003) 202–6, Ash (2003) 218–21, Baier (2003), Woodman (forthcoming). That Atticus is the main interlocutor in the *de Legibus* passage can hardly have been without attraction for Pliny: he casts his own addressee, Titinius Capito, in the role of Cicero's favourite correspondent, now transposed from dialogue to letter. Further Ciceronian parallels in 5.8 are listed at Marchesi (2008) 254.

[45] Cic. *Off.* 1.116 'Those whose fathers or ancestors won glory by outstanding performance in a particular field generally devote themselves to excelling in the same way themselves... Some, indeed, add to that inherited from their fathers praise that is all their own' (trans. M.T. Griffin and E.M. Atkins). For Pliny's familiarity with the *de Officiis*, see Stinchcomb (1935–6), Korfmacher (1946–7).

[46] For *honestas*, nevertheless, as a virtue in Pliny letters, see Méthy (2007) 30–42, 48–58.

fully below). As suggested at the beginning of this chapter, the consular status of Spurinna is perhaps one (unmentioned) reason why he is a better model for the Younger than the Elder could ever be. Pliny, nevertheless, finds other, more tactful ways of making his point. For in letters 3.1 and 3.5 Pliny offers detailed descriptions of the daily routines of first the living Spurinna and then of his long-dead uncle. The proximity of the first two of these letters within Book 3 – not to mention the extensive vocabulary shared by each[47] – appears to invite readers to make a comparison between the typical daily routines of Spurinna and uncle Pliny. Nor is the subject a trivial one. For in the words of Ker (2004) 216, 'In the moralizing tradition of Roman literature... there was a strong tendency to see a person's use of time as an indicator of his or her moral and social identity.' In this sense letter 3.5 is parallel to 6.16, since there was a marked tendency also to understand the narrative of a subject's death as a microcosm of the life.[48]

At the very end of the nine-book collection, furthermore, Pliny responds to a request for information on his own summer and winter routines at his Tuscan and Laurentine villas (9.36, 9.40).[49] These letters will enter the argument of this chapter at a slightly later stage, but it will be useful to have information on their contents alongside the letters on the daily schedules of Spurinna and the Elder Pliny. The context in which the descriptions are given means that they are not fully commensurable. For example, letter 3.1 explicitly presents the schedule of Spurinna as one maintained in retirement after a lifetime of achievement (3.1.11–12), while that for the Elder Pliny in 3.5 details his routine during a life still devoted to public service at Rome (3.5.14).[50] Nevertheless, the joint impact which these letters make on the careful reader can perhaps best be conveyed by a tabular summary of their contents. Such a tabular analysis will also do much to elucidate the argument which follows.[51]

---

47 See the exhaustive list at Henderson (2002a) 200–2. For a detailed treatment of letters 3.1 and 3.5, see Henderson (2002b). On 3.5, see also Lefèvre (2009) 123–6 [= (1989) 115–18].

48 See Henderson (2002a) 80, citing Sen. *Ep.* 12.

49 As is often pointed out, these letters are clearly inspired by Seneca's response to a request to outline the order of his day in letter 83; Pliny's letter 3.1 also shows significant parallels in its detailing of an elderly man's routine. See Henderson (2002a) 63–5, 195 n. 7.

50 In addition, while 3.1 gives a systematic and linear description of the routine of Spurinna, the schedule of the Elder Pliny must be extracted by the reader from 3.5 (albeit with little difficulty). Finally, the description of the Younger's routine in 9.36 is that of a consular orator at his country villa in summer, although 9.40 gives some balance by presenting his routine in winter at his villa near Rome as not totally different in kind from the summer routine at the Tuscan villa.

51 Grateful acknowledgement is made of Leach (2003) 164, 165 in respect of her summaries of the routines in 3.1 and 9.36 (reproduced here with small supplements). See also Lefèvre (2009) 242–5 [= (1987) 258–62].

Spurinna: 3.1.4–9	**Elder Pliny: 3.5.8–14**	**Younger Pliny: 9.36**
Summer and winter routine in retirement at villa	*Summer and winter routine of working life*	*Summer routine* in secessu *at Tuscan villa*
1. One hour meditation in bed after waking	1. Start work (in winter) four or five hours before dawn	1. Early waking about sunrise; working out ideas in the dark
2. Three-mile walk while conversing or reading a book	2. Before dawn, visit Emperor Vespasian	2. Secretary enters; dictation period
3. Seated activity, either reading or conversing	3. Attend to official business in hand	3. Walk on the grounds to continue thinking
4. Seven-mile carriage ride with wife or friends	4. Return home and spend any spare time on *studia*	4. Drive and more concentration
5. One-mile walk	5. Simple meal	5. Short sleep
6. Writing period in seclusion: lyric poems in Latin and Greek	6. Lie in sun (in summer): book read and notes taken	6. Another walk

7. Bath preparation [with variations hereon for summer and winter]
  a. Naked exercise in the sun
  b. Vigorous game of catch
	7. Cold bath, food, snatch of sleep	7. Reading Latin or Greek speech aloud to improve digestion

	8. More *studia* 'as if on a new day'	8. Another walk
8. Bath	9. Dinner: book read and notes taken	9. Oiling and bathing
9. Short rest with reading	10. Rise from dinner (for bed) during light hours (in summer) or as soon as darkness falls (in winter)	10. Dinner with reading
10. Formal dinner interspersed with performances		11. Literary performance
	[While on *secessus* in the country, time is entirely devoted to *studia*, apart from actual time spent in water during bath]	12. Another walk with conversation [Schedule may be varied by substituting horseback for carriage ride or by hunting. Time may also be spent with tenants. Variations for routine at the Laurentine villa in winter in 9.40 include no siesta, getting up earlier or going to bed later, and substitution of legal work for literary performance.]

Before beginning our analysis of these letters, one oddity requires comment: despite the importance of epistolary communication in the Roman world generally and Pliny's circle in particular, no one here – not even Pliny himself – seems to build in separate time specifically for the lengthy and time-consuming business of writing letters. (The closest Pliny comes to acknowledging the time spent on keeping up with one's correspondence is found in letter 1.10.9 (quoted above p. 21), where he complains about the many business letters he must compose.)

At any rate, reversing the order in which the 'schedule' letters appear in Book 3, we focus first on letter 3.5 and the Elder Pliny. After providing information on the Elder's routine in 3.5.8–14 (summarized above), the Younger begins to comment on his uncle's devotion to *studia* and his astonishing rate of literary production (3.5.15–20). It is in this last part of the letter that Pliny betrays an awareness of the pressures placed on him by the figure of the Elder. For example we learn – to return to a subject raised earlier in connection with the Vesuvius letters – that his uncle criticized him for walking when he might have dedicated the time instead to study through being carried in a sedan chair (3.5.15–16). But, in contrast to the seriousness applied in 5.8 to the question of adopting his uncle's literary genre, here any thought of modelling oneself on the Elder is brushed lightly aside:

itaque soleo **ridere** cum me quidam studiosum uocant, qui si comparer illi sum **desidiosissimus**. ego autem tantum, quem partim publica partim amicorum offi-cia distringunt? quis ex istis, qui tota uita litteris **assident**, collatus illi non quasi somno et **inertiae** deditus erubescat? (3.5.19)[52]

Hence I am in the habit of laughing when some people call me studious, who if compared with him am the idlest of the idle. *I* only, distracted as I am partly by public calls, partly by those of friendship? Who of those who devote their whole lives to letters, when compared with him, will not blush like some addict of sleep and idleness?

Potential comparison with the Elder provokes in the Younger neither guilt nor grave reflection on how one's life-course might be changed, but rather personal amusement. He appears content to occupy a middle position between the Elder (who combined a life of official service and high literary productivity) and those who devote their entire lives to literature (and produce less than the Elder). It is conceded that the Elder's (non-senatorial) *occupationes* (3.5.18) placed severe constraints on his time. Yet a partial explanation for the Younger's contentment appears to be offered by the information that he must deal both with 'public duties' and those laid on him by friends. That is to say, posts on the senatorial *cursus honorum* such as his recently demitted treasury position (see Chapter 1 and Appendix 1), plus private service in the law courts.

The Younger, then, is aware of the personal example set him by the Elder in the organization of his time and effort, yet declines to treat it with the

---

[52] The closeness of the (highlighted) language to Pliny's letter to Tacitus on his *otium*-soaked hunt-ing practices in 1.6.1 is worth pondering: *ridebis . . . inertia mea . . . ad retia sedebam*, 'you will laugh . . . my idleness . . . I was sitting by the nets . . .'. On this letter, see further below p. 121 n. 56.

seriousness reserved for other subjects. It is then a matter of keen interest when we return to letter 3.1, and read at both beginning and end of its lengthy description of Spurinna's daily schedule the following:

... neminem magis in senectute, si modo senescere datum est, aemulari uelim; nihil est enim illo uitae genere distinctius. (3.1.1)

... there is no one whom I would sooner take for my model in old age, provided always it is given to me to grow old; for nothing can be better arranged than his mode of life.

hanc ego uitam uoto et cogitatione praesumo, ingressurus auidissime, ut primum ratio aetatis receptui canere permiserit. (3.1.11–12)

Such is the kind of life I look forward to on my own account in wish and in thought, and which I shall enter on with the greatest eagerness so soon as a regard for my advancing years shall permit me to sound the retreat.

Spurinna's lifestyle receives an explicit endorsement which is withheld from that of the Elder: the regime of the former is the one to which Pliny (eventually) aspires.[53] This raises the question of what makes the former more attractive. By comparison with Spurinna, the daily schedule of the Elder clearly lacks variety and periods of relaxation. Variety is of course a key feature not only of the Younger's life, but also of his literary output in both prose and verse, and of the *Letters* themselves. (In the felicitous formulation of Johnson (2000) 622, 'The fascinating structure of Spurinna's regimen ... is worthy of a poetry book ... or ... any art that counterpoises a unifying structure with elaborate variation.') Where Spurinna's varied daily routine exercises both body and mind (3.1.4), the corpulent Elder (6.16.13), who went everywhere in a sedan chair (3.5.15–16), displays a firm focus on *studia* when official business does not intervene. Indeed, the Younger writes the reader a licence to see an even greater contrast between the pair:

in secessu solum balinei tempus studiis eximebatur (cum dico balinei, de interioribus loquor; nam dum destringitur tergiturque, audiebat aliquid aut dictabat). (3.5.14)

In the country, only his bathing-time was exempted from study (when I say bathing, I am speaking of the moment of immersion, for while he was being rubbed and dried he was read to or dictated).

The Younger carefully notes slight variations in routine for summer and winter in all four of his most detailed 'schedule' letters (see the table above),

---

53 Cf. Cova (2001) 65–6. For Spurinna's schedule versus that of the Elder Pliny, see further Henderson (2002a) 76–80, (2002b) 268; for Spurinna's alone, see further Johnson (2000) 621–3, (2010) 36–9.

but the biggest variation of all occurs in the case of the Elder's differing practices in the city and in the country. In the country, whatever variety there has been in the Elder's days is replaced with a single-minded devotion to *studia*. Indeed, in the Vesuvius letters, we saw the adolescent Pliny attempting to reproduce this monomania even in the most catastrophic of circumstances. The contrast with Spurinna could hardly be greater, since he, in his retirement, is permanently *in secessu* at his country villa. Where Spurinna in the country weaves reading and writing into the fabric of his broader personal and social activity, for the Elder Pliny reading and writing are his preferred sole activities when away from the city.[54] (As will become clear in letter 5.6, the Younger – who in all probability inherited his Tuscan villa from the Elder – uses his time in the country rather differently; see Chapter 7.)

Despite the adult Pliny's endorsement of Spurinna's varied programme and the withholding of endorsement from the Elder, the reader is not yet empowered to view the former as modelling himself on the latter. For Spurinna is explicitly a model for retirement (3.1.1, quoted above). Furthermore, the immediately preceding book is filled with evidence of hard work in the law courts and elsewhere (2.8, 2.11, 2.12, 2.14) and accompanying literary production (2.5, 2.19), and complaints about overload and frustration are loud and long (2.8).[55] On this evidence, the Younger is actually modelling himself instead on the Elder's schedule of work while in the city.[56] Characteristically, this is a 'loose end' which Pliny ties up for the reader – although we must wait, as so often in the collection, for Book 9 to provide the crucial letter.[57] For here, as laid out above, Pliny in two letters describes to the aspiring young aristocratic orator Fuscus Salinator (already glimpsed in Chapter 2) his daily schedules in summer and winter. Pliny's

---

[54] Contrast the Elder's own – and potentially somewhat different – account of how he uses his time at *HN praef.* 18.

[55] On the key role played in Book 2 by letter 2.17 on Pliny's Laurentine villa, and the direct engagement of this letter with 3.1 on the routine of Spurinna, see Chapter 7.

[56] A letter in Book 1 had also revealed tendencies similar to the Elder's when in the country, since at 1.6.2 Pliny reveals to Tacitus his practice of hunting with notebook in hand. However, in a companion letter in Book 9 also addressed to Tacitus such mania has rather faded. For in 9.10.2 literary studies must be pursued with restraint (*Mineruae . . . seruiendum est, delicate tamen ut in secessu et aestate*, 'One must serve Minerva, delicately, however, in a manner suitable to being in the country and in summer'), even when there is no hunting. An attitude of which the Elder would hardly approve. For the key role (once more) of Book 9 in revising earlier attitudes, see below. For the complex series of literary and structural issues raised by 1.6 and 9.10, see Marchesi (2008) 118–35 and Edwards (2008), with references to earlier literature, also Chapters 5 and 6 in this volume.

[57] For the highly significant letters 9.36 and 9.40, see also Chapters 6 and 7. For letter 3.12, however, as already an instantiation of the mean between the Elder and Spurinna, see Henderson (2002a) 131–2.

routine while *in secessu* at the Tuscan estate (9.36) does display emphases and objectives different from those attributed to Spurinna's in 3.1. In the formulation of Leach (2003) 161–2,

the divisions of Pliny's day . . . include more studious pastimes against Spurinna's greater proportion of recreational: his longer rides and walks, ball-playing and verse composition. While allowing for health-promoting activities on the grounds that they are mentally refreshing, Pliny emphasizes the dedication of his leisure time to productive work and thus to the interaction of *otium* with *negotium*.[58]

(And the opportunities for healthy activities may be reduced by the intrusion of legal work at the villa close to Rome, in 9.40.) Nevertheless, the same principles of daily variety and the exercise of body and mind are central to Pliny and Spurinna at their country villas in a way that is quite untrue of the Elder Pliny.[59] Similarities in terms of early morning time spent in the bedroom, the alternation of physical and seated activities, periods of composition, and readings before and during dinner – all combine to explain retrospectively the attraction of Spurinna's regime for Pliny. A transition in retirement into such a daily schedule will for Pliny be not only appropriate but also virtually seamless, requiring only a change of emphasis.

Yet a smooth transition is not the only factor which explains Pliny's preference for Spurinna over the Elder. Here we return to a key sentence at the end of the first letter of Book 3, where Pliny explains why the regime of Spurinna is not yet appropriate:[60]

interim mille laboribus conteror, quorum mihi et solacium et exemplum est idem Spurinna; nam ille quoque, quoad honestum fuit, obiit officia, gessit magistratus, prouincias rexit, multoque labore hoc otium meruit. igitur eundem mihi cursum, eundem terminum statuo . . . (3.1.11–12)

Meanwhile I am exhausted by a thousand labours, in which Spurinna is at once my solace and my example. For he, too, as long as it became him, discharged offices, held magistracies, governed provinces, and it was by hard work that he became entitled to this leisure. I propose, then, to myself the same course and the same goal . . .

The 'thousand labours' will be evident to any reader of Book 2, although we discover as Book 3 progresses that all the hard work has paid off, with Pliny's

---

[58] Not that Pliny is consistent on the matter outside these set-piece 'routine' letters: 7.4 seems to imply a summer regimen at the Laurentine villa rather close to Spurinna's.

[59] Cf. esp. 3.1.4 (on Spurinna) *nec minus animum quam corpus exercet*, 'he exercises his mind no less than his body', and 5.6.46 (on the Tuscan villa) *nam studiis animum, uenatu corpus exerceo*, 'for my mind I exercise by study, and my body by hunting'.

[60] Cf. the very similar language of exemplarity in retirement after a lifetime's senatorial service applied to Pomponius Bassus, at 4.23.2, 4.

ascent to the consulship. And it is precisely this which makes Spurinna such a good model for Pliny: he too has known the onerous tasks and responsibilities which are the lot of the consul (not to mention governor of provinces). The Younger plans to arrive at the same final destination as Spurinna by taking the very same path along the *cursus honorum*. The Elder, as we learn in Book 5, is taken most seriously as a model in the area of choice of literary genre, while the Vesuvius letters of Book 6 make it clear that imitation of the Elder's obsession with *studia* belongs to the past of Pliny's youth. The consular Pliny must choose appropriate fellow consuls as his model, and not equestrian procurators who focused too narrowly on *studia*. In the words of Bernstein (2008b), 'The admonitory image of the ceaselessly toiling Elder Pliny shows the dangers of subordinating a life entirely to *studia*, whilst the laudatory account of Spurinna's *otium* suggests that a distinguished public career must come first. The good life according to Pliny involves the pursuit of renown and adherence to moral obligation as well as *otium*.'[61]

SILIUS ITALICUS AS NEGATIVE EXAMPLE IN BOOK 3

For all the respectful distance put between himself and his uncle, the Younger Pliny is careful not to leave the Elder isolated in Book 3. It may be noted that both 3.1 and 3.5 are embedded within a sequence of letters heavily freighted with senior figures, many of them of consular rank. Thus after the description of Spurinna's routine in 3.1, Corellius Rufus makes an appearance in 3.3 as a spur to proper action in finding a tutor for his grandson, while, following the memorialization of the Elder Pliny in 3.5, we find in 3.7 a long obituary letter devoted to the record of the consular poet Silius Italicus. Furthermore, in between the latter epistles Pliny is discovered in 3.6 giving instructions for the erection of a striking statue of an old man in his home town, on whose base is to be recorded Pliny's 'name and titles' (3.6.5), i.e. the consulship of AD 100 which is the understood context for much of Book 3. A series of interconnecting themes runs through this complex sequence of letters which mark Pliny's ascent of the *cursus honorum*: rank and status, exemplarity, conduct in old age and the remembrance of a man's career.[62]

---

[61] See also Henderson (2002a) 132–3 on letter 3.6 as evidence of concerns with differences of status from the Elder, and 165–6 for this letter as marker of the passing of filial subordination to the Elder.

[62] In the felicitous words of Henderson (2002a) 65 (which may be applied to the whole of the sequence of 3.1–7), 'To mark his emergence as an elder statesman Pliny . . . make[s] the third book reverberate with his mighty consecration of gerontology.'

Letter 3.7 on Silius Italicus – yet another consular of north Italian extraction[63] – resonates with notable power within this sequence, and indeed with many letters elsewhere on Pliny's 'elders and betters'. It reports Silius' suicide – the first in the collection since the death of Pliny's admired elder Corellius Rufus in letter 1.12, with which it invites comparison. The information that Silius, consul in 68, is the last of Nero's consuls to die (at 3.7.9–10) also invites comparison with the record of Verginius Rufus, himself a Neronian consul (in 63). Pliny's observation at 3.7.3 – that Silius 'had injured his reputation under Nero (he was believed to have turned informer voluntarily)' – may also bring to mind Regulus, another man with a tarnished record under Nero (1.5.1, 3). Unlike Regulus, however, Silius is said to have redeemed himself under later emperors (3.7.3).[64] Nor can we exclude here others with a debatable record to defend in the terrible events of 68–9, particularly (once more) Verginius Rufus.[65]

Here we concentrate on the role which letter 3.7 has in the sequence 3.1–7 as a negative exemplar in relation to the competing regimes of both Spurinna and the Elder Pliny.[66] In a short passage in the obituary letter for Silius, Pliny gives a summarizing account of how Silius, after his final service as proconsul of Asia (3.7.3), spent his days at leisure in Rome before he retired fully to Campania:[67]

fuit inter principes ciuitatis sine potentia, sine inuidia: salutabatur colebatur, multumque in lectulo iacens cubiculo semper, non ex fortuna frequenti, doctissimis sermonibus dies transigebat, cum a scribendo uacaret. (3.7.4)

He was among the chief men of the state, possessing no power and arousing no hostility. He had many visitors and much attention shown him, and, reclining a good deal on a couch in his apartment (always thronged, though not from regard to his fortunes), he passed the days in learned discourse, when he had leisure from writing.

Like the Spurinna of 3.1, Silius has visitors, conducts improving conversations and devotes his time to writing (3.1.4, 7). But Spurinna in his old age

---

[63] See Syme, *RP* 4.132 [= (1982) 476], 4.380–1 [= (1983) 109–10], 7.488.

[64] Silius' well-borne grief for his dead son (3.7.2) will also contrast with the extravagance of Regulus' grief in letters 4.2, 4.7; see Henderson (2002b) 283. For Regulus, see Chapters 1 and 2.

[65] The Elder Pliny is likewise defended by hints of a retarded career under Nero, at 3.5.5; but for scepticism on such retardation, see Beagon (2005) 4.

[66] For Silius as a 'back-to-front' Spurinna by compensating for his life through his retirement, see Henderson (2002a) 115. On letter 3.7, see also Lefèvre (2009) 142–5 [= (1989) 118–23].

[67] For Pliny's failure to mention Silius' (possible) successful practice in the Centumviral court during these very years – where Martial hails him as a new Cicero (7.63) – see McDermott and Orentzel (1977) 25, 32, Henderson (2002a) 116–17. For the prominence, by contrast, awarded Regulus in the same court, see Chapter 2.

proves more active than Silius in his (presumably) younger days in Rome: the former is soon out of his *lectulus* (3.1.4), and retires to his *cubiculum* to write at a set time of the day, not before vigorous exercise (3.1.7).[68] The resulting poetry written by the two men attracts significantly disparate praise from Pliny:

scribit enim et quidem utraque lingua lyrica doctissima; mira illis dulcedo, mira suauitas, mira hilaritas, cuius gratiam cumulat sanctitas scribentis. (3.1.7)

For he writes lyrical poems with great skill, in Greek, too, as well as in Latin. There is a wonderful sweetness about them, a wonderful attractiveness and light-heartedness, and their charm is enhanced by the purity of the writer's own life.

scribebat carmina maiore cura quam ingenio, non numquam iudicia hominum recitationibus experiebatur. (3.7.5)

He wrote poems with more care than ability, and occasionally tested the taste of the public by reciting them.

The lyric poetry of one is hailed as a remarkable success: indeed, its charm is increased by the *sanctitas* of the author. The verses of the other, so the literary Caninius Rufus (cf. 1.5, 2.8) is informed, are uninspired.[69] One can only draw the conclusion that, in a version of *talis... oratio qualis uita*, 'as the speech, so the life' (Sen. *Ep.* 114.1), the moral reputations of the authors are mirrored in the quality of their verses. In Silius' case, a chec-qered career (with a morality to match) coincides with a mixed appraisal of his verse: strong on *cura*, weak on *ingenium*.[70] The lukewarmness of Pliny's judgement is confirmed later in the collection when we learn that another verse-writing consular and veteran of 68–9 composed excellent verse: Verginius Rufus wrote poetry fit to be included in a list which begins with Cicero, Calvus and Asinius Pollio (5.3.5).

However, the greatest beneficiary of the judgement that Silius' works did not match *ingenium* to *cura* is the Elder Pliny. In the chronological catalogue of the Elder's works produced by Pliny in the opening sentences of letter 3.5, the Elder's very first work is described in pointed terms as follows:

---

[68] Here the active Spurinna is cast in the role of desirable intermediate between the self-indulgent Silius and the hyper-active Elder Pliny of 3.5.

[69] For the leisured Caninius as 'just the right audience to give Silius an appreciative hearing', see Henderson (2002a) 105–9.

[70] Note also Pliny's comments on Silius' materialistic excesses (*emacitas*) at 3.7.8 in terms of multiple and neglectful villa ownership and fondness for luxury goods. By contrast, Spurinna is not only unattached to his luxury goods (3.1.9), but spends all his time at one villa in 3.1 and invests in it deeply (the others he undoubtedly owned going unmentioned). For letter 3.7 as critical of Silius, see also Johnson (2010) 40–1.

'De iaculatione equestri unus'; hunc cum praefectus alae militaret, **pari ingenio curaque composuit.** (3.5.3)

'On throwing the javelin from horseback, one book'; this he wrote, with as much care as ability, during his campaigns as commander of the cavalry.

That is to say, the Elder's very first work, written while on military service in Germany, displayed the exemplary combination of *cura* and *ingenium* which Silius' later poetic productions – written in leisure-filled semi-retirement – so conspicuously lacked.[71] The production of literature, as we have seen, is intimately linked in Pliny's mind to the organization of one's daily routine. Hence the two daily regimes of the Elder and Silius are laid before the reader for judgement. The routine of Silius in 3.7.4 is divided between writing and receiving visitors, where the latter converse in learned style with Silius as he lies on his couch in his *cubiculum*. Such is the life of this leading man of the state. Rather different is the life of the still-active Elder in 3.5, who squeezes his *studia* in while visiting Vespasian and attending to official duties (cf. *in amicitia principis*, 'in friendship with the emperor', 3.5.18, and *amicitia principum*, 'friendship with emperors', 3.5.7). The Elder has no callers (he does the calling), no learned discussion (books written by others are the object of the Elder's thirst for learning). Friends who attempted to initiate learned discussion – by stopping a reader who mispronounced his text – were likely to find themselves silenced (3.5.12): *tanta erat parsimonia temporis*, 'so great was his economy with time' (3.5.13). And the literary results of these two lifestyles are polar opposites in quality – and indeed in the space required to discuss them in the *Letters*. In this way, while making clear his preference for Spurinna over the Elder as his model, Pliny also makes clear the superiority of the Elder over consulars like Silius Italicus.

CORELLIUS RUFUS, VERGINIUS RUFUS AND THE LIMITS OF EXEMPLARITY

We turn our attention finally to two remaining admired elders who have received frequent mention above. If the limits of the exemplarity of Spurinna and particularly the Elder Pliny receive respectful qualification,

---

[71] The parallel also highlights a contrast: *scribebat carmina maiore cura quam ingenio* are the only words spent on Silius' massive epic, while the equivalent words in 3.5 are only the first in a long trawl through the extensive bibliography of the Elder; cf. Henderson (2002a) 108–9. (Nevertheless, for suggestive connections between Pliny's portrait of Silius and the text of the *Punica*, see Henderson (2002a) 109–13.)

the same is true also of Verginius Rufus and especially Corellius Rufus. An exploration of the limits of the exemplarity of the latter pair will also serve as bridgehead to a theme of some importance within the letters, namely Pliny's growing sense of his own exemplarity to the elite of Rome's younger generations.

Pliny maintains a high-minded emphasis on the role of Corellius and Verginius as sources of personal inspiration.[72] Corellius is the object of Pliny's intimate admiration (*quem ego cum ex admiratione diligere coepissem... magis admiratus sum postquam penitus inspexi*, 'whom, when I had begun to love him owing to my admiration for him...I admired still more after deep contemplation of him', 4.17.4), and the wisest man of the age, whose advice Pliny sought on every matter (9.13.6); while Verginius is hailed as a cherished exemplar of old-fashioned virtue (*nobis... quaerendus ac desiderandus est ut exemplar aeui prioris, mihi uero praecipue*, 'We... have to miss him and regret him as a model of a bygone age; I, for my part, particularly', 2.1.7; cf. 2.1.12).

It is worth adding here that more traditional exemplary figures drawn from Roman history are conspicuous by their rarity (or lack of prominence) in Pliny's *Letters*. Such men are reserved largely for the more public context of the *Panegyricus*.[73] In the private context of the *Letters*, Pliny's quartet of admired elders – alongside such heavyweight senior *amici* as Iulius Frontinus, Arrius Antoninus and Iulius Servianus[74] – effectively take the place of traditional exemplary figures.[75] By contrast, in both his correspondence and speeches, Cicero had demonstrated a more conventional focus on exemplars from Rome's glorious past, such as Scipio, Laelius and Camillus. In his letters, Seneca appears to have restricted the use of traditional exemplary figures so evident in his other prose works,[76] and was prepared to admit contemporary figures (including himself).[77] Nevertheless, when explicitly emphasizing the need to keep constantly in mind a personal

---

[72] As Hoffer (1999) 146 points out, no mention is made of legacies undoubtedly received.

[73] See Gowing (2005) 123–30, who analyses Pliny's argument that Trajan has eclipsed the heroes of the Republic in terms of exemplarity.

[74] For the thrice-consul Frontinus' connection with Pliny, cf. 4.8.3 (nominator for priesthood), 5.1 (personal adviser), 9.19 (loved equally with Verginius), and see Chapter 3. The twice-consul Arrius Antoninus receives three friendly letters on the subject of his poetry (4.3, 4.18, 5.15), while at 10.2 it is revealed that the aristocratic Iulius Servianus, consul for the second time in 102, acquired the *ius trium liberorum* from Trajan for Pliny. Servianus appears as addressee in the *Letters* at 3.17 and 6.26, and is mentioned also at 7.6.8 and 8.23.5. On this figure, see also Chapter 5.

[75] Nevertheless, Pliny's elders are often said to possess antique virtues, as in the *laudatio* of Verginius cited above; see further Méthy (2003), who provides a detailed analysis of the few 'great figures of the past' in Pliny's *Letters*.

[76] See Mayer (1991) 158–60.

[77] Cf. *Ep.* 66, 83.13, Mayer (1991) 147, 149 with n. 15, Richardson-Hay (2006) 101–5.

model – in line with the emphases of many philosophical traditions – he is mainly thinking of exemplars from the past rather than those drawn from personal experience.[78] In a letter near the end of his first book, for example, quoting a dictum of Epicurus on living daily under the imagined eye of a personally chosen role model (*aliquis uir bonus nobis diligendus est ac semper ante oculos habendus, ut sic tamquam illo spectante uiuamus et omnia tamquam illo uidente faciamus,* 'we must cherish some good man and hold him always before our eyes, so that we live, as it were, under his gaze, and do everything as if he sees it', *Ep.* 11.8–9), Seneca illustrates it for Lucilius by suggesting a choice of Cato or the more attractive Laelius (11.10, 25.5–6; cf. 104.21).

For Pliny it is Corellius – recently passed away in Book 1 – who plays this guiding role. After news of the heroic suicide of Corellius, Pliny laments that he has lost 'a witness to my life, a guide and a master', and fears above all that he will now live 'more carelessly' (*uereor ne neglegentius uiuam,* 1.12.12).[79] Furthermore Pliny suggests for the deceased Corellius a strongly visual role in his memory and mental life, akin to that recommended by Seneca. For example, as explanation of his willingness to take up a court case on behalf of Corellius' daughter, he cites the presence of Corellius himself in his mind's eye: *obuersatur oculis ille uir quo neminem aetas nostra grauiorem sanctiorem subtiliorem tulit,* 'Before my eyes is that great man, the best man of his age for dignity, purity and acuteness of judgement' (4.17.4–5).[80] However, not only are Pliny's models drawn from his lived experience, but the emphasis on his visualization of them is also significantly different from Seneca. The Stoic letter-writer expects that a model in the mind's eye will affect above all the secret inner life: *aliquem habeat animus... cuius auctoritate etiam secretum suum sanctius faciat,* 'The soul should have some person . . . on whose authority it can make even its inner sanctum more holy' (*Ep.* 11.9). Pliny, as is his norm, shows no concern for the Senecan 'inner life',[81] nor does he place much emphasis on the

---

[78] See Richardson-Hay (2006) 344–7 on *Ep.* 11.8–10. On the exemplars offered by Seneca to Lucilius (and on letter 11 in general), see Henderson (2004) 16–18. In *Ep.* 32.1 Seneca takes an even more radical step by suggesting that Lucilius live as if Seneca himself were watching. For the moral function of *exempla* in Seneca's letters, see Mayer (1991) 165–8.

[79] For an analysis of letter 1.12, see Hoffer (1999) 141–60 and Carlon (2009) 77–80.

[80] For the deceased Verginius in Pliny's mental vision, where the emphasis falls more on desire for the departed rather than on exemplarity per se, cf. 2.1.12, 6.10.1–2.

[81] Pliny in fact looks outward: his visualization of Corellius is based on a deep and personal knowledge of a living man who kept nothing 'inside' secret from him: *inspexi enim penitus: nihil a me ille secretum,* 'For I did contemplate him thoroughly. He had no secret from me' (4.17.5). For the 'turn inwards' as a feature of Seneca's letters, see Edwards (1997). For the fate of the concept in Pliny's

philosophical exemplarity of his models. Rather, they are presented largely as staunch upholders of the Roman tradition of public service and virtue.[82]

Nevertheless, while Pliny's choice (and use) of exemplars may be read as significantly different from the epistolary practice of both Seneca and Cicero, such a choice inevitably brings problems. The limitations of the long dead are more easily forgotten, while the more recently deceased – as we have seen already in the case of the Elder – inevitably raise the question of how to define oneself against them. As noted earlier, in the obituary letter for Corellius in 1.12, Pliny both asserts the role of 'guide and master' for Corellius and expresses the fear that he will now live 'more carelessly'. Subsequent letters both substantiate this claim for Corellius' influential role in the past, and provide solid evidence that Pliny goes on to live with exemplary care precisely because of the influence of Corellius' memory – particularly in relation to the latter's family.[83]

But during Corellius' lifetime, it appears that there were limits to his personal exemplarity. Pliny is careful to delay this revelation until – yet again – Book 9, although to understand its impact we must return to letter 4.17.[84] Here Pliny documents Corellius' support during the early stages of his career as he sought and performed his offices (4.17.6). Particularly significant here is Pliny's anecdote about how, when others praised him in front of the emperor Nerva, Corellius maintained his silence, before adding:

'necesse est' inquit 'parcius laudem Secundum, quia nihil nisi ex consilio meo facit.' qua uoce tribuit mihi quantum petere uoto immodicum erat, nihil me facere non sapientissime, cum omnia ex consilio sapientissimi uiri facerem. (4.17.8–9)

'I must', he said, 'be more sparing of my praises of Secundus, inasmuch as he does nothing except by my advice.' In this remark he attributed to me what it would have been extravagant to ask for in my prayers; namely, that I did nothing except with the utmost wisdom, inasmuch as all that I did was by the advice of the wisest of men.

Pliny confirms Corellius' assertion that he always acted on the latter's advice, and adds a compliment about the *sapientia* of Corellius (and his own for following him). That he was beholden to the advice of Corellius seems further confirmed in the opening letter of the following book, where

---

letters, see Leach (1990) with the revisions of Riggsby (1998); cf. the discussion in Chapter 6 of Pliny 4.6.

[82] Corellius, it is true, dies like a Stoic hero (cf. esp. 1.12.10);, but he is very much a practical Roman Stoic, superior to the Greek Stoic who appears two letters earlier in 1.10; see Hoffer (1999) 147.

[83] Cf. e.g. 3.3, 4.17, 5.1, 7.11.   [84] On this letter, see also Carlon (2009) 85–8.

it is told how during the reign of Domitian Pliny called in Corellius and Frontinus – Rome's 'most respected men' at the time – to arbitrate in an inheritance dispute (5.1.5–6). Pliny reports that he conducted himself in accordance with their advice (*ex consilii sententia . . . inquam*, 'in accordance with the opinion of the council . . . I said', 5.1.6). Yet in Corellius' last appearance in the collection, his status as dispenser of wisdom undergoes revision. In 9.13 – a letter whose importance emerged in Chapter 1 – Pliny provides the context for his attempted prosecution of Publicius Certus. He reveals how he informed Corellius at the last minute of his intentions, but did not consult him first on the matter:

omnia ego semper ad Corellium rettuli, quem **prouidentissimum** aetatis nostrae **sapientissimumque** cognoui: in hoc tamen contentus consilio meo fui ueritus ne uetaret; erat enim cunctantior cautiorque. (9.13.6)

I always referred everything to Corellius, knowing him for the most far-seeing and wisest man of our times. On this occasion, however, I was content with my own counsel, fearing that he would put his veto on it, for he was inclined to hesitation and caution.

At 4.17.10 Pliny had labelled Corellius as *prouidentissimus*, 'most far-seeing' and immediately prior to that – as seen above – had proudly put on display Corellius' implication that all of Pliny's actions (*omnia*) were extremely wise since he acted on the advice of the wisest of men (*sapientissime . . . ex consilio sapientissimi uiri*, 'with the utmost wisdom . . . by the advice of the wisest of men'). In the passage quoted from 9.13, the same cluster of terms appears once more in the context of relations between Pliny and Corellius, only for them all to be swept away by a shocking assertion. Corellius was not consulted, because he was (habitually) rather hesitant and cautious.[85]

The shock of this belated revelation about Corellius' limitations as exemplary elder – and Pliny's trust in his own powers of judgement even amid the tumultuous events of 96–7 – is compounded by the fact that Pliny applies the language of exemplarity to his own actions in the same letter. For he reveals that his desire to prosecute Certus was motivated by a determination to set an example for others to follow ('I . . . was incited by public justice, by the disgraceful character of the deed, and by a consideration of the example to be made [*exempli ratio*]', 9.13.3), and labels stories about Certus' dying vision of being menaced by an armed Pliny as

---

[85] Potentially even more troubling is another letter late in the collection (8.14), in which Pliny writes to the learned jurist Titius Aristo about the *dearth* of senatorial examples in his youth; cf. esp. 8.14.8. On the role of Book 8, see further below.

primarily useful for the example they set ('Whether this was true or not I would not venture to say positively; it is important to the example set [*interest tamen exempli*] that it should be held to be true', 9.13.25).[86] The revelation empowers the reader – as seen also in Chapter 1 – to return to the early books of the correspondence and to read them with fresh eyes. For letter 9.13 shows us that before the death of Corellius, Pliny was already in the process of becoming his own guide.[87] Even in 1.12 we may now find intimations of independence from Corellius, for Pliny's absence here from the final deathbed scene (1.12.9–10), as Hoffer (1999) 156 suggests, serves the subtle purpose of avoiding the creation of a 'father-son dynamic . . . the absent Pliny is not really a subordinate, obediently receiving deathbed wishes and commands'. Above all, beneath the often polite and deferential persona of Books 1 and 2, we are invited to detect a steely self-confidence.

The examination of the limits of the exemplarity of Verginius Rufus is conducted rather more subtly, but again is linked to a suggestion that it is Pliny himself who may now consider himself a model to others. At the time of his death Pliny had hailed Verginius as 'a model of a bygone age' (2.1.7).[88] Later in Book 6 – as seen in Chapter 2 – Pliny has occasion to visit his grave, which lies inside Verginius' old estate on the Tuscan coast.[89] Ten years have elapsed since the great man's death (6.10.3), and Pliny is afflicted both by a vain desire to see and be with the dead man (6.10.1, 2), and by grief at seeing his tomb still unfinished by his heir (6.10.3–5). The marker of the elapse of time is important, since it alerts us to the potential difference between the busy advocate of Book 2 and the consular orator of Book 6. In the very next letter, indeed, it is now Pliny's turn to be exemplary. For here he celebrates a 'a day . . . most joyful, and to be marked by me with the whitest of stones' (6.11.3). This effusion is justified by his encounter with two young orators already glimpsed in Chapter 2 – Ummidius Quadratus and Fuscus Salinator (also the addressee of 9.36 and 9.40, discussed above) – who prove their worth by looking to Pliny as their model:

---

[86] For Cicero's use of himself as an *exemplum* both in the letters and elsewhere, see Lowrie (2007).

[87] Cf. Hoffer (1999) 156, 159. For a complementary reading of 9.13, see Carlon (2009) 95–8.

[88] For a sophisticated analysis of Pliny's account in 2.1 of the funeral of Verginius and the *laudatio* of Tacitus as in dialogue with the *Agricola*, see Marchesi (2008) 189–99. For Verginius in Pliny, see also Lefèvre (2009) 23–36.

[89] At 6.10.11 the estate is said to belong now to the mother of Pliny's previous wife (immediately prior to Calpurnia): further evidence of the close connection between Verginius and Pliny's family. Family connections and property mingle together also in letters concerning the family of Corellius; cf. 7.11, 7.14.

ipsi me ut **rectorem**, ut **magistrum** intuebantur, et iis qui audiebant me aemulari, meis instare uestigiis uidebantur . . . quid . . . mihi optatius quam me ad recta tendentibus quasi **exemplar** esse propositum? (6.11.2, 3)

they directed their glances at me as their guide and teacher, and seemed to those who heard them to be imitating me and treading in my footsteps . . . What . . . can be more desirable for me personally than that I should be set up as a kind of model to men who have noble aims?

Not only has Pliny become, as Corellius had been to him in his youth, both *rector* and *magister* (*uitae meae testem rectorem magistrum*, 'a witness to my life, a guide and a master', 1.12.12) to young men, but, a decade after the death of Verginius, it is Pliny himself who has achieved the status of *exemplar*. As we argue in Chapter 2, the significant juxtaposition of letters is a key element in Pliny's artistic arrangement of his books. And here the reminder that Verginius died a decade ago – placed next to an insistence on Pliny's own status as model – has its own point to make.

A few letters earlier in the book Pliny had placed similar emphasis on his role as model to the young, while praising the young and fatherless Iulius Naso for choosing Pliny for personal imitation: *me certe, ut primum sibi iudicare permisit, ad amorem imitationemque delegit*, 'me, certainly, as soon as he permitted himself to form a judgement, he selected as the object of his affection and imitation' (6.6.5). The aggregation of these themes – the death now long ago of former exemplars and Pliny's emergence as model in his own right – may alert us to the pivotal role played by Book 6 in the development of the themes which have been the subject of this chapter. The memory of both Verginius and Corellius is perpetuated right to the end of the collection (9.13.6, 9.19), although the exemplarity of each receives significant qualification in the process. More significantly Pliny's last living model, Vestricius Spurinna, disappears from the collection at letter 5.17 – just after the first and last mention of Pliny's older consular colleague Cornutus Tertullus as an expressly exemplary presence in 5.14[90] – while the final named appearance of the Elder Pliny in the collection here in Book 6,[91] as shown at the beginning of this chapter, is accompanied by a strong implicit suggestion that Pliny's close imitation of the Elder was confined to the years of his adolescence. Pliny, it is true, did not hesitate

[90] In 5.14 he is hailed as *exemplar antiquitatis*, 'model of antiquity' (3), and Pliny avers that he revered him like a father (5), adding that together they cherished 'almost all those of either sex whom our epoch has produced as worthy of imitation [*aemulandos*]' (4).

[91] The Elder does turn up – deliberately unnamed – near the end of Book 9, where the Younger's tale of the African dolphin in letter 9.33 implicitly invites positive comparison with the Elder's account of the same dolphin in *HN* 9.8; see Stevens (2009).

to apply the language of exemplarity to himself even in earlier books of the collection,[92] and the letters themselves en masse are a deliberate display of exemplarity in a general sense (a lesson not lost on later letter-writers who model themselves and implicitly their behaviour on Pliny's decorous letters).[93] Nevertheless, it can be argued that the clustering here of significant language and juxtapositions in Book 6 is a signal of Pliny's growing self-consciousness about his role and responsibility as model to those around him, particularly the young.[94]

That self-consciousness, as Neil Bernstein has shown,[95] reaches its apogee in Book 8, where Pliny most fully develops the idea of a role for himself as symbolic father to a series of young men. Just as Verginius Rufus had shown Pliny the affection of a parent in his own youth (2.1.8), and Corellius Rufus had acted as guide and master, so now Pliny – revealed as himself still childless in Book 8 (8.10, 11) – seeks to act as substitute father and mentor to Rome's young elite. In letter 8.14 Pliny looks back to an ideal age when young men aspiring to rise up the *cursus honorum* learned by listening and taking the advice of fathers or father-figures:

inde honores petituri adsistebant curiae foribus, et consilii publici spectatores ante quam consortes erant. suus cuique parens pro magistro, aut cui parens non erat maximus quisque et uetustissimus pro parente. (8.14.5–6)

Hence candidates for public office stood by the doors of the senate house, and were spectators of the national council before becoming members of it. Each had his own father for an instructor, or to him who had no father the oldest and most illustrious citizens stood in the place of one.

The concern for the education of those without their own fathers resonates strongly with Pliny's own experience as mediated through the *Letters*. More importantly, it resonates strongly with other letters in Book 8, in particular its immediate predecessor (8.13) and one later in the book (8.23). In letter 8.13 Pliny responds to the news that the young Genialis is using Pliny's

---

[92] E.g. 1.8.8, 17; 3.18.2, 4.24.7. It will not have escaped Pliny's notice that Seneca generates *exempla* from the letters of e.g. Augustus and Cicero at *Breu.* 4–5 (see Chapter 6) and *Ep.* 97.

[93] For Pliny's self-presentation in the *Letters* as a source of authoritative advice, see Guillemin (1929) 32–51. Seneca's aspiration to exemplary status had emerged towards the end of his life, and he begins to use himself explicitly as an *exemplum* with some frequency for the first time in the *Letters*; see Mayer (1991) 68–9, and cf. e.g. Sen. *Ep.* 98.13.

[94] Cf. e.g. 7.1.7, 7.11.8, 7.33.9; 9.13.3, 25 (quoted above in the context of Corellius and the attempted prosecution of Certus). Cf. the stirring words of Tac. *Hist.* 1.3.1 *non tamen adeo uirtutum sterile saeculum ut non et bona exempla prodiderit*, 'but the age was not so barren of virtue that it did not produce good models'.

[95] Bernstein (2008a). (For slavery as alternative dominant theme in Book 8, see Whitton (2010).) Nevertheless, letters actually addressed to the younger generation are rare in Pliny, certainly by comparison with Cicero; see Leach (2006).

speeches as texts to study with his own father. In his response, Pliny 'is enable[d] . . . to claim a place for himself within the privileged father–son dynamic' (Bernstein (2008a) 216). Pliny exclaims:

Probo quod libellos meos cum patre legisti. pertinet ad profectum tuum a disertissimo uiro discere, quid laudandum quid reprehendendum, simul ita institui, ut uerum dicere adsuescas. uides quem sequi, cuius debeas implere uestigia. (8.13.1–2)

I approve of you having read my little books in company with your father. It helps your progress to learn from a man of the highest eloquence what deserves praise and what censure, and at the same time to be so trained as to learn to speak the truth. You see whom you ought to follow, in whose footsteps you ought to tread.

Pliny provides the content on which the father–son educative process proceeds. In particular, 'Through his praise of their activities, Pliny has indirectly laid claim to the authority to evaluate Genialis' moral and intellectual development at the hands of his father. Pliny thereby suggests that the work of fatherhood can be shared between the elder Genialis and other authoritative figures such as himself' (Bernstein (2008a) 218). A similar dynamic pervades Pliny's obituary letter for the young Iunius Avitus in letter 8.23, where the writer reflects on what made Avitus so distinctive in his generation:

suffragio meo adiutus in petendis honoribus fuerat; ad hoc ita me diligebat, ita uerebatur, ut me formatore morum, me quasi magistro uteretur. rarum hoc in adulescentibus nostris . . . statim sapiunt, statim sciunt omnia, neminem uerentur, neminem imitantur, atque ipsi sibi exempla sunt. sed non Auitus . . . (8.23.2–3)

I assisted him with my support when he was a candidate for office; add to this, that he so loved and revered me that he treated me as the moulder of his character, as his master, so to speak. A rare thing this in the case of our young men . . . They are all at once wise; they all at once know everything; they revere no one; they imitate no one, and are indeed themselves their own models. Not so Avitus . . .

Pliny performs the same range of roles for Avitus as Corellius and Verginius had done for him. And Avitus, it appears, was like Pliny fatherless at a young age (8.23.8). Pliny's attentiveness to Avitus is thus to be understood as a kind of symbolic fatherhood – a relationship perhaps signalled in the echo inside *formatore morum* of Horace's praise of his father's instruction (*Sat.* 1.4.120–1 *sic me | formabat puerum dictis*, 'in this way he shaped me as a boy with his words').

In sum, the *Letters*, with their emergent narrative of Pliny's growing exemplarity to promising members of Rome's younger generations, put together a story of hope and anticipation – stretching far into the future – while simultaneously developing an ever more densely detailed retrospective interpretation of the example set by Pliny's seniors. As for the anticipated future, Pliny was not wrong about it, at least from a purely personal point of view. For, as has often been noted, it is remarkable how many of Pliny's younger correspondents went on to achieve high office and position in the years after Pliny's death.[96]

If the final books of the collection witness the growth of Pliny's sense of himself as a model to the young, they also mark the emergence of a man who is – in Pliny's apparent estimation at least – a highly imitable contemporary, namely Cornelius Tacitus. In Book 7 Pliny explicitly confesses for the first time the depth and long-standing nature of his admiration for Tacitus and his literary-rhetorical talents:[97]

equidem adulescentulus, cum iam tu fama gloriaque floreres, te sequi, tibi 'longo sed proximus interuallo' et esse et haberi concupiscebam. et erant multa clarissima ingenia; sed tu mihi (ita similitudo naturae ferebat) maxime imitabilis, maxime imitandus uidebaris. (7.20.4)

For my part, when I was a very young man, while you were already flourishing in renown and glory, I yearned to follow after you, both to be accounted and to be 'second to you, though great the space between'. Yet there were in existence many men of brilliant genius; nevertheless you seemed to me (owing to the similarity of our dispositions) to be the one most capable of being imitated, and most worthy of imitation.

Tacitus here appears for the first time explicitly as a model to be imitated. The heady words of praise heaped on Tacitus bear comparison with the tributes offered to Pliny's trio of elderly northern consulars, and are all the more remarkable for being addressed directly to a living person.[98] Tacitus is no father-figure, to be sure. But Pliny's sense of competitiveness with Tacitus is both lively and strong: as with his elders, this is a sense of 'inferiority' to be worked through. However, fuller consideration of that relationship must wait until the next chapter, where it will be exposed as rather more fraught than is usually supposed.

---

[96] See e.g. Sherwin-White (1966) 157, Henderson (2003) 116–17. Some – such as Septicius Clarus, who opens the nine-book collection, and Fuscus Salinator, who closes it – would indeed achieve high office before having themselves or their families fall foul of Hadrian. In the attractive formulation of Syme, 'A group of senior personages, meeting early in the reign of Antoninus Pius to celebrate the eightieth birthday of their dead friend [Pliny], could have exchanged notable reflections on the paradoxes in the life of men' (*RP* 2.494 [= (1960) 378], with *RP* 2.492–4 [= (1960) 376–8] for the fates of Clarus and Fuscus).

[97] For discussion of this passage, see also Chapter 5.   [98] Cf. also e.g. 8.7.1.

Pliny's peers
Reading for the addressee

Letters are a natural medium for maintaining and recording friendship between writer and addressee, and ancient letter collections often seem to assume readers are as interested in those epistolary friends as they are in the letter-writers themselves.[1] Cicero's letters, in particular, bear witness to relationships developed over decades, and they are valued for what they tell us about his interactions with contemporaries in the highest echelons of society, as well as with his closest and oldest friend, Atticus. In Nepos' eyes, the sheer volume of correspondence addressed to Atticus was itself testimony to the strength of the friendship:

quamquam eum praecipue dilexit Cicero, ut ne frater quidem ei Quintus carior fuerit aut familiarior. ei rei sunt indicio praeter eos libros, in quibus de eo facit mentionem, qui in uulgus sunt editi, undecim uolumina epistularum ab consulatu eius usque ad extremum tempus ad Atticum missarum. (Nep. *Att.* 16.3)

Nevertheless, Cicero was particularly fond of him: so much so that not even his brother Quintus was dearer or closer. To prove the point, apart from the books in which Cicero mentions Atticus, which have been published, there are eleven rolls of letters, sent to Atticus from the time of Cicero's consulship right down to the end. (trans. N. Horsfall)

Maintaining Chapter 4's focus on selective study of Pliny's associates and on varied modes of reading, we move on now from consideration of his relationships with mentors and protégés and turn to an introductory study of a selection of the peers and colleagues who people his collection; this is intended to take 'sighting shots', as it were, to establish the boundaries and varieties of Pliny's friendships, and, in particular, to assess the criteria we might use in order to make our selection of important individuals.

In this chapter, we offer first a brief account of some markers of friendship to be found in the letter collection, and then more specific studies of five

---

[1] See now White (2010) 60.

letter cycles devoted to friends and colleagues who seem to be singled out either (like Tacitus) by the frequency of Pliny's address or (like Calvisius Rufus or Calestrius Tiro) by an accumulation of friendly vocabulary and motifs in their epistolary 'narratives': Calestrius Tiro, Voconius Romanus, Cornutus Tertullus, Septicius Clarus and Cornelius Tacitus.[2] To some extent, we must once again work against the grain of the collection in order to make our selection of Pliny's particular intimates, since Pliny's books, unlike Cicero's, are not organized by addressee.[3] Indeed (Book 10 aside), each contains a startlingly wide variety of addressees and epistolary friendships.[4] Pliny's apparently miscellaneous design allows him to present a programme for living well, in which individual letters and letter cycles, 'realistically' arranged to reflect a busy life full of encounters with associates of all kinds, cumulatively exemplify his equitable treatment of friends both eminent and relatively humble. This theme is then skilfully woven into the larger tapestry of the collection, and (precisely by eschewing organization by addressee) Pliny suggests that the management of one's (epistolary) relationships is but another aspect of a life of balanced variety.

ADDRESSEES AND LETTER COLLECTIONS

Letter books were often identified and even arranged according to addressee.[5] We have already seen an ancient reader's response to the letters to Atticus, but even in the *ad Familiares* collections, the organization by addressee means that little or no effort of research is required to find 'the next letter' written to any given individual.[6] The inclusion also of letters *from* some of these addressees merely supports and enhances the reader's interest in Cicero's correspondents themselves. The prime example is Caelius, whose letters fill Book 8 of the collection, and who also dominates much of Book 2, but there are other figures – such men as Trebatius (*Fam.* 7.5–22), Munatius Plancus (*Fam.* 10.1–24), Brutus (*ad Brut.*) – with

---

[2] For a selection of Pliny's other addressees, see Appendix 4; for bibliography, see Appendix 3.

[3] See Chapter 1. For a similarly selective approach, which seeks to identify specific classes of associates (such as Pliny's 'literary friends'), see White (1975) 299. For other, more thematic, ordering schemes in the Ciceronian collections, see now White (2010) 54–6.

[4] Cf. Bütler (1970) 94, 'fast jeder der 247 Briefe der ersten neun Bücher wird so zu einem Dokument der Freundesliebe und der weitreichenden Beziehungen ihres Verfassers.' See also Chapter 2.

[5] See, among many possible examples, Gellius' reference to the letters of Augustus *ad Gaium nepotem* (*NA* 15.7), or to those of Caesar to Oppius and Balbus (*NA* 17.9.1), or to Fronto's reference to books of letters from Cicero to Brutus and to Axius (*ad Anton. Imp.* 3.8.3). See also above p. 14 n. 26. For Caesar's letters, in particular, see Ebbeler (2003).

[6] For our commitment to reading the majority of Pliny's letter cycles according to the internal sequence across the collection, see the Introduction to this volume.

whom we can see Cicero's relationship developing and changing within the sequences of the letters which he addressed to them. In-jokes confirm and build upon established relationships as the letters proceed, and repetitions and reiterations of friendly intercourse all help us to think we can imagine our way into the company of men upon whose conversations we are eavesdropping over periods of weeks, months or even years. And of course, the letters to Caesar (almost entirely lost) leave a tantalizing gap in our understanding of the latter part of Cicero's life.[7]

The expectation of development across an epistolary cycle with one addressee underpins Seneca's epistolary programme of philosophical instruction, too, to rather different effect. Seneca addresses a single friend, Lucilius, on the model (consciously articulated in *Ep.* 21.4) of Atticus in Cicero's collections. We see less development in the personal relationship between writer and addressee than we might have found in Cicero's letters, but the collection still gives the sense of progress in the shared endeavour of philosophy upon which the relationship is founded, as Lucilius' journey along the road to *sapientia* is guided by (for example) Seneca's gradual introduction of longer, 'harder' letters in the later books, in which he moves away from the memorable quotations and maxims which served as entertaining pedagogical props to ease the early learning stages. The intensity of focus here generated by the use of a single addressee suits a project which is founded upon a philosophical withdrawal from the hurly-burly of city life (e.g. *Ep.* 7 and *Ep.* 8), and upon an aversion to dependency upon a multitude of friends (*Ep.* 9) or even to an excess of intellectual influences (*Ep.* 2); Seneca can meditate in epistolary 'privacy' upon the nature of friendship and the effects of human stimulus, in the company of just one like-minded addressee.

In Pliny's collection, by contrast, it can be difficult (without such aids as the ancient indices or modern prosopographical works) to keep up with the constantly changing crowd of faces among his addressees, and to select the most significant friendships in his life:[8] Book 10 aside, letters to any given individual are scattered throughout the first nine books, and no single addressee dominates the collection. It is often harder still to evaluate addressees' characters and interests, since separate letters to the same individual may seem to cover vastly different topics. Cross-references specifically to an earlier letter to the same addressee are relatively rare,[9]

[7] Suet. *Iul.* 56.6.

[8] For Pliny's organizational techniques, see Chapters 1 and 2. For Pliny's innovations in this regard, see Marchesi (2008) 18.

[9] E.g. 7.29 and 8.6, both addressed to Montanus about the Pallas inscription.

and two letters to the same addressee positioned near one another within a book (like the famous 6.16 and 6.20) are rarer still.[10] When such marked pairings or sequences do occur, their impact is all the greater, since the collection's usual demand that the reader constantly change direction and adapt to a different addressee, a new tone or a fresh topic is temporarily suspended as we are offered something familiar and reminded of something recently read. Pairs such as the famous Vesuvius letters (6.16 and 6.20) acquire a monumental quality from their mutually reinforcing positions; even if the event they describe, or the 'celebrity' addressee (Tacitus) were not irresistibly interesting in themselves, their placement so close together would signal a pause, as it were, at an important staging post in Pliny's epistolary autobiography.[11] Apart from these exceptional cases, however, the distribution throughout the collection of, for example, letters *ad Voconium* contributes to the 'reality effect' of a collection which claims to be a set of casually assembled gatherings of seemingly unrelated texts, put together 'as they came to hand' (1.1.1).[12]

MARKERS OF FRIENDSHIP

Pliny's collection, then, confounds the expectations of readers conditioned by the Ciceronian collections, and invites us into a highly populated world to meet a different individual in each successive letter, disrupting sequences of letters which would, in other collections, have been grouped together. Nevertheless, obvious indicators, such as affectionate language, mock-abusive teasing (e.g. in 1.15), or anecdotes of private life, can help us select key addressees. Topics such as concern for someone's health, too (although a natural epistolary topic), may be both an indicator of friendship and a trigger for heightened emotionalism in expressing affection.[13] Finally, certain modes of writing might feel more acceptable within the confines of closer intimacy: praise and blame, for example, are given more free rein in letters to close friends. Self-praise, especially, although usually frowned

---

[10] Cf. 2.11 and 2.12, on the Marius Priscus case.

[11] That they are not immediately juxtaposed reinforces the sense of loose chronological realism (if not real chronology) which Pliny builds into his collection. The interposition of three letters between 6.16 and 6.20 gives the impression that Tacitus has had just enough time to read 6.16 and reply to beg for more of the story; see also Chapter 2 on this kind of 'reality effect'. On pairs of letters, see Marchesi (2008) 25. The ancient indices would have thrown such design features into high relief.

[12] Marchesi (2008) 24.

[13] Pliny himself naturally refers to a range of degrees of friendship, e.g. 4.17.2 (*non plane familiaris sed tamen amicitia*, 'if not an absolute intimacy, still a friendship'). On affectionate language in late republican epistolography, see Hutchinson (1998) 17, Hall (2009) 63–71, 206–7.

upon, becomes more permissible in a letter to an addressee close enough to be an *alter ego*.[14] Even certain aspects of enmity (relatively uncommon in Pliny's letters) seem carefully contained in letters to Pliny's closest friends. It is striking, for example, that several of Pliny's attacks on Regulus occur in the shelter of an especially close relationship with his addressee: the first letter about this great enemy, 1.5, is also the first to Voconius Romanus, whom he claims as one of his closest friends, and to whom he can reveal such inner thoughts as would not – unlike his *facta* or *dicta* – be the subject of public record (1.5.17). The first letter to Calvisius Rufus (2.20) is also about Pliny's hostility to Regulus, and later it is another unusually close friend, Maturus Arrianus, who receives the obituary for Regulus (6.2) which we have already discussed in Chapter 2.[15]

Friendship vocabulary can guide the reader's selection too. *Noster*, for example, when used of a mutual friend, often seems to indicate particular warmth,[16] and although *amici* and *amicitiae* abound in the letters, the term *contubernalis* is considerably more restricted in its use, suggesting a degree of familiarity normally associated with a familial household (Ummidia's grandson, for example, lives in her *contubernium*, as Pliny's wife was raised in that of Calpurnia Hispulla).[17] Indeed, when applied to friends, *contubernalis* denotes those who are in and out of one's house every day or with whom one has had some daily interaction in the past.[18] Pliny's *contubernales*, first mentioned early in 1.2, include his closest confidants (none, as it happens, are women) or oldest associates, such as Romatius Firmus (1.19.1), Voconius Romanus (2.13.5; 10.4.1), Calvisius Rufus (1.12.12; 4.4.1) and Suetonius Tranquillus (1.24.1; 10.94.1), as well as the unnamed group of those who act as a kind of literary advisory council for Pliny, and are mentioned in 1.2.5 and 6.33.11 (the last a letter to Voconius Romanus).[19]

---

[14] Gibson (2003).

[15] We know too little about Attius Clemens, the addressee of 4.2 (on Regulus' excessive mourning for his son) to be able to assess his significance in this context; he receives only one other letter, although it is one of the collection's foundation stones in the opening sequences of Book 1 (1.10, about Euphrates). The two letters to Attius share an interest in the correlation between appearance/public behaviour and true virtue.

[16] For *noster* as typically used of fellow-Cisalpines, see Sherwin-White (1966) 419. On the language of friendship in Pliny's predecessors, see Konstan (1995) 335 and *passim*; for a more wide-ranging survey of notions and vocabulary of friendship in Roman culture, see Konstan (1997) 122–48.

[17] 7.24.3; 4.19.6. See *TLL* s.v. 792.50–793.46.

[18] See Johnson (2010) 145–6. Cicero, for example, complains that C. Arrius has become a *contubernalis* by dint of constantly turning up in the villa at Formiae and impeding Cicero's studies instead of taking himself off to Rome (*Att.* 2.14.2; 2.15.3). Sherwin-White (1966) 152 briefly surveys the terms Pliny uses for his friends (principally *familiaris*, with *amicus* used of acquaintances, and *contubernalis* or *sodalis* reserved for especially treasured individuals). For the *contubernium* as 'a regular metaphor of literary friendships', see Sherwin-White (1966) 178.

[19] For *contubernalis* in this sense, see *TLL* s.v. 790.82–791.39.

As a hallmark of quality, the term is also one of the key mechanisms of smoothing the way of patronage, and it is especially common in the context of recommendations or performance of favours.[20] In 1.19, for example, Pliny sets out for Romatius Firmus the reasons for a gift of sufficient cash to bring this addressee up into the equestrian census bracket. 1.24 backs Suetonius' wish to buy a small farm, and 2.13 recommends Voconius to its addressee.[21] All three are Pliny's *contubernales*. In return, *contubernales* may support Pliny with advice or consolation: so Calvisius at 1.12.12 is the man to whom Pliny confides his fear that Corellius' death diminishes his own commitment to living well.[22]

Nevertheless, as an aid to selection of important addressees, even such strongly marked vocabulary of friendship is largely useless to any *first-time* reader of Pliny who lacks access to, for example, a good modern concordance, and its impact upon a sequential reading of the collection will be subtle and cumulative. Nevertheless, the design of Pliny's collection does give some discreet help to the sequential first-time reader, in that most of those who seem closest to Pliny appear first in Book 1, either as addressees or in the body of a letter,[23] and most of the names in Book 1 reappear later in the collection.[24] A few cycles are confined to the later books: Rosianus Geminus' six letters, for example, are housed in the last three books of the collection (in each case at opposite ends of each book) and then capped with a letter of recommendation on his behalf at 10.26.[25] Otherwise, no new correspondent in Books 3, 5, 6, 8 and 9 receives more than three letters in total. Moreover, lone letters (i.e. one-off letters to individuals who appear nowhere else in Pliny) are rarer in Book 1 than in any other except Book 8.[26] All other books have at least three letters which are the only ones to the addressees in question, and some (Books 9 and 6, for example) have many more (eight and six letters respectively).[27]

---

[20] See also Johnson (2010) 145–7.

[21] Cf. 4.4, where Pliny vouches for Varisidius Nepos by citing his connections with his own *contubernalis*, Calvisius Rufus (Varisidius' maternal uncle). Similarly, at 4.27 Sentius Augurinus is *contubernalis* to both Spurinna and Antoninus; his position as *contubernalis* of respected elders guarantees the excellence of his character.

[22] Cf. 3.19.1.

[23] We focus in this chapter on the male addressees who dominate the collection. On the gender balance in the letters ('237½ letters to about 100 different men and 9½ letters to 7 different women') – and on the significant shift in those statistics in the letters to known relatives – see Hoffer (1999) 133.

[24] The inevitable uncertainties as to the identity of e.g. any given Maximus makes all these figures a little impressionistic, but one can still observe overall trends and patterns.

[25] 7.1, 7.24, 8.5, 8.22, 9.11, 9.30.   [26] Only 1.4 and 1.16 are certainly lone letters, as are 8.13 and 8.18.

[27] On the distribution of correspondents throughout the books, see Sherwin-White (1966) 65–9, also Chapter 2.

So Pliny starts his reader off gently – and also, perhaps naturally, compliments many addressees by including them in his first book. Further books can then present the reader with familiar faces as way-markers in the prosopographical forest. Moreover, a conscientious user of the ancient indices, conditioned by the addressee-focused corpora of Cicero and Seneca, who wanted to scan the collection for important addressees would have been able to select with relative ease the cycles of letters to the most frequently addressed individuals;[28] nevertheless, even that most useful of the selective reader's tools would have offered striking visual confirmation not only of the collection's resistance to traditional groupings of letters by addressee but also of the remarkably small numbers of letters attached to the names of even the most frequently recurring individuals. No book on Pliny is complete, for example, without the reminder that Tacitus is Pliny's most frequent addressee, but it is sobering to realize that we are talking about only eleven letters.[29] So if we want to determine which of Pliny's addressees were most important to him on the basis of numbers alone, we can observe that the recipients of six or more letters in the collection, in descending order of number of letters received, are: Tacitus, Calpurnius Fabatus, Voconius Romanus, Maturus Arrianus, Macrinus, Calvisius Rufus and Rosianus Geminus. Nevertheless, the value of such a focus on numbers is limited, since even those designated as *contubernales* are not necessarily the recipients of a larger number of letters (witness Suetonius Tranquillus, addressee of four letters,[30] Calestrius Tiro, who is marked as especially close in 7.16 but receives only four letters, and Romatius Firmus, who receives only two).

However, Pliny is careful gradually to build up a certain amount of detail about selected people in his collection, and to confirm, as it were, the importance of some addressees by including a third-person 'reference' (or even a potted biography) for them later in the collection – a cohesive narrative device which might in many cases be hidden from a selective reader who used the indices to trawl for his chosen addressee.[31] One gets a slightly better picture, then, by counting letters to *and about* any given individual and considering their interplay: in numerical terms alone, that would give Calestrius Tiro a total of seven letters, for example, and bring

---

[28] On the ancient indices, see further Chapter 2, with Appendix 2.

[29] Compare that number with e.g. Cicero's seventeen letters to Trebatius in *Fam.* 7.6–22, or the fourteen letters to Decimus Brutus (*Fam.* 11.5–8, 12, 14–18, 21–2, 24–25).

[30] For bibliography on Suetonius and Pliny, see Appendix 3.

[31] Contrast the convenient placement of Cicero's letter to Caesar *on behalf of* Trebatius (*Fam.* 7.5) at the head of the sequence of letters addressed *to* Trebatius (*Fam.* 7.6–22).

Tacitus and Voconius Romanus up to fourteen and ten letters respectively.[32] All three of these men will receive attention later in this chapter.

In a sense, however, and at the risk of impossibly circular argument, all addressees in Pliny's letter collection are the writer's *amici*, simply by virtue of receiving a letter (a token of friendship in itself) and the honour of a place in the published collection. Nevertheless, although many of those who receive larger numbers of letters are marked as special friends,[33] those to (or about) whom he writes in the warmest terms are not necessarily among his most frequent addressees.

An extreme example is the quiet-living Transpadane wit, Atilius Crescens, to whom no letter is addressed anywhere in the collection.[34] He is twice mentioned in passing in the early books, on both occasions as the source of a witticism or clever observation,[35] but later Pliny sketches a history of deep mutual affection:

hunc ego non ut multi, sed artissime diligo. oppida nostra unius diei itinere dirimuntur; ipsi amare inuicem, qui est flagrantissimus amor, adulescentuli coepimus. mansit hic postea, nec refrixit iudicio sed inualuit. sciunt qui alterutrum nostrum familiarius intuentur. nam et ille amicitiam meam latissima praedicatione circumfert, et ego prae me fero, quantae sit mihi curae modestia quies securitas eius. (6.8.1–2)

He is one whom I cherish, not after the vulgar fashion, but with my whole heart. Our native towns are separated by one day's journey only. Our love for each other began – and this is the most fervent kind of love – when we were mere striplings. It endured to after years, and far from being cooled, was strengthened by our mature judgement. Those who are most intimately acquainted with either of us know this. For, not only does he widely proclaim and circulate his friendship for me, but I too make no secret of the interest I feel in his modest life, his repose, and his security.

This is a man of little money and no influence, whose value to Pliny appears to lie solely in his wit and his open acknowledgement of their friendship. As we have already noted in Chapter 2, Book 6 combines letters about Pliny's *negotium* with instances of intense private affection, the language

---

[32] A brief summary of the figures (the 'raw' number of letters to someone/the expanded figure including letters about or mentioning someone): Tacitus (11/14), Fabatus (9/10), Voconius (8/9), Maturus(7/8), Macrinus (6/7), Calvisius (6/8), Rosianus Geminus (6/7). On these criteria, it might also be worth adding Calestrius Tiro (4/7), Suetonius Tranquillus (4/7), Paulinus (5/8), Cornelius Ursus (5/5), Fuscus Salinator (3/5, and another important inhabitant of the later collection who is first introduced in Book 7) and Julius Servianus (2/5). No letter mentions Romatius Firmus as a third party.

[33] Tacitus, as we shall see later in this chapter, is a significant exception.

[34] For Atilius' origins at Bergomum, see Syme, *RP* 5.449, 453 [= (1985a) 332, 336.]

[35] 1.9.8, 2.14.2.

of which is suffused throughout several of the letters. 6.8, which intercedes upon Atilius' behalf in the process of recovering a debt, shows Pliny's dedication even to relatively humble northern friends who have chosen a life of *quies* – in fact his defence of Atilius' position is framed in some of the most aggressive and assertive terms to be found in the entire collection.[36] This letter sits well in Book 6, which is also (in parallel with its dominant interest in *negotium*) a book about protégés and, more specifically, about the protection and promotion of the interests of one's friends: not only does it contain the two letters about Pliny's support of the candidature of Julius Naso (6.6 and 6.9), but it is in Book 6 that we first meet Fuscus Salinator and Ummidius Quadratus (6.11), both future protégés of Pliny.

A considerably more distinguished friend, Julius Servianus, is only twice addressed in the collection (3.17, an anxious inquiry about his well-being, and 6.26, a letter of congratulation upon his daughter's betrothal to Fuscus Salinator), but even these two rather short letters have been read as evidence of a particularly close relationship.[37] Although Sherwin-White classifies 3.17 as only a 'courtesy note', for example, he detects 'a special intimacy' with this addressee, observing that 'nowhere does Pliny express such strong fears for an absent friend, save for his sick wife'. In this case, the 'special intimacy' – if such there was – is represented in a minimalist letter which has been stripped of *Realien* in order to maintain the focus upon emotion:

rectene omnia, quod iam pridem epistulae tuae cessant? an omnia recte, sed occupatus es tu? an tu non occupatus, sed occasio scribendi uel rara uel nulla? exime hunc mihi scrupulum, cui par esse non possum, exime autem uel data opera tabellario misso. ego uiaticum, ego etiam praemium dabo, nuntiet modo quod opto. ipse ualeo, si ualere est suspensum et anxium uiuere, exspectantem in horas timentemque pro capite amicissimo, quidquid accidere homini potest. uale. (3.17)

Can all be well, that your letters have ceased for some time past? Or perhaps all is well, but you are busy? Or you are not busy, but you have few or no opportunities of communicating with me? Relieve me of this uneasiness which is too much for me: pray relieve me of it, even at the cost of sending a special messenger. I will pay him his expenses and make him a present into the bargain, provided only he

---

[36] E.g. in the slightly combative imaginary exchange between his addressee and himself (*quorsus haec?... iterum dices 'quorsus haec?'*) and Pliny's assertion in both Greek and Latin that Atilius will suffer injury over Pliny's dead body. Cf. Cicero's observation in *de Amic.* 57 that one may behave more aggressively in defence of a friend than on one's own behalf. For a reading of this letter within the sequences of its book, see Chapter 2.

[37] On this man, suffect in 90, consul again (with Licinius Sura) in 102, and the husband of Hadrian's sister, Domitia Paulina, see Syme, *RP* 2.770 [= (1969b) 232], 3.1158–9, 1166ff. [= (1979b) 287–9, 296ff.], 5.525–6 [= (1985d) 44–5]. Servianus appears in three other letters: 7.6.8, where he appears as *iudex* in a poisoning case, 8.23.5, which records his friendship with the late Junius Avitus, and 10.2, where we find him as the instigator of the emperor's gift to Pliny of the *ius trium liberorum*.

brings me the news I long for. For myself, I am well, if one can be said to be well who lives in suspense and anxiety, hourly expecting and dreading on the account of his loved friend every possible accident which can befall man. Farewell.

In terms of the letter collection itself, the relationship between the two men seems to come out of nowhere: Pliny shows himself worrying over a long hiatus in a correspondence of which this is the first visible sample in the collection.[38] The letter opens with questions and speculations about Servianus' circumstances, and reveals Pliny fearing the worst.[39] The bones of the letter are very simple:

1. What is happening to prevent you writing?
2. I would like a letter from you.
3. I am well, but anxious, fearing for your safety.

This common epistolary pattern allows for considerable creative freedom. Ovid's *Heroides* I, for example, shows Penelope speculating about Ulysses' circumstances, outlining her efforts to obtain news of him, summarizing her current situation, and enumerating the anxious fantasies she has endured during the Trojan War and in the long years of his absence.[40] As usual in Pliny, however, 3.17 gives no specific information about the addressee's current circumstances (the *occupationes* which keep him from writing are left unspecified), and it is not until we reach the last sentence that we realize that Servianus might be in imminent physical danger. What Pliny offers here is, in fact, a concise template for any anxious letter ever written,[41] soliciting in return the most basic epistolary communication (*si uales bene est, ego ualeo*).[42]

Letter 6.26, by contrast, is a kind of prose epithalamium, addressed, rather unusually, to the bride's father, on the occasion of his daughter's engagement to one of Pliny's new protégés, Fuscus Salinator. The

---

[38] For Pliny's habit of suggesting a background of ongoing epistolary relationships, see also Chapter 8.

[39] This is one of the rare Pliny letters to acknowledge the mechanics of postal delivery (which were a much more frequent motif in Cicero's letters: White (2010) 11–15), and the emotional significance of the letter's content is to be measured by Pliny's management of such practical matters: he will pay a reward in addition to the messenger's normal travel allowance *as long as he gets the news he wants*.

[40] On *Heroides* I, see Kennedy (1984).

[41] See Hoffer (1999) 48 n. 10 for parallels in Seneca and Ovid. Cf. 2.2.

[42] This letter, and others like it, provide unnerving pockets of 'silence' in a collection which otherwise gives the impression of busy conversations between Pliny and those of his circle – hence, perhaps, the whiff of the atmosphere of the *Heroides*, where silence and loneliness dominate. One should note the juxtaposition of this letter about a long break in communication with the contrastingly lengthy 3.18, which gives an account of Pliny's delight that his friends have just willingly spent three days at his recitation of the *Panegyricus*. We find a similarly stark contrast between the brief 1.11 (which worries about Fabius Iustus' long epistolary silence) and the lengthy account of Pliny's special relationship with Corellius in 1.12.

bridegroom is appropriately praised in splendid terms, but the central figures of the letter are the bride's father and his friend Pliny. Their intimacy seems touchingly confirmed when Pliny imagines himself one day lifting Servianus' newly born grandchildren from his arms, to cradle them as if he were himself their proud progenitor:

quam felix tempus illud, quo mihi liberos illius nepotes tuos, ut meos uel liberos uel nepotes, ex uestro sinu sumere et quasi pari iure tenere contingeret. (6.26.3)

How happy the time, when it will be my good fortune to receive from your arms his children and your grandchildren – just as if they were my own children or grandchildren – and to hold them in mine, as though I had an equal right to them!

Anticipation of the baby in arms is traditional in epithalamia,[43] as is the expectation that the newborn will look like his father (*superest ut auum te quam maturissime similium sui faciat*, 'all that remains is that he should, as soon as possible, make you the grandfather of young ones like himself', 6.26.3), but nowhere else are the characters around that baby set up in this configuration. In keeping with Pliny's regular emphasis on his own good relationship with older relatives of his coevals or protégés, bridegroom, addressee and writer are all linked with one another in friendship and affection, and the staging of this imaginary scene brings Pliny into the inner sanctum of the family.

Both letters to Servianus, then, seem to offer snapshots of emotional intimacy in a relationship which constructs itself within the confines of these individual letters as unusually close, but which has relatively little wider impact in the collection as a whole. Neither letter gives us any information about the background to their relationship or about its history and development. Shared interests are kept from view (although one might say that the shared interest in this case is Fuscus, newly met earlier in this very book, at 6.11). Moreover, that Servianus was one of Trajan's most important lieutenants is nowhere suggested, and it is only later, in an obituary letter for a shared friend, that we discover something about his military career:

quod ille obsequium Seruiano exactissimo uiro praestitit! quem legatum tribunus ita et intellexit et cepit, ut ex Germania in Pannoniam transeuntem non ut commilito sed ut comes adsectatorque sequeretur. (8.23.5)

What deference he paid to that most accomplished man Servianus, when the latter was Legate and he was military tribune. He so appreciated and at the same time captivated Servianus that in his march across from Germania to Pannonia

---

[43] See e.g. Catull. 61.209–18.

he followed him, not as being one of his army, but as a companion and personal attendant.

Here Avitus' exemplary behaviour towards Servianus on campaign parallels in the military sphere the devotion and respect he had shown to Pliny, his political patron, while in Rome (8.23.2). If Servianus was serving abroad when 3.17 was composed, then we have another instance of Pliny's tendency to de-emphasize military life[44] and of his habit of encouraging re-reading of early letters in the light of fresh information offered late in the collection. That the final reference to Servianus in 10.2 (where we discover that Servianus recommended Pliny to Trajan for the *ius trium liberorum*) emphasizes the interest the two men take, one way or another, in each other's progeny seems almost too neat to be coincidental, especially as both letters, in different ways, also concern the hopes of a new bridegroom for future children. But we need to read the whole sequence and balance earlier letters with later ones in order to pick up such patterns and echoes.

Letters 3.17 and 6.26, then, although both cast in emotional terms, give us – considered as individual items – relatively little to go on if we read Pliny's letters (as we sometimes read Cicero's) in order to understand a relationship with an addressee. Indeed, Sherwin-White's note of a 'special intimacy' in so limited a correspondence should make us ask how we can really identify intimacy in an epistolary collection, and what signals – if any – the letters emit to help us distinguish particularly close friends. Moreover, the way in which the apparently unconnected topics of 3.17 and 6.26 are separately echoed in later letters about Servianus to other addressees reminds us to re-examine sequences to and about Pliny's more frequent addressees in order to see how he builds his epistolary friendship narratives with the subtlest of touches and in cumulative brushstrokes.

CALESTRIUS TIRO

We begin with an important 'mini-cycle' of letters (7.16, 7.23, 7.32) in which Pliny smoothes the way for his friend, the newly proconsular Calestrius Tiro, to break his journey to Baetica with a visit to Calpurnius Fabatus at Ticinum. We have already seen in Chapters 2 and 3 the subtle associative allusions and significant juxtapositions which link Tiro with Fabatus' granddaughter, Calpurnia (and which also thereby help to mark out this

---

[44] Cf. 9.2, where it is implied, but without detail, that Sabinus may be on campaign. Cf. also Chapters 1 and 2 on this tendency in Books 1 and 6 respectively, and on Pliny's consistent portrayal of Trajan as *ciuilis princeps*.

friendship as a special one), and this little set of letters in Book 7 builds upon that association: the reward for the attentive reader is an unexpected extra coherence and structure in the relationships between Tiro and *two* members of Pliny's family.[45] Here, in an important 'checklist' for close friendships, Pliny vouches for Calestrius as a mirror-image of himself:

Calestrium Tironem familiarissime diligo et priuatis mihi et publicis necessitudinibus implicitum. Simul militauimus, simul quaestores Caesaris fuimus. ille me in tribunatu liberorum iure praecessit, ego illum in praetura sum consecutus, cum mihi Caesar annum remisisset. ego in uillas eius saepe secessi, ille in domo mea saepe conualuit. (7.16.1–2)

I have an intimate regard for Calestrius Tiro, who is attached to me both by private and public ties. We served in the army together, and we were Caesar's quaestors together. He preceded me in the tribuneship, in virtue of his having children, but I overtook him in the praetorship – Caesar having remitted me a year. I have often enjoyed the retirement of his country seats, and he has often recovered his health at my house.

Shared professional experience and near-parallel careers are anchored by deep roots of private friendship, as both men regularly (*saepe* is repeated) stay in each other's houses for relaxation or convalescence.[46] This more 'private' information might seem of little use or interest to Fabatus, given that his business with Calestrius is legal rather than personal, but it sets the scene well for Pliny's efforts to forge a new three-way relationship between Calestrius, Fabatus and himself. The next in the series, 7.23, builds upon the domestic familiarity between Pliny and Calestrius by recommending that Fabatus accept the visit in his *cubiculum* (the most private space of his house, into which only important visitors might expect to be received) rather than travelling to a more formal meeting. Calestrius, after all, is practically family:

quin immo denuntio, ut illum et domi et intra domum atque etiam intra cubiculi limen exspectes. etenim, cum a me ut frater diligatur, non debet ab eo quem ego parentis loco obseruo, exigere officium quod parenti suo remisisset. (7.23.1–2)

Nay, further, I enjoin on you to wait for him at home, and, what is more, inside your house, and even inside your chamber. For truly, since he is cherished by me as a brother, he ought not to exact from one whom I look up to as a father an attention which he would have excused in the case of his own father.

---

[45] On a comparable pairing in Catullus 50 and 51 of the poet's relationships with Licinius Calvus and with Lesbia, see Finamore (1984).

[46] Long shared experience could also be offered as preamble and justification for any act of patronage (e.g. 1.19.1). Cf. also 6.8 and Laelius' words in Cic. *de Amic.* 15.

Pliny can vouch for the travelling proconsul as a brother rather than as an official of the state, as the gradual rhetorical progress towards the most intimate part of the house (forget Milan, meet him at home, inside the house – even better: in the *cubiculum* . . .) elegantly illustrates, anticipating a swiftly accelerating relationship between two men who are still strangers to one another.[47] 7.32, the final letter in the mini-cycle, gives no indication whether or not Fabatus acted on Pliny's suggestion, but does imply that the visit went well and the job got done, to the shared credit of Pliny and Fabatus. This is a narrative of successful triangulation of relationships, but the whole sequence depends upon Pliny's established familiarity with both men even in the most private spaces of their lives.[48]

VOCONIUS ROMANUS

For the sharing of one's life with a close friend *in secessu* or in town, one can look to another letter of recommendation, this time addressed to Priscus on behalf of Voconius Romanus (2.13).

> hunc ego, cum simul studeremus, arte familiariterque dilexi; ille meus in urbe ille in secessu contubernalis, cum hoc seria cum hoc iocos miscui. (2.13.5)

> When we were fellow-students I had a close and intimate regard for him; he was my daily associate in town and country; with him I shared my serious and my sportive hours.

Voconius has been Pliny's companion in life's miscellany from early youth, sharing *otium* and *negotium*, sobriety and jest – a special privilege which may be read as all the more significant in a collection built upon miscellaneity. He is perhaps better drawn than many of Pliny's addressees, since two letters recommend or praise him, namely 2.13 (to Priscus) and 10.4 (to the emperor).[49] His name crops up remarkably regularly throughout the correspondence, with only three out of all ten books lacking a letter to or about him. Moreover, three of the letters to Voconius are in immediate proximity to key letters to Tacitus, and it seems possible that a reader might be expected to pick up on this sort of cluster, consciously or not – and the ancient indices, of course, would facilitate such an observation.

---

47 On a comparable journey from public to private space, cf. 1.3.1 with Hoffer (1999) 32. On the *cubiculum*, see Riggsby (1997).

48 See Rees (2007) for the triangulation of relationships by means of recommendation letters. One should note that Calestrius is one of the figures whose career is followed in a chronological fashion in the letters (winning gubernatorial appointment, 6.22; movement north via Fabatus' house, 7.16, 7.23, 7.32; work in his province, 9.5).

49 Syme, *RP* 2.480ff. [= (1960) 364ff.], 5.488 [= (1985b) 183].

We are rarely far from one of the Tacitus letters, since they are well dis-
tributed throughout the books (missing only from Books 3 and 5), but
three instances like this seems unlikely to be accidental.[50] 1.5, the first letter
in the collection about the enmity with Regulus, is followed by the famous
note to Tacitus about Pliny's success in catching boar (1.6). In Book 6,
the first of the two Vesuvius letters (6.16) follows a rather catty anecdote
about Iavolenus Priscus sent to Voconius.[51] Finally, the pattern is reversed
in Book 8, where the letter to Voconius about the Clitumnus (8.8) immediately follows a short one to Tacitus about an exchange of manuscripts.
Moreover, 2.1, the letter about Verginius Rufus' funeral (including Tacitus'
spoken eulogy), is actually addressed to Voconius himself. Pliny's attempts
to match himself with Tacitus (see below) seem to be mirrored in the regular presence of his great contemporary in the proximity of letters addressed
to some of his very closest friends – another feature which might have been
relatively easily observed by users of the ancient indices.

That the figure of Voconius is important not only for his own sake,
but also for the landscaping of the collection – that he should stand out
above the mass of lesser correspondents, in other words, as a kind of
navigational landmark for the reader who might otherwise be confused
by the mass of addressees – may also explain similar associative place-
ments and important commonalities of theme in the letters to this one
addressee.

We have already remarked on the 'safety catch' Pliny puts on his letters
about his only advertised enemy in addressing them only to his very closest
friends. One should note, too, that 1.5 (the condemnation of Regulus),
is followed in the Voconius cycle by a letter about one of Pliny's great
men of the past: 2.1, on the funeral of Verginius Rufus;[52] an eagle-eyed
user of the indices (or enthusiastic re-reader of the collection) might also
notice a comparable sequencing in Books 2–3, where 2.20, the final letter
of the second book (and the first addressed to Calvisius Rufus), denounces
Regulus' shameless legacy-hunting, before 3.1 (also to Calvisius) extols
Spurinna's admirable retirement, thus making a parallel shift from negative
to positive *exemplum* in the first two letters to each of these important
correspondents.

Letter 2.1 fulfils multiple functions. It serves as an epistolary equivalent
to Tacitus' spoken eulogy at the grand public ceremony, it provides an

---

[50] A similar tantalizing coincidence of juxtaposition – this time a coincidence of topic rather than
addressee – may be observed for the two letters addressed to Julius Servianus (3.17 and 6.26) which
we have discussed above, both of which immediately precede a letter about the consular speech of
thanks to the emperor.

[51] See further Chapter 2.   [52] On Verginius Rufus, see further Chapter 4.

account of the death (or at least the first causes of it), it situates Pliny himself in relation to the great man, and finally it presents itself as a private act of mourning in the arms of a friend (*quibus ex causis necesse est tamquam immaturam mortem eius in sinu tuo defleam*, 'these are the reasons which oblige me to pour my griefs into your bosom for a death which seems almost premature', 2.1.10). The process is reminiscent of 1.12, to Calestrius Tiro, in which Pliny mourns the death of Corellius Rufus, in words, moreover, already spoken to Calvisius Rufus (*in summa dicam, quod recenti dolore contubernali meo Caluisio dixi: 'uereor ne neglegentius uiuam'*, 'to sum up, I will repeat what in the freshness of my grief I said to my friend Calvisius, "I fear I may live more carelessly for the future"', 1.12.12). In both 1.12 and 2.1, although biographical material dominates, it is the need to share grief with close friends which provides the impulse for composition; a letter itself implicitly contributes to the fight against the *neglegentia* which Pliny fears after his loss of two great mentors.[53]

Once the reader has met Voconius in these two letters, 2.13, the letter of recommendation to Priscus on Voconius' behalf, further defines the relationship (and Voconius' personal and intellectual qualities) in ways which will underpin the remainder of the cycle. The lifelong connection between the two men, begun in student days, has recently been crowned by Pliny's successful petition to the emperor for the *ius trium liberorum* for his friend. Pliny refers only rarely in the first nine books to his acts of patronage in intercession with the emperor, and so it seems appropriate that this cycle will end with a letter to Trajan (10.4) seeking Voconius' promotion to senatorial status, and confirming his supreme importance even among Pliny's closest friends: *inter quos sibi uel praecipuum locum uindicat Voconius Romanus, ab ineunte aetate condiscipulus et contubernalis*, 'among these, Voconius Romanus claims for himself, I would say, even the first place, my schoolfellow and companion from early life' (10.4.1).

Voconius' achievements in advocacy, combined with unusual epistolary skill, make him a man who seems to mirror Pliny, as 'another self':[54]

ad hoc ingenium excelsum subtile dulce facile eruditum in causis agendis; epistulas quidem scribit, ut Musas ipsas Latine loqui credas. (2.13.7)

Add to this an intelligence of a lofty character, subtle, agreeable, ready, accomplished in pleading causes. As for the letters he writes, you would imagine the Muses in person were talking Latin.

---

[53] That Calvisius is also the addressee of 3.1, on Spurinna, reinforces the pattern visible in the first three books of Pliny confiding in his closest friends on the subject both of special enemies and treasured mentors.

[54] For close study of 9.7, another letter linking Voconius' activities (in this case his building projects) with Pliny's own, see Chapter 7.

This intellectual friend is an ideal addressee for the remaining letters at the heart of the cycle, which include a request to mark up corrections to the *Panegyricus* (3.13.5),[55] the account of Priscus' bad behaviour at a poetic recitation (6.15), and a crucial letter on the *pro Attia Viriola* (6.33), in which Pliny ascribes to Voconius an expertise in his speeches which recalls Atticus' role as Cicero's 'Aristarchus':

in summa solent quidam ex contubernalibus nostris existimare hanc orationem (iterum dicam) ut inter meas ὑπὲρ Κτησιφῶντος esse: an uere, tu facillime iudicabis, qui tam memoriter tenes omnes, ut conferre cum hac dum hanc solam legis possis. (6.33.11) [56]

In short, some of our friends generally consider this speech as being the 'Pro Ctesiphonte' of my speeches; whether truly, you will most easily judge, who have them all so well in your memory as to be able to compare them with this, while reading this alone.

Voconius has primacy among these literary *contubernales*, as the final arbiter for the speech after their preliminary reviews. Moreover, perhaps in keeping with Voconius' unusual role as Pliny's Aristarchus, three letters to Voconius break Pliny's habit of reticence in naming his own works: 3.13 identifies the *Panegyricus*, 6.33 the *pro Attia Viriola*, and 9.28 the *pro Clario*.[57]

Voconius is further distinguished in the collection by Pliny's unusual and repeated emphasis on Voconius' epistolary output – a rare instance of the representation, even in *oratio obliqua*, of the correspondence of another writer in Pliny's collection. His letters have already been praised in 2.13, but in 9.28 they earn a whole letter in their own right:

post longum tempus epistulas tuas, sed tres pariter recepi, omnes elegantissimas amantissimas, et quales a te uenire praesertim desideratas oportebat ... adicias alias te litteras curiosius scriptas mississe; an acceperim quaeris. non accepi et accipere gestio. proinde prima quaque occasione mitte adpositis quidem usuris, quas ego (num parcius possum?) centesimas computabo. (9.28.1, 4–5)

After a long interval I have received your letters – three at the same time, however – all of them very choice and friendly compositions, and such as letters coming from

---

[55] Such reciprocal *Korrekturarbeit* is requested or offered in several letters throughout the collection, not all of them addressed to those who seem otherwise especially close confidants (for a summary list of letters on this topic, see Bütler (1970) 37 n. 33). We should notice that Pliny's comments on the work of others start later than his letters asking for help for his own work. On frank criticism of literary work as the mark of friendship which is most characteristic of this collection in particular, see Morello (2007); cf. Roller (1998) 293.

[56] This is close in tone to Cicero's letters about his own work to Atticus, including *Att.* 1.14, which we have already discussed in Chapter 3. For the importance of 6.33 within Book 6, see Chapter 2.

[57] On Pliny's reticence about his works, see Morello (2003) and cf. Chapter 1.

you should be, particularly when they are so greatly desired . . . You add that you sent me another letter more carefully composed, and you ask whether I have received it. I have not received it, and I long to do so. Accordingly, send me a copy at the very first opportunity, with something added to it by way of interest, which I shall compute (can I put it lower?) at twelve per cent.

Pliny conveys a bustling epistolary exchange; in a single letter he summarizes three from Voconius, all covering epistolary topics familiar from Pliny's own books: greetings to a third party, a recommendation, a complaint about the *uindemia*, a report on current literary work, compliments on the *pro Clario*, and a promise to join Pliny when called upon. Finally, Pliny's report of Voconius' letters tantalizes readers with the prospect of a more consciously literary one, which has not arrived.

Pliny's characterization of Voconius' missing epistolary tour de force (*curiosius scriptas*, 'more carefully composed') is reminiscent of Pliny's own collected letters (*curatius scriptae*, 'written with rather more than usual care', 1.1.1). In 8.8, indeed (also to Voconius), Pliny has already provided us with a template for literary correspondence between these two men; this letter sketches the attractions of the Clitumnus spring, and begins by declaring Pliny's certainty that if Voconius had already ever seen this beauty spot he would have narrated his visit to Pliny – presumably in *litterae curiosius scriptae*. Pliny got there first.

Pliny's expectation in 9.28 that the more 'artificial' kind of letter would be delivered normally should make us wary of dividing the correspondence of Pliny's circle into 'real' letters and the 'artificial/literary' ones which have become luxury items upon which interest might be charged for late delivery.[58] 8.8 is, it seems, the perfect embodiment of Pliny's commitment to the digressive, descriptive style which he draws from historiography; nevertheless, the three letters Pliny has received from Voconius are *elegantissimae*, so even these are not routine letters. Pliny's summary in 9.28 hardly reflects their elegance, and some of the topics seem comparatively banal, but by naming only bare topics, without illustrative quotation, Pliny enhances by contrast his own elegant turns in 9.28 and further highlights the role of form and style in letters.[59] It is, moreover, entirely appropriate that a letter about many subjects and several separate pieces of work (the three

---

[58] Guillemin (1929) 133–4.

[59] He showcases two metaphors: the financial metaphor at the end of the letter is a rather audacious demand for epistolary 'interest' payments (especially given that Pliny has just paid one letter in return for three), but we should see that Voconius in his turn has apparently described himself as a would-be runaway (slave) from his domestic responsibilities (though here it is Pliny who plans to put fetters on him – *pace* Sherwin-White (1966) 511: 'Pliny cannot be *threatening* Romanus with the grievous bonds of business, as in the metaphor of II.8.2–3').

letters from Voconius, the work about Pliny he is currently polishing, the literary letter which has not yet arrived) is positioned late in the collection and immediately before a short note about Pliny's dedication to variety in his studies (*ego uariis me studiorum generibus nulli satis confisus experior*, 'I try my hand at various kinds of literature, not being sufficiently confident about any of them', 9.29.1).

CORNUTUS TERTULLUS

We move on from these two friends, linked to Pliny by youthful companionship and intellectual affinities, to the case of an older senatorial associate. Cornutus Tertullus,[60] Pliny's colleague both at the *aerarium* and as consul (and later also his successor in Bithynia), receives only two letters in the collection, placed in reasonably close proximity (7.21 and 7.31), but one other letter, 5.14, is entirely devoted to him, and he appears also in 2.11, 2.12 (both to Maturus Arrianus on the Priscus case), 4.17 (on the case against Caecilius on behalf of Corellia) and 9.13 (on Pliny's handling of the *de Heluidii ultione*). Information about him is carefully measured out and progressively reinforced in these letters, and one can read a kind of narrative across even this rather disparate sequence, as Pliny establishes and reprises the themes of finance (an expertise they have in common) and collegiality (Cornutus is several times referred to as *collega*), and, above all, uses these few letters to his older colleague to bolster his own association with Corellius and Helvidius.

Cornutus first appears in his role as consul designate (Pliny's own status as such is not advertised) in the rather Sallustian senatorial debate on the actions to be taken against Marius Priscus (2.11), urging that Priscus himself be banished and all monies acquired by him confiscated and placed in the *aerarium*. In 2.11 and 2.12, he is portrayed as a man of probity with an interest in financial good practice, and one, moreover, who is appropriately well disposed towards Pliny and his fellow advocate in the case, Tacitus. As we shall see, it is part of the function of Cornutus in the 'plot' of the letters to yoke Pliny to those with whom he most wants to be associated. Here that target is – once again – Tacitus.[61] Cornutus' next appearance, however, finds him paired with Pliny as the particular friend of Corellius:

---

[60] Syme, *RP* 2.478 [= (1960) 362], Lefèvre (2009) 42–3.
[61] Pliny's efforts to put himself in Tacitus' circle by positioning friends and colleagues in close proximity to the items in the Tacitus cycle may be a response to the situation observed most recently by Johnson (2010) 72: 'however well connected Tacitus and Pliny may have been, they kept different company'. Cf. Syme (1958) 112-13.

quin etiam moriens filiae suae (ipsa solet praedicare): 'multos quidem amicos tibi ut longiore uita paraui, praecipuos tamen Secundum et Cornutum.' (4.17.9)

More than this, on his death-bed, he said to his daughter (she tells the story herself), 'I have prepared for you many friends, in virtue of my long life; but the chief of them are Secundus and Cornutus.'

That shared friendships are the foundation of their own relationship[62] is further attested by 5.14, a letter which takes Cornutus' appointment as *curator uiae Aemiliae* as the inspiration for an account of their relationship:

una diligimus, una dileximus omnes fere quos aetas nostra in utroque sexu aemulandos tulit; quae societas amicitiarum artissima nos familiaritate coniunxit. (5.14.4)

We love in unison, and have loved in unison, almost all those of either sex whom our epoch has produced as worthy of imitation; a partnership in friendships which has bound us together in the closest intimacy.

These friendships clearly include those with Corellius and his daughter but remain unspecific enough to suggest wider possibilities. Then there is the bond of shared public office (*uinculum necessitudinis publicae*, 5.14.5) – this is the first and only explicit acknowledgement of the parallelism of their careers, as Cornutus is introduced as the ideal colleague (*collega quasi uoto petitus*, 'my colleague, as though accorded to my prayers'). That was the period when Cornutus' value as *exemplar antiquitatis* was of most service to Pliny, as he says that he regarded him almost as *magister* and *parens*.[63] That quasi-hortatory role of Cornutus as *exemplum* is served also by the new appointment as *curator uiae Aemiliae*, which spurs Pliny back to his own duties as curator of the Tiber's banks.

It is only once these foundational elements are in place that the two letters actually addressed to Cornutus make proper sense. The letters keep good company in Book 7: the first falls between missives to Tacitus and to the illustrious Pompeius Falco, while the second is followed by letters to Calpurnius Fabatus and (again) Tacitus.[64] 7.21 purports to respond to Cornutus' urgings that Pliny nurse himself carefully through a serious bout of eye trouble, and perhaps seems out of place in the relationship at first glance, since it is not about public duties or about friendship with Corellius.

---

[62] McDermott (1971) 90.   [63] On Pliny's other exemplary elders, see Chapter 4.
[64] We should also note that Pliny's colleague in the Priscus case, on which Cornutus gave a favourable *sententia*, was – once again – Tacitus (2.11.2).

Pliny frames his letter as an act of obedience to a man he addresses specifically as *collega* (*pareo, collega carissime, et infirmitati oculorum ut iubes consulo*, 'I am all obedience, my dearest colleague, and am attending, as you bid me, to the weakness in my eyes,' 7.21.1). The invocation of Cornutus as *collega* consciously recalls the letter in Book 5 which introduced Cornutus to Pliny's wider readership and to posterity.[65] Pliny's pose of obedience[66] recalls his respect for Cornutus (as quasi *magister*), but as the relationship develops, Pliny implicitly draws Cornutus into the intimate space of the *cubiculum*, and introduces him to his 'sickbed' routine (a process similar to the one Pliny fosters in the development of a new relationship between Fabatus and Calestrius Tiro). Unusually, Pliny here shares aspects of his *studia* with Cornutus,[67] showing himself here following his uncle's example and taking full advantage of a journey in a litter to hear (since he cannot read) something important.

Letter 7.31, an introduction for Claudius Pollio, who is keen to make Cornutus' acquaintance, brings us back to the shared interest which dominates the cycle, namely finance. We know from 2.11 about Cornutus' interest in diverting Priscus' funds to the *aerarium* (and as colleagues at the *aerarium*, he and Pliny would have expertise in common). Here Pliny vouches for Pollio's probity in financial matters, and his talent for accounting, having observed him during his military service, when Pliny himself was in charge of financial investigations, and watched his later career in the field of finance. Once again, however, Corellius is the kingpin mutual friend; in this case he selected Pollio and drew him out of retirement specifically to assist him on land commission – Pollio, then, is 'one of us'.

Although but a final brief reference to Cornutus, 9.13.16 caps the earlier information about their shared association with Corellius and moves attention to a different shared association, this time with the family of Helvidius Priscus. In this letter about Pliny's *de Heluidi ultione*, as we pointed out in Chapter 1, one can see Pliny distancing himself from reliance on Corellius, fearing the old man's cautious conservatism. Cornutus here is seen acting on behalf of Helvidius' daughter, for whom he had been assigned as tutor;

---

[65] For *caritas* for Cornutus as his consular colleague, see *Pan.* 90.3–93; 91.6. For the suggestion that Pliny's use of *carissime* here implies quasi-imperial condescension on Pliny's part (on the model of Trajan's frequent use of the term in addressing Pliny himself), see McDermott (1971) 90–1, who takes issue with Sherwin-White's view that this rare vocative marks this as a 'genuine letter' and an indication of real tenderness in Pliny's view of this man.

[66] We should notice how often Pliny adopts the pose of obedience – starting with the innovative dedicatory letter to Septicius (on the innovation, see Janson (1964) 119).

[67] As Sherwin-White (1966) 443 points out, there are otherwise few traces of intellectual interests shared between them.

he appears only briefly, but the echo of his less formal relationship with Corellius' daughter suggests that the reader should be ready to link the two sets of shared associations and to pick up on Pliny's narrative of professional friendship in which his colleague in public life is also his colleague in controversial private loyalties.[68]

SEPTICIUS CLARUS AND PLINY'S EGALITARIANISM

We move on to Septicius Clarus, whose prominence as dedicatee (and first addressee) of the whole collection has attracted comment. The senatorial Clarus was at this stage still a relatively shadowy figure, whose major career success, as far as we can tell, came under Hadrian, after Pliny's death.[69] Hoffer reads the choice of this dedicatee as an implicit declaration that Pliny needs no patron and feels no obligation to 'dedicate upwards'; Clarus (the 'representative addressee') is 'merely an empty place-holder, who could be replaced by any other friend'.[70] For Gowers, however, the choice of Clarus was an advertisement for Pliny's shrewdness as well as for his modest pretensions: confident of Clarus' future success, Pliny dedicates his work to him as an investment for the future.[71]

In the wider context of the collection, the mixed social and career status of his correspondents is an important aspect of Pliny's portrait of his friendships. As Syme puts it, 'he has not been at pains to solicit illustrious names'; in the first two books of the collection, only Tacitus is certainly consular, and in those books we meet a remarkable number of the men Syme famously calls 'Pliny's less successful friends' – local dignitaries and associates from the north, such as Caninius Rufus, Romatius Firmus and Plinius Paternus, or from the provinces, such as the Saguntine Voconius Romanus.[72]

The duty to treat all one's friends alike is also a striking motif in the letters to Clarus and others. As part of his depiction of healthy relationships within a social circle, Pliny reshapes into kindlier epistolary form a conventional satiric topic of invidious distinctions between important and unimportant friends. The motif of Pliny's frugal dinners, for example, introduced in 1.15, is developed and explained to Avitus in 2.6, a letter which sets out Pliny's

---

[68] On 9.13, see Carlon (2009) 58–64.

[69] On the status of Pliny's addressees in general, see Chapter 2.

[70] Hoffer (1999) 22. We should note, however, Hoffer's view of 'the entire corpus' as a 'flattering tribute to the emperor and the existing power structure'.

[71] Gowers (1993) 272. One wonders why Tacitus, his most frequent addressee, might not have been a more obvious choice of dedicatee if Pliny wished to invest in the long-term survival of his work.

[72] Syme, *RP* 2.489 [= (1960) 374].

egalitarian agenda and offers a negative *exemplum* of invidious behaviour (*quid debeas fugere*, 'an example of what you should shun', 2.6.7). Here Pliny has dined with a man who thought himself an elegant society host but betrayed vulgarity by serving different grades of food and wine, according to the status of his three groups of guests (inner circle, *minores amici*, and freedmen).[73] Pliny – safely protected from any suspicion of unworthy motives by his position in the top class of guests – objects specifically to the grading and classification of friends (*nam gradatim amicos habet*, 'for he puts his friends into categories', 2.6.2) and reports his own rule that all should eat alike at his house; potentially ruinous expense is neatly avoided if the host simply drinks the same wine he serves to his humblest guests.

The lesson is not only one of frugality and modesty, but of making the right sorts of distinctions in life. Pliny's dinner host, however, has made distinctions between friends, but seated the opposed vices of *luxuria* and meanness side by side at the same table:

quorsus haec? ne tibi, optimae indolis iuueni, quorundam in mensa luxuria specie frugalitatis imponat . . . igitur memento nihil magis esse uitandum quam istam lux-uriae et sordium nouam societatem; quae cum sint turpissima discreta ac separata, turpius iunguntur. (2.6.6–7)

To what end all this? In order that the show which some people make at their tables may not impose on you, my young friend, with your excellent disposition, under the guise of economy . . . Remember, then, that there is nothing more to be avoided than this strange association of extravagance and meanness – vices which are loathsome enough when separate and asunder, and still more loathsome when they are combined.

This is the only explicit reference to *luxuria* in the letters, and Pliny's treat-ment of it is carefully nuanced.[74] It is not *luxuria* that is the problem here (nor the awareness of social differences), but the ostentatious distinctions made between those to whom *luxuria* is offered and those who are visibly excluded from it. In a refocusing of a hackneyed topic to serve the agenda of this ever-friendly author of letters, *luxuria* is shown to be inimical to amicable hospitality.

Three letters of Book 9 return to the theme of egalitarian behaviour, and inquire into the nature of real generosity. 9.5, to Calestrius Tiro, discusses the friendly treatment to be meted out to all classes of provincials when in

---

[73] For a satiric version of this kind of behaviour in a host, see Juvenal *Sat.* 5.

[74] On Pliny as 'curiously silent' on the subject of *luxuria* by comparison with most other writers of his era (including – especially – his uncle), see Leach (2003) 149; cf. Chapter 7 on the careful handling of *luxuria* in Pliny's villas.

service abroad while insisting gently upon the preservation of appropriate distinctions, 'for if these are confounded, disordered and intermingled, nothing can be more unequal than this very equality' (*nihil est ipsa aequalitate inaequalius*, 9.5.3). In 9.9, Colonus has expressed sorrow at the death of Pompeius Quintianus, and Pliny approves that he retains his affection for a dead friend instead of turning his attention only upon the living or, as some do, only on the living *and successful* ('for they forget the unfortunate, no less than if they were dead', 9.9.1). The *exemplum* in this perfectly integrated letter is the late Quintianus himself:

et hercule is fuit Quintianus, quem diligi deceat ipsius exemplo. felices amabat, miseros tuebatur, desiderabat amissos. (9.9.2)

And, by Hercules, Quintianus was a man who ought to be cherished on the strength of his own example. He loved the successful, defended the wretched, mourned for the lost.

The successful and the wretched are still kept in separate conceptual categories but Pliny insists that they should be *treated* alike. Finally, in 9.30, Pliny draws a lesson about true generosity from the behaviour of another mutual friend, Nonius. One should never, he says, be generous only to those who can reciprocate – such a practice is really just a form of hunting:

uolo enim eum, qui sit uere liberalis, tribuere patriae propinquis, affinibus amicis, sed amicis dico pauperibus, non ut isti qui iis potissimum donant, qui donare maxime possunt. hos ego uiscatis hamatisque muneribus non sua promere puto sed aliena corripere. sunt ingenio simili qui quod huic donant auferunt illi, *famamque liberalitatis auaritia petunt.* (9.30.2–3)

For I will have it that the truly generous man gives to his country, his relations, his connections, his friends; I speak of his *poor* friends, not like those who choose as the objects of their donations such as can best make a return. I consider these people with their presents – all smeared with bird-lime, and furnished with a hood – to be not so much bringing forth out of their own as clutching at other people's property. Those are of a like character, who take from one what they give to another, seeking through avarice a reputation for generosity.

Like 2.6, with which we started this part of our discussion, 9.30 offers a paradox: a reputation for liberality may in fact be unjustly won by avaricious practices (*famamque liberalitatis auaritia petunt*, 'they seek through avarice a reputation for generosity', 9.30.3). In Pliny's better world, true generosity to others begins with personal frugality:

primum est autem suo esse contentum, deinde, quos praecipue scias indigere, sustentantem fouentemque orbe quodam socialitatis ambire. (9.30.3)[75]

Now the principal thing is to be content with one's own; after that, to support, to cherish, and, as it were, to encompass in a circle of fellowship those whom one knows to be particularly in need.

Egalitarian behaviour is important for Pliny; the famous letters about his kindness to his slaves are just a little further along the same spectrum.[76]

If one reads 1.1 in this context, the choice of Clarus seems inspired. There are remarkably few letters to this (relatively) modest addressee (only four in the whole collection, two of which are to be found in the first book).[77] That in itself, as we have seen in the case of even the closest of associates, such as Calestrius Tiro (also the recipient of only four letters), is not out of line with the pattern of the collection. All the letters, however, centre upon some aspect of social and literary friendship: 1.15 chastises Clarus for choosing a vulgarly expensive dinner party over simple fun at Pliny's house, 7.28 is Pliny's answer to an anonymous complaint that he overpraises his friends, and 8.1 expresses concern over the illness of a favourite reader, Encolpius. In 2.9, Pliny's expression of anxiety about the political ambitions of Clarus' nephew, Clarus is marked not as an illustrious citizen (despite his eloquent name) but as a man of endearing personal qualities: *habet auunculum C. Septicium, quo nihil uerius nihil simplicius, nihil candidius nihil fidelius noui*, 'he has for his maternal uncle C. Septicius, than whom I have never known a sincerer, more straightforward, more guileless, more reliable man', (2.9.4). These letters encompass, then, the private friendship between two men who ought to share simple meals and bookish chat, the wide circle of unnamed friends, and the writer's affection even for his social inferior – a good sample, in other words, of Pliny's friendly interactions.[78]

Moreover, letters do not communicate with the powerful and the celebrated alone; although Cicero's *familiares* include the prominent figures of his day, Atticus, the single dominant addressee in the surviving letter corpora, is a wealthy *eques* and the names of several other Ciceronian correspondents do not necessarily raise the heart rate. It seems likely, indeed, that some, at least, of Cicero's addressees would have been almost as

---

[75] See also Bütler (1970) 127–8.   [76] For Pliny and slavery, see Appendix 3.

[77] 1.1, 1.15, 7.28, 8.1.

[78] Pliny does not tell us about (but might have expected his contemporary audience to know) Septicius' Transpadane origin, which made him an ideal first addressee for a collection full of Transpadane addressees.

unfamiliar to Pliny's readers as Pliny's are to us.[79] Moreover, what little we know about the collection of letters which Cicero planned in his lifetime suggests that the impulse to publish came not from his most powerful friends, but from Atticus and Cicero's freedman, Tiro (*Att.* 16.5, *Fam.* 16.17), so that Pliny's ascription of encouragement to publish to a still relatively modest friend sits well within the tradition. Seneca, too, will not have lacked a pool of powerful addressees, even at the precarious stage of his life when the *Epistulae Morales* were probably composed, and yet he chose Lucilius. A collection of letters *in prose*, then, would not necessarily have been expected to be 'dedicated upwards'.

TACITUS

Finally, however, we turn to Pliny's epistolary engagement with one of the collection's greatest figures, Tacitus,[80] only to find important contrasts between the Tacitus cycle and almost all the other 'friendship' cycles we have considered. Although Tacitus is famously Pliny's most frequent addressee in the first nine books, for example, Pliny nowhere uses any of the vocabulary of special intimacy in relation to him: he is not *contubernalis* or even *amicus*.[81] At least one passing reference to him, at 4.15.1, seems almost ostentatiously understated (see below, n. 93). Letters which mention him in the third person dwell upon his position as consul or his grand reputation as an orator and budding historian, but not upon any emotional attachment between the two men.[82]

Some readers would like to trace developments in this relationship as the books unfold. Sherwin-White, for example, discerns greater formality in the six letters addressed to Tacitus in Books 1–6 than in the five letters of 7–9, which he sees as a semi-separate 'interconnected series', and traces the source of 'the literary friendship which emerges suddenly in 7.20' at 6.16 and 6.20 (Pliny's accounts of the eruption of Vesuvius written at Tacitus' request).[83] This is in many respects a natural reading of the Tacitus cycle, but it does not fully represent the complexity of Pliny's engagement with

---

[79] Nevertheless, for three-quarters of Cicero's correspondents in the *ad Familiares* as senatorial in status, and for the evident interest of the collection's editor in the social identity and prominence of the correspondents, see White (2010) 60–1.

[80] For bibliography on Tacitus and Pliny, see Appendix 3.

[81] As Sherwin-White (1966) 100 points out, 'Tacitus is never *noster.*'

[82] 2.1, 2.11, 9.23. 4.15 comes close to linking Pliny into a nexus of Tacitus' friends, since it recommends a young man, Asinius Rufus, who is close to both Tacitus and Pliny.

[83] Sherwin-White (1966) 100.

his most famous addressee, which starts, indeed, with greater informality than Sherwin-White suggests.

The opening letter in the sequence, 1.6, suggests a stronger personal relationship between the two men than we will find in any subsequent letter. It begins, after all, with laughter at Pliny's own expense (*ridebis, et licet rideas*, 'laugh you will, and laugh you may'); epistolary laughter – in Cicero's collection, at least – is a natural marker of emotional engagement and understanding between correspondents, and Pliny is certainly playing upon such cues here.[84] Tacitus' mockery is ostensibly based, moreover, on personal knowledge of Pliny's character – or at least of the aspects of it which Pliny chooses to showcase in his 'Paradebriefen': *ego, ille quem nosti* ('I, the man you know'), Pliny says, as he boasts of uncharacteristic success in the boar hunt.[85] '*Ipse?*' ('Yourself?') says Tacitus, and Pliny's 'answer' acknowledges that his incredulity is well founded: *inertia* and *quies* are indeed the salient characteristics of Pliny's temperament, he admits, and boar hunting is rather physical and energetic for such a man – indeed he is a rather sedentary sort of hunter (*sedebam*, 1.6.1), sitting by the nets thinking and making notes, and one who finds Minerva (i.e. literary work) as well as Diana in the mountains.[86]

This letter, short though it is, is rich and complex in its agenda, and it is all the more important to understand its place in the collection and in the Tacitus cycle itself because it finds its pair in another letter about hunting (this time announcing a dearth of boar) in Book 9:

cupio praeceptis tuis parere; sed aprorum tanta penuria est, ut Mineruae et Dianae, quas ais pariter colendas, conuenire non possit. itaque Mineruae tantum seruien-dum est... itaque poemata quiescunt, quae tu inter nemora et lucos commodis-sime perfici putas. oratiunculam unam alteram retractaui; quamquam id genus operis inamabile inamoenum, magisque laboribus ruris quam uoluptatibus simile. uale. (9.10)

I am desirous of obeying your precepts, yet such is the scarcity of wild boar that Minerva and Diana (who, according to you, should be worshipped in company) cannot be brought together. So Minerva alone must be served... Hence my poetry – which *you* think can be most suitably turned out among groves and words – is dormant. I have retouched one or two of my small orations. Yet this

---

[84] For Cicero's liking for friendly humour in letters, see *Fam.*2.4.1. For nuanced discussion of Cicero's epistolary humour, see Griffin (1995); Hutchinson (1998) 172–99; Hall (2009) 49–52, 164–5.

[85] On *ille quem nosti* generally (and as an echo of Catull. 22.1), see Marchesi (2008) 118 n. 30.

[86] Pliny often defines himself in contrast to whichever 'foil' he is dealing with: in comparison with his vigorous uncle he is *desidiosissimus* (3.5.19), and Tacitus here knows him as a man of *inertia*, but the frivolous Martial shows him hard at work in the service of *tetrica Minerua* (3.21.5).

kind of work is ungrateful and displeasing, and resembles rather the labours than the pleasures of the country.

This apparently repetitive selection of letters at beginning and (near) end of the cycle is unusual in the collection, and has drawn comment, as readers have tried to explain (or explain away) the similarities between the two letters. Sherwin-White notes, for example, that the hunt is less successful than in 1.6, that Pliny produces literary work while travelling, rather than during the hunt, and that the Diana–Minerva motif is here ascribed to Tacitus rather than to Pliny (and that 'the two notes are not closely linked even on this ground'). Nevertheless, the first and the penultimate letters in the Tacitus series, for all their differences in emphasis, are clearly non-identical twins. By Book 9 Pliny can play upon the unexpectedness of 'prosaic' work during a country retreat, having already established (as we have seen in Chapter 3) his commitment to poetic work while on the road. Moreover, Pliny's emphasis on productiveness in Book 1 is now balanced by a more doleful anxiety that he cannot produce the work he would wish to; this reworking of the theme of writing and productivity is entirely in keeping with the wider shift in emphasis between Book 1 (the book, as we have already said, of literary renaissance under Trajan) and Book 9 (which is coloured already in 9.2 by an apparent sense of inadequacy and productive failure).

Friendship is not entirely the point of these letters, although they assume familiarity between the two men. That the same advice has been given by Tacitus to Pliny in 9.10 as was delivered by Pliny to Tacitus in 1.6 reflects one of the two dominant motifs of the entire cycle: their parity in careers, status and *studia*. The foundations of this theme are laid in Book 2. The book contains no letters addressed to Tacitus, but he appears as Pliny's colleague in the prosecution of Marius Priscus (2.11.2), and as the consular eulogist for Verginius Rufus (2.1.6) – in the latter case matched by Pliny not at the event itself but in the letter which becomes the written (and longer-lasting) equivalent of the spoken eulogy. In 6.9, however, this motif comes to the fore, in a rather prickly reply to Tacitus' request that Pliny support Julius Naso's candidature. Pliny insists here on complete parity between himself and Tacitus in relation to this candidature: not only might he have written the same exhortation to Tacitus had he been the one absent from Rome, but he claims joint status in any future appeals on their young protégé's behalf: *tu tamen censeo alios roges; ego precum tuarum minister adiutor particeps ero*, 'however, I vote that you canvass other people; *I* will act as agent, assistant, and partner in your applications' (6.9.2). His expectation that either one of them could act as primary or secondary supporter of this young man mirrors, in the political sphere, the implication of 1.6. and 9.10 that either one of them could offer the same epistolary advice about literary work in the countryside.

Pliny needed, in fact, no encouragement to support Naso, and is already working hard on Naso's behalf. That Tacitus has got it wrong is immediately clear to the linear reader who has arrived at 6.9 after having encountered, at 6.6, a long letter to Minicius Fundanus in support of this very candidate:

suscepi candidatum, et suscepisse me notum est; ego ambio, ego periclitor; in summa, si datur Nasoni quod petit, illius honor, si negatur, mea repulsa est. (6.6.9)

I have taken in hand a candidate, and it is known that I have taken him in hand. The canvass is mine, the danger is mine. In short, if Naso gets what he asks, his will be the honour; if he fails, the defeat will be mine.

Pliny insists that his involvement in Naso's candidature is public knowledge; that this is pointed becomes clearer in 6.9, where it again seems everyone *except Tacitus* knows that Naso is one of Pliny's special protégés.[87]

Letter 7.20 takes the theme of parity back into the literary sphere, as Pliny returns a draft of Tacitus' work with his comments, remarking on the pleasure to be found in their exchange of work, once again emphasizing that they take turns in doing the same tasks for each other (*nunc a te librum meum cum adnotationibus tuis exspecto. O iucundas, o pulchras uices!*, 'And now, I am expecting from you *my* book with *your* notes. What a delightful and charming interchange!' 7.20.2). Once again, the motif of public knowledge is important ('it will be universally related [*usquequaque narrabitur*] in what concord . . . we lived', 7.20.2). The letter then offers a remarkably competitive (if respectful) history of the development of Pliny's own fame and career:

equidem adulescentulus, cum iam tu fama gloriaque floreres, te sequi, tibi 'longo sed proximus interuallo' et esse et haberi concupiscebam . . . quo magis gaudeo, quod si quis de studiis sermo, una nominamur, quod de te loquentibus statim occurro. (7.20.4–5)

For my part, when I was a very young man, while you were already flourishing in renown and glory, I yearned to follow after you, both to be accounted and to be

---

[87] See further below on issues of knowledge in this relationship. One should note also the cumulative message of other letters in the immediate vicinity of 6.9, including 6.8 (on behalf of Atilius Crescens), 6.10 (on the disgraceful neglect of Verginius' memory), 6.11 (on Pliny's delight in Fuscus and Ummidius) and 6.12 (on his willingness to act on behalf of a friend of Fabatus, which contrasts strongly with the tetchiness of 6.9: *tu uero non debes suspensa manu commendare mihi quos tuendos putas*, 'you, assuredly, ought not to hold your hand in recommending to me those persons whom you think worthy of support', 6.12.1)

'second to you, though great the space between' . . . I the more rejoice then that, whenever the conversation turns on intellectual pursuits, we are named together, that to people speaking about you my name at once presents itself.[88]

As Pliny gradually comes to equal Tacitus in reputation, he highlights the foundation of mutual encouragement which supports both men's achievements in *studia* (*alterum alterius studia fouisse*, 'each to have furthered the studies of the other', 7.20.3).[89]

The final letter to mention Tacitus, 9.23, develops the theme of parity of reputation between the two men still further.[90] This is Pliny's famous account of a recent conversation with Tacitus:

frequenter agenti mihi euenit, ut centumuiri cum diu se intra iudicum auctoritatem grauitatemque tenuissent, omnes repente quasi uicti coactique consurgerent laudarentque; frequenter e senatu famam qualem maxime optaueram rettuli: numquam tamen maiorem cepi uoluptatem, quam nuper ex sermone Corneli Taciti. narrabat sedisse secum circensibus proximis equitem Romanum. hunc post uarios eruditosque sermones requisisse: 'Italicus es an prouincialis?' se respondisse: 'nosti me, et quidem ex studiis.' ad hoc illum: 'Tacitus es an Plinius?' exprimere non possum, quam sit iucundum mihi quod nomina nostra quasi litterarum propria, non hominum, litteris redduntur, quod uterque nostrum his etiam ex studiis notus, quibus aliter ignotus est. (9.23.1–3)

Often it has happened to me, when pleading, that the Centumviri, after keeping for a long while to their judicial dignity and gravity, have suddenly – as though vanquished and compelled to the act – risen from their seats in a body and applauded me. Often have I obtained from the Senate the highest glory I had aspired to. Yet never have I received greater pleasure than lately from what was told me by Cornelius Tacitus. He related how a Roman knight was sitting by him at the last Circensian games. After a conversation of a varied and learned character, the gentleman asked him, 'Are you from Italy or the provinces? ' He replied, 'You know me, and from your reading too.' Upon which the other inquired, 'Are you Tacitus or Pliny?' I cannot express how delightful it is that our names, as though belonging to literature, and not to human beings, are thus connected with literature; that each of us is known by means of his pursuits, even to those to whom he is otherwise unknown.

---

[88] Pliny habitually calibrates his own public position within the 'right' circle of people by reference to that of Tacitus. In 4.15, for example, he numbers himself and Tacitus together among the good men revered by Asinius Rufus, and links all three of them by similarities of character (*cum sit ad conectendas amicitias uel tenacissimum uinculum morum similitudo*, 'since, for the cementing of friendships, the strongest of all ties is to be found in a resemblance of characters', 4.15.2).

[89] For a new reading of the relationship between the works of Tacitus and Pliny, arguing that Tacitus can be shown in several instances to be the imitator of Pliny, see Woodman (2009) 32–5. For a nuanced reading of Pliny's competitive engagement with Tacitus, see Whitton (2012).

[90] However, on the identification of the unnamed historian of 9.27 with Tacitus, see most recently Whitton (2012) 363–4.

Here, at last, Tacitus himself vouches for Pliny's reputation, not in a letter, but in a conversation which Pliny records for posterity in this final book (which focuses especially, as we have remarked elsewhere, upon letters which confirm Pliny's literary success and wide, enthusiastic readership). Competitive elements abound in this letter, which is also reminiscent of earlier letters in the cycle. Tacitus' *nosti me*, for example, spoken to the unnamed stranger at the circus, echoes Pliny's address to Tacitus in 1.6: *ego, ille quem nosti*, 'I, the Pliny whom you know', and this final letter in the cycle meditates upon themes of knowledge and reputation.[91] In 1.6 Tacitus 'knew' Pliny as a man lacking in physical energy but was about to be given to understand Pliny's dogged commitment to literary work. By 9.23, Tacitus' confident/hopeful riddle *nosti me, et quidem ex studiis*, 'you know me, and from your reading too', gets a disturbingly ambivalent reply: you could be Tacitus, but maybe you are Pliny. Even strangers in a crowd know Pliny perhaps as well as they know Tacitus, it seems. The personal acquaintance inherent in *ego, ille quem nosti* is consciously and explicitly downgraded, as Pliny celebrates the readjustment of knowledge in which names belong only to literature and not to the men themselves.

If we were in any doubt about who might ultimately come out on top after this iconic moment of uncertainty (*Tacitus es an Plinius?* 'Are you Tacitus or Pliny?'), the second anecdote of 9.23 gives us the answer. Here Pliny reports another similar encounter of his own with a stranger, this time at a dinner party – but this time Pliny is identified without hesitation, and he has risen in his own mind to the heights of fame reached not by Tacitus but by Demosthenes:

recumbebat mecum uir egregius, Fadius Rufinus, super eum municeps ipsius, qui illo die primum uenerat in urbem; cui Rufinus demonstrans me: 'uides hunc?' multa deinde de studiis nostris; et ille 'Plinius est' inquit. uerum fatebor, capio magnum laboris mei fructum. an si Demosthenes iure laetatus est, quod illum anus Attica ita noscitauit: οὗτός ἐστι Δημοσθένης, ego celebritate nominis mei gaudere non debeo? (9.23.4–5)

That distinguished man Fabius Rufinus was my neighbour at table, and above him was one of his townsmen, who had come to Rome that day for the first time. Rufinus, pointing me out to him, said, 'Do you see this gentleman?' and proceeded to talk at length of my literary pursuits. Said the other, 'It must be Pliny.' To acknowledge the truth, I enjoy a great reward from my labours. Why, if Demosthenes was rightly delighted because an old woman of Athens recognized him in these terms, 'This is Demosthenes!' ought not *I* to rejoice in the celebrity of my name?

---

[91] Cf. Hor. *Sat.* 1.9.7.

It is hard not to read this letter as another example of what Hoffer calls Pliny's bad faith.[92] Although Pliny has insisted upon the equality of the relationship, this letter puts him ahead of Tacitus in the recognition stakes. Pliny is correctly identified to his face; Tacitus met with a degree of uncertainty and a further riddle.[93]

It may also be significant that this letter about Tacitus chatting to a neighbour in the circus comes in the same book as Pliny's only letter about the *Circenses*, in which he describes them as *otiosissimae occupationes*, 'the idlest of occupations', and assures his friend Calvisius that he would rather spend the time writing than watching entertainments of that kind (*omne hoc tempus inter pugillares ac libellos iucundissima quiete transmisi*, 'I have been passing all this time between my writing-tablets and my books in the most delicious calm,' 9.6.1). Tacitus seems to like such entertainments, but by 9.23 we already know that Pliny puts his time to better use in literary *labor*.[94] Indeed, he manages to create in the midst of the urban festival period an environment and a life which is reminiscent not only of the Laurentine villa (*Laurentinum meum, hoc est libellos et pugillares, studiosumque otium repetam*, 'I shall return to my house at Laurentum, in other words, to my books and my writing-tablets and my studious retirement,' 1.22.11) but also of the peaceful hunting scene of 1.6 in which Pliny recommends to Tacitus that he carry *pugillares* with him on a hunt, in addition to *panarium et lagunculam*.[95]

Pliny's collection depicts a courteous world, in which Pliny accords even-handed treatment to a wide variety of his peers. Conversely, the courtesy and mutual admiration of some of these associations co-exist with just a little more tetchy self-positioning than has sometimes been acknowledged, as Pliny seeks to establish his own status as equal to that of a famous

---

[92] Hoffer (1999) 227.

[93] This passage may help to explain the odd *scis quem uirum* ('you know what *he* is') of Pliny's reference to Tacitus in 4.15 – whom you know and whom you recognize are important issues in the Tacitus sequence.

[94] The placement of 4.16 and 4.13 in close proximity in their book may betray a similarly competitive agenda. In 4.13.10 Pliny depicts Tacitus surrounded by a *copia studiosorum* ('a great number of learned persons') from whom Tacitus could select a suitable teacher for the youth of Pliny's home town; in 4.16 we see Pliny approaching the Centumviral court surrounded by such extraordinary crowds, all paying their respects to *studia*, that an aristocratic young man could get his tunic torn in the crush (and yet remain, kept decent only by his toga(!), to hear Pliny out). See also Whitton (2012) 356, 357 on the placement of 9.14 (to Tacitus) immediately after the account of Pliny's greatest senatorial triumph in 9.13, and on other similar juxtapositions in Pliny's collection.

[95] Cf. 9.36.6: *uenor aliquando, sed non sine pugillaribus, ut quamuis nihil ceperam non nihil referam*, 'occasionally I hunt, but not without my note-books, so that, if I fail in *taking* something, I may at any rate have something to *bring home*'.

contemporary; it is the reader *of the cycle* who is well placed to see this phenomenon unencumbered by the distractions of nearby letters within the books addressed to other associates and discussing different topics. Nevertheless, Pliny achieves subtle effects by placing close friends and colleagues near Tacitus in the collection, implicitly creating a shared circle of associates. Further, by allowing the reader to contrast (for example) the modest anxiety he expresses in 6.6.2 ('I am exercised by hope as well as troubled by fear, no longer feeling like one who has served the office of consul') when recommending Iulius Naso to Fundanus, and the fulsomeness of his praise of his protégé, with the crisp brevity of his response to Tacitus' efforts on the same candidate's behalf, he rewards the reader who takes the trouble to set the letters to this most stellar of addressees in the wider context of their books and the collection as a whole.

CHAPTER 6

Otium
How to manage leisure

In this chapter we look at another facet of Pliny's obsession with time management: his marked interest in the proper use of *otium* ('leisure').[1] Where military or gubernatorial service might often in Cicero's collections have necessitated an exchange of letters, in Pliny it is frequently the retreat into *secessus* which prompts correspondence; indeed, somewhere between 20 and 38 per cent of the letters in most of the first nine books discuss the fruits and pursuits of *otium*, a far greater percentage than we find anywhere in Cicero. Pliny's hope for well-deserved *otium* in later life is mirrored by the theme's increased prominence in later books, a marriage of structure and ideas which furnishes one of the collection's most significant implied narrative drives (later thrown into reverse, of course, in the busy professional Book 10).[2] Nevertheless, although Book 9, home of the two great letters about Pliny's daily routines in the *otium*-rich environments of his villas, seems to make the strongest statement of the theme,[3] *otium* dominates the collection before then. Indeed, in a now familiar pattern, the letters of Book 9, in which Pliny replies to his protégé Fuscus Salinator's request for specific details of Pliny's own routine, seem merely to satisfy a need generated by the prominence of the *otium* theme throughout the earlier books. It is as if Pliny acknowledges, at last, the obvious requirement, just as he only openly acknowledges the importance of Cicero as *epistolographical* model at the opening of the final book.[4]

Book 7, in particular, stands out for its rich vein of letters (almost 70 per cent of the book) about the use, misuse or unavailability of *otium*, including 7.2 on Pliny's reluctance to send his work to a busy Iustus, 7.3 on Bruttius Praesens' continuing absence from Rome, 7.4 on Pliny's poetry, 7.9

---

[1] For bibliography on the subject, see Appendix 3.
[2] See Chapters 1 and 8 on the loose sense of chronological development which is built into the collection. For the change of pace in Book 10, and the degree to which Pliny 'effaces his leisure' in Book 10 and 'presents his gubernatorial self as a workaholic', see Woolf (2006a) 105.
[3] See Leach (2003) 162. On 9.36 and 9.40, see Chapter 4.   [4] See Chapter 3.

on Fuscus Salinator's study programme, 7.13 on Ferox's effortlessly elegant letters and 7.24 on Ummidia Quadratilla's frivolity.[5] This startling preponderance makes Book 7 the complement (in a typically Plinian oscillation of tone and subject matter) to Book 6, in which, as we argued in Chapter 2, *negotium* dominates, with *otium* relegated to a handful of letters.[6]

In this chapter, we take a mixed approach to reading the letters, starting from close reading of single letters, and moving on to a more thematic survey. We set the scene with 1.9 and 1.10, where Pliny first adumbrates his time-management problems, before returning to sequential reading of the opening letters of Book 1, this time highlighting Pliny's self-confessed propensity for idleness.[7] We argue that Pliny's letters on *otium* need to be seen in the context of Seneca's ideas on the subject, and that Pliny is defining himself rather carefully in relation to this epistolographical predecessor. We move on to the images and metaphors which Pliny draws from his leisure activities (especially hunting, dining and farming) to illuminate his self- and time-management. Finally, in keeping with our belief that even thematic study of the collection is enriched if we allow the design of Pliny's collection to guide the reader's interpretative experience, we devote the final part of this chapter to a sequential reading of the *otium* motif in the first part of Book 7 (as a representative sample), before closing with another study of a single letter, 7.24, which stands out for its unusual focus on women's *otium*.

MONITORING *OTIUM* AND ROUTINE: THE SENECAN TRADITION

The broad spectrum of Pliny's leisure activities encompasses hunting, dinners, conversations, tourism and even work on the grape harvest. However, our fiscally expert author scrupulously follows Cato's dictum that one should be able to return profit sheets and 'accounts' for *otium* and *negotium* alike;[8] indeed, he devotes considerable attention to time and motion studies, worrying about the degree to which his own *otium* is productive rather than merely idle, and urging his friends, too, to put leisure time to best use. The prime leisure pursuit, however, is always study and literary work,[9] and

---

[5] For a stimulating reading of Book 7, see Fitzgerald (2007a).

[6] The prominence of silence as a theme in Book 7 (Fitzgerald (2007a) 203) likewise contrasts with Book 6, in which successful communication and public speech dominate.

[7] For a more fully 'autobiographical' reading of Book 1, including 1.9 and 1.10, see Chapter 1.

[8] Cic. *Planc.* 66.

[9] Reading, too, Pliny suggests, belongs in *otium* (*quasi per otium lego*, 'read it as though quite at my ease', 6.20.5); this might prompt us to include in the broad category of '*otium* letters' his epistolary responses to his friends' literary work.

in this respect Pliny subscribes to an elite tradition which includes Cicero's famous *otium litteratum* and Seneca's declaration that '*otium* without literary work is a death'.[10] Nevertheless, in many respects, Pliny's engagement with previous work on *otium*, particularly that of Seneca, is complex and subtle.

The proper use of *otium* is a common motif in Seneca, not only in the letters, but also in the dialogues (particularly, of course, the *de Otio*, but also the *de Breuitate Vitae*), and his strictures on pointless *otium* and misguided *otiosi* are often trenchantly expressed in detailed catalogues of useless pursuits. In *Breu.*12, for example, Seneca castigates as *desidiosa occupatio* ('lazy activity') or *iners negotium* ('sluggish business') time wasted on hairstyling, worthless musical accomplishments, gourmandising, sunbathing, travelling in litters or useless literary work. He reserves his harshest criticisms, however, for those who insist upon strict routine even in trivial activities and who create a fuss, for example, if they are late for their daily drives. Above all, he attacks those who rely on others to help maintain a daily routine, needing someone else to tell them when to eat, when to bathe, when to take a swim and so on (*Breu.* 12.6); naturally, philosophy is the foundation of well-managed *otium*.[11]

Pliny ignores many of these 'useless' activities (musical accomplishments and hairstyling, in particular), but his treatment of, for example, sunbathing, dining and travelling in litters is consistently more positive than Seneca's.[12] However, he shows a comparable disapproval of excessively fixed routines, and the flexibility and moderation of the 'approved' daily routines described in 3.1, 9.36 or 9.40 reflect a reluctance to prescribe too rigidly.[13] Pliny is content to vary his routine when it seems right to do so and even, as we shall see, cheerfully to give up the treasured enjoyments of *otium* when his health requires it.

Moreover, the *otium* which he describes in 9.36 and 9.40 is carefully presented as a life of relaxed alternation between physical and intellectual activities. Literary work and intellectual conversation absorb his attention, but other activities appear in an adaptable daily schedule:

---

[10] Cic. *Tusc.* 5.105, Sen. *Ep.* 82.3. André (1966) is still indispensable for the study of the complex intellectual history of the concept of *otium*; cf. Bütler (1970) 41–57, Gamberini (1983) 103–9, Méthy (2007) 353–78.

[11] E.g. *Ep.* 55.3.

[12] See e.g. 3.1.8, 1.15, 7.21. On Seneca's letters, see the works listed in our Appendix 3.

[13] For Pliny's moderate and balanced approach to time-management throughout the collection, see also Chapter 4.

non numquam ex hoc ordine aliqua mutantur; nam, si diu iacui uel ambulaui, post somnum demum lectionemque non uehiculo sed, quod breuius quia uelocius, equo gestor. (9.36.5)

At times some changes are made in the above disposition. For if I have been a long while on my couch, or walking, it is only after a nap and a reading that I take the air, not in a carriage, but – which takes less time, as being more rapid – on horseback.

The key is always an appropriate balance between repetition and variety: after Pliny has spent the first waking period thinking out his work, he begins a repetitive process of having it taken down ('I call for my amanuensis, and, letting in the daylight, dictate what I have put together; he goes away, is recalled, is dismissed afresh [*abit rursusque reuocatur rursusque dimittitur*],' 9.36.2). Thereafter, the day proceeds steadily, as Pliny continues to think and dictate in turn, pursuing his thoughts in different environments (as he walks or rides while meditating), by turns snoozing, walking, reciting, then walking again.

CONSTRAINTS AND FAILINGS

By contrast, Pliny bemoans the constraints upon time in the city which impede the productivity which is characteristic of well-managed *otium* – an obsession with time pressure which seems modern and familiar and which emerges very early on in the collection.[14] 1.9 and 1.10, in particular, stage conversations (real or hypothetical) about Pliny's dissatisfaction with his busy urban existence. The first defines the issue in familiar Senecan terms; the second counters with a (different) philosopher's answer, which discourages 'Senecan' yearnings for a private and contemplative life.[15]

In 1.9 Pliny describes a sensation common to any elite resident of the city (*si* quem *interroges*, 'if you were to ask *anyone*', 1.9.1): looked at in hindsight, the ceremonies and the debts to friendship which cram an urban day seem insignificant in the aggregate.

mirum est quam singulis diebus in urbe ratio aut constet aut constare uideatur, pluribus iunctisque non constet. nam si quem interroges 'hodie quid egisti?', respondeat: 'officio togae uirilis interfui, sponsalia aut nuptias frequentaui, ille me ad signandum testamentum, ille in aduocationem, ille in consilium rogauit.' haec

---

[14] Cf. 2.8.2–3, 2.14.1, 3.1.11, 3.12.1–2, 3.21.5, 8.9, 9.35. On *distringor* see Morello (2003) 188 and Bütler (1970) 41.

[15] For consideration of 1.9 in the context of traditions of satiric criticism of city life, see Méthy (2007) 330–3. For more on 1.9, see Chapter 1.

quo die feceris, necessaria, eadem, si cotidie fecisse te reputes, inania uidentur, multo magis cum secesseris. (1.9.1–3)

It is astonishing how good an account can be given, or seem to be given, of each separate day spent in Rome, yet that this is not the case with regard to a number of days taken in conjunction. If you were to ask anyone, 'What have you been doing today?' he would reply, 'I have attended at the ceremony of a youth's coming of age, I have helped to celebrate a betrothal or a wedding. One has invited me to the signing of his will, another to attend a trial on his behalf, another to a consultation.' These things seem indispensable at the time when they are done, but when you come to reflect that you have been doing them day after day, they strike you as mere frivolities; and much more is this the case when one has retired into the country.

Such urban activities are absorbing and important when looked at as separate items (or separate days), and Pliny seems to apply his accounting metaphor (*ratio constare*) to good effect: if he is busy doing things like this for his friends and associates, his 'accounts' balance. Similarly, in 1.3, we have already seen another context in which multiple activities call upon one's time in any given location (or type of location): so, in 1.3 Pliny imagines Caninius enjoying in turn each of the delights of his villa at Comum, or giving way to the demands of managing his estate, and frequently called away from such pleasures. Such pleasures are merely ephemeral distractions, however, and Pliny urges his friend to stick to one thing: the laborious *studia* which will provide an immortality to remain his own, even after heirs have taken over his material possessions. 1.9 shows Pliny himself seeking a similar focus after the frenetic variety of social and professional life in the city. Life in the Laurentine villa, by contrast, seems to be largely defined by absence of disruptive influences (noise, spoken criticism, emotional upheaval), and a freedom from the uncomfortable moral compromises required by urban life:

nihil audio quod audisse, nihil dico quod dixisse paeniteat; nemo apud me quemquam sinistris sermonibus carpit, neminem ipse reprehendo, nisi tamen me cum parum commode scribo; nulla spe nullo timore sollicitor, nullis rumoribus inquietor: mecum tantum et cum libellis loquor. (1.9.4)

I hear nothing, I say nothing, which one need be ashamed of hearing or saying. No one about me gossips ill-naturedly of anyone else, and I for my part censure no one, except myself, however, when my writings are not up to the mark. I am troubled by no hopes and no fears, disquieted by no rumours: I converse with myself only and with my books.

The Laurentine villa is a natural location for *otium* ('I shall return to my house at Laurentum, in other words, to my books and my writing-tablets and my studious retirement [*hoc est libellos et pugillares, studiosumque otium repetam*],' 1.22.11);[16] it is also relatively close, so *secessus* is readily available for Pliny ('it is only seventeen miles distant from the town, so that having got through all you had to do, you can go and stay there with your day's work already secured and disposed of,' 2.17.2).[17] Pliny gives an impression of solitude – a partial misrepresentation, since he was most unlikely to be actually alone at the villa,[18] but the point is the contrast between city life, where anyone could call upon his time, and villa life where there is time for reading, writing and physical exercise. Conversation there is to be had with one's books, and the critical voice of urban life becomes the healthy *self*-criticism of the author contemplating his own work.[19] To extend the ancient accounting metaphor, we should note a contrast also in the 'account sheets' Pliny returns for his time: those for his urban life contain multiple routine entries which generate no long-term profit, but, paradoxically, under several headings in the accounts for life at Laurentum, he enters only a zero (*nihil audio, nihil dico, nemo, neminem, nulla, nullis*) and yet anticipates a generous profit, as the landscape itself assists his literary work (*quam multa inuenitis, quam multa dictatis*, 'how many thoughts do you suggest to the imagination and dictate to the pen', 1.9.6).

Finally, Pliny invites not only his addressee but also, by implication, the 'everyman' with whom one might have this imaginary conversation to choose such peaceful study:[20]

proinde tu quoque strepitum istum inanemque discursum et multum ineptos labores, ut primum fuerit occasio, relinque teque studiis uel otio trade. satius est enim, ut Atilius noster eruditissime simul et facetissime dixit, otiosum esse quam nihil agere. uale. (1.9.7–8)

In the same way do you too, my friend, at the first opportunity, turn your back upon all that bustle, and idle hurry-scurry, and utterly inane drudgery, and give

---

[16] For Pliny's deliberately selective picture of the Laurentine villa, of which his enticing description in 2.17 is designed to offer a counterweight to 2.11–12, see Chapter 7. On his more positive attitude in Book 6 to the distractions of his professional life, see Chapter 2.

[17] As Leach points out, however, Pliny here 'contrives a sharp break that highlights his theme' by omitting any reference to the journey from Rome to the Laurentine villa; the sudden change of perspective here serves to emphasize the psychological distance travelled even to this, the closest to Rome of all Pliny's villas: Leach (2003) 157. For Pliny's *urban* leisure at the close of the day's business, see 3.21.5.

[18] For more on 2.17 and on the millionaires' row on the Laurentine shore (including the likelihood of frequent callers), see Chapter 7.

[19] We should notice, too, that this letter implicitly rejects the events of a normal urban day as epistolary material: it is only with hindsight that this kind of letter may be produced.

[20] Cf. 1.3.3.

yourself up to study or even to repose. It is better – as friend Atilius says, with as much wisdom as wit – to have nothing to do than to do nothing.

On the face of it, this is a Senecan position. For Seneca, real literary and rhetorical achievement is impossible for a man who is preoccupied with his business and social duties (*Breu.* 7.3). Like Pliny, Seneca enumerates the distractions and troubles of a life of *negotium*:

ille reus quot dies abstulit? quot ille candidatus? quot illa anus efferendis heredibus lassa? quot ille ad irritandam auaritiam captantium simulatus aeger? quot ille potentior amicus, qui uos non in amicitiam sed in apparatum habet? (*Breu.* 7.7)[21]

Of how many days has that defendant robbed you? Of how many that candidate? Of how many that old woman wearied with burying her heirs? Of how many that man who is shamming sickness for the purpose of exciting the greed of the legacy-hunters? Of how many that very powerful friend who has you and your like on the list, not of his friends, but of his retinue?

He adduces *exempla* of three public men who complained of their *negotium* or longed to escape into *otium* as Pliny does: the emperor Augustus, Cicero and Livius Drusus (*Breu.* 4.2–4, 5.1–3). He begins in relatively indulgent vein by summarizing a letter from Augustus to the senate, in which the *princeps* consoled himself for his burdens with the hope of well-earned *otium* upon completion of his public tasks – a worthy revelation for a letter, it seems (*Breu.* 4.2–4).[22] By contrast, the difficulties in *otium* of Cicero and Livius Drusus are much less sympathetically treated. Cicero is criticized because he failed to behave as a *sapiens* and to grasp the intellectual and moral opportunities of an enforced period of *otium* (*Breu.* 5.3), Drusus because the failings of his own turbulent personality (rather than any external circumstances) prevented him from enjoying *otium*, and – worse still – he realized his mistakes too late (*sero... querebatur, Breu.* 6.2). Seneca, then, is scathing about those who complain either about *otium* or the lack of it, when the opportunity to enjoy it and use it well lay within their grasp: only the emperor among his *exempla* escapes censure.

---

[21] Cf. *Breu.* 3.2, where Seneca reckons up the amount of time worldly pursuits and associates can steal from a life, and *Breu.* 14.3, on the social whirl. For the emptiness and pointlessness of a poorly managed 'busy life', cf. *Tranq.* 12.4. and also 12.2: *horum si aliquem exeuntem e domo interrogaueris: 'quo tu? quid cogitas?' respondebit tibi: 'non mehercules scio, sed aliquos uidebo, aliquid agam,'* 'If you ask one of these as he comes out of the house: "Where are you going? What have you in mind?" he will reply to you: "Upon my word, I really do not know, but I shall see some people, I shall do something."'

[22] One should note that it is the *epistolary* legacy of Augustus and Cicero upon which Seneca draws for information about their dissatisfactions. We might set Pliny's 3.1.12 on his own hopes of *otium* in retirement in the same tradition as Augustus' alleged dreams of *otium* late in life.

Seneca's criticism of those who bemoan excessively busy lives is similarly robust at *Ep.* 106.1, a letter which plays upon one of the most clichéd epistolary openings, namely an apology for long silence due to pressure of business.[23] As so often, he brusquely assigns the management of time to each individual's personal responsibility and insists that it is one's own failure to make correct choices about how to spend one's days which is the thief of vacation time:[24]

tardius rescribo ad epistulas tuas, non quia districtus occupationibus sum. hanc excusationem caue audias: uaco, et omnes uacant qui uolunt.

I reply to your letter rather tardily, not because of pressure of business. Do not listen to this excuse; I have free time, and so does everyone who wishes to have free time.

Finally, in *Ep.* 68, a central text for anyone interested in the interrelationship between Pliny's letters and Seneca's work on this topic, Seneca contrasts the disruptive influences of the forum with the peace of rural retirement, and urges upon Lucilius a self-critical dialogue with himself of which Pliny's inner conversations in 1.9 are strongly reminiscent:

cum secesseris, non est hoc agendum, ut de te homines loquantur, sed ut ipse tecum loquaris. quid autem loqueris? quod homines de aliis libentissime faciunt, de te apud te male existima: assuesces et dicere uerum et audire. Id autem maxime tracta quod in te esse infirmissimum senties. (*Ep.* 68. 6)

When you withdraw from the world, your business is to talk with yourself, not to have men talk about you. But what shall you talk about? Do just what people are fond of doing when they talk about their neighbours – speak ill of yourself when by yourself; then you will become accustomed both to speak and to hear the truth. Above all, however, ponder that which you come to feel is your greatest weakness.

As usual, Pliny takes the pragmatic view that talking to oneself in *otium* (an important motif in 1.9.6) is not part of the searching out and exterminating of one's own vices, but contributes to literary refinement and productivity.

Nevertheless, Pliny discusses issues relating to the choice of *otium* over *negotium* in similar terms, and seeks a philosopher's advice. Just as 1.9 bemoans the restriction on Pliny's virtuous and productive solitude, its complement, 1.10, enumerates the tasks which prevent Pliny from indulging his wish to spend time in the company of his erudite friend, Euphrates:

---

[23] Pliny offers a brief list of such excuses in 2.2.2.   [24] Cf. *Ep.* 22.9.

nam distringor officio, ut maximo sic molestissimo: sedeo pro tribunali, subnoto **libellos**, conficio **tabulas**, **scribo plurimas sed illitteratissimas litteras**. soleo non numquam (nam id ipsum quando contingit!) de his occupationibus apud Euphraten queri. (1.10.9–10)

For I am engrossed in the discharge of an office as highly irksome as it is important. I sit on the bench, countersign *petitions*, make up *accounts*, and *write a vast number of most unliterary letters*. I am in the habit of complaining to Euphrates occasionally (for how seldom do I get the chance of doing even this !) about my employment.

Once again, Pliny is entering daily life into an account sheet, calculating activities and output. Here he depicts himself producing writing of all kinds *except* the literary work which requires *otium*.[25] Nevertheless, Euphrates urges Pliny to consider his public and legal work as the better part of a truly philosophical life.

ille me consolatur, affirmat etiam esse hanc philosophiae et quidem pulcherrimam partem, agere negotium publicum, cognoscere iudicare, promere et exercere iustitiam, quaeque ipsi doceant in usu habere. mihi tamen hoc unum non persuadet, satius esse ista facere quam cum illo dies totos audiendo discendoque consumere. (1.10.10)

He consoles me, and goes so far as to assert that it is a function, and indeed the noblest function of philosophy, to conduct public affairs, to investigate, to judge, to exhibit and exercise justice, and to put in practice what these very philosophers teach. Yet one thing alone he cannot convince me of: that it is better to be thus engaged, than to consume whole days in listening to him and learning from him.

Pliny's claim to be unconvinced that his public career is the better part of philosophy is disingenuous, perhaps, but the letter does establish a hierarchy of activities: the demands of friendship come first, followed by the obligation to the state; the pleasures of intellectual conversation should be a relatively rare indulgence. Later, in 8.9, Pliny will say that it is precisely the longed-for *studia* from which he is barred by the *negotia* imposed by friends which confirm that *amicitiae officium* must take precedence over *studia* as well as over the inclination to rest in idleness:

olim non librum in manus, non stilum sumpsi, olim nescio quid sit otium quid quies, quid denique illud iners quidem, iucundum tamen nihil agere nihil esse: adeo multa me negotia amicorum nec secedere nec studere patiuntur. nulla enim

---

[25] Cf. for different readings of the 'hierarchy' of Pliny's work in 1.9.2, Hoffer (1999) 112–13 and Leach (2003) 157. For the public servant whose attention is demanded by professional reading matter rather than literary work, cf. Mart. 11.1.

studia tanti sunt, ut amicitiae officium deseratur, quod religiosissime custodien-
dum studia ipsa praecipiunt. uale.(8.9)[26]

For a long time I have taken neither book nor pen in hand. For a long time I have
not known what rest is or repose, or, in short, that state, so idle yet so agreeable,
of doing nothing and being nothing. To such a degree do the multitude of my
friends' affairs debar me from seclusion and study. For no studies are of such
importance that the office of friendship should be abandoned on their account –
indeed, that this office should be most religiously guarded is a matter which is
taught us by these very studies.

In 1.10, it is also clear that Pliny's public work is not expected to keep him
from Euphrates altogether: he can, after all, complain to the great man of
his frustrations (1.10.9).

Pliny's two letters, then, balance each other in their representation of
conversations about *otium* and in the different positions espoused in them
on a 'Senecan' dilemma (longing for philosophically healthy *otium* vs appreciation of philosophically justifiable *negotium*). They also offer contrasting
images of *otium* in both rural and urban environments: whereas the *otium*
of philosophical peace and literary productivity which Pliny envisioned in
1.9 was explicitly non-urban and solitary (and his addressee was advised to
seek such *otium*), the retreat to philosophy in 1.10 – although denied to
Pliny as a full-time state, like the *secessus* of 1.9 – is to be found in the city. In
a familiar pattern of oscillation in juxtaposed letters, then, Pliny explores
a similar issue in two radically different settings and enacts a different
perspective (and outcome) in each case.

As in 1.9.7, the addressee is urged to profit from the opportunity to talk
to Euphrates:

quo magis te cui uacat hortor, cum in urbem proxime ueneris (uenias autem ob
hoc maturius), illi te expoliendum limandumque permittas. (1.10.11)

So all the more do I exhort you, who have the spare time, directly you come to
town (and you ought to come sooner on this account), to put yourself into his
hands for the purpose of being perfected and finished.

Paradoxically, only the genuinely leisured (like Attius Clemens), who are
at liberty to spend all their time in the idyllic setting of a villa like Pliny's
Laurentine, may spend time in the city putting themselves into the hands
of this philosophical craftsman for intensive polishing and refining – as if

---

[26] This letter is startlingly juxtaposed with the *otium*-rich 8.8 on tourist attractions at the Clitumnus
spring. For other similarly sharp contrasts between adjacent letters, see Chapter 8.

they are themselves the products of the neoteric literary craft to which such terms belong.[27]

In these letters, then, Pliny expresses the want of *otium* to (at least) four interlocutors – the unnamed speaker of 1.9.2, Minicius Fundanus (the addressee of 1.9), Attius Clemens (addressee of 1.10) and Euphrates – and it is the fourth of these who brings consolation (*ille me consolatur*) and settles Pliny's inner conflict. Both letters insist, either explicitly or implicitly, that *otium* is for literary work – and concomitantly that any written work produced in *negotium* is partly defined by its lack of literary qualities. Above all, they confirm Pliny's commitment to variety and alternation of tasks: he cannot spend whole days talking with Euphrates (single-mindedness, as 1.9.5–7 has suggested, is only possible during finite and relatively brief periods of *otium*), but he does, on his brief visits, voice a recurring complaint about the way his busy urban life divides up his days into worldly tasks without leaving time for any more edifying activity, and wish for a better balance between professional and intellectual life.

MAKING A FEATURE OF IDLENESS

Reading Pliny in the light of Seneca reveals the degree to which he has 'modestly' depicted himself as no refusenik philosopher, but as an 'everyman' – educated, of course, and still elite, but with the aspirations that anyone like him might recognize and share. He feels the kinds of pressures and longings which Seneca *proficiens* exhorts us to ignore or discard as inappropriate to a true *sapiens*, and presents himself as an ordinary man, with ordinary human failings. One of the failings he highlights in particular allows him, however, to implement Seneca's advice on the management of *otium*. Seneca's *Ep.* 68 famously instructs Lucilius to avoid boasting about *otium*: he should hide himself away in retirement (*absconde te in otio*) but also conceal the retirement itself (*sed et ipsum otium absconde*). Inactivity, Seneca says, should be ascribed to some unenviable factor, such as ill-health, physical frailty – or plain laziness:

nunc ad illud reuertor quod suadere tibi coeperam, ut otium tuum ignotum sit. non est quod inscribas tibi philosophiam ac quietem: aliud proposito tuo nomen impone, ualetudinem et imbecillitatem uocato et desidiam. gloriari otio iners ambitio est. (*Ep.* 68.3)

---

[27] On neoteric stylistic terms, see e.g. Batstone (1998). For this vocabulary used of the refinement of oratorical talent in the young, see Quint. *Inst.* 2.4.8.

I now return to the advice which I set out to give you – that you keep your retirement in the background. There is no need to fasten a placard upon yourself with the words: 'Philosopher and Quietist'. Give your purpose some other name; call it ill-health and bodily weakness, or mere laziness. To boast of our retirement is but idle self-seeking.

Ostentatious *otium* draws too much attention, thereby defeating its purpose (*cum secesseris, non est hoc agendum, ut de te homines loquantur, sed ut ipse tecum loquaris*, 'When you withdraw from the world, your business is to talk with yourself, not to have men talk about you,' *Ep. 68. 6*).

Seneca's last-named smokescreen, *desidia*, is skilfully deployed in Pliny's first book. Paradoxically, it might seem, for a man who will claim by 1.9 to be overburdened with *negotium*, Pliny's collection begins in varieties of idleness, and he sustains the motif throughout the opening sequence of letters, reinforcing it with an accretion of associated themes, in order to build towards the larger theme of the complex relationships between *otium* and *negotium*, and between idleness and labour, before he takes up his complaint about professional distractions.[28] Another sequential reading of the opening letters of the collection will illustrate.

The dedicatory epistle to Septicius Clarus shows Pliny publishing his letter collection only modestly and at a friend's request. The collection appears nonchalantly constructed, the letters supposedly arranged in the order in which they came to hand. Nevertheless, they are selected from those on which he has expended 'rather more than usual care' (*si quas paulo curatius scripsissem*).[29] The same combination of care in composition and casualness in publication is sustained and developed in 1.2, as Pliny sends Arrianus a speech on which he has lavished *more care* than on any previous work; this immediately trumps the letters (written only *paulo curatius*) and advertises Pliny as an orator.[30] However, the effortfully crafted speech contrasts with his persona: Pliny claims to be a naturally idle man, prone to long periods of sloth (*longae desidiae*, 1.2.3) from which the effort of polishing the speech has roused him ('provided only I was capable of being roused [*excitari*]', 1.2.3). He reiterates his claim to temperamental idleness in 1.8.2 ('you must not, however, expect anything in the shape of new work from an idle man [*ab homine desidioso*]').[31] In 1.2.4, moreover,

---

[28] For an 'autobiographical' solution to the problem of comparable contradictory 'time signals' in Book 1, see Chapter 1.

[29] See Chapter 8.   [30] See Mayer (2003) on this as Pliny's primary goal.

[31] Compare the apparent hesitance in letters 1.1 and 1.2 (*si quas paulo curatius scripsissem* ~ *si modo is sum*). For the production of literary work *per desidiam et otium*, cf. 7.13.2.

he gives a specific example of the stylistic care expended on the speech which complements the focus on his own idleness, and highlights the 'Ciceronian' digressions and showpiece passages in which he has most considered the reader's pleasure and his own; these constitute departures from the 'main road' of a speech into '*loci amoeni*', as it were (*quotiens paulum itinere decedere non intempestiuis amoenitatibus*, 'whenever a pleasant topic, not unseasonably introduced, suggested to me a pleasant divergence from the beaten road', 1.2.4). Pliny depicts himself as easily tempted, even in his labours, down the paths to repose, which he finds in the *otium* of literary genre as much as in the lived experience at his villas. Even his decision to publish this speech is motivated by laziness (*audis desidiae uotum*, 'do you hear the wish of indolence?' 1.2.6): one must publish *something* and this is already to hand and more or less finished.[32] Naturally, the reader will remember from 1.1 that the same is true of the letter collection itself.

Letter 1.3 initially seems thematically unlike 1.2, since it sketches ordinary activities of *otium* (walking, swimming and sunbathing) rather than the literary labour of 1.2, but the setting of the letter – the pleasances of Comum (*suburbanum amoenissimum*, 'that most charming of villas') – once more suggests the pull towards *otium* and pleasure which was expressed in Pliny's pride in the *amoenitates* of his speech (1.2.4). Nevertheless, 1.3 is the first to make explicit the requirement that *otium* be productive (*effinge aliquid et excude*, 'fashion and produce something'), and Pliny begins to blur the distinction between *otium* and *negotium*, urging Caninius to devote every energy to literary work:

hoc sit negotium tuum hoc otium; hic labor haec quies; in his uigilia, in his etiam somnus reponatur. (1.3.3)

Let *this* be your business, *this* your relaxation, this your labour this your repose; in this let your waking and even your sleeping time be employed.

There is a paradox built in here already: Caninius is to bring *negotium, labor, uigilia* into his *secessus* (*in alto isto pinguique secessu*, 'in that deep and comfortable retreat of yours').[33] An *otium* letter is already refocused

---

[32] On idleness as characteristic of the modern orator, cf. the harsher strictures of Sen. *Controu.* 1 *praef.* 10. Cf. by contrast Seneca's positive account of Porcius Latro, who was given to laziness interspersed with furious bursts of work (Sen. *Controu.* 1 *praef.* 13–15); one might compare John Keats' need for alternation of 'indolence' and 'energy' (see Woodman (1974) 53).

[33] For Pliny's habit of bringing the *inamoenum* into his villa retreat by revising earlier work, see 5.8.6 and 9.10.3 ('I have retouched one or other of my small orations. Yet this kind of work is ungrateful and displeasing [*inamabile inamoenum*], and resembles rather the labours than the pleasures of the country [*magisque laboribus ruris quam uoluptatibus simile*]').

upon *labor*, and all our 'normal' categories begin to fall into creative confusion.[34]

In 1.4 we are still in the world of the villa, as Pliny writes to his mother-in-law about the hospitality he has received at her villas and about her servants' care for his comfort. The theme of the 'diversion' from a road is still present (*deuerteris*) as is that of the laziness built into Pliny's life. This time it is his servants who mirror his own laziness: unafraid of the gentle master whose habits they reflect, they might nevertheless stir themselves to provide for someone else the hospitality they do not trouble to offer him.[35]

Letter 1.5 interrupts this sequence of pleasures with a difficult professional encounter – one which (in another typically Plinian oscillation of mood and image) shows Regulus displaying a servile fear which Pliny's slaves had entirely lacked.[36] However, the motifs of pleasures and pleasances recur in 1.6 (discussed further below and in Chapter 5), which reinforces Pliny's image as an idler. Here Tacitus is expected to be surprised to find Pliny doing something as energetic as hunting, and Pliny reassures him that Pliny (*qua* huntsman) is still a sluggish and studious fellow (*non tamen ut omnino ab inertia mea et quiete discederem*, 'yet not so as entirely to deviate from my inert and sedentary ways', 1.6.1). This is no energetic woodland trek, but a meditative sit-down (*sedebam*) beside the nets with writing materials to hand, in a wilder version of the *locus amoenus*, in which gods may be found roaming (*experieris non Dianam magis montibus quam Mineruam inerrare*, 'you will find by experience that Minerva as well as Diana rambles over the mountains', 1.6.3). Once again the distinction between work and leisure is blurred. The physical activity of hunting to which Pliny refuses to give his full attention serves above all to stimulate him mentally, just as the *contentio dicendi* had done in letter 1.2 (*me... excitauit*, 'roused me' ~ *animus excitetur*, 'the mind is roused'; cf *cogitationis incitamenta*, 'incentives to reflection', 1.6.2).

Finally, 1.7 and 1.8 revives the theme of Pliny's obedience to his friends (in accepting a professional engagement and in preparing work for publication), before Pliny turns to the expressions of frustration and regret in 1.9 and 1.10 which we have already discussed.

---

[34] Lefèvre (2009) 239 [= (1987) 253–4].

[35] Vocabulary cues: *deuerteris* (1.4.2) ~ *itinere decedere* (1.2.4), *neglegenter* (1.4.3) ~ *neglectae* (1.1.2), *excitantur* (1.4.4) ~ *excitauit* (1.2.3). Cf *balineum* (1.4.1) ~ *balineum* (1.3.1). This whole episode is driven by letters: just one old letter from Pompeia allows Pliny to make his own epistolary arrangements to visit her villas (1.4.1).

[36] We might compare the maxim that 'all the wicked are slaves', Cic. *Parad.* 35 (cf. *Parad.* 40 on fear and slavery).

Space constraints preclude further detailed sequential study of Book 1 here, but we can already see the picture gradually becoming more complex as one letter follows another. In 1.13, Pliny maps the boundary of acceptable idleness in the literary sphere and makes his only claim to diligence in these early letters of Book 1: he devotes time to hearing the literary work of others (*prope nemini defui*, 'I have failed scarcely anyone,' 1.13.5). Pliny measures the evils of the literary world of contemporary Rome precisely in terms of an excess of *otium* and the resulting failure to give a day its proper value:

nunc otiosissimus quisque multo ante rogatus et identidem admonitus aut non uenit aut, si uenit, queritur se diem (quia non perdidit) perdidisse. sed tanto magis laudandi probandique sunt, quos a scribendi recitandique studio haec auditorum uel desidia uel superbia non retardat. (1.13.4–5)

Nowadays, the idlest people, though they have had a long invitation and frequent reminders, either do not come at all, or, if they do come, complain that they have lost a day, just because they have *not* lost one. All the more then should we praise and approve those who are not discouraged in their zeal for writing and recitation by this laziness, or else superciliousness, of their audiences.

These *otiosissimi* look back on time spent performing a duty for friends, and worry that it has been wasted, just as Pliny had (as *negotiosissimus*) in 1.9. The damage done to friendships and to literary productivity here makes *desidia* into an unacceptable vice, in which Pliny himself, of course, never indulges.[37]

In 1.20 an impatient audience potentially militates once more against a writer's self-disciplined commitment to writing well. This letter, the 'answer' to Tacitus' *Dialogus*, and addressed to Tacitus himself, presents lengthy composition as a strategy for ensuring a speech's effectiveness;[38] by implication briefer exposition is the mark of the less conscientious speaker. Here Pliny sketches again the potentially disastrous interrelation (first introduced in 1.13.5) between the idleness of an inadequate audience and the writer's commitment to his craft:

[37] Cf. 9.32, where Pliny labels himself *delicatus* for choosing not to write long letters while remaining eager to receive them: again brevity is a sign of idleness, but Pliny's idleness stops short of his performance of duty as addressee, auditor, or recipient of another's writing. Just how far this pose as a *delicatus*, however, matches the reality is called into question by the juxtaposition of this letter with one of the longest and most overtly 'artful' letters of the Book, namely 9.33, on the dolphin.

[38] For more on the relationship between Tacitus' works and those of Pliny, see the works listed in our Appendix 3.

'at est gratior multis actio breuis.' est, sed inertibus quorum delicias desidiamque quasi iudicium respicere ridiculum est. nam si hos in consilio habeas, non solum satius breuiter dicere, sed omnino non dicere. (1.20.23)[39]

'But to many short speeches are more agreeable.' So they are; to do-nothing folks, whose lazy whims it would be ridiculous to look to, as if they could decide the point. If you took counsel of these people, it would be best not merely to speak briefly, but not to speak at all.

There is, then, a story being told in the letters of Book 1, which are at least partly about whether or not one makes an effort in life, particularly in *otium*.[40]

ACTION AND IMAGE IN *OTIUM*

In documenting this effort and recording the productivity of his leisure time in his 'accounts', Pliny draws on the traditional pursuits of rural *otium* to illuminate his vision of the relationship between leisure and literary work. Hunting, for example (although never explicitly included in any of the great 'routine' letters), appears already in 1.6, the first letter to Tacitus.[41] Pliny boasts that he has on this occasion caught three boar,[42] but even if the day's sport had been more disappointing, the well-organized huntsman would not have returned without spoils (*meditabar aliquid enotabamque, ut si manus uacuas, plenas tamen ceras reportarem*, 'I thought over a subject and made my notes about it; so that, though my hands were empty, I might take back my note-book at any rate well-filled,' 1.6.1).

Letter 2.8 brings a variation. Here Pliny asks Caninius (also the addressee of 1.3 on productive leisure at Comum) how he spends his time at his estate:

---

[39] Cf. 4.16.3 *studeamus ergo* **nec desidiae nostrae praetendamus alienam**. *sunt qui audiant, sunt qui legant, nos modo dignum aliquid auribus dignum chartis* **elaboremus**, 'let us follow our intellectual pursuits, then, *and not allege other folks' slothfulness as an excuse for our own*. There are those who will listen, there are those who will read, if only we take pains to produce what is worthy of people's ears or of the paper on which it is written.' For another denunciation of the modern oratorical world as shackled by *desidia*, cf. 6.2.5. For a more traditional (and aggressive) statement of the incompatibility of *uirtus* and *desidia*, see Cic. *Sest.* 138.

[40] In 3.1.12 Pliny says he will delay extended *otium* until he is old enough to escape the charge of *inertia* (*cum inertiae crimen effugero*); his management of his *otium* during his prime, however, is a delicate balancing act. One should note that Pliny's references to his own *desidia* peter out after Book 4. On Pliny's declaration in 2.2.2 that he is enjoying *studia* and indolence together (both the products of *otium*), see Chapter 7; not only does 2.2 offer a salutary contrast to the *negotium*-rich tone of Book 2, but it also makes the reader reflect back on *desidia* and *studia* as persistent motifs in Book 1.

[41] Cf. Ludolph (1997) 168 on 1.6 as the axis of the *Paradebriefen*. For more on this letter, along with others to Tacitus, see Chapter 5.

[42] On a possible punning reference to Tacitus' Aper in the *Dialogus*, see Edwards (2008) 50; cf. Murgia (1985) 181.

*studes an piscaris an uenaris an **simul omnia**?* ('are you studying or fishing or hunting or *all these things at once*?' 2.8.1).[43] He contrasts Caninius' active (but consistent and convenient) *otium* with his own constrained life in which one task follows (and overlaps with) another in endless sequence. In a development of the hunting motif, he uses an important image of entrapment:

numquamne hos artissimos laqueos, si soluere negatur, abrumpam? . . . tot nexibus, tot quasi catenis maius in dies occupationum agmen extenditur. (2.8.2)

Shall I never be able to break through, if unable to loosen them, these bonds which so closely confine me? . . . So numerous are the coils, so numerous the links, so to speak, by which the chain of my occupations is daily extended.

This time Pliny is not beside the nets but *in* them, not hunter but hunted.

Pliny extends his manoeuvre of substitution (in which written work is the product of an unrelated country pursuit) to the domain of farming, too. In 4.6, for example, he contrasts the literary harvest from his Laurentine villa, where he writes prolifically, with more orthodox crops from other properties:

ibi enim plurimum scribo, nec agrum quem non habeo sed ipsum me studiis excolo; ac iam possum tibi ut aliis in locis horreum plenum, sic ibi scrinium ostendere.[44] (4.6.2)

For there I write a great deal, and improve, not the land (which I have not got), but *myself* by means of study; and just as in other places I can show you a full barn, so here I can actually show you a full escritoire.

The property without fertile acres is paradoxically the only one to show a profit, just as an unsuccessful hunt may yet provide a full 'bag' at the end of the day.[45]

---

[43] Also perhaps a joke: one can't hunt *and* fish *and* study all at the same time. This ratchets things up from the comparatively restrained multi-tasking of 1.6 (where Pliny is doing only two things at a time).

[44] Cf. *plenas . . . ceras* (1.6). Notice here that Pliny cultivates himself, and there are echoes of Seneca, who also expects *otium* to be well invested and to show a profit: *tota, ut ita dicam, in reditu est*, 'the whole of it, so to speak, yields income', *Breu.* 11.2. See Riggsby (1998) 85 on this letter as showing one of the relatively few traces in the collection of 'the new cultivation of the self' which has long been detected from Seneca onwards (arguing that Pliny takes a generally conservative approach to questions of 'the self'). It is noteworthy in 4.6 that Pliny's 'self-improvement' in *otium* is but enrichment of productive terrain, as it were, rather than refinement of the self: as the land will bring forth crops, so Pliny will bring forth writings. See also Myers (2005) 120–1 on this passage and on Pliny's *otium* in general.

[45] Contrast 5.2, where Pliny is unable to respond in kind to a gift of edible birds, but can send something written (here just a letter – *epistulas **steriles***, 'a *barren* letter') instead.

Balancing literary against agricultural production is again the theme of
8.15, where Pliny feels free to send Iunior multiple works to read because he
knows that his addressee will have time on his hands during this year's poor
uindemia. Finally, 9.16 pulls all the threads together: Pliny has neither time
nor inclination to hunt because of a depressingly meagre grape harvest, but
at least he has some new poetry to show for his time away:[46]

deuehimus tamen pro nouo musto nouos uersiculos tibique iucundissime exigenti
ut primum uidebuntur deferuisse mittemus. (9.16.2)

However, in the place of new wine, I am drawing off some new verses, and, as you
are so polite in requiring them, will send them to you as soon as they shall seem
to have laid aside their fermentation.

Given all this, it is a mildly pleasing joke that in 9.20 Pliny implicitly
combines the hunting and farming motifs, thanking a man named Venator
for a letter about Pliny's books which has arrived while Pliny is busy with
the *uindemia*.

In 9.10, another letter to Tacitus, the 'hunting 'n' writing' motif takes
a new turn. This time boar are in short supply, and Pliny turns instead to
solely literary activities and to his normal relaxed mode (the one Tacitus
was surprised to see interrupted in 1.6), as he works *delicate tamen ut in
secessu et aestate* ('delicately, however, in a manner suitable to being in the
country and in summer').[47] Tacitus has recommended that he write verse
on his country outing, but Pliny (having composed some light verse on
the journey and in odd moments since arrival) chooses instead to revise his
speeches, a task explicitly defined as a choice of *labor* over *uoluptas*:

itaque poemata quiescunt, quae tu inter nemora et lucos commodissime perfici
putas. oratiunculam unam alteram retractaui; quamquam id genus operis inamabile inamoenum, magisque laboribus ruris quam uoluptatibus simile (9.10.2–3)

Hence my poetry – which *you* think can be most suitably turned out among groves
and woods – is dormant. I have retouched one or two of my small orations; yet
this kind of work is ungrateful and displeasing, and resembles rather the labours
than the pleasures of the country.

Instead of purely pleasurable activities, Pliny is now devoting himself to
harsher labours, while verse (the natural product of *otium*) takes a rest in
the country (*quiescunt*). The amorous shepherds of Vergil's *Eclogues* have
given way, as it were, to the hard-pressed farmers of the *Georgics*.

---

[46] For Pliny's image as a relatively unsuccessful farmer, see e.g. 8.2.1.
[47] For literary work (in this case reading) during *otium* when hunting is off the agenda, cf. Mart. 12.1.
See Marchesi (2008) 121.

One of the keys to all this is the piquant unexpectedness of Pliny's practice.[48] Nobody who knows Pliny would expect him to go hunting, much less to catch anything, but so he does. As a huntsman, however, he remains above all a *littérateur* (again, an unexpected feature: even in the most conventional depictions of poets languishing in lyric rapture in the woods, they are not usually to be found sitting by the hunting nets). Even when Pliny matches his persona to his situation (*delicate tamen ut in secessu*, 9.10.2), he deliberately 'fails' to match activity to environment: instead of poetry in the countryside, he takes on the more laborious and unattractive task of revising old speeches for publication; if Diana cannot be found in the mountains, Pliny will fulfil the 'service to Minerva' (*Mineruae tantum seruiendum est*, 9.10.2) which we already know from the passage of Martial quoted in 3.21.5 as the focus of Pliny's working days in town (*totos dat tetricae dies Mineruae*, 'to the stern Minerva he devotes all his days', 3.21.5). Just as in 1.2, then, Pliny's special brand of idleness produces the serious prose which he can publish.

BOOK 7 AND ITS *OTIUM* CYCLE

Time, then, to turn to the study of the single book in which *otium* dominates, and to examine how Pliny's *otium* theme is played out in a coherent sequence in which the proper use of leisure improves both the man and his writing.

Pliny presents a model for the life of order, routine and restraint, in which *otium* belongs within a life of 'managed variety'. The dominant obsession of Book 7, in particular, is the proper design of life, and eighteen of its thirty-three letters (letters 1, 2, 3, 4, 5, 9, 12, 15, 16, 17, 19, 21, 23, 24, 26, 27, 30, 31) relate in some way to annual or daily routines or to time management. These include eleven which are either explicitly about physical health or illness or use language with a medical colour (1, 3, 5, 19, 21, 23, 24, 26, 27, 30, 31). A further seven letters refer (however briefly) to the tension between *otium* and *negotium* or to the *studia* which are the fruit of *otium* (6, 7, 13, 20, 22, 25, 33). That leaves only letters 8, 10 (both of which follow up earlier letters), 11, 14 (both about estate management), 18 (about the financial management of munificence), 28 (about Pliny's alleged exaggeration of his friends' virtues), 29 (about Pallas' inscription) and 32 (which closes the book's sequence of letters to Fabatus).

---

[48] Cf. the 'discrepancy between his authoritative public persona and his ludic poetic persona' in 7.4 (Marchesi (2008) 80). The 'unexpectedness' of a scholar in *otium* is exemplified too in 7.25 on the quiet-living Terentius' erudition. For Pliny as a poet, see also Appendix 3.

The majority of this book's letters, then, belong in an intricate nexus of pieces about routine/*otium*/study/health, and are arranged, according to Pliny's frequent practice, in loose 'daisy chain' sequences whereby a letter is linked to the immediately preceding letters by one or more images or motifs (not necessarily the dominant motif in each case). This feature of Pliny's book design further encourages the linear, sequential reading which allows us to follow Pliny's signposts through the book; as a sample of the method and its fruits, we offer here a reading of the first part of Book 7, before we turn at last to a study of 7.24, which depicts a situation in which two very different family members successfully devote themselves to *otium* and to study respectively while living peacefully together in the same house.

Letter 1's anxiety at Geminus' 'persistent ill-health' (*pertinax ualetudo*, 7.1.1) introduces the theme of Pliny's management of his own health, which will recur in letters 21 and 26 (the latter a quasi-philosophical letter on how illness makes us better people).[49] Illness brings *otium* perforce, but a balance between flexibility and self-discipline in the daily routine is essential for convalescence. If necessary, for example, normal well-regulated bathing habits (an important element of a daily leisure routine, even for the Elder Pliny), should be abandoned (7.1.5).[50] For Seneca an excessive attachment to bathing routines (especially when dictated or monitored by others) betrayed a misplaced devotion to *otium*; Pliny takes a pragmatic approach, in which his own temperance and self-restraint during illness becomes a model of sensible flexibility.[51]

Letter 2 shifts attention from routines of single days to seasonal fluctuations of the year. Pliny refuses to send Iustus his verse ('which even from idle folks [*otiosis*] can scarce obtain a moment of their useless time') until the autumn, when evenings, at least, may be free for such *nugae*; in fact, he defers even his selection process until the quieter season (*hieme demum... quaeram quid potissimum ex nugis meis tibi exhibeam*, 'in winter at last... I shall consider which of my trifles I may best show to you', 7.2.2). The letter itself – already part of a careful selection, and short,

---

[49] As Sherwin-White (1966) 402 points out, the focus upon Pliny's own 'morbid states' is peculiar to this book. For health as an epistolary motif, see e.g. Sen. *Ep.* 54, on his struggles with asthma, and *Ep.* 78, where he writes about how he himself responds philosophically to illness (including, at 78.11, a confident assertion that any sense of deprivation from fasting or refraining from drink soon dies away and such treatments should be undertaken calmly).

[50] Cf. 2.8.2, where Pliny uses a sick man's longing for wine and baths as a simile to illuminate his longing for *otium*.

[51] *Breu.* 12.6. However, for Seneca's own epistolary commitment to balance and variety of activity during a period of illness, see *Ep.* 78.5; once again, the worst course is to give way to uninterrupted *otium* (*ne indulgeas otio*).

so as to avoid intruding upon Iustus' 'incessant occupations' (*adsiduis occupationibus*, 7.2.1) – embodies and illustrates Pliny's restraint and consideration.[52]

Motifs of change, flexibility and restraint are picked up in new ways by letter 3, which adumbrates yet another type of alternation between periods of time.[53] The 'persistent illness' of letter 1 and the 'incessant occupations' of letter 2 are followed by the 'persistency' (*perseuerantia*) of Praesens' commitment to 'uninterrupted [*perpetua*] absence' in rural *otium*:

> tantane **perseuerantia** tu modo in Lucania, modo in Campania? 'ipse enim' inquis 'Lucanus, uxor Campana.' iusta causa longioris absentiae, non **perpetuae** tamen. quin ergo aliquando in urbem redis? (7.3.1)

> Still the same *persistency* on your part in remaining at one time in Lucania, at another in Campania! 'Why,' say you, 'I myself am a Lucanian and my wife is a Campanian.' Good grounds these for a more protracted absence from town; but not, however, for an *uninterrupted* one. Why not return then at some time to Rome?

Praesens changes location but not environment: he remains in the world of the villa, spending his time exactly as he pleases, on a diet (the dining image is Pliny's own) of unremitting pleasure. Pliny recommends that Praesens' appetite for *otium* be healthily sharpened by a serving of the city's more bitter challenges, and his pleasures aroused from the lethargy (*languescant*) induced by overindulgence.

This addressee, who has kingly freedom to dispose of his own time (*quousque regnabis?* 'How long will you continue to play the king?' 7.3.2), is polar opposite to Iustus in letter 2, whose time is not his own. Indeed, Pliny's strictures recall Cicero's discussion (in similarly 'regal' language) of the freedom exercised by those who retreat from public life:

---

[52] Pliny characteristically conceals what exactly is keeping Fabius Iustus so busy. For argument that he is currently on military campaign (based very largely upon the language of this letter), see Syme (1970) 110–18; for an alternative view of Iustus' occupations as those of an overburdened landowner, see Sherwin-White (1966) 403. Pliny solves a comparable seasonal dilemma at 9.25, by sending his poetic 'birds' to flutter among the eagles in the care of his soldier addressee, but in 7.2 there is something reminiscent of the farmers in Vergil's *Georgics* who have time for jollity in the dark evenings of the winter when they can no longer toil outside in every waking hour (*G.* 1.299–301); on Pliny's engagement with the *Georgics*, see most recently Power (2010). Pliny designs his letter, short though it is, to have the widest possible frame of reference, and his lack of specificity about his addressee's work assists him in this project. The focus is on the season, the shortness of time and the matching shortness of the letter.

[53] Pliny shows himself alternately pandering to and resisting his own inclinations: he allows himself *amoenitates* in his writing (1.2.4) but suggests that physical *amoenitates* should be resisted or used to further such writing (e.g. at 1.3.3 or 1.24.3–4).

uixeruntque non nulli in agris delectati re sua familiari. his idem propositum fuit, quod regibus, ut ne qua re egerent, ne cui parerent, libertate uterentur, cuius proprium est sic uiuere, ut uelis. (*de Officiis* 1.69–70)

Some of them, too, lived in the country and found their pleasure in the manage-ment of their private estates. Such men have had the same aims as kings – to suffer no want, to be subject to no authority, to enjoy their liberty, that is, in its essence, to live just as they please. (trans. Miller)

Such freedom must be kept within healthy bounds, and the language of time-limits dominates the first part of 7.3 (*longioris, perpetuae, aliquando, quousque*) until an insistent *TEMPUS EST* ('high time', 7.3.3) recalls Prae-sens to Rome.[54]

Variety, and the habitual good use of time which might otherwise be wasted, dominate letter 4's agenda. Pliny tells Pontius that he has written poetry of various kinds since he first tried his hand at tragedy at the age of 14, and he highlights the changes of place involved in the history of his poetic career (*e militia rediens*, 'on my return from military service'; *in Laurentino*, 'at my house at Laurentum'; *in urbem reuersus*, 'on my return to town') which have trained him to expect journey times (*maxime in itinere*, 'principally when travelling', 7.4.8) to be routinely productive of verse. 'Gaps' of time (often irregularly spaced: *mox*, 'soon'; *post longam desuetudinem*, 'after being long out of practice') might be used for speedy composition (*exiguo temporis momento*, 'in a remarkably short space of time'; *hos quoque non minus celeriter*, 'these too with no less speed'), but the central example of such free time is a sleepless summer afternoon at the Laurentine villa. Pliny's summer studies in this letter contrast with his reluctance to send his (military?) friend Iustus anything to read until wintertime (7.2), while – unlike Praesens, who journeys only between one villa environment and another (7.3) – he shuttles regularly between city and villa.[55] Variety of place is matched, moreover, by variety of genre, as Pliny experiments with different types of verse (*plura metra*).

We have already discussed (Chapter 3) the subtle links between letter 4 and letter 5, in which Pliny expands upon his commitment to things poetic by playing out a poetic topic in prose. We have also noted (in Chapter 2)

---

[54] We might recall also Pliny's implicit criticism of the Elder Pliny's unceasing labours (discussed in Chapter 4); Pliny is meditating, then, in a long sequence of letters across the entire collection, upon the right balance in life between labour and leisure, as he locates his associates, his elders and himself along the spectrum of activity which has overwork at one end and constant self-indulgent leisure at the other.

[55] This seems to echo his uncle's strictures on making productive use of journeys by taking litters rather than walking (3.5.16), though he means here journeys to and from the city, not within the city itself.

the parallels between the passionate language used in Book 6 of (and to) the two addressees of these letters, Calestrius Tiro and Calpurnia. However, in this context, we should note that in 7.5 Pliny suffers (as an *exclusus amator*) not because an elegiac mistress is playing him tricks, but because even in Calpurnia's absence he helplessly maintains his normal routine of visits to her rooms (*quibus horis te uisere solebam*, 'at the times when I was in the habit of looking in on you', 7.5.1), and must retreat forlorn when he cannot see her. It is his inability to adjust his habit which exacerbates unhappiness.

Pliny's remedy for his elegiac suffering, however, is – characteristically, and in line with his recommendations to Praesens – to return to professional forensic labour. As so often, this makes him a kind of anti-hero in the genre to which he alludes: a real elegiac poet would reject the business of the forum in favour of a life devoted to verse and a girl. In this instance the excessive busyness of public life is better for Pliny than the well-regulated routines of *otium*. Without Calpurnia, sleep is impossible, but there is no suggestion that he is using his wakefulness productively at home; the only remedy is the 'wearing down' of the sufferer by hard work – precisely the kind of 'wearing down' which he urged upon Praesens in letter 3 as a healthy corrective for unremitting pleasure (*terere*, 7.3.3 ~ *conteror*, 7.5.2).[56]

Letter 6 then completes the return from poetic *otium* to oratorical *negotium* with an example of the work to which Pliny flees at the end of letter 5. Letters 7.6 and 7.10 form a final pair in a sequence of letters (which began at 5.20) about Pliny's representation of Varenus against the Bithynians. At the close of the letter, when Pliny tells us that all parties now await the final judgement of the princeps, he highlights in this professional context the familiar theme of alternation between *otium* and *labor*:

nam dies ille nobis pro Vareno aut securitatem et otium dabit aut intermissum laborem renouata sollicitudine iniunget. (7.6.14)

For, the day when it is given will either put us at rest and at ease for Varenus, or will force us to resume our interrupted labours with renewed anxiety.

Pliny reminds us here that intermittence and change of situation dominate professional activity too.[57]

---

[56] Note also *molestias*, 3.5 ~ *miseria curisque*, 5.2. For solace to be found in literary work during times of worry, cf. 8.19.1. We should note also the echo of 3.1.11, where Spurinna himself is both *solacium et exemplum* ('at once my solace and my example') for Pliny's disciplined application of himself to grinding professional labours (*conteror*) when what he really wishes for is the true *otium* of the honourably time-served statesman (see Chapter 4).

[57] Variety and alternation within the book is now matched in the Varenus sequence, as, by contrast with the extensive speech reported in 5.20, Pliny asserts the value also of the pithy retort or even of

The theme of alternation between work which prevents *studia* and the satiety of *otium* which in turn eventually sends a man back to work dominates letter 7 to Saturninus. This (with 8 to Priscus and 15 to Saturninus) begins a letter series about the friendship which Pliny has fostered between the two men. The letter acknowledges a now familiar pattern in Saturninus' life:

te negotiis distineri ob hoc moleste fero, quod deseruire studiis non potes. si tamen alteram litem per iudicem, alteram (ut ais) ipse finieris, incipies primum istic otio frui, deinde satiatus ad nos reuerti. (7.7.2)

I am sorry to hear that you are engrossed by business, for this reason, that you are unable to devote yourself to literature. However, when you have concluded one case before a judge, and (as you tell me) settled the other in person, you will begin, first, to enjoy your leisure where you are, and then, when you have had enough of it, to think of returning to us.

Letter 7 recalls letter 3 in its insistence that even when *otium* has been achieved, it will be only temporary, and Pliny uses the same language of satiety and return in both cases (*tempus est te **reuisere** molestias nostras . . . ne uoluptates istae **satietate** languescant*, 'it is time you should revisit our worries . . . that these pleasures of yours may not languish through satiety' ~ **satiatus** *ad nos **reuerti***, 'when you have had enough of it, to think of returning to us').

Letter 8, however, meditates further upon friendship, and offers a different perspective upon these themes of persistence and change: unlike both professional and leisure activities, one's friendships should not be brief or intermittent. Pliny assured Saturninus in Letter 7 that time would increase his friendship with Priscus (7.7.2); now, to Priscus, he predicts the relationship's longevity (*nec ad breue tempus*, 'and for no short time', 7.8.2) at least partly because of Saturninus' innate *constantia* (*quod habet maximam in amore constantiam*, 'he is principally distinguished for the remarkable consistency of his affections', 7.8.3).

Letter 9 is a nodal letter for the book, and – like the 'routine' letters at the end of Book 9 which share the same addressee – give the reader what he has been wanting for some time. The opening picks up a theme from 7.3: like Praesens, Fuscus is enjoying an extended period of *secessus* (*quo **iam diu** frueris*, 'which you have now for some time enjoyed', 7.9.1), but in this instance Pliny does not urge his addressee to return to the bustle of city life but advises him what *studia* are most useful in *otium* (*utile in primis*, 'it

---

silence (*non minus interdum oratorium esse tacere quam dicere*, 'there are times when it is no less the part of an orator to hold his tongue than to speak', 7.6.7).

will be particularly profitable', 7.9.2). The focus on utility, a curious one, perhaps, from one who started out in Book 1 as a lover of the digression and other *amoenitates*, suits Pliny's Quintilianic project of training the young orator. It is entirely characteristic of him that he thinks *otium* should be put to such a use, and that he highlights the effort one should lavish upon these exercises.

Once again, although selection of activity is important, variety is the key. The student should alternate between languages, between reading and writing, between imitation of models and revision of past work, between the pugnacious style appropriate to oratory and the simpler language of epistles, between letters and historical vignettes, between prose labour and verse relaxation (*fas est et carmine remitti*, 'even poetry is a fitting relaxation', 7.9.9). The 'variety in dining' metaphor which Pliny used on Praesens (7.3.5) mutates into a 'variety in farming' metaphor for Fuscus (*ut enim terrae uariis mutatisque seminibus, ita ingenia nostra nunc hac nunc illa meditatione recoluntur*, 'for as soils are refreshed by varying and changing the seeds, so are our minds by exercising the thoughts now in one direction, now in another', 7.9.7).

Short practice exercises are in order, since Fuscus is in temporary *secessus* rather than lengthy *otium*. Even his poetic attempts should be in a short genre: epic is unsuitable (*non dico continuo et longo*, 'I don't say long and sustained poems', 7.9.9) because it needs uninterrupted *otium*, whereas epigram and lighter verse of other kinds relaxes the mind and punctuates more serious activity (*apte quantas libet occupationes curasque distinguit*, 'forms a suitable interruption to occupations and business, however important', 7.9.9). There is also a further unexpected benefit: not only is it as good a stylistic exercise as the translation assignments Pliny recommended in 7.9.2, but it also serves as an emotional safety valve, a means to express polar extremes of mood and tone.[58]

Letter 7.9 crowns this first series in Book 7 about time management, variety and routines. It touches on several of the most important features of Plinian *otium*, and it should be read as a standard-bearer for the genre and one of the most important interpretative keys to the collection, arguing explicitly that even an extended period of *secessus* should be broken down into short chunks of time and small literary tasks.[59]

Thereafter, letter 10 returns us to the world of *negotium* (otherwise relatively rare in this book, balancing out against the very minor role of

---

[58] 4.14.3.
[59] See Leach (2003) 161 on the greater number of separate elements in Pliny's 'daily routine' than in Spurinna's; cf. also Chapter 4. For more on 7.9, in particular, see Chapter 3.

otium in Book 6), as it completes the story of letter 6, on the Varenus case, while letter 11, in justifying to his wife's grandfather his decision to sell inherited land to Corellia at a discount, reprises the theme of *amicitia* which appeared in letters 7 and 8. The cyclical pattern (literary work – professional work – friendship) which was established in letters 4–8 has now been repeated in letters 9–11.

Readers willing to extend this sequential reading of Book 7 will find all these motifs reworked and recycled in the later letters. Letter 15, for example, also implicitly contrasts his addressee's situation with that of Praesens in letter 3, for whom *otium* meant doing whatever he wanted (*te omnia alia quam quae uelis agere moleste ferrem*, 'that your occupations are everything but what you could wish would be a subject of regret to me', 7.15.2), while letter 21 again highlights Pliny's self-restraint during illness.[60] Here the struggle it costs him to abstain from reading and writing during an episode of eye trouble contrasts with the easy renunciation of baths and wine in letter 1; here too, his physical self-discipline is assured, but nevertheless also supported by the presence of an unnamed *custos* (presumably, as Sherwin-White surmises, one of his doctors). Ill health enforces *otium*, then, with careful management and rationing of the more personal routines of *otium*, but which can also resemble *negotium* in barring the sufferer from books and pens (cf. 8.9.1 *olim non librum in manus, non stilum sumpsi*, 'for a long time I have taken neither book nor pen in hand').[61]

UMMIDIA QUADRATILLA

Finally, we turn to another nodal letter within the book, the obituary for Ummidia Quadratilla (7.24), which meditates upon a previously unexplored facet of *otium*: the nature and effects of women's *otium*. Pliny sketches for Rosianus Geminus (the addressee also of 7.1) a moral tale, tinged with affection and good humour, about the impeccable legacy and fundamentally sound values of a racy old lady.[62] Not only has Ummidia left an admirable will,[63] but her grandson Ummidius (with Fuscus one of Pliny's special protégés in 6.11) is a credit to her, having turned out chaste,

---

[60] On this letter, see Sherwin-White (1966) 428. For more on its addressee, Cornutus, see Chapter 5.

[61] For an epistolary assertion that ill health should affect only the body, and not one's normal intellectual activity, see Sen. *Ep.* 78.20–1, where even the process of wrestling with the disease is but another way of pursuing philosophical *studia*.

[62] On Ummidia Quadratilla, see Carlon (2009) 189–91, 204–11, Sick (1999).

[63] See Sherwin-White (1966) 431 on the parallel with Domitius Tullus' will in 8.18.

hardworking, studious and respectful. Despite her enthusiastic patronage of pantomimes and love of leisure games, Ummidia conscientiously protected Ummidius from moral contagion:

> uixit in contubernio auiae delicatae seuerissime, et tamen obsequentissime. habebat illa pantomimos fouebatque, effusius quam principi feminae conuenit. hos Quadratus non in theatro, non domi spectabat, nec illa exigebat. audiui ipsam cum mihi commendaret nepotis sui studia, solere se, ut feminam in illo otio sexus, laxare animum lusu calculorum, solere spectare pantomimos suos, sed cum factura esset alterutrum, semper se nepoti suo praecepisse abiret studeretque; quod mihi non amore eius magis facere quam reuerentia uidebatur. (7.24.3–5)

In the society of a grandmother addicted to pleasure he lived a life of extreme steadiness, and yet of compliance with her wishes. She had pantomimists in her employ, and interested herself more warmly in them than became a woman of her high rank. Neither at the theatre nor at home did Quadratus witness the performances of these men, and she did not require him to do so. I have heard her say herself, when commending to me her grandson's studious pursuits, that being a woman, with that leisure (*otio*) which is the lot of her sex, she was in the habit of relieving her mind by a game of draughts, or by watching the performances of her pantomimists; but that whenever she was about to do either of these things she always bade her grandson go off to his studies; and she seemed to me to do this from a sense of what was due to the youth as much as from her love for him.

This incongruous pair co-exist harmoniously in the same house because of Ummidia's clear-headed distinction between masculine *studia* and feminine *otium* (*in illo otio sexus*, 'that leisure which is the lot of her sex'); she is represented as aware of the dubious respectability of her tastes (though not, perhaps, as aware as she should be: she enjoys mimes *effusius quam principi feminae conuenit*, 'more warmly than became a woman of high rank'). She is by her own admission a frivolous old lady (and all the more fun to meet in a collection otherwise populated by soberly exemplary women),[64] but she knows what is really worthwhile: not her own life but that of her grandson. She fosters Ummidius' *studia* by encouraging more productive use of time she herself spends on frivolity but by lining up suitable masculine supervision;[65] in this case, of course, that means Pliny, who has her policy in this regard from her own lips (*cum mihi commendaret nepotis sui studia*, 'when she commended to me her grandson's

---

[64] On 7.24 making a pair with 7.19 on Fannia, see Fitzgerald (2007a) 210 n. 47.

[65] Ummidia acts as a kind of *praeceptor* (*semper se nepoti suo praecepisse abiret studeretque*, 'she always *instructed* her grandson to go off to his studies', 7.24.5) – a position analogous, in its way, to that of Pliny the Elder, who leaves his nephew studying when he sets sail towards Vesuvius.

studious pursuits', 7.24.5). As a result, Ummidius' complete ignorance of her actors' work before he attended the tribute performance after her death can be marked out as a wonder (*miraberis, et ego miratus sum*, 'you will be astonished, and so was I', 7.24.6), and the satisfactory education of a worthy master for the house (7.24.8) as a cause for joy.[66]

This is an *otium* letter, but it is not really *about* Ummidia's *otium*, although that topic is one of its most appealing elements. It is a letter about good guardianship and *reuerentia* on both sides of a familial relationship, and it shows how masculine propriety might co-exist with feminine (here distinctively urban) *otium* without harm to a family. It is also a letter about inheritance and tradition, and the protection of the new generation. It is entirely characteristic of Pliny that the first thing he is interested in in 7.24 is Ummidia's well-balanced will, while his last reflection is upon the good match between the tradition of her house (which once belonged to the consular lawyer Cassius Longinus) and the temperament and talent of its newest heir:

> implebit enim illam Quadratus meus et decebit, rursusque ei pristinam dignitatem celebritatem gloriam reddet, cum tantus orator inde procedet, quantus iuris ille consultus. (7.24.9)

> For my friend Quadratus will worthily fill it and become it, and once more restore to it its ancient dignity, celebrity and glory, since there will issue thence as great an orator as Cassius was a jurisconsult.

The result of Ummidia's *otium* – so utterly unlike that of Fuscus in 7.9, but (in its way) equally well managed – is, once again, a polished master orator, on the model of Pliny himself. Even a slightly reprehensible *otium*, then, may be redeemed by the production of something worthwhile and long-lasting; here Ummidia has left a testament to her fundamental observance of good values in the form of her grandson, and he in his turn will have a long posterity.[67]

---

[66] For contemporary concerns about the effect of careless rearing which allows young men to acquire a taste for theatre and for gladiators, cf. Messalla's strictures in Tac. *Dial.* 29.3.

[67] We might usefully compare the picture of Pliny working in peace in his *diaeta* (2.17.24) while the revels of the Saturnalia are going on elsewhere in his house (see discussion in Chapter 7); Ummidius is the image of Pliny both in his capacity to treat an older relative with reverence, despite differences in temperament, and in his separation from, and tolerance of, the more frivolous pleasures of others. 7.24, then, prepares the way thematically for Pliny's revelation that he spends long hours at the Laurentine villa on the unappealing task of revising his speeches. In this respect, too, 7.24 is the contrasting complement to Pliny's letters about his uncle, since it discusses the raising of a 'Plinian' orator by an elder who is too devoted either to work (in Pliny the Elder's case) or to pleasure (in Ummidia's).

CONCLUSION

Pliny's letters on *otium*, then, convey a set of didactic moral messages about the value of effort in life, and about the human need for variety in activities and preoccupations; they call upon their readers and addressees to make good use of leisure for long-term profit as well as for immediate refreshment. The letters themselves, however, are often instantiations of well-managed and thoughtful *otium* (as Fitzgerald says, 'the letter's the thing').[68] Connors rightly observes that smallness of scale and informality of tone are typically appropriate to a genre to be enjoyed in *otium*;[69] letters, then, are an ideal example of such a genre in Pliny's hands.

Indeed, one could argue that Pliny develops the letter as the prose genre most appropriate to *otium*, and the medium in which life's variety and repetitiveness alike may be most aptly depicted.[70] The life Pliny describes throughout his letter collection is one of variety and constant interruption, and such a life is faithfully represented in a complex design of sequences of short 'pieces' in which each one may adopt a radically different tone and topic from its immediate predecessor. If Pliny (paradoxically) seems to return to the same themes too often, repeatedly recycling his insistence on variety and alternation in life, it should perhaps be remembered that repetition is itself often a distinctive feature of epistolary communication; not only does a letter-writer say the same sorts of things to lots of different addressees, but letters record repeated thoughts because of their rootedness in 'today's moment' (hence the repetitiveness of the *Tristia*, of the *Heroides* and even of Cicero's collections). Any given letter-writer's 'signature' obsessions will be built into his or her letters in this way: Ovid's own misery in Tomis, the reproaches of his abandoned *Heroides*, Cicero's enraged despair at the death of the *res publica*, Fronto's hypochondria – and Pliny's commitment to variety. The design of Pliny's letter collection, indeed, preserves two very different 'reality effects' in offering variety and change of topic from letter to letter, while also mirroring and instantiating life's repetitiveness across any given book as a whole.

---

[68] Fitzgerald (2007a) 210.   [69] Connors (2000) 208.

[70] We should notice that even the locations Pliny recommends for *otium* foster and enhance variety and alternation between work and play (e.g. 8.8.4: *iucundum utrumque per iocum ludumque fluitantibus, ut flexerint cursum, laborem otio otium labore uariare*, 'it is an agreeable change for those who are afloat for sport and pastime to vary toil by repose or repose by toil, according as they shift their course').

Pliny's letter collection, in its variety and regularity alike, might also be
understood as a 'Senecan' study of man. For Seneca, *otium* is only properly
devoted to *studia*, but for him this means study of natural science and/or
moral philosophy.[71] Pliny, however (unlike his uncle), largely eschews traditional scientific study, and rare exceptions only prove the rule. In 4.30,
for example, he sends Licinius Sura a little puzzle from Pliny country (a
'local delicacy', as it were) in the form of a topic for scientific inquiry: the
possible reasons for the tidal behaviour of a small spring near Comum.[72]
However, just as he balances a refusal to write history (5.8) with a readiness
to supply 'historical' raw material to others (7.33), here Pliny leaves the
science to Licinius (in so far as the *recusatio* form allows), and confines his
ambitions to the descriptive writing in which he has declared his interest
in 1.2.[73]

A different kind of Plinian 'science', however, may be found in the first
of the great 'routine' letters, 3.1:

me autem ut certus siderum cursus ita uita hominum disposita delectat. senum
praesertim: nam iuuenes confusa adhuc quaedam et quasi turbata non indecent,
senibus placida omnia et ordinata conueniunt, quibus industria sera turpis ambitio
est. (3.1.2)

And for my part, just as the stars with their fixed course, so do the lives of men best
please me when they are methodical, and this particularly in the case of old men.
In young men a certain confusion as yet, and a certain disorder, so to speak, are
not unbecoming: a general repose and regularity are suitable to age, a time when
activity is out of date and ambition is discreditable.

Echoing Seneca's expectation that a gentleman's leisure time is best devoted
to scientific study of nature and its patterns, Pliny redefines his private
interest in people and their disposition of daily life as a study comparable to
that of astronomy: the regularity and fixedness of astronomical movements
are best matched by the well-regulated lives of old men rather than the
chaotic and restless ones of the young who still have their way to make
in the world. Pliny's letter collection studies the lives of others, instructs
his friends in how to follow (or avoid) the patterns of those lives, and
illustrates his own progress towards the perfectly ordered life (as revealed
at last in the 'routine' letters about himself late in the final book of the

---

[71] Sen. *Helu.* 8.6.

[72] The term he uses, *quaestio* (4.30.1), itself recalls Seneca's *Quaestiones Naturales*.

[73] Pliny the Elder, too, briefly discusses the phenomenon at *HN* 2.232; cf. *HN* 2.102 and Sen. *Q. Nat.*
6.16–17.

'literary' collection). It may not be too fanciful to suggest that although the letters purport to show Pliny engaging in literary study, the object of his contemplation which is most obviously on show, and which is most appropriately sketched and annotated in this genre, is the study of man and how man learns to act out ordered and controlled movements through life's variegated chaos.

CHAPTER 7

Reading the villa letters
9.7, 2.17, 5.6

Topos and topography persist in reacting with one another... To someone walking across... Dublin with Joyce, the scene will offer critical reflections on the text – not truth, despite the hard reality of streets and buildings, but another interpretation.

L.T. Pearcy, *Bryn Mawr Classical Review* 2002.07.07

The opulent modern resort of Bellagio nestles at the end of a long promontory which divides the lower half of Lake Como into the two forks of an upside down letter 'Y'.[1] Visitors to the town may tour the gardens of the Villa Serbelloni, which occupy the high ground of the promontory towering above Bellagio, and enjoy the views towards the Alps as they begin to rise north and west, with the Swiss border around 20 kilometres distant as the crow flies. If visitors now turn their gaze down the west fork of the lower lake, their attention will soon be caught by a smaller promontory jutting out a few kilometres away on the far side of the lake, which shelters a gently curving bay that is the shorefront of the modern village of Lenno.

Renaissance viewers knew how to interpret this scene, and proposed the high ground above Bellagio and the curving shoreline of Lenno as candidates for the location of Pliny's villas in the Lake Como area. In the first half of the sixteenth century, the learned Benedetto Giovio (1471–1545), native of Como, had already suggested Bellagio as the site for one of Pliny's villas. By 1570, Lenno had joined Bellagio in its association with Pliny. In a map published that year by Abraham Ortellius, the wording of *Letters* 9.7.3 (quoted later below) is adapted to mark Bellagio with the legend *in iugo huius prom. fuit villa Plinii quam Tragediam appellare solebat*, 'On the ridge of this promontory was the villa of Pliny which he called "Tragedy",' and Lenno with *hic olim Villa Plinii quam Comediam appellare solebat*, 'Here

---

[1] See the map found at the beginning of the present volume. For the many locations identified for Pliny's villas around Lake Como, see du Prey (1994) 3–14. For the long history of visitors to Lake Como in search of Pliny's villas, see Allain (1901–2) III.vii–xvii, lxxxvii–cii, 505–16.

once was the villa of Pliny which he called "Comedy".'[2] For Ortellius and his readers these have become the locations for a pair of villas described by Pliny in Book 9, where Comedy is said to stand in her characteristic slippers (*socculi*) low on a curving bay, while Tragedy towers on the platform heels worn by tragic actors (*cothurni*) well above the water on a high ridge which divides two bays.[3]

Letter 9.7 and its reception encapsulate, in fact, much of the fascination of Pliny's country villas: tourism, archaeology, the interaction of text and topography, and – with two villas which bear the names of literary genres – the suspicion that Pliny's residences may also bear the weight of his literary aspirations. Indeed letter 9.7 and (particularly) Pliny's earlier letters on his most famous properties – the Laurentine villa on the shore near Rome (2.17) and the Tuscan villa near ancient Tifernum (5.6) – have accumulated a massive bibliography since the Renaissance quite out of proportion to their status in the context of Pliny's *Letters* as a whole.[4]

The present chapter follows on from its predecessor inasmuch as it investigates a particular context for Pliny's *otium*; various intersections will emerge also with the portions of Chapter 4 devoted to Pliny's obsession with the management of his daily routine. The chapter begins by adopting the reading habits of the anthologist, extracting for study the three best-known letters on Pliny's villas (2.17, 5.6 and 9.7). As noted in the Introduction and (particularly) Chapter 2, the *Letters* are open to this piecemeal approach, and these three villa letters do respond to attempts to read them in isolation or – even better – in relation to one another. The immediate starting point is the Tragedy and Comedy letter introduced above (9.7). The many layers of this short piece – literary, historical, archaeological – are separated out and used in turn to ask questions about related features of the two longer villa letters in Books 2 and 5. In the process, fresh perspectives are gained on the mechanics of the collection, e.g. how later letters significantly alter our perceptions of earlier letters.

We follow this with a more intensive focus on 2.17 and 5.6, where we investigate the literary and ethical context for the description of a villa and

---

[2] Reproduced at du Prey (1994) 4–5.

[3] According to Allain (1901–2) III.viii n. 3, Giovio (Benedict Jovius) – historian of Como and author of the inscriptions underneath the statues of the Elder and Younger Plinii which decorate the façade of Como's cathedral (McHam (2005) 476–82) – was the first to identify Bellagio as the site of Tragedy; for that identification in his *Historiae Patriae Libri Duo*, see Giovio (1982) 232–3. On Giovio and his archaeological researches around Lake Como, see Zimmerman (1995) 4–5, 291–2 n. 9; for the strong association also of his brother Paolo with Plinian 'sites' on the lake, see du Prey (1994) 5–6; Zimmerman (1995) 161, 188–9; Lauterbach (1996) 132–6.

[4] For bibliography on the villa letters (and more generally on estates and Pliny's role as landowner in the *Letters*), see Appendix 3.

study the particular character of Pliny's descriptions of his properties and
the agenda behind them. The goal here is a deeper appreciation of Pliny's
talent for generating complex symbols for both himself and his letters.
In ancient thought the villa, like a man's speech, might be taken to be a
direct reflection of character,[5] and Pliny takes advantage of this so that his
villa letters come to embody his persona and mirror his various social and
literary agendas.

At the mid-point of the chapter we abandon the piecemeal approach
of the anthologist, and emphasize the benefits of reading Pliny's two most
intensively studied villa letters within their original contexts in Book 2 and
Book 5. Here we demonstrate that the pair play organic – and hitherto
unnoticed – roles within their books. That role for the Tuscan villa in Book
5 is intimately connected with the figure of the Elder Pliny (the object of
separate study already in Chapter 4) – long suspected as the owner of
the villa prior to the Younger. The *Letters* are scanned for clues to that
ownership, and questions are asked about how we are to read 5.6 in the
context of inferences – themselves encouraged by Book 5 as a whole – to
be made about the Elder as former occupier of the site.

Recent excavations, in fact, appear to confirm that the Younger inherited
the Tuscan villa from the Elder (of which more below), and in the final
sections of the chapter we turn our attention to the archaeology of Pliny's
villas. Here we argue – against the apparent consensus of literary critics –
that attempts to track down the sites of Pliny's estates represent a form of
authentic reaction to the villa letters. We demonstrate also the contributions
made by recent archaeological work to contextualizing Pliny's villa letters,
and suggest ways in which the excavations can deepen our understanding
of the purpose of these letters.

Taken as a whole, the larger purpose of this chapter is to demonstrate
the ability of letters within the collection to prosper under a wide range of
critical approaches, stretching from the metaliterary to the archaeological.
The varied approaches applied to Pliny's villa letters exemplify the critical
possibilities for the collection as a whole. Significantly, these approaches –
where they have not simply ignored one another – have often been at war.
Letters 2.17, 5.6 and 9.7 present a particularly good vantage point from
which to view the strife and its accompanying rhetoric of denunciation.
Literary critics insist that Pliny's descriptions of his villas serve literary and
symbolic agendas which have little to do with the provision of a floor plan

---

[5] See e.g. Bodel (1997) 5–6 on Sen. *Ep.* 86 (cf. Bodel (1997) 13 on Sen. *Ep.* 12.1); Henderson (2003)
120–4; Leach (2003) 154 on Cic. *Off.* 1.138–4. See also Myers (2005) 105–6, and cf. Cato *Agr.* 4.45.

or the data on villa life and rural management so beloved of economic historians. Architects and garden designers, nevertheless, have found in these same letters inspiration for their own villa plans and reconstructions. They in turn express fears of the limitations that archaeological discoveries might place on their creativity, only for archaeologists – ignoring both them and the literary critics – to apply themselves to a variety of locations stretching from Lake Como to the old Roman shoreline south of Ostia.[6] The present chapter seeks to integrate these approaches by way of demonstrating the ability of the villa letters to absorb (nearly) every sort of critical pressure. In this sense the villa letters stand duty in this chapter for the collection as a whole.

LETTER 9.7: TRAGEDY AND COMEDY ON LAKE COMO

Letter 9.7, perhaps the least often anthologized of the villa letters, is found in a book which is itself critically neglected. But Book 9 emerges in the present study – especially in Chapters 1 and above all 8 – as crucial to understanding how the collection asks to be read, and in the present chapter we shall see once again how letters in Book 9 may demand that earlier items be re-read in a new light. The more immediate purpose of a study of 9.7, however, is to introduce the issues raised by Pliny's villa letters, and to show how this short epistle helps us to make a first approach to the more complex letters on the Tuscan and Laurentine properties.

  In Book 9 almost one-quarter of the forty letters are set in or focus on Pliny's estates, including four out of the five closing epistles (9.36, 37, 39, 40). Letter 9.7 offers information to Voconius Romanus[7] on Pliny's building plans for two properties on Lake Como, although a passing remark makes it clear that these do not comprise the totality of his holdings there:

huius in litore plures meae uillae, sed duae maxime ut delectant ita exercent. (9.7.2)

There are several villas of mine on the shore of this lake, but two of them, while they greatly delight me, exercise me in an equal degree.

Pliny, we infer, owned three and probably more properties on the lake itself (to say nothing of agricultural holdings in the broader area). And what applies to his northern holdings may apply to his estates elsewhere. For Pliny, as a wealthy member of Rome's elite, will have owned numerous villas and estates scattered over Italy – like his grandfather-in-law

---

[6] Bergmann (1995) remains essential reading on methodological disagreements over the villa letters. For a bibliographical review of work produced on Pliny's estates, see Anguissola (2007).

[7] On this significant correspondent, see Chapter 5.

Calpurnius Fabatus, who, in addition to his estates in Comum, owned properties in Campania (6.30) and at Ameria in Umbria (8.20). Pliny did not put the whole of his life into the letters, such as the close connection he evidently had with Hispellum in Umbria, but which is barely visible in the correspondence.[8] One inference is that we should not see the properties mentioned by Pliny as reflecting the totality of his holdings, but rather as the product of a personal choice which included some and excluded others.[9] If, for example, Pliny, like many of his class, owned a villa on the Campanian coast, he withholds that information from us. Even among those houses mentioned by Pliny, not all receive equal emphasis. In particular his urban residence appears but once,[10] and at that in passing as he attempts briefly to summarize the first ten lines of an epigram by Martial which explains in riddling terms how the Muse may cross town to reach Pliny's house: *adloquitur Musam, mandat ut domum meam Esquilis quaerat, adeat reuerenter*, 'He addresses the Muse, commands her to seek my house on the Esquiline, and approach it respectfully' (3.21.5).[11] Pliny (subtly) makes it clear – since Martial does not – that his house was in the premier residential district of the Esquiline; but there are good reasons for the brevity of the elucidation. The advertisement of the self through one's house at Rome was hardly encouraged by the imperial system (contrast Cic. *Off.* 1.138, 140) and could flourish more easily at country residences.[12] At any rate, there is every reason to believe that Pliny owns more villas than he describes, and that those which are described have been carefully picked out with advertisement in mind.

The two Lake Como villas described by 9.7 are emphatically conceived as a pair linked by their internally opposed qualities:

altera imposita saxis more Baiano lacum prospicit, altera aeque more Baiano lacum tangit. itaque illam tragoediam, hanc appellare comoediam soleo, illam quod quasi cothurnis, hanc quod quasi socculis sustinetur. (9.7.3)

---

[8] See Champlin (2001), who shows that Pliny had strong ties with Umbria (as evidenced in the important inscription found at Hispellum: *CIL* 6.1552 = 11.5272, reproduced in Appendix 1 p. 272 n. 16), but that these ties are systematically underplayed in the *Letters* in favour of promoting links with his native town of Comum.

[9] For one reconstruction of the number of villas owned by Pliny, see Duncan-Jones (1982) 19–24.

[10] The house also appears by implication as Pliny's physical point of departure for short journeys within Rome (1.5.8, 5.9.1, 8.21.2–3) and no doubt as the scene of his many recitations (for the *domus* as the preferred locale for the *recitatio*, see White (1993) 293, Johnson (2010) 47–8). Unlike in the *Panegyricus* (Roche (2011b)), the distinctive landmarks and topography of Rome itself also largely go missing in Pliny's letters. On the city in epistolography, see Clark (2007).

[11] Mart. 10.20.1–10, with Henderson (2002a) 50–5; cf. Förtsch (1993) 17 n. 55. On Pliny's engagement with this poem, see also Chapter 3.

[12] See Bodel (1997) 7, 18–20, 31–2.

One of them, placed on the rocks, after the fashion of Baiae, overlooks the lake; another, similarly after the fashion of Baiae, is at the edge of the lake. Hence I am in the habit of calling the former 'Tragedy' and the latter 'Comedy', because one is supported as it were by high buskins, and the other by low slippers.

Tragedy on her ridge contrasts with the shore-side Comedy; cf. the same emphasis at 9.7.4 (quoted below). These contrasts are further elaborated in the remainder of the letter in a variety of ways, ranging from the view commanded by each to the opportunities offered either for fishing from the bedroom or watching fishermen ply their trade below. This emphasis on contrasting heights will remind readers of something revealed earlier about the Laurentine and Tuscan properties. The former is on the beach (2.17.27), while the latter is at the top of a (deceptively) high incline.[13] Readers are being encouraged to look back, as so often in Book 9. We are invited to re-read the Laurentine and Tuscan properties and epistles – though apparently built and composed separately – as an artistically conjoined and contrasting pair. And if we do look back, we will discover that the seaside Laurentine villa is exposed to the elements, while the Tuscan villa is calm; the former is rather compact (it is said to have numerous neighbouring properties along the shoreline), while the latter extends over a larger area (there are few neighbours, Pliny says, near the Tuscan villa). As du Prey rightly insists, 'it is obvious that Pliny liked writing pendant letters as much as he liked living in pairs of houses'.[14]

This encouragement to think of villas in terms of internally contrasting pairs receives an emphatic boost at the very end of Book 9, where Pliny describes his personal routines at the Tuscan (9.36) and Laurentine (9.40) villas. As argued in Chapter 4, the programmes of work here outlined ask to be read against the personal routines of Spurinna and the Elder Pliny as they appear in Book 3.[15] In the context of the present chapter, we note that the two villas are explicitly divided into summer residence ('You ask how I dispose of my day in summer-time at my place in Tuscany', 9.36.1) and winter residence ('You enquire what of all this is changed in winter-time at my Laurentine villa', 9.40.1). Here there are further signs of a design to convert these two villas, as described in Books 2 and 5, into a binary

---

[13] *uilla in colle imo sita prospicit quasi ex summo: ita leuiter et sensim cliuo fallente consurgit, ut cum ascendere te non putes, sentias ascendisse*, 'Situated at the bottom of a hill, my villa commands a view as if it were on the summit; so gentle and gradual is the unperceived rise that you realize you have made an ascent, without knowing you have been ascending' (5.6.14).

[14] Du Prey (1994) 13, 118. For the influence of such pairings on later architects, see du Prey (1994) 5, 37–8, 253–4, 333 n. 53. On the importance of alternation (of activities and places etc.) as a theme within Pliny, see Chapter 6.

[15] On letters 9.36 and 9.40, see also Chapter 6.

polarity to match the Lake Como properties described earlier in Book 9. As Tragedy is to Comedy, so the summer of the Tuscan villa is to the winter of the Laurentine villa.[16]

The contrast in Book 9 between this latter pair of villas is consistent, in some respects, with details found in the texts of the villa descriptions of 2.17 and 5.6. Pliny tells us that the Laurentine villa is only 17 miles from Rome (2.17.2, quoted below p. 220 n. 60), while in Book 10 we learn that the Tuscan estate is 150 miles distant (10.8.6), requiring a journey of five days or so to reach it (Sherwin-White (1966) 574–5 ad loc.). As such, the Laurentine is a plausible candidate for the normal winter residence, when Pliny must be in Rome to attend to business in court and senate. Furthermore, as Rossiter (2003) 356–9 notes, the Laurentine is buffeted by winds (2.17.4, 17), while the Tuscan has only 'a benign wind which circulates cool air through the dining room' (5.6.29); the benefits of shade are emphasized throughout 5.6, while 'at Laurentum [Pliny] is more concerned with how the building keeps its occupants warm', whether by means of the sun or man-made heat; and there are baths at both establishments, but the ones in the Tuscan property are mentioned for their ability to keep the bather cool. Nevertheless, the text of 2.17 contains plenty of references to summertime residence at the Laurentine villa (2.17.10, 17, 19), and references elsewhere in the collection bear this out (e.g. 7.4). Similarly elements of 5.6 emphasize the winter attractions and amenities of the Tuscan villa (e.g. 5.6.24, 28, 31, 34).[17]

Rossiter (2003) 359–60 suggests that Pliny's polarization of his villas in this way might simply be an example of elite posturing, in thrall to claims about the attractions of spending the seasons at different villas. We take also the lesson that Pliny is retrospectively imposing on the villa letters of Books 2 and 5 an emphasis which the texts themselves do not consistently support. And in this he has largely succeeded, as the assumption derived from 9.36 and 9.40 – that one villa is for winter and the other for summer – is firmly embedded in the scholarly literature. Not only, then, may Pliny be detected in the act of sculpting his villas so that they offer artistic contrasts as pairs, but we learn also that later letters may impose significant agendas on – even alter our perception of – earlier ones. Similarly, we have already seen in Chapter 1 that a single letter in Book 9 may initiate a significant re-reading of various letters in Book 1.

---

[16] Hoffer (1999) 34–5, 41 notes that Caninius Rufus' Comum villa in 1.3 already combines the virtues of Pliny's summer and winter residences. For a reading of this villa letter, see Hoffer (1999) 29–44.

[17] See also Förtsch (1993) 26–9.

Later letters also disclose facts about Pliny's Tuscan and Laurentine residences that reveal the villa tours of Books 2 and 5 to have been adapted to Pliny's needs in context for a particular effect. For example the *otium*-rich atmosphere of letter 5.6, with its emphasis on informality and relaxation, fosters an image of the Tuscan villa as an island of personal tranquillity. In Pliny's own words, *altius ibi otium et pinguius eoque securius: nulla necessitas togae, nemo accersitor ex proximo, placida omnia et quiescentia*, 'the leisure there is more profound, more calm, and consequently less liable to interruption. There is no need to put on one's toga; no callers from nearby; everything is peaceful and quiet' (5.6.45). Letter 9.36, by contrast, not only reveals the existence of erudite members of Pliny's *familia* with whom the villa owner might converse, but also the arrival of neighbours (*interueniunt amici ex proximis oppidis*, 'friends interrupt with visits from neighbouring towns', 9.36.5). The appearance of friends from nearby is not necessarily inconsistent with the absence of neighbours who invite Pliny out, but the contrast in spirit between the two letters is palpable. Equally striking is the belated introduction of a wife onto the set of the Tuscan villa (9.36.4), from which she has been heretofore rigorously excluded. Other letters, particularly in Books 7–9, hem the property in with tales of agricultural woe. And, as we shall see later, the image of the Laurentine villa of 2.17 suffers even more radical revision from the final letter of Book 9.

Returning to discussion of 9.7, if the names which Pliny gives to his properties, as Bergmann (1995) 416 points out, hint strongly at Pliny's willingness to project literary aspirations onto his villas, they point also to Pliny's entry into a literary game. In letter 9.7 two villa-women – Tragedy, Comedy and villas all being feminine in gender – effectively present themselves before a male viewer:

sua utrique amoenitas, et utraque possidenti ipsa diuersitate iucundior. haec lacu propius, illa latius utitur; haec unum sinum molli curuamine amplectitur, illa editissimo dorso duos dirimit; illic recta gestatio longo limite super litus extenditur, hic spatiosissimo xysto leuiter inflectitur; illa fluctus non sentit haec frangit; ex illa possis despicere piscantes, ex hac ipse piscari, hamumque de cubiculo ac paene etiam de lectulo ut e naucula iacere. (9.7.3–4)

Each of them has its special charm, and each is more attractive to the owner by its contrast with the other. One enjoys a nearer, the other a more extended view of the lake; one, with a gentle curve, embraces a small bay, the other, situated on a lofty summit, separates two small bays from each other; there a promenade stretches for a long way, in a straight line, above the shore, here it gently curves in the shape of a spacious terrace-walk; one of them does not feel the waves, and the other breaks them. From the former you can look down on the people fishing, from the latter you can fish yourself, and throw your line from your room, and actually from your bed almost, just as from a skiff.

Readers are being asked here to remember the Choice of Herakles (Xen. *Mem.* 2.1.21–34).[18] In this famous story, the hero meets Virtue and Vice (Arete and Kakia), where – as in Pliny – the contrasting physical charms of the female entities are catalogued (*Mem.* 2.1.21–4). Furthermore, just as Vice holds out to Herakles the prospect of pleasure and Virtue that of toil (*Mem.* 2.1.23–5, 27–30), so Pliny remarks on the delight offered, and the work entailed, by his two villas (9.7.2, quoted above p. 203).[19] However, Pliny's more immediate model is *Amores* 3.1,[20] where Ovid encounters the opposing poetic genres of Elegy and Tragedy:

> uenit odoratos Elegia nexa capillos,
>   et, puto, pes illi longior alter erat.
> forma decens, uestis tenuissima, uultus amantis,
>   et pedibus uitium causa decoris erat.   10
> uenit et ingenti uiolenta **Tragoedia** passu:
>   fronte comae torua, palla iacebat humi;
> laeua manus sceptrum late regale mouebat,
>   Lydius alta pedum uincla **cothurnus** erat

There came Elegy with coil of odorous locks, and, I think, one foot longer than the other. She had a becoming form, the thinnest of garments, the expression of a lover, and the fault in her feet added to her grace. There came, too, raging *Tragedy*, with mighty stride: on her scowling brow her locks lay in disorder, her robe trailed on the ground; her left hand swayed wide a kingly sceptre, and on her feet was the high bound Lydian *cothurnus*. (trans. G. Showerman and G.P. Goold, adapted)

Once more two 'women' present themselves before a male viewer, with their contrasting attributes systematically detailed. Clearly Pliny has taken this idea of poetic women and their footwear from Ovid, and given his

---

[18] 'High' and 'low' are written into the context for this tale, since Socrates quotes from Hesiod on the high road to Virtue and the easy road to Wickedness (*Mem.* 2.1.20, quoting Hes. *Op.* 285ff.). On this context, and the vigorous afterlife of the story in Ovid and beyond, see Gibson (2007) 72–6.

[19] For Pliny's collapse here of the polarities of the original, see below. The polarities of pleasure/pain and delight/effort – and their potential for collapse – are among Pliny's most characteristic motifs; see Chapter 6 on *labor* and *otium* (esp. 8.8.4), and for examples using *exercere* and *delectare* vel sim., cf. 2.14.1 (quoted above, p. 72), 6.7.3, 6.8.6, 7.9.12. Esp. relevant here is Pliny's description of the pain and pleasure derived from his mother's estates (almost certainly also in the Comum area): *me praedia materna parum commode tractant, **delectant** tamen ut materna*, 'The farms inherited from my mother are not treating me well; yet they delight me as coming from my mother' (2.15.2). In context these 'painful' estates also form a binary opposition with the purely pleasurable Laurentine estate described just two letters later in 2.17.

[20] Cf. also Ov. *Am.* 2.10.5–8. Pliny's older contemporary Silius Italicus produces a version in which Scipio encounters Virtus and Voluptas (*Pun.* 15.18–128).

villa high on a promontory the same platform boots of Tragedy, while his shoreline villa is given the low-heeled slipper in fact often associated elsewhere with Comedy.[21]

Where Herakles goes on (of course) to choose Arete, Ovid emphasizes the equal but contrasting attractions of both Tragedy and Elegy before choosing the latter – yet with a promise to return eventually to the former (*Am.* 3.1.61–8). Pliny's own contribution to this literary dialogue is to insist also on the equal and opposite attractions of his villa-women-genres, but to let it become apparent that no choice needs to be made (9.7.3, quoted above), such that he can decide to carry on building with both (*hae mihi causae utrique quae desunt adstruendi ob ea quae supersunt*, 'These are my reasons for adding to each what is wanting, in view of the advantages already enjoyed by both', 9.7.4). That Pliny does not have to make up his mind – despite his use of an Ovidian Choice of Herakles as a structuring device for the letter – is an enviably sophisticated way of drawing attention to the fact that, while one of his villas may be the equivalent of Ovid's Tragedy, his other villa is *not* Elegy, much less Kakia.[22] To put it another way, there is nothing wrong nowadays with building two equally beautiful villas. Far from being locked into a moral polarity, one can find oneself instead in the neutral territory of (not) choosing between two equally morally inoffensive but stylistically opposite genres. In Pliny, both roads now lead to virtue (and style),[23] and – as ever – he manages the feat of doing both of two opposed things at once.

The interplay of 9.7 with the Choice of Herakles constitutes fair warning that Pliny is not simply describing houses. Literary games are evident also in the comparison between Homer's shield of Achilles and his own description of the Tuscan villa in 5.6 (of which more later). But these amusements are harnessed to make a contribution to an older ethical debate in fact

---

[21] Cf. Ov. *Rem. am.* 375–6, Quint. *Inst.* 10.2.22. On the complex literary history and symbolism of the *cothurnus* and the *soccus*, see Gibson (2007) 28–9, 72–3. More generally, the linguistic division of Pliny's villas into 'hard' (Tragedy) and 'soft' (Comedy) recalls the same apportioning of feminine and masculine characteristics to Arete-Tragedy and Kakia-Elegy evident in the texts of both Xenophon and Ovid. E.g. Comedy in Pliny: *sinum molli curuamine . . . leuiter inflectitur*, 'with a gentle curve [embraces] a small bay . . . it gently curves' (noting also the string of diminutives at 9.7.4); and Tragedy: *editissimo dorso . . . recta gestatio . . .* 'on a lofty crag . . . a promenade [stretches] in a straight line . . .'. Cf. esp. Ov. *Am.* 3.1.9, 11 (on Elegy; quoted above).

[22] Cf. *Fast.* 5.1–110 where, in another version of the Choice of Herakles, Ovid is unable to make up his mind between the Muses' competing explanations for the name of the month of May. Plato's *Symposium* likewise ends with Socrates insisting on the artistic equivalence of tragedy and comedy.

[23] In the context of Book 9 this message is reinforced by the contrasting message of 9.3, where Pliny insists on the necessity of personal choice between opposing styles of life (9.3.2) but also displays uncharacteristic tolerance of those who choose the mortality of absolute leisure over the immortality achieved through hard work (on literary studies).

raised at the very beginning of the letter: *aedificare te scribis. bene est, inueni patrocinium*, 'You write that you are engaged on building. That is good, I have found my defence' (9.7.1). The verb *aedifico* and cognates have strong resonances in Roman moral discourse. Pliny's fellow northern Italian Cornelius Nepos had written in praise of Atticus that *nam cum esset pecuniosus, nemo illo minus fuit emax, minus aedificator*, 'for although he was well off, no one was less inclined to buying or building' (*Att.* 13.1) – indeed Atticus allegedly owned no suburban or seaside villa, and his country estates were few (*Att.* 14.3) – and Juvenal would soon write 'Caetronius was a builder [*aedificator*]', in condemnation of a man who built 'now on the curving shore of Caieta, now on the heights of Tibur' (*Sat.* 14.86–7).

But the content of Pliny's letter rather defuses these criticisms: building is not an ethical dilemma, but an aesthetic option, even where both options resemble the shoreline of Baiae (9.7.3, quoted above), whose attractions had received traditional condemnation in Seneca's letters.[24] Needless to say, Pliny is not being too controversial here. For alongside this older and harsher tradition of the condemnation of private building as *luxuria*,[25] there had grown up in recent times a tradition of positive praise for the luxury dwellings of wealthy patrons, where magnificent estates are made to reflect the culture and taste of their owners.[26] Pliny turns this tradition to account when writing in praise of his own villas, which are conspicuous less for the luxury of their appointments than for the reflection they provide of Pliny's own highbrow tastes for literary games.

Yet, for all that Pliny's northern villas are sculpted into a contrasting pair and freighted with symbolism, the archaeology of Lake Como still offers us something of value for understanding letter 9.7. There is in fact no convincing material evidence for the locations of Tragedy and Comedy.[27] The closest connection between Pliny and Bellagio comes in the form of an inscription discovered in the vicinity which records the presence of a member of the *gens Plinia*, identified by Syme with the addressee of two letters later in Book 9.[28] Nevertheless, the local traditions feeding into

---

[24] Pliny perhaps means particularly to collapse Seneca's polarity between fortress houses built on the heights of Baiae (good) versus pleasure palaces built on the shores of Baiae (bad), found at *Epist.* 51.11–12. However, a crucial term in Seneca's text is corrupt; see Bickel (1958).

[25] Cf. e.g. Lucr. 3.1060–7, Varro *Rust.* 1.13.6–7, Sall. *Cat.* 12.3, 20.11–12, Petron. *Sat.* 120.88, Sen. *Tranq.* 2.13–14; D'Arms (1970) 40–3, 116–20; Bergmann (1991) 62–4; Leach (2003) 149–52.

[26] See Leach (2003) 152–4 and Myers (2005) 103–11 on Martial and Statius.

[27] See Allain (1901–2) III.viii–x, xiii–xiv, 506–10 for an unwitting evocation of the meagreness of the evidence.

[28] *CIL* 5.5521 M. Plinius Sab[...: identified by Syme, *RP* 7.510 n. 104 with the Sabinianus of 9.21, 24. In the sixteenth century, Benedetto Giovio reported a find on the high ground above Bellagio of

Abraham Ortellius' map of Lake Como appear to have been responding to the inner logic of 9.7. Consequently Lenno and Bellagio possess real interpretative power. For these sites are clearly visible from each other, although there is no specific requirement in the text of letter 9.7 that the same should obtain for the pair of villas named Comedy and Tragedy. But if a visitor were to cross by boat between them – still the most convenient method of transport around Lake Como – and, viewing both locations from a midpoint, were to ask himself (*sic*) which he preferred, then he would be replicating the visual dynamic implicit in the Choice of Herakles which in fact also animates the epistle in Book 9 (even if the need to make a choice is here ultimately removed). Lenno and Bellagio, in other words, offer an arrestingly good topographical interpretation of the text.

LETTERS 2.17 AND 5.6: CONTEXTS, CONTENTS, CHARACTER

Letter 9.7 on the villas of Lake Como has acted as a useful introduction to the literary, historical and archaeological issues raised by Pliny's villa letters in Books 2 and 5. We have seen that in Pliny a villa description may be anything but neutral or objective. Rather villas may be selected from a larger available group, visibly shaped so as to form contrasting pairs (and this a product of letters late in the collection shaping our perception of earlier books), or deployed as ciphers in a literary game which is also designed to tell us something about the character of the owner. Finally, we have seen that the actual Italian landscape may interact with a letter to enhance a reading of its text.

It is now time to turn our attention more closely to letters 2.17 and 5.6, treating first their contexts and contents, followed by reflections on the quality and character of those contents.

It has often been observed that the villa tour, although foreshadowed in earlier literature (above all Horace), does not take definitive shape as a literary exercise until the mid first century AD, where, as Guillemin (1929) 142 suggests, standard subjects for description are glimpsed in Seneca's fifty-fifth letter on the Baian complex of Servilius Vatia.[29] Nevertheless, it is Pliny's older contemporaries Statius and Martial who give decisive impetus

---

'fragments of a broken *monumentum* of a certain Marcus Plinius' (Giovio (1982) 233). (For members of the *gens* in the region, see Bacchiega (1993).) The spring mentioned at Pliny 4.30 is also preserved at the modern Villa Pliniana near Torno on Lake Como; cf. du Prey (1994) 6, also Meulemans (1913).

[29] For a full survey of the Roman tradition of description of estates – with a special emphasis on gardens – see Littlewood (1987).

to what Stephen Hinds has happily named the 'poetics of real estate'.[30] Their descriptions of the residences of wealthy patrons set a precedent for Pliny in the description of his own residences – where, of course, Pliny may speak as owner rather than client. In *Siluae* 1.3 Statius praises the artifice and luxury of the estate of the Epicurean *littérateur* Manlius Vopiscus, whose villa occupies both sides of the river Anio at a site above Tibur, while *Siluae* 2.2 offers a detailed panegyric of Pollius Felix's costly establishment on the heights at Surrentum.[31] What is new here in Statius, as Guillemin (1929) 142 suggests, is that a reader is taken on a celebratory tour *inside* the house. Previous efforts had concentrated largely on the façade of the villa and surrounding grounds. Seneca happily described the grottoes and artificial streams in the estate of Servilius Vatia, but a visit inside the austere residence of Scipio at Liternum provokes moral disapprobation of contemporary bathing luxury (*Ep.* 86.4–13; cf. 89.21, 90.7–10, 25, 43; 122.8), and elsewhere reflections on personal senescence and decay (12.1–2).

With Statius and later Pliny, furthermore, not only do certain elements of the external description of the estate begin to show signs of formalization,[32] but so already do the elements of internal description including architectural features exposed to the elements (Stat. *Silu.* 2.2.50, Pliny 2.17.5) and baths with both indoor and outdoor amenities (Stat. *Silu.* 1.3.44, 2.2.17–19, Pliny 2.17.11).[33] One might go further and observe, with Myers (2005) 111–13, that the two villas of Statius are paired, like those of Pliny: one inland and one seaside villa; one at ground level and one raised high above its environment.

Yet for all the similarities, one difference is striking. The interiors of Pliny's villas contain little in the way of luxury materials or commodities, so conspicuous in the *encomia* of Statius (e.g. *Silu.* 1.3.34–7, 47–57; 2.2.63–72, 83–97). The Elder Pliny, it is worth observing, had made clear his own hostility to luxury establishments (*HN* 9.170, 36.6, 36.109), and suggestions of extravagance are accordingly moved out into the gardens of the Younger's villas.[34]

---

[30] Hinds (2001). For bibliography on Pliny's relations with the poetry of Martial and Statius, see Appendix 3.

[31] *Silu.* 1.3 effectively throws down the gauntlet to Pliny, for a location on the *ager Laurens* is listed among those that must give way to the villa of Manlius Vopiscus (*Silu.* 1.3.83–4, quoted below p. 232 n. 111). On *Silu.* 2.2, see further Bergmann (1991) 51ff., Newlands (2011) 12–15, 120–57.

[32] See Guillemin (1929) 142. For the parallel emphasis in Pliny and Statius on views from the villa (Stat. *Silu.* 1.3.18–19, Pliny 5.6.7), see further Bergmann (1991) 58, 59–61, noting their denunciation in Sen. *Ep.* 89.21.

[33] Further examples in Guillemin (1929) 142–3.

[34] Note especially the costly marble fixtures and setting of the *stibadium* described at 5.6.36–40; see further Hoffer (1999) 35, Leach (2003) 155–6, Myers (2005) 116–17.

Moving from context to content, we begin with the observation that letters 2.17 and 5.6 are respectively the third-longest and longest of all Pliny's epistles. Although their contents defy brief summary,[35] it can nevertheless be observed that the tours proper both end at the same point, with Pliny's description of that part of the estate in which he can most fully hide himself away: the *diaeta* or private suite of rooms inside the Laurentine villa (2.17.20–4) and the *zothecula* or hidden alcove in the gardens of the Tuscan villa (5.6.38–40).[36] There is likewise a shared similar grand structure, with opening friendly response to an earlier query or remark by the addressee (2.17.1, 5.6.1–3), a setting of the villa in its landscape (2.17.2–3, 5.6.4–13), and a long central section on the interior of the villa (2.17.4–24, 5.6.14–31) followed by a focus on surrounding amenities (2.17.25–9, 5.6.32–40).[37]

Yet if the architecture of the two letters is similar, the same does not hold for the character of their descriptive contents. Du Prey (1994) 21, observing that later architects have generally preferred to sketch the Laurentine villa, attributes this to the fact that the Tuscan villa letter, with its emphasis on recreation and informality, shows more 'easygoing amorphousness' and is perhaps rather vaguer in its descriptions than the Laurentine. Nevertheless, both letters lack architectural precision, and in general Pliny is stronger on general orientation, views from the villa and the effects of the seasons than he is on internal decoration or architectural framework.[38] In fact, it would not be too much to say that the letters are tortuously hard to follow.[39] As if it were not hard enough to visualize three-dimensional space from a purely textual description, Pliny ramps up the difficulty for the reader. For, by the reckoning of Riggsby (2003) 170, the two letters list 'thirty-eight and twenty-eight distinct rooms respectively, as well as ten un-segmented suites and numerous courtyards and other outdoor areas. Of these, he describes the shape of only two and the furnishings of a few more. Nor does he generally tell us what the spaces were used for.' In view of this it comes as no surprise to learn that Pliny's villa letters made their first appreciable impact in Renaissance and early modern times not on the design

---

[35] For a list of features mentioned by Pliny in their 'narrative' order, see Tanzer (1924) 44, 108.

[36] Cf. Chapter 5 for a sequence of letters in Book 7 in which Calestrius Tiro is invited into increasingly private domestic spaces.

[37] See further Förtsch (1993) 25–9, Goalen (2001) 43–4.

[38] Du Prey (1994) 26; cf. du Prey (1994) 118.

[39] Du Prey (1994) 27–8; cf. Bergmann (1995) 409–10 on puzzling omissions and technical terms found in 2.17 and 5.6. Contrast Pliny's willingness in the nearby 2.19.5–8 to discuss the difficulties in comprehending a technical legal case.

of houses, but rather on gardens.[40] Perhaps it is Pliny's idea of a joke to make the reader work hardest precisely when he is describing his arenas for *otium*.

Yet the very difficulty – like the gaps in Pliny's epistolary autobiography identified in Chapter 1 – is also undoubtedly alluring. In the words of du Prey (1994) 28, 'The sauntering, meandering quality of Pliny's villas... suggests a flexibility of planning to the would-be emulator who takes Pliny at his word.'[41] Hence the variety of floor plans and restitutions proposed by scholars and architects over the last centuries – the very subject matter of du Prey's book on *The Villas of Pliny: From Antiquity to Posterity*.[42] Further enlightenment on why Pliny's villa letters are hard to follow – or easy to interpret in a great variety of ways – is provided by Riggsby (2003) 169–70, who points out that the villa letters, despite the strong sense of movement through space often noted as a feature of the letters (e.g. by du Prey (1994) 26), ultimately provide neither maps of the residences nor itineraries through them.[43] Here 'rooms [are not] generally given an orientation relative to each other. Instead of direction [or route], Pliny merely notes adjacency. Instead of left, right, forward or the like, one reads simply adverbs like *hinc, inde, mox*, or *deinde* or verbs like *adnectitur, adhaeret, adiacet*, or *adplicitum est*.' The result is 'a set of isolated islands', where 'what carries the weight of his description is a plethora of names – thirty in fact', and the notion of an itinerary through the villas 'is an illusion created by the inherently linear nature of a letter'.[44]

LETTERS 2.17 AND 5.6: THE LITERARY AND SOCIAL AGENDA

Are then these vague and tortuous villa letters the product of a mere amateur,[45] an example of failed description? It is fair to say the majority of recent critics have interpreted Pliny's 'failure' to offer a full or realistic visualization of his estates as one indication that the letters have another agenda. One obvious possibility is that the villas are largely the starting point for a virtuoso literary performance in the ecphrastic mode. Such is suggested not only by the numerous parallels noted above with earlier examples of the genre, but also by the coda to letter 5.6, where Pliny defends

---

[40] See du Prey (1994) 28, 32–5.
[41] Cf. Bergmann (1995) 417–18, also Hunt (2001) 32 on the similar attractions of Horace's estates.
[42] On the reception of Pliny more generally, see Appendix 3.
[43] Cf. Bergmann (1995) 410; cf. also Bergmann (1991) 57 on similar qualities in Stat. *Silu.* 2.2.
[44] See further Riggsby (2003) 171–5 for Pliny's description in qualitative rather than quantitative terms.
[45] Cf. du Prey (1994) 8–9, 23–5.

the length of his description by aligning it with ecphrases in the *Iliad* and *Aeneid*:[46]

uides quot uersibus Homerus, quot Vergilius arma hic Aeneae Achillis ille describat; breuis tamen uterque est quia facit quod instituit . . . non enim excursus hic eius, sed opus ipsum est. similiter nos ut 'parua magnis', cum totam uillam oculis tuis subicere conamur, si nihil inductum et quasi deuium loquimur, non epistula quae describit sed uilla quae describitur magna est. (5.6.43–4)

You see the number of lines in which Homer and Vergil describe, the one arms of Aeneas, the other those of Achilles; yet each of them is brief, because he is only doing what he proposed to do . . . here is no digression on his part, it is the very work he has to do. Similarly, in my case (to compare small things with great), when I am trying to set the whole villa before your eyes, provided I say nothing alien to the subject and as it were out of the way, it is not the letter which gives the description, but the villa which is described, that is of great size.

Not only has epic enterprise and planning gone into the description of the Tuscan villa,[47] but – so the analogy allows – as the ecphrasis of the shield of Achilles is to the *Iliad*, so the description of Pliny's villa is to his collection of letters. All three share the fruits of intense artistic labour, and all are parts of larger works. And from Pliny's acknowledgement of ecphrastic self-consciousness in letter 5.6, it is a short step towards seeing that the villa descriptions are a meditation on the letter-form as a work of art. Ever since the fourth book of Vergil's *Georgics*, the description of a garden's design might be taken to represent the literary skills of the author in the handling of his material, while the artifice of the villa and gardens described by Statius certainly mirror the extravagant poetics of the *Siluae*.[48] In 5.6 Pliny encourages a similar understanding of his own texts by drawing an explicit comparison between the experience of walking round his impressive villa and of reading the lengthy letter which describes it: 'Nor was I afraid that you would be wearied with reading what you would not weary of seeing in person, especially as you might rest at intervals, if so disposed, and laying down the letter, often take a seat, as it were [*depositaque epistula quasi residere saepius posses*]' (5.6.41).

The analogy between villa and letter offers the reader a licence to understand the terms of the description of the building as embodying Pliny's

---

[46] For 5.6 not just as an example of ecphrasis, but as an extended theoretical discourse on the problem of description and representation, see Chinn (2007).

[47] Note that Pliny also assimilates his 'greatest ever' speech to the shield of Aeneas in 6.33.1 (quoted above p. 40) with a citation from Verg. *Aen.* 8.439, and there awards himself the analogical role of master craftsman (Vulcan).

[48] See Myers (2005) 105, 107, 111, Newlands (2002) 119–98.

literary programme for his epistolary project. If the stated aim of the letter is to describe the *whole* villa (5.6.44, quoted above), then, in the summary of Myers (2005) 123, 'he justifies the enumeration of *minutiae* not just in this letter, but in the collection as a whole . . . The desire to visit (or own) his estate created by reading the letter (2.17.29) . . . translates into an appetite for Pliny's writings . . . The emphasis on the *uariatio* of the landscapes and the *dispositio* of the estates coincides with rhetorical precepts and with the composition of his *Epistles*.'[49] One might add that the villas, described as essentially collections of rooms of varying function, have much in common with the 'managed miscellaneity' which is a feature both of Pliny's life and his letter collection; see further Chapter 8.

Many readers have sensed more generally in the letters what Bergmann has called an 'insistently metaphorical quality' ((1995) 410). This perception can be related in part to the influence exerted on many readers by knowledge of a mnemonic exercise famously recommended by Pliny's old mentor Quintilian (*Inst.* 11.2.18, 20), where a public speaker learns to order his material and lodge it in the memory by fixing it to a tour through a great house, beginning with *uestibulum, atrium*, and so on into the *cubicula* and beyond.[50] The approach may yet be taken further; one critic has argued that we are viewing here 'rhetorical exercises . . . the letters follow the typical steps of an *argumentatio*, in which Pliny uses Greek terms and concepts to demonstrate his erudition'.[51]

Nevertheless, for all the allure of uncovering hidden or coded meanings in 2.17 and 5.6, there is one obvious way in which these letters are about something other than – yet closely connected to – the buildings themselves. For they necessarily offer a portrait of their owner. At the outset of the chapter mention was made of the tendency within elite Roman culture to see the villa – like style of speech – as a reflection of the character of the man. The virtual absence of other human figures is one clue to the fact that 2.17 and 5.6 are self-portraits.[52] So too are Pliny's insistence on the ultimately modest size of the estates; the striking absence of such interior details as sculpture, paintings or furniture (with the exception of the bookcase in 2.17.8 and the wall-painting of birds in 5.6.22); and the scant attention given to accommodation for slaves and freedmen (cf. 2.17.9). Together these omissions and emphases create a very particular image of

[49] Cf. Henderson (2002a) 15–20, (2003) 119, 121–2; also McEwen (1995).
[50] See further Goalen (2001) 45, more generally Baroin (1998), Bergmann (1994).
[51] A. Drummer, as reported by Bergmann (1995) 408; cf. Bergmann (1995) 409–10.
[52] For the distinction here from the villas of Cicero, which are often the scenes for dialogue between interlocutors, see Scivoletto (1989).

the owner: a man who stands unimpeded in our full view, unconcerned with the mundanities of daily life, and the epitome of good taste yet never extravagant. The approach can be extended to the very details of the houses which Pliny chooses to emphasize or reveal: the Tuscan villa, at the top of a rise but beneath a higher slope (5.6.14), can be seen to reflect Pliny's place on the social ladder; the visibility of the Laurentine villa on the shore and Pliny's obsession there with catching sunlight (2.17.7, 20, 27) speak of Pliny's ambitions and love of 'conventional approval, imperial benevolence, glory and honour'.[53]

THE LAURENTINE VILLA IN THE CONTEXT OF BOOK 2

For all the insistence by critics on seeing the villa letters as fundamentally a portrait of their owner, it can be argued that viewing the letters in isolation from their immediate contexts results in a significantly incomplete appreciation of the quality of the image. In order to gain a fuller appreciation of the portrait, we abandon – as promised at the beginning of this chapter – the piecemeal approach of the anthologist and now read the letters within the context of the book in which each is found.[54] Indeed Pliny, by comparing his Tuscan villa letter to the Shield of Achilles – an ecphrasis which is organically connected to the larger literary work of which it is a part – implicitly issues the reader with an invitation to read his villa letters within their surrounding literary contexts. As will become evident below, it is the function of letter 2.17 to act as thematic counterweight to a repeated emphasis in Book 2 on a growing mound of business. In turn it will be seen that, despite a larger tendency to see 'the villa as the man', Book 2 makes it plain that 2.17 can offer only a very partial picture. For a truly rounded expression of his character through his homes, Pliny would need to provide a detailed description also of his Esquiline town house; but, for reasons already noted at the beginning of this chapter, a consular orator in Pliny's day would have reason to refrain from such a naive piece of self-display. The full expression of a person's character through their country residence (or routine there) is possible only for a character like Spurinna in letter 3.1, who has retired to his villa for the evening of his life after a lifetime's public service. Pliny, by contrast, still has much to offer, and his villas – scenes of *otium* – cannot express this fully.

---

[53] See Henderson (2003) 120–4, (2002a) 17, 20; also Bergmann (1995) 409, Myers (2005) 114–15, 119–20.

[54] For a catalogue of the contents and addressees of letters in Book 2, see Appendix 2.

The first seven letters of Book 2 display characteristic *uarietas* in their subject matter, including courtesy notes (2.2), descriptions of a dinner party (2.6), and the happy report of a statue voted for Spurinna and his son (2.7). Letter 2.8 sounds a warning note: business is piling up for Pliny: 'For fresh business is always growing on to the old, and yet the old is not yet complete. So numerous are the coils, so numerous the links, so to speak, by which the chain of my occupations is daily extended' (2.8.3). This is borne out to some extent by the letters which follow, and in the process we receive a thematic corrective to the second letter of the book, where Pliny was able to declare: *ipse ad uillam partim studiis partim desidia fruor, quorum utrumque ex otio nascitur*, 'I am myself at my villa, in the enjoyment partly of study, partly of indolence: leisure is the parent of both' (2.2.2). For in 2.11 and 12 Pliny gives an account of his role in the trial of Marius Priscus, while 2.14's weary report of decline in courtroom standards begins with an assertion of preoccupation with legal business (2.14.1, quoted above p. 72). Such preoccupations find a reflection in the speech which Pliny has been asked to recite before an audience in 2.19, but where he fears the demanding technicalities of the speech might put an audience off.[55] Alongside this avalanche of legal business Pliny puts on display his performance of a series of personal *officia*.[56] Furthermore, while Pliny makes enquiries after the *otium* of *others* in their estates in a sequence of letters in the middle of the book,[57] it is only towards the end that Pliny returns to the theme hinted at briefly in 2.2 and expatiates on the leisure that he enjoys at *his own* Laurentine estate in 2.17.

Thematically, it will now be seen, 2.17 serves as a counterbalance to all the emphasis in Book 2 on hard work and personal duties. In particular, at 1,086 words long, 2.17 is clearly meant to act as a counterweight to 2.11–12, which themselves together weigh in at 1,084 words long.[58] 2.17 and 2.11 (with 2.12) in fact tower over the book like twin peaks and as such ask to be read in tandem. Together they give a full portrait of the two

---

[55] Compare similarly 2.5, where Pliny refers to a recently completed speech on municipal property for a civil suit.

[56] See 2.9 (canvassing for the elections of a protégé), 2.13 (a letter of recommendation), 2.16 (dealings with matters of inheritance even outside the Centumviral courts) and 2.18 (a search for a tutor for an old friend's children).

[57] Cf e.g. 2.8 (to Caninius Rufus on his Comum estates), 2.11.24–5 (request for news of the fruit-trees and vines of Arrianus' lands), and 2.15 (an enquiry into the pleasure given Valerianus by his newly purchased estates).

[58] This is in the context of a book where the next longest letter contains 396 words, and the shortest contains 51 words; for a useful provision of word counts for each letter in the nine-book collection, see Carlon (2009) 227–39. For further comment on the near symmetry here between 2.11/12 and 2.17, see Whitton (2010).

sides of Pliny's life: preoccupation with legal affairs versus the leisure of the Laurentine villa. Hence, as suggested earlier, the villa cannot give a full picture of the character of its owner. Such a thing can be provided only by a careful reading of the book in which the Laurentine villa is set. In order for 2.17 to perform the role of *otium*-rich counterweight to public duties of 2.11 and 2.12, anything overly suggestive of *negotium* and *officium* must be removed from the villa (or downplayed). As we have seen, letter 2.17 is largely a list of rooms in the Laurentine villa, but does end up with a detailed description of Pliny's beloved *diaeta* where he can bury himself away from the rest of the house:

in hanc ego diaetam cum me recepi, abesse mihi etiam a uilla mea uideor, magnamque eius uoluptatem praecipue Saturnalibus capio, cum reliqua pars tecti licentia dierum festisque clamoribus personat; nam nec ipse meorum lusibus nec illi studiis meis obstrepunt. (2.17.24)

After taking myself into this annexe, it seems to me that I have got away even from my villa, and I derive especial enjoyment from it at the Saturnalia, when the other parts of the establishment are ringing with the freedom and festive shouts of that season; for then I am no obstacle to the games of my household, nor are they to my studies.

Here is Pliny's haven for *studia*. Both this *diaeta* and the tour of the villa which precedes it are largely kept free of the taint of legal business or cares of estate management. As we are manoeuvred from dining room to gymnasium to ball-court to baths to swimming pool to covered walkway to garden – and the views of sea or landscape which each provides – only the faintest of hints of mundane cares reach the reader, with the occasional mention of a granary here or brief discussion there of how supplies are obtained.

That 2.17 has been deliberately tidied up in this respect is suggested above all by a passage in the very final letter of the nine-book collection:[59]

si agendi necessitas instat, quae frequens hieme, non iam comoedo uel lyristae post cenam locus, sed illa, quae dictaui, identidem retractantur, ac simul memoriae frequenti emendatione proficitur. (9.40.2)

If there is any pressing necessity for appearing in court (as there often is in winter), there is no longer place for a comedian or a lyrical performer after dinner, but I often go over again what I have dictated, and at the same time my memory is helped by this frequent revision.

---

[59] On the broader significance of this passage, see Chapter 8.

Now it appears that the Laurentine villa is the habitual scene in the winter months of preparation for appearances in court. No time, under these circumstances, for after-dinner entertainment, but Pliny must revise his dictations with a view to improving his upcoming performance. In 2.17 Pliny had allowed readers to make the inference that the undescribed Esquiline house was the only scene of such preparation for appearances in the nearby courts;[60] but we now stand corrected. Pliny reveals here in Book 9 what he did not choose to emphasize in Book 2: that the Laurentine house was a place for long nights of labour. This belatedly reveals the extent to which 2.17 has been largely cleared of unwelcome 'business' in order to turn it into a counterweight to the emphasis elsewhere in Book 2 on legal work.[61] Had Pliny revealed in 2.17 that a suite of rooms was reserved for working on his courtroom speeches, that would have somewhat muddied the clarity of the contrast.

That 2.17 can only express one aspect of Pliny's character finds confirmation soon after in 3.1, where Pliny visits the residence of Spurinna. Here we gain a fresh perspective on the exemplarity of this senior figure. As shown in Chapter 4, Spurinna now spends all his time at his villa following a fixed daily routine. Pliny professes admiration for Spurinna's way of life, but ends the letter by making it clear that such a life cannot yet be his lot (3.1.11–12, quoted above pp. 120, 122). If 2.17 lets us see that Pliny's life already resembles Spurinna's at least when he is in residence at the Laurentine villa, the reference in 3.1.11 to being 'exhausted by a thousand tasks' reminds us that the rest of Pliny's life is rather more like the rest of Book 2. Having a good time all the time at one's villa is only for the elderly and retired – that is to say, by conventional Roman thinking, for the marginalized.[62]

The contrast is further reinforced by a reversal in descriptive technique between the two letters. For if 2.17 is in effect a catalogue of room names where associated activities must be inferred by readers,[63] then letter 3.1 is a list of activities whose physical location is left largely to our imagination. Not only is the geographical site of Spurinna's country villa left unspecified (3.1.1; contrast 2.17.2), but the rooms and

---

[60] Cf. 2.17.2 (on the Laurentine villa) *decem septem milibus passuum ab urbe secessit, ut peractis quae agenda fuerint saluo iam et composito die possis ibi manere*, 'It is only seventeen miles distant from Rome, so that having got through all you had to do, you can go and stay there with your day's work already secured and disposed of'; cf. the quotation at 3.21.5 of Mart. 10.20.14–18.

[61] In this context, the repeated emphasis in 2.17 on shelter from the elements makes particular thematic sense (in addition to the veristic sense, where protection from the elements is a necessary feature of a seaside villa).

[62] Riggsby (1998) 85–6.   [63] See Riggsby (2003) 170.

spaces in which his daily activities are conducted go unnamed: *lectulo continetur... ambulat... considit... uehiculum ascendit... ambulat... scribit... mouetur pila... lotus accubat... adponitur cena...*, 'he lies on his couch... walks... sits down... steps into his carriage... walks... writes... a ball is thrown... after his bath he lies down... dinner is served...'. The only room actually named in 3.1 is the *cubiculum* where Spurinna composes his verse in the afternoon (3.1.7). Put another way, where 2.17 operates by means of nouns (*gymnasium, balineum, triclinium*), 3.1 operates by verbs (*mouetur pila, lotus accubat*). The thoroughgoing extent to which this reversal in descriptive technique is sustained suggests a very deliberate artistic experiment by Pliny. Spurinna's villa is not allowed to compete in our imaginations with the nearby Laurentine. Not only that, but the combination of essential sameness and profound difference implicit in the mirror-image reversal perhaps encourages the reader to ask how Pliny's life is similar to Spurinna and in what sense it radically differs. Pliny cannot adopt the same mode of description for both himself and Spurinna, as his life is shared with Spurinna only during the short intervals of time spent at the Laurentine villa.

THE TUSCAN VILLA IN THE CONTEXT OF BOOK 5

Letter 5.16 may be shown (more briefly) to have a close relationship with other letters in its book.[64] Our analysis will culminate with speculation about the prior ownership of the Tuscan villa, which in turn will allow the introduction in the final part of the chapter of an important intersection between text and topography. The goal, as stated earlier, is to create an example of the integration of literary and historical or archaeological approaches.

A subtle thematic thread runs through a number of letters in Book 5, evoking the memory of the Elder Pliny. Pliny's adoptive father was notoriously hostile to poetry, yet the Younger defends his own practice of the art in letter 5.3 with a long list of senatorial figures – many of whom are rather better known as orators or generals than as versifiers.[65] Sherwin-White's acute observation that 'The list suggests the pedantic learning of Pliny's uncle' allows us in turn to suggest that the Younger is deliberately using a characteristic mannerism of the *Natural History* – the learned catalogue of practitioners – to defend a type of activity to

---

[64] For a catalogue of the contents and addressees of letters in Book 5, see Appendix 2.
[65] For the hostility of the Elder to poetry, see *HN* praef. 1 and Gibson (2011a).

which the Elder appears to have been hostile.[66] The Elder comes back into view in letter 5.5, where the story of a nocturnal apparition to the writer C. Fannius will remind readers of the only other 'literary' dream in the correspondence, namely that reported for the sleeping Elder Pliny in 3.5.4. The dreams are a reverse image of one another: the visitation of Drusus Nero to the over-achieving Elder Pliny leads to a twenty-volume historical work (designed to preserve the memory of the former), while the appearance of the emperor Nero to Fannius accurately predicts the death of Fannius well before the completion of his multi-volume work on the victims of that emperor. The letter ends with a plea to complete unfinished works that the Elder Pliny would surely have found pleasing (5.5.7–8). The Elder makes his only explicit appearance in Book 5 in the nearby eighth letter (discussed in Chapter 4), where the Younger contemplates following the example of the former by writing a historical work. This letter shows strong links with 5.5: the Younger's fear that writing a history will impede the publication of his revised speeches (5.8.6–7) is bolstered by memory of the death of Fannius prior to completion of his life's work (and the contrasting example of the Elder Pliny).

The theme of the completion of literary tasks continues in 5.10, where Pliny, a slow publisher by his own admission in this letter, urges Suetonius to bring forth his long-anticipated 'perfected and completed work'. As is often the case with Pliny, the actual title of the work in question is not mentioned; but it may well be the *De Viris Illustribus*.[67] If this conjecture is correct – and the work was certainly known to Pliny's circle through his poetic advertisement of its imminence (5.10.1) – then an interesting situation results. For a biographical sketch of the Elder Pliny would appear in Suetonius' book or section on illustrious historians – a sketch whose composition was likely aided by the Younger's own letter 3.5 on the works and days of the Elder.[68] The appearance of the Elder is of course somewhat spectral here, but the close connections with nearby letters allow the alert reader to suspect a special purpose in the cajoling of Suetonius.

It is in this context of the evocation of the memory of the Elder Pliny that we return to letter 5.6 and ask: where did Pliny's adoptive father

---

[66] Sherwin-White (1966) 317. Ovid's list at *Tr.* 2.431–42 of risqué poets who came to no harm is also relevant; see Chapter 8.

[67] First suggested by Macé (1900) 66–77 and doubted by Sherwin-White (1966) 338, Wallace-Hadrill (1983) 52–3, 59, Kaster (1995) xliv; but for a new argument in favour of this work, see Power (2010).

[68] See Syme, *RP* 7.496 n. 1, also Sherwin-White (1966) 220, 374. A new text and discussion of the entry on the Elder Pliny, apparently derived ultimately from the *De Viris Illustribus*, can be found in Reeve (2011); see also Baldwin (1983) 399–405, Wallace-Hadrill (1983) 50–9, Gibson (2011a) 204. For Suetonius and Pliny, see also Appendix 3.

own estates? It has in fact long been suspected that the Tuscan estates were inherited by the Younger from the Elder.[69] If this speculation were correct, then a whole layer of new meaning would be added to letter 5.6. The routine of *otium* strongly implied throughout the Tuscan villa letter would take on a particular point. The Younger lets us see his pleasure garden, with topiary (5.6.16–17); a *piscina* for swimming (5.6.25); a court for ball games (5.6.28); numerous dining rooms for different kinds of dinner parties (5.6.21, 29–30, 36–7); a hippodrome and formal gardens, whether for walking or riding (5.6.32–6); and so on. The Elder, as we know from letter 3.5 (discussed in Chapter 4), would hardly approve of the Younger ordering his existence with the help of these amenities. The benefits to Pliny of this villa are summed up in the final paragraph of the letter: *ibi animo, ibi corpore maxime ualeo. nam studiis animum, uenatu corpus exerceo*, 'Here, both mentally and bodily, I am in especial vigour; for my mind I exercise by study, and my body by hunting' (5.6.46). By contrast the Elder, thoroughly focused on literary endeavour *particularly* when in the country (3.5.14, quoted above p. 120), would have led a very different life on this same estate.

Of course, the Tuscan estate may have looked very different in the Elder's time. In this connection, the comments of Pliny on the design of the villa are significant: *indulsi amori meo; amo enim, quae maxima ex parte ipse incohaui aut incohata percolui*, 'I have indulged my partiality; for I am partial to what was in great part laid out by myself or completed by me after it had been laid out' (5.6.41). From this it can be inferred that, while the site was not virgin land (as we might expect if owned previously by the Elder), it nevertheless required substantial work from the Younger. The Younger, so we might interpret, has effectively built his own villa on and over a site owned by the Elder, no doubt incorporating his buildings but substantially extending (or completing) the design. A better metaphor for the Younger's relationship with the Elder could hardly be discovered.[70] The result, in any case, is a massive edifice which the Elder – tactfully not mentioned here – would hardly have found fit for his own purposes.

Tact aside, the Younger has reason not to mention the Elder's ownership of the villa to Domitius Apollinaris, who hailed from Vercellae in the very

[69] See e.g. Sherwin-White (1966) 265, 322; Syme, *RP* 7.502; Nicols (1980) 368–9; Duncan-Jones (1982) 19; cf. the opinions of the excavators (Uroz Sáez (1999b), Braconi (2003) 48).

[70] Indeed, for once the Younger has been able to do something otherwise impossible in his relationship with the Elder. In 5.8.7, after mentioning the Elder as an *exemplum*, the Younger urges his addressee to remember that *quidquid non est peractum, pro **non incohato** est*, 'whatever is not perfected is as though it had never been begun'. The Elder left no work unfinished, except perhaps for his villa: *incohata percolui*, adds the Younger.

heart of 'Pliny country'.[71] He is unlikely to have needed the explanation. But how could readers possibly intuit this unmentioned 'fact'? Inference and elimination will get readers a good length of the way there.[72] There is nevertheless one clue buried deep within the text of the letter which points to the Elder Pliny. In describing the agricultural conditions of the villa's farms, the Younger notes the particularly intensive amount of effort needed in the act of ploughing: *tantis glaebis tenacissimum solum cum primum prosecatur assurgit, ut nono demum sulco perdometur*, 'the soil is so stiff and rises up in such huge clods when first cut into, that it is only by a course of nine ploughings that it can finally be reduced' (5.6.10). The same observation is in fact made by the Elder Pliny:

quarto seri sulco Vergilius existimatur uoluisse, cum dixit optimam esse segetem quae bis soles, bis frigora sensisset. spissius solum, sicut plerumque in Italia, quinto sulco seri melius est, in Tuscis uero nono. (*HN* 18.181)

When Vergil said that the best crop is one that twice has felt the sun and twice the cold, he is taken to have desired a fourth ploughing before sowing. Where the soil is rather dense, as it usually is in Italy, it is better to plough five times before sowing, but in Tuscany nine times. (trans. H. Rackham, adapted)

Sherwin-White ad loc. speculates that the two Plinii are talking from experience; hence the possibility of their successive ownership of the villa. It is perhaps not too much to entertain the possibility also of allusion.[73] One could assume that the subject of Book 18 of the work – agriculture – made it one of the most prominent volumes so far as elite landowners were concerned. Furthermore, the Elder's (typically competitive) reference to Vergil in the passage from Book 18 arguably raises the passage to the memorable.[74] But, for all that, it is perhaps best to think of this parallel as not so much an allusion as a reward lying in wait for readers of the Younger who know their text of the Elder well. And that reward includes the opportunity to grasp the fact that the Tuscan estate is inherited from the Elder and so to read letter 5.6 from a new angle, where the reader can

---

[71] See Syme, *RP* 7.588–9, 601.

[72] E.g. when Pliny mentions identifiable properties owned by his father or mother, these always appear in the vicinity of Lake Como (e.g. 7.11.5). And when Pliny tells us that he was adopted as *patronus* of Tifernum near the villa when he was 'still little more than a boy' (4.1.4), the implied date matches up well with one of the few other dates given in the collection, namely the death of the Elder Pliny when the Younger was in his eighteenth year (6.20.5); cf. Sherwin-White (1966) 265.

[73] For instance, Pliny expects a single rare adjective to perform the work of allusion to the epistolary preface of the *Natural History*; see Gibson (2011a) 189–93 on the use of *duriusculus* in 1.16.5 to allude to *HN* praef. 1 and a controversy over the 'harshness' of Catullus.

[74] See Bruère (1956), Howe (1985) 570–2.

see that the Elder Pliny is the palimpsest over which this *otium*-rich text is written.

I'LL DIG WITH THIS: THE PEN VERSUS THE SPADE

What the context of letter 5.6 encourages, the letter itself implies and historians have long suspected may now be confirmed at long last by archaeology. In addition to the 150 or so brick stamps bearing the initials CPCS (i.e. C. Plinius Caecilius Secundus) found at a villa site in the upper Tiber valley – of which more in due course – there have been found a number of brick stamps bearing the initials CPS (Caius Plinius Secundus),[75] i.e. in this context distinctively those of the Elder Pliny.[76] This new and potentially significant discovery raises the question of the intersection between text and topography – already glimpsed in the Lake Como letter at the chapter's outset – in a particularly urgent manner.

Literary critics, almost on principle, have sometimes displayed scepticism about – bordering on hostility towards – the excavation of sites with literary associations. And it is fair to say that approaches which downplay the materiality of Pliny's villas and emphasize the ecphrastic, metaphorical and 'poetological' aspects of letters 2.17 and 5.6 represent something of a consensus among literary critics of the last three decades. Indeed, some have even gone so far as to argue that Pliny's villas are entirely notional constructions.[77] We challenge this consensus and seek the integration of approaches. First, by arguing for the authenticity of archaeological investigation as a response to letters 2.17 and 5.6, and secondly by outlining the contribution made by recent archaeological work on Pliny's Tuscan and Laurentine villas to contextualizing these great villa letters.

In letter 9.7 Pliny is rather imprecise about the exact location of Comedy and Tragedy. As anyone who has ever visited Lake Como will know, curving shorelines and raised promontories are not rare in the neighbourhood.[78]

---

[75] The latter were published for the first time in Uroz Sáez (2008) 130, 142 figs. 17, 18. It is clear from other brick stamps collected on site that the estate, after the ownership of M. Granius Marcellus in Augustan times, eventually passed into imperial possession (and thence to the Plinii); see Braconi (1999b) 34–5; Uroz Sáez (1999a) 46, (1999b) 192–3, 195; (2008) 124–31; Braconi and Uroz Sáez (2008) 111–19. Granius Marcellus appears in Tac. *Ann.* 1.74.3 in a context which demonstrates links with Pliny 1.9.5 and 10.8; see Woodman (2009) 34–5.

[76] On the nomenclature of the Elder and Younger, see further Chapter 4.

[77] For some representatives of this tradition, see Bergmann (1995) 408. But for a classic example of the light thrown on literature by archaeology, see Will (1982) on Hor. *Carm.* 1.4.

[78] As already noted by Benedetto Giovio in the context of his identification of Bellagio as a site for 'Tragedy': *multi autem apud Larium sunt sinus, multa item dorsa, sed . . .* , 'There are however many bays on Lake Como and just as many ridges; but . . .' (Giovio (1982) 232).

However, as we move further south and closer to Rome – towards the regions that many of Pliny's friends would find more accessible and more familiar – Pliny begins to provide ever more precise information on the whereabouts of his estates.[79] Letter 4.1 had already revealed that the Tuscan estate lies close to the town of Tifernum Tiberinum (modern Città di Castello),[80] of which Pliny is *patronus*, and letter 5.6 supplies further indications of location. The estate lies under the Apennines (2), in an area which resembles an amphitheatre (7), while the villa itself is located at the top of a gentle rise underneath a larger hill (14, quoted above p. 205 n. 13). Enough detail for the location to be tentatively identified in the late seventeenth century (see below). However, it is for the Laurentine – the residence closest to the capital – that Pliny provides the ancient equivalent of a postal address.[81] The villa (as already noted) is said to be seventeen miles from Rome (2.17.2), and is approachable by two routes:[82]

aditur non una uia; nam et Laurentina et Ostiensis eodem ferunt, sed Laurentina a quarto decimo lapide, Ostiensis ab undecimo relinquenda est. (2.17.2)

There is access to it by more than one road, for the Laurentine and Ostian roads lead in the same direction; only you must branch off from the Laurentine at the fourteenth milestone and the Ostian at the eleventh.

This narrows the location to a particular and readily identifiable stretch of the coast road running south of Ostia (later the Via Severiana). Further indications of precise position emerge towards the end of the letter:

frugi quidem homini sufficit etiam uicus, quem una uilla discernit. in hoc balinea meritoria tria . . . (2.17.26)

Indeed a man of moderate requirements might be provided for even at the village, which is separated from me by one villa only. In this village there are three public baths . . .

Contemporaries and later visitors might readily identify this village as the 'uicus Augustanus' (originally perhaps 'uicus Laurentium') – probably the only settlement of this kind on the stretch of coast delimited by Pliny.[83]

---

[79] This hierarchy of details about location is also related to the ostensible motivation for each letter: 9.7 is a response to the news that Voconius Romanus is building on his properties too; 5.6 takes the initial form of an assurance to Domitius Apollinaris that his villa is in a healthy part of central Italy; while 2.17 climaxes in an invitation to Gallus to visit his villa.

[80] For the identification, see Bonomi Ponzi (1999) 15.

[81] This is in itself significant, for Pliny, although a frequent traveller the length and breadth of Italy, rarely shows any interest in details involving distances, routes or location; see Cova (1999).

[82] For a modern map showing the ancient roads, see Ricotti (1984) fig. 3.

[83] See Ricotti (1987) 123; but contrast the apparently more cautious Purcell (1998) 22, 24 n. 73.

The closer his villas to Rome, the more clearly Pliny wished his readers to know their exact location; Pliny, it can be suggested, *wanted* his villas to be tracked down. And this can be related to an argument made by Bodel (1997), that Roman villa owners – in a phenomenon related to the belief that house reflects character – invested heavily in the idea that their residences outside Rome might preserve their name for centuries to come. Indeed even before Pliny's day there are traces of a 'tourist' industry centred on the villas of the famous,[84] including the villa of Scipio the Younger at Liternum visited by Seneca and the subject of his *Ep.* 86. Similarly a passage in the Elder's *Natural History* implies that Cicero's *Cumanum* estate in Campania was the object of tourism in the Flavian era (*HN* 31.6–8).[85] Furthermore, the locations of famous men's villas or ancestral homes were a topic of interest to Pliny's younger contemporary Suetonius, not only in his lives of the Caesars (e.g. *Aug.* 6, 94.6–7),[86] but also in the lives of famous literary men (e.g. *domusque ostenditur circa Tiburni luculum*, 'his house is pointed out in the environs of the small grove of Tibur', *Vita Hor.*). But Pliny did not have to rely on his villas finding their way in the world by word of mouth alone: he had his letters to reinforce their fame. As Bodel (1997) 17 insists of the Tuscan estate described by Pliny in letter 5.6, 'both the autobiographical letter and the personally-designed Tuscan villa were meant to perpetuate the reputation of their author. In writing about his country house Pliny bolsters both supports of his anticipated fame.' Letter and country villa form a mutually reinforcing bond: the physical villa – as one more route to posthumous fame – is quite as important to Pliny as its textual description.

Architects perhaps use the main body of 2.17 and 5.6 – the descriptions of the residential villas – for purposes for which they are not designed. (Yet, such 'misuse' of the texts has been deeply creative and one of their sources of fascination.) By contrast, attempts to use the information provided on villa location appear to run with the grain of Pliny's text. Useful counter-examples are provided by attempts to find the villas of Ovid and Horace near Rome, where the poets' level of textual imprecision on their location is similar to that offered by Pliny for his Lake Como villas.[87] In Ovid we find

---

[84] See Bodel (1997) 5. The profound impact made by visiting the habitual locales of the famous dead is a topic for discussion already at Cic. *Fin.* 5.1–6.

[85] The passage is discussed *in extenso* by L. Morgan (2007); for the history of the site as a destination for visitors (perhaps owned in the Younger's time by Silius Italicus), see L. Morgan (2007) 127–35, also D'Arms (1970) 207–8.

[86] Cf. Pliny's prediction of a tourist trade for sites associated with Trajan at *Pan.* 15.4.

[87] For reported discoveries of Ovid's suburban villa in 2000, see Gaertner (2005) 455; a location near the intersection of the Via Clodia and Via Flaminia is implied at *Pont.* 1.8.43–5. For the long tradition

no implicit encouragement to track down his estates, no suggestion that the poet sees his villa as a route to the perpetuation of his name. Similarly Horace, for all his devotion to the Sabine farm, sees no value in the estate for anyone other than himself. In sum, when we attempt to locate Pliny's Tuscan or particularly the Laurentine villa, we are arguably responding to a text which allows for the possibility of readers who might actually want to travel in their minds to – even physically track down – the villa sites of the 'famous' Pliny the Younger.[88] And Pliny's amicable persona will assure posthumous visitors of a warm welcome, certainly by contrast with the prickly Horace of the *Epistles*, whose ghost is more likely to be encountered setting dogs on literary tourists.

ARCHAEOLOGY IN TUSCANY/UMBRIA AND THE *AGER LAURENS*

Whatever critics might feel about the validity of excavating literary sites, we cannot ignore the fact that the site of Pliny's 'Tuscan' villa has been located in the upper Tiber valley on the Umbria–Tuscany border,[89] while the general site of the suburban villa on the shore of the *ager Laurens* has been intensively investigated since the 1980s. Neither site solves the 'problems' of letters 2.17 and 5.6 – arguably the problems are multiplied – but both, in any case, have something to tell us about these letters.

As noted earlier, enough information is provided in letters 4.1 and 5.6 for the site of Pliny's Tuscan villa to have been identified in the seventeenth century, by Francesco Ignazio Lazzari (1633–1717), a native of the region.[90] That site lies around eight kilometres above Città di Castello in the vicinity of the attractive Comune di San Giustino – where the text of letter 5.6.13

---

of attempts to locate the site of Horace's Sabine villa, see Frischer (2001). Various details implying a particular location near Licenza north-east of Rome are liberally scattered (e.g. *Carm.* 1.17.1–12, *Epist.* 1.10.49, 1.14.3, 1.16.4–8, 1.18.104–5), but the clues they provide are riddling (cf. Frischer (2001) 76).

[88] The descriptions by Statius of the villa of Pollius Felix (*Silu.* 2.2) arguably allow for a similar reading; for identifications of the villa here, see D'Arms (1970) 220–2, Bergmann (1991) 66 n. 3.

[89] Pliny always refers to this estate as 'Tuscan' (e.g. 5.6.1 *Tuscos meos*), although it is clear from other references that it lay within the region of Tifernum Tiberinum (e.g. 4.1.3–4), which is located in Umbria, according to Pliny *HN* 3.53. The 'conflict' is attributable to the Augustan imposition of regional boundaries which did not respect earlier ethnic divisions, as in the case of Tifernum, which appears originally to have been Etruscan; see Sisani (2008). Ironically, the Augustan regions leave their only substantial historical trace in the *Natural History*; see Bispham (2007).

[90] For a history of attempts to locate Pliny's Tuscan villa, see du Prey (1994) 74–81, Braconi (1999b) 21–3. Extracts from Lazzari's manuscript are transcribed at Braconi and Uroz Sáez (2001) 212–13 n. 3.

has been elegantly incised so as to run the length of the modern central square. More precisely, it is to be found next to the hamlet of Pitigliano on a site including a large raised area known until the nineteenth century simply as 'Colle',[91] and fields a little below known locally as the Campo di Santa Fiora.[92]

As Pliny's description demands, we find here a locality at the top of a deceptively rising incline which itself shelters beneath the foothills of the Apennines with a view of the great bowl of hills which surround the Tiber and its valley. Initial archaeological findings at the site were given authoritative publication in 1999 under the editorship of Paolo Braconi and José Uroz Saéz.[93] Here was revealed the discovery on the Campo di Santa Fiora of over fifty roof tiles and other masonry bearing Pliny's initials (CPCS);[94] around one hundred more would be added to this total in the final phase of the excavations, which lasted into the early years of the new century.[95] Buildings belonging largely to the agricultural and productive part of the villa were uncovered at first, mostly in a very poor state of preservation.[96] By the 1970s agricultural activity had drastically lowered the level of the site, apparently destroying much that had been preserved into the twentieth century; the remains that may be seen there today are mostly from beneath the ancient floor level.[97] Later work revealed a further substantial structure in front of the previous excavations a little further down the incline, apparently a temple and portico complex (perhaps that described by Pliny in letter 9.39).[98]

From the excavations, it is clear that the part of Pliny's estate which has been discovered is the *pars rustica*: the residential part of the villa – the

---

[91] Pliny has succeeded in stamping his name on the landscape: the 'hill' and its village have subsequently become known as Colle Plinio (Braconi (1999b) 22); and early modern scholars interpreted Pitigliano (wrongly) as a vernacular corruption of Pliniano (du Prey (1994) 74–7).

[92] For a map, see Braconi (2001) 738, or Braconi and Uroz Sáez (1999) 18. For possible links between the (vanished) church of Santa Fiora and cults in Pliny's time on the site, see Braconi (2001).

[93] Summarized in English by Marzano (2007) 110–14, 150–1, 736–7. For a briefer advance summary of the findings and their interpretation, see Braconi (1998).

[94] Uroz Sáez (1999a).

[95] Uroz Sáez (2008). These and other finds will be displayed at a museum dedicated to the archaeology of the upper Tiber valley, set up for opening in nearby Celalba at the Villa Graziani (whose former owner, G. Magherini Graziani, played a significant role in the confirmation of the site in the nineteenth century; see Braconi (1999b) 21).

[96] Braconi (1999b) 24–36.   [97] See Braconi (1999a) 20, (1999b) 23–4.

[98] See Braconi and Uroz Sáez (2001) and, with illustrations of tentative reconstructions, Braconi and Uroz Sáez (2008) 114–17. It appears likely that, in the phase before Pliny's ownership of the estate, the buildings on the Campo di Santa Fiora comprised the villa complex of a previous owner, Granius Marcellus, which was subsequently remodelled by Pliny to become the heart of his *pars rustica*.

pars urbana – in all likelihood lies further up the slope on top of Colle
Plinio, inside the grounds of the magnificent walled estate belonging to
the Marchesi Cappelletti.[99] But of excavation inside these walls – where
local oral tradition insists on the existence of underground remains[100] –
there is no possibility whatever.[101] Yet the discovery of the *pars rustica* is a
matter for excitement rather than disappointment, since we have here the
dark side of Pliny's Tuscan moon. In particular, from the viewpoint of the
present chapter, the excavations have much to tell us about the selectivity
of Pliny's self-portrait in 5.6. The existence of a *pars rustica* is certainly
implied in other letters, although often the reader must infer from cross-
reference that Pliny is talking specifically about the Tuscan estate.[102] Letter
5.6 opens with a description of the fertile fields which surround the villa.
But in that same letter there is no mention of the substantial complex of
agricultural and related buildings on the modern Campo di Santa Fiora;
Pliny's gaze rests on the elite residence atop the Colle Plinio.[103] Here, at
least in letter 5.6, is a man who rises both metaphorically – and (as we
can now see from the topography) literally – above the mundanities of the
tenant farmers and agriculture from which his vast personal wealth was
derived.

It was noted earlier that Pliny provides virtually a postal address for his
Laurentine villa, apparently restricting the site of his residence to a short
stretch of coast on the *ager Laurens*.[104] He 'neglects' only to say whether
his house is the second villa to the north or to the south of a village that is
in all probability to be identified with the *uicus Augustanus* in the modern
presidential estate of Castelporziano. If to the south, it perhaps lies under
or near the site of the residence known as the 'Villa Magna' in the vicinity
of Grotte di Piastra inside the presidential estate; if to the north, then
under or near the site of the villa known locally as villa di Plinio (or 'la
Palombara') situated in the neighbouring public park of Castelfusano.[105]

---

99   See Braconi and Uroz Sáez (2008), esp. 109 fig. 5.

100 Braconi and Uroz Sáez (2001) 216 n. 12, (2008) 106.

101 To the possible relief of at least some modern architects; see Du Prey (1994) 80–1.

102 E.g. 4.1.3, 4.6.1, 9.15–16, 9.20, 9.36.6; cf. 7.30.2–4, 8.2, 9.37, 9.39.

103 For visual representation of the gap between the two complexes, see Braconi and Uroz Sáez (2008)
     108–9 figs. 4–5. For a reconstruction of agricultural practices at the Tuscan villa site, see Braconi
     (2008).

104 For a cultural study of the coast of the *ager Laurens*, see Purcell (1998). On the history of attempts
     to locate Pliny's Laurentine villa here, see du Prey (1994) 82–106. For the story of excavation along
     the Laurentine shore as a whole, see Claridge (1997–98), (forthcoming b); cf. the account given by
     Lanciani (1909) 306–31.

105 For maps, see Ricotti (1984) fig. 3, Claridge (1997–98) fig. 4, Lauro and Claridge (1998) 40 (fold
     out plate I).

The remains of neither villa, in fact, appear to approximate very closely to Pliny's description.[106] This is perhaps unsurprising. Not only did the residences of the Laurentine shore undergo remodelling in antiquity by successive owners, but the coast and its sites have suffered extensive silting since antiquity and in modern times plundering along with dense (and damaging) forestation. Furthermore, Pliny tells us at 2.17.20 that he was responsible for building only one wing of the Laurentine villa; hence there is a reduced chance of identifying a house as his through brick stamps.[107]

Rather more significant, in a sense, is what the general survey of the shoreline of the *ager Laurens* as a whole can tell us about Pliny's letter. First, the village to which Pliny refers may have been a substantial settlement even in his day (although it would reach its maximum development after Pliny's time).[108] Secondly, survey and excavation along the shoreline reveal a seafront that was increasingly crowded with villas and other buildings as time went on, but that even in Pliny's time was something of a millionaires' row of magnificent residences.[109] Such 'crowding' does appear fleetingly in the body of the letter (e.g. 2.17.12, 21 *a tergo uillae*, 'villas behind'), and more explicitly in two late sentences.[110] But this is not the dominant impression yielded by letter 2.17, where Pliny prefers to emphasize the villa's remoteness. He is careful to convey the information that the villa is best reached on horseback rather than in a carriage, as the road turns sandy and narrow or passes through woods and open fields (2.17.2–3). And emphasis falls repeatedly on peace, tranquillity and seclusion (2.17.2, 10, 13, 17, 22–4), as well as on the natural elements of sun, sea and wind (and

---

[106] On the villa di Plinio in the Castelfusano estate, see De Franceschini (2005) 260–4 and the excavation report of Ramieri (1995), which show that nothing yet links the villa with Pliny. For the 'Villa Magna' in the Castelporziano estate, see likewise De Franceschini (2005) 265–7. The 'discovery' of Pliny's Laurentine villa was announced to the Anglophone world by Ricotti (1987) 182–4; for excavation reports, based on modest digs, see Ricotti (1983) [*non vidi*], (1984), (1985), (1988). However, aside from the problem of the dates of what has been excavated (Lauro and Claridge (1998) 47), the contrast between the extravagant reconstructions of Ricotti (e.g. (1985) fig. 2) and the map produced by Lauro and Claridge ((1998) 45 fig. 11) of exiguous actual discoveries tells its own story.

[107] Cf. du Prey (1994) 84.

[108] Context and initial excavation reports are provided by Patterson (1985); Claridge (1985), (1988), (1998), (forthcoming a).

[109] For a detailed catalogue of finds up to 1991, see Lauro and Claridge (1998); cf. a summary in English by Marzano (2007) 306–9, 312–29.

[110] 2.17.26 (quoted above p. 226), 27 *litus ornant uarietate gratissima nunc continua nunc intermissa tecta uillarum, quae praestant multarum urbium faciem, siue mari siue ipso litore utare*, 'The coast is ornamented in the most pleasing variety by the roofs of villas, now continuous, now spaced out, so as to give the appearance of a number of towns, whether you look at them from the sea or from the shore itself.' Cf. Pliny's revelation that the Laurentine has no attached lands at 4.6.2.

the exposure to or shelter from each). This image is congruent with Pliny's careful preparation for it in Book 1, where the Laurentine is hailed *o mare, o litus, uerum secretumque* μουσεῖον, 'Oh sea and shore, true and secret haunt of the Muses' (1.9.6), and described as a place of *studiosum otium,* 'studious leisure' (1.22.11).

It can be suggested that Pliny's emphasis on remoteness is part of the literary and cultural tradition of the *ager Laurens*. For this 'primitive' area was associated with various primeval Italian figures connected to the prehistory of Rome. Here also Aeneas landed for the first time near Rome (and the Trojans later settled), and here king Latinus had his mythical city, now long 'disappeared' – which added to a sense of remoteness for the area in later times. Many of these associations for the Laurentine shore had been given classic shape – and hence for men of Pliny's generation had become culturally fixed – in the second half of the *Aeneid,* from the moment Aeneas spies the *ingens lucus* from his ship (Verg. *Aen.* 7.29).[111] But in reality, as the archaeological record strongly suggests to us, we might guess that Pliny had little chance of avoiding the kinds of social calls and other intrusions from friends, neighbours and locals which are such a feature of Cicero's epistolary records of stays in his various villas.[112] Perhaps Pliny's de-emphasis of the likely reality here has a political edge. Would Trajan find it reassuring to hear that his senatorial elite were *not* regularly in and out of each other's houses, even when in close physical proximity?

With this particular example of disjunction between text and site, surely Pliny risked disappointing the literary tourist? In fact, the utter certainty of readers who will check metaphor-laden description against openly available physical reality has not stopped writers from provoking the disorientation of their audience, or readers from enjoying both the conjunction and the disjunction between text and location. In the words of L.T. Pearcy that form the epigraph to this chapter, 'the scene will offer critical reflections on the text – not truth, despite the hard reality of streets and buildings, but another interpretation'. In the case of the Laurentine shore it can be suggested that readers of the *Letters* familiar with the area – whether in antiquity or today – are supposed to enjoy the disjunction between the seaside haven of the text and the stretch of expensive residences now

---

[111] See the brilliant analysis of Purcell (1998) 18–21, 25–7 and cf. esp. the preface to the description of Vopiscus' Tibur villa at Stat. *Silu.* 1.3.83–4 *cedant Telegoni, cedant Laurentia Turni | iugera Lucrinaeque domus,* 'Let the acres of Telegonus and the Laurentian acres of Turnus yield, and the Lucrine homes.'

[112] See D'Arms (1970) 50–1, 61. It is worth adding that the Vergilian palace and city of Latinus no doubt conferred cultural capital on owners of magnificent villas in the area, and also granted licence for literary architectural description.

confirmed by archaeology. In fact, the interpretation of the text provided by the Laurentine shore is one that allows the reader of 2.17 to grasp Pliny's determined (even wilful) creation of an atmosphere of isolation and retreat. In this locale, Pliny and his villa (in all its aspects) may take centre stage, despite the location of the residence on a shoreline next to a busy village in the midst of a string of millionaire estates.[113]

---

[113] For the disjunction between the praiseworthy wilderness constructed by Pliny's text and the reality of a well-supplied luxury zone for villa owners, see also Purcell (1998) 23, 24–5. For villa owners who tried – unlike Pliny – to match modest dwellings to the cultural 'mood' of the landscape, see Purcell (1998) 25–6.

CHAPTER 8

The grand design
How to read the collection

Design matters in Pliny's work, and that makes it all the more important to take a holistic approach to the collection. We have now looked at the varied and subtle ways in which Pliny embeds each epistle within its immediate environment, binding it to its predecessor and successor with a shared allusion, or with echoes (however faint) of image, theme and vocabulary, sometimes inviting us, by a complex series of allusive moves, to dig in the gaps between letters for information about author and addressees. We have also examined (with particular attention to Book 6) Pliny's symmetrical balancing of letters at beginning and end of a book unit, and the dividends available to the alert reader who asks himself how such phenomena might influence a re-reading of the book. We have noted where the cumulative dominance of a single theme or thematic cluster within a book invites interpretation, or where important figures loom over whole books: so, in Chapter 2, we remarked upon the surprisingly long shadow cast over Book 7 by the figure of Domitian, after Book 6 has been cast as Trajan's book.

Further, we have considered the effects achieved by balances and contrasts which are built into the design of the collection or of individual books. So, for example, we have suggested that Pliny balances Book 7, dominated by *otium*, as a counterweight to the professionally laborious preoccupations of Book 6 (see Chapters 2 and 6), while at book level he leavens the *negotium* which dominates Book 2 with a single attention-grabbing letter about a villa's *otium*-rich atmosphere (see Chapter 7), or highlights in 3.1 the blissful relaxation of a well-earned *secessus* in old age (Chapter 4) before further exploring in the remainder of Book 3 a cluster of themes related to the *cursus honorum* which should precede the prize of retirement.[1]

---

[1] We should note that the locations in which Pliny sets the beginning and end of Book 3 provide vivid confirmation of this point, since the book opens in Spurinna's villa (3.1), where verse in the

Pliny reasserts his commitment to variety and miscellaneity on every page, as even juxtaposed letters contrast with one another, topics and moods seem to oscillate from one letter to the next, and whole books pull Pliny's 'epistolary life' back into balance by, for example, offering rest after labour or by bringing him (and 'us') back south from Comum in Book 6 before recording Calestrius Tiro's journey northwards to visit Calpurnius Fabatus in Book 7 (see Chapter 2).[2] Pliny preserves the documentary appearance of the collection by eschewing reference (after the dedicatory epistle) to the collection as a whole or to book units. Nevertheless, he achieves a balance in the collection between a marked miscellaneity at page level and the highly symmetrical architecture of the collection, a marriage of opposites which allows the work to achieve a resolution of sorts while still seeming to reflect life's teeming reality.

The result is a collection which can appeal to readers at different stages of engagement with the text: the first-time reader, who is constantly shown something new or pointed down a different path (e.g. by a different addressee or a superficially abrupt change of topic), and who might be tempted, by the text itself, or by the indices which may have been attached to each book, to take an anthologizer's approach;[3] the systematic and comprehensive (even 'encyclopaedic') reader, who starts at the beginning and continues all the way through to the end, taking each book as it comes and as a whole; and finally to the (often surprised) re-reader, who finds himself, at the end of the collection, reconsidering and re-interpreting clues laid before him in Book 1 in the light of later information.

After many years of work in tandem on this author, this book's two authors have come to a shared respect for the craftsmanship and subtlety to be found not only in the letters themselves but in their disposition into skilfully structured book units and a distinctive collection. Neither of us is an anthologizing reader by instinct, although (as we said in the introduction to this volume) in our studies of letter cycles and recurrent motifs we have necessarily read as anthologizers, for interpretative convenience. We share a commitment to reading and interpreting each of these letter books as a whole, and we both also recognize the power of a linear reading of the letters, whether that be in short sequences or over whole books, and we have endeavoured throughout this book to outline the rewards available to the

---

daytime is perfectly acceptable, and ends with Martial's image of Pliny in his house on the Esquiline, working so hard that Martial's poetry must wait respectfully for its host's attention (3.21.5). On this as the sole mention of Pliny's town house in the collection, see Chapter 7.

[2] Cf. König (2007a) 272 for comparable oscillations between moods in Alciphron's fictional letters.

[3] For the collection's hospitable encouragement to an anthologizing reader, see Chapters 2 and 7.

reader who responds to Pliny's encouragement to re-read. Our approaches diverge a little in the way we treat such holistic readings: where architectural order and structure stand in slightly higher relief for Gibson, Morello's approach tends to be more loosely associative, taking up Pliny's invitation to look for accumulations of themes, and allusive echoes. Nevertheless, our different roads have converged at several places, and ultimately brought us to the same interpretative destinations.

For example, Gibson's chapter on the elders in Pliny's life (Chapter 4) and Morello's on his use of *otium* (Chapter 6) both evaluate time management as a dominant motif in the letters. Similarly Gibson on the possibilities of a biographical reading of the collection (Chapter 1) and Morello on Pliny's episto-literary models (Chapter 3) both note that Pliny withholds until the very last book(s) of the collection some crucial material about his life, his philosophy (and practice) of *otium*, or his approach to his literary oeuvre. Gibson on Book 6 (Chapter 2) and Morello in this final chapter on the collection's 'grand design' both commit to the interpretative power of reading beginnings and ends against one another in order to define Pliny's agenda within those terminus points. Gibson's Chapter 7 on Pliny's villas emphasizes (like Morello in this chapter) the collection's invitation to re-read, but also examines (and harmonizes) a range of 'anthologizing' approaches, in the process re-integrating the villa letters (too often considered in isolation) into the context of their books and the collection as a whole. Gibson in Chapter 4 and Morello in Chapter 5 examine the narratives contained in letter cycles which cross book boundaries (in this case defining those cycles by reference to a deceased 'elder and better' or by addressee), while both Gibson's study of Book 6 (Chapter 2) and Morello's of Book 7 (Chapter 6) assess the power of reading a single book both as a whole and as part of a balanced pair within the collection's grand design.

In this chapter we step back once more to look at the bigger picture, and to think again about the sustained cycles and the fleeting gestures towards symmetry within the work which help to maintain coherence in such a variegated collection. As we shall see in this chapter, some of the literary echoes which underpin the overall design are heard only late in the collection, yet again encouraging reconsideration of earlier book patterns, and so we begin with a reconsideration of the relationship between the beginning and the end of the nine books; we then move on to assess the effect upon the reader's experience of Pliny's work created by the addition at the end of the collection of a tenth (and quite different) book.

BEGINNINGS AND ENDS ONCE MORE: BOOK I AND BOOK 9

As we noted in our reading of Book 6 (Chapter 2), beginnings and ends at book level are set in a careful symmetry which seems to highlight Pliny's commitment to books of letters as whole units; in recent years, readers have begun to notice similar phenomena at collection level, and as more links and correspondences between Book 1 and Book 9 have been noted and subjected to interpretation, our view of the collection and of Book 9 itself has changed significantly.[4]

Book 9 seems unlike Books 1–8 in that it contains a much larger number of letters (forty letters, to thirty addressees), most of them rather short. Traditional readings of Book 9's place in the collection have tended to interpret these novel qualities negatively, as symptomatic of decline. The dominant voice is that of Sherwin-White, who notes that 'the forty letters include only twelve of any substance' and that 'at first sight IX might seem to contain a miscellany of letters from Pliny's files covering the whole period from I to VIII'. Sherwin-White observes the shift of focus towards private and domestic topics (with only 9.13, on the Certus affair – now long past – dealing with important public affairs), and remarks upon the inclusion of twenty-eight minor letters which he categorizes under the (relatively trivial) headings of Admonitions or Courtesy notes, suggesting that such thin gleanings as remain in Pliny's archives (perhaps including items rejected during the preparation of earlier books) have been hastily edited, to meet the print deadline, as it were, before his departure for Bithynia.[5]

Murgia, too, has less faith than the present authors in the clarity and precision of Pliny's organizational patterns,[6] but still thinks that Sherwin-White gave Pliny 'insufficient credit for artistry', on the basis of the astonishing reprise of the 'hunting 'n' writing' motif of 1.6 in 9.10, a feature which contributes to the valedictory quality of Book 9.[7] Similar responsions might also prompt readers to recognize other letter 'pairs' in the two books. 9.1, for example opens with Pliny's exhortation (*saepe te monui*) to Maximus to publish a work which has been too long in gestation, an

---

[4] On the design of the collection, with special reference to (deceptive) closure devices, see Whitton (2011).

[5] Sherwin-White (1966) 39–40, 49–50. One should note, however, that Sherwin-White does also highlight important links between key letters of Books 7–9 (including the implication in 9.19 that 6.10 could already be read in published form).

[6] 'If Pliny was at all concerned with arranging letters in patterns, it certainly was not a dominating concern', Murgia (1985) 200. For nuanced criticism of Murgia's position, see Bodel (unpublished).

[7] On the 'valedictory' tone of Book 9, cf. Leach (2003) 162.

apparent echo of Pliny's own concession in 1.1 to repeated encouragement from Septicius Clarus (*frequenter hortatus es*). Similarly, 9.13 'balances, and in effect answers' 1.5, since both letters treat the contrasting behaviour of Regulus and of Pliny in the immediate aftermath of Domitian's death; again it is up to the reader to catch the echo in the early part of each letter: *post Domitiani mortem* ∼ *occiso Domitiano*.[8] 9.26, too, is thematically linked with two letters on oratorical style in Book 1, namely 1.2 and (especially) 1.20, sharing not only the topic but the stylistic feature of an unusual density of Greek words.[9]

PLINY AND THE ART OF READING

Above all, the importance of beginnings and ends is once again signalled by a feature highlighted by Barchiesi (and after him by Marchesi): an opening letter (1.1) addressed to a long-standing admirer of Pliny's letters named Clarus is appropriately 'answered' by a closing letter (9.40) to another devotee, this time a star of the new generation named Fuscus.[10] We move from 'light' to 'dusk' across the collection, as it were, just as within the smaller compass of the final letters of Book 9 summer at the Laurentine villa (9.36) turns to winter at the Tuscan house (9.40). Barchiesi persuasively contrasts the patronage exercised by Clarus ('Mr VIP') with the admiration of Fuscus ('Mr Almost Famous'); these addressees' names eloquently reflect the narrative drive we noted in Chapter 4, in which we are invited to follow Pliny's progress from protégé to patron in his own right. The similarities which are masked by their names also bring a sense of completion to the collection: both, crucially, are admirers who stimulate the production of more of the letters which they admire.

Letter 9.40 suggests once again that Book 9 is partly about reconsideration of Pliny, as it contains – in almost the final sentence of the collection – one of Pliny's characteristic passages about his commitment to reconsidering, revising, and rewriting his own work: *si agendi necessitas instat, quae frequens hieme, non iam comoedo uel lyristae post cenam locus, sed illa, quae dictaui, identidem retractantur,* 'if there is any pressing necessity for appearing in court (as there often is in winter) there is no longer place for a

---

[8] Hoffer (1999) 66.

[9] In addition, Leach (2003) 162 notes that positioning of letters about rural *otium* close to beginning of 1 and end of 9 suggests a 'final conceptualization of the collection as a whole'. Cf. Marchesi (2008) 116 for a specific, if understated, link (via allusion to the *Aeneid*) between 1.2 and 9.14.

[10] Barchiesi (2005) 330–2, Marchesi (2008) 250. We have already noted Pliny's willingness, more pronounced than is usually acknowledged, to play upon addressees' names; see Chapter 2.

comedian or a lyrical performer after dinner, but I often go over again what I have dictated' (9.40.2).[11] The apparently lazy Pliny of Book 1 now shows himself eschewing more relaxed literary pleasures and staying up late to work even at his villa. The collection's movement away from Septicius Clarus (as the symbolic marker of the collection's opening) is clear when we notice that these abandoned *comoedos... uel lyristen* (1.15.2) were precisely the entertainments on offer at the festive evening Septicius had failed to attend in Book 1. As Barchiesi rightly says, then, of Pliny's focus on 'rewriting' in 9.40:[12]

Pliny is ostensibly speaking only about his oratory, not about letters, but as far as this letter belongs to its place in the book, the implication must be that letter-writing too is not a casual occasional production when such an important author is the writer. Hence an invitation to revisit the entire nine-book opus as a true collection, planned, rewritten and improved, by a self-conscious author and a perfectionist.

We might understand this letter as applying also to our reading strategies in the letter collection itself: as readers, we too should consider returning to, and refining, interpretative work already done.[13] It is entirely in keeping with Pliny's practice that we find such signals at the very end of the collection of private letters. Moreover, it reflects and supports the literary mission which he has already defined for himself in 5.8, the famous letter in which he resists Titinius Capito's encouragement to turn his hand to historiography. He does so on the grounds that he has been involved in some important cases (5.8.6) and needs to devote all his energies to revising (*retractare*) his speeches, not only to preserve them for posterity, but also because he is only now – after the decades of work since he began to speak in the forum in his nineteenth year of age – coming to appreciate what his profession really entails (*nunc demum quid praestare debeat orator, adhuc tamen per caliginem uideo*, 'I only now perceive, yet still through a mist, what is required of an orator', 5.8.8). Pliny's modesty makes him revise and review even the work in which he has professional expertise, and his message to his readers to think again about everything they have learned in their earlier experience as readers of his collection reflects his attitude to his own career.[14]

However, Pliny is merciful to the first-time reader, and hospitable to those who find it easier to deal with long texts by breaking them up into

---

[11] A similar stress on the value of thorough revision of work may be found in 9.35.2, 9.36.2.
[12] Barchiesi (2005) 332.   [13] This approach is central to Chapters 1 and 7, in particular.
[14] On 5.8, see Woodman (forthcoming) and the brief discussion in Chapter 4.

manageable chunks or by reading selectively. Similar instructions for us as readers in how to handle Pliny's letter collection may also be implicitly delivered in letter 9.4 to Macrinus – again a letter ostensibly about Pliny's oratory. Pliny's prescriptive directions to the reader make this brief cover-letter (or 'courtesy note') into a 'user's manual' or 'quick start leaflet' to the long speech it accompanies:

uererer ne immodicam orationem putares, quam cum hac epistula accipies, nisi esset generis eius ut saepe incipere saepe desinere uideatur. nam singulis criminibus singulae uelut causae continentur. poteris ergo, undecumque coeperis ubicumque desieris, quae deinceps sequentur et quasi incipientia legere et **quasi cohaerentia**, meque in uniuersitate longissimum, breuissimum in partibus iudicare. uale.

I should be afraid you would think the oration, which you will receive with this letter, of immoderate length, if it were not of such a kind as to seem to have many beginnings and many endings. For under each separate charge is contained as it were a separate cause. So, at whatever point you begin, or at whatever place you leave off, you will be able to read what next follows both in the light of a new commencement and a *connected sequel*, and so to pronounce me, if extremely long as to the whole, yet extremely short as to the separate parts. Farewell.

As so often, Pliny does not specify which of his speeches he has sent, but it seems likely that he is referring to the *in Caecilii Socios*, which he has already mentioned in 3.4 (addressed to this same Macrinus) and in the much longer 3.9 (to Cornelius Minicianus). 3.9, too, repeatedly emphasizes the complex variety in the case, which involved multiple charges and multiple defendants.[15] Pliny outlines the decision he took (together with his colleague, Lucceius Albinus) to break the case down into a series of semi-separate actions. Their aim was partly to spare their stamina as speakers, and partly to retain the attention and goodwill of an audience who might otherwise be bored and exhausted by the single marathon case. Above all, the piecemeal approach seemed the most useful strategy for containing, managing and winning an enormous legal and oratorical endeavour:

nam nos quoque tam numerosum agmen reorum ita demum uidebamus posse superari, si per singulos carperetur. (3.9.11)

For we, too, saw that so numerous an array of accused could only be got the better of, on condition of being attacked singly.

This letter goes on to report the twists and turns in the case; moreover, its apparently casual structure carefully mirrors the stop-start quality of

---

[15] 'It involved many points [*fuit multiplex*] and required frequent pleadings, presenting much variety [*cum magna uarietate*]' (3.9.2).

the linked prosecution(s), as Pliny at first appears to present a sustained narrative in his usual tightly designed letter format, but then twice 'reopens' the letter, as if to add something extra which had been (almost) forgotten.

At 3.9.27–8, for example, we think we have reached the end of the story, as Pliny excuses the letter's length by reminding his impatient addressee of the mass of material which needed to be included ('remember that a letter is not a long one which embraces so many days and trials, so many defendants, in short, and so many cases');[16] however, he begins again at 3.9.28, to capture some part of the tale he had almost forgotten (*succurrit quod praeterieram*, 'something occurs to me which I had passed over'), and then does the same thing again at 3.9.36 ('I ask myself whether I have again omitted anything [*an aliquid omiserim rursus*], and again an omission has nearly occurred [*rursus paene omisi*]').

This is a natural epistolary mode, one might say, but such a structure is very far from Pliny's usual practice in this collection. Perhaps in consequence, he feels obliged to mark the 'real' ending of the letter very clearly in the final sentence:

hic erit epistulae finis, re uera finis; litteram non addam, etiamsi adhuc aliquid praeterisse me sensero. (3.9.37)

This shall be the end of my epistle, really and truly the end; I won't add a single letter, even though I should still feel that I have left something out.

Pliny here ensures that his concerns about length and about the best ways to divide up the material are allowed to spill over from the prosecution itself into his own letter to Minicianus.

If we read 9.4 against this background, it seems clearer that Pliny employs an advocate's expertise in dividing a long work into manageable sections, each with a kind of new beginning and its own ending; the focus in 3.9 is mainly upon the speakers themselves, and only secondarily upon the audience, but in 9.4 Pliny issues quasi-prefatory directions that the *reader* should allow himself false endings, as it were, and beginnings chosen at whim: since the speech reads like something which is constantly beginning and ending, it could be picked up or left off at any point.

Here in 9.4, then, Pliny tells us short works can be put together into long works, and long works divided, provided that they are appropriately

---

[16] Concerns about length are a common signal of closure in Pliny's letters (e.g. 1.20, 2.5, 2.11, 4.11). Here the self-consciously never-ending quality of the letter's account of the speech modestly and humorously reflects Pliny's awareness that his exhaustive and lengthy speech made substantial demands upon its original audience (demands which now need to be minimized for the new readership).

structured by their author, and that their reader is willing to adapt his reading method to suit the challenge. Oratorical works of this kind, Pliny would have us believe, do not necessarily demand sequential reading *from start to finish*, and indeed might offer themselves equally naturally to a 'partitioning' approach and to multiple reading sessions, in which the reader himself determines where to begin and end. In this way, Pliny helps the reader who is approaching such a text *for the first time*, giving encouragement to look at parts rather than the whole.

There is a natural move for us to make here: the letter collection itself – as a work with many addressees, many beginnings and endings, many pieces of modest length within a more complex structure – is open to the same treatment. We might also be reminded, when we read Pliny's assurance that he will not add a single 'letter' (*littera*) to 3.9, even if he realizes that he has overlooked something else, of the contrasting approach he promised to take to the construction of a collection of epistles ('I shall hunt up such other letters [*epistulas* – there is here no ambiguous *litteras*] as still lie neglected, and if I write any fresh ones, I will not withhold them', 1.1.2). In the case of both the letter collection and the complex, multi-part speech, we can read from cover to cover (in which case the work is really rather long) or in chunks, starting anywhere and enjoying the 'quasi-coherence' (cf. *quasi cohaerentia*, 9.4.2) as each letter builds upon the one immediately before it. Pliny implies, nevertheless, a commitment to sequences (however short) and to the pleasures of juxtaposition, and readers must 'manage' their own task of dealing with such phenomena: just as Pliny breaks up a long, formless day into a series of manageable and coherent tasks, or a complex speech into readable sections, so we are invited to break up our reading task.[17]

Pliny has treated the skilled technique of reading (or listening) in earlier letters, too. In a letter on the *Panegyricus*, for example (a work which, he would have us believe, shares with his letters a relatively weak reliance on *materia* and a proportionally greater dependence upon *cura* and the writer's craft), he hopes that his ideal reader/listener will approach the speech equipped with a sensitivity to compositional order and a keen appreciation of the delivery and the arrangement of the speech:

---

[17] Cf. the invitation in 5.6.41 to pause for rest in the epistolary tour of the Tuscan villa (see Chapter 7). This is not, one should note, an open invitation to anthologize at random, since attention to sequences remains vital; Pliny is, however, suggesting that it may be up to us to control our own sequential progress through his texts. For encouragement to a reader to delimit his own reading, cf. Mart. 10.1.1–4 with Holzberg (2004–5) 213–14.

in ceteris enim lectorem nouitas ipsa intentum habet, in hac nota uulgata dicta sunt omnia; quo fit ut quasi otiosus securusque lector tantum elocutioni uacet, in qua satisfacere difficilius est cum sola aestimatur. atque utinam ordo saltem et transitus et figurae simul spectarentur! nam inuenire praeclare, enuntiare magnifice interdum etiam barbari solent, disponere apte, figurare uarie nisi eruditis negatum est. (3.13.2–3)

For, while in the case of other subjects, their very novelty keeps the reader attentive; as to this one, everything has been made known, published, said over and over again. The consequence is that the reader, grown in a manner indolent and careless, is free to attend to the mode of expression only, a point in which it is very difficult to give satisfaction, when it is the only one that is made the subject of criticism. And I would that the arrangement at least, and the transitions and the figures of speech were equally attended to; for brilliancy of invention and grandeur of diction are to be found sometimes even among the untutored; whereas harmony in arrangement and variety in ornamentation are in the power of the learned only.

Liberation from the demands of novel content affords the discerning reader a kind of intellectual *otium* (*quasi otiosus securusque*, 'in a manner indolent and careless', 3.13.2), in which he can better engage with the sophisticated display of technique.[18] Pliny highlights in particular the virtues of *ordo* ('arrangement') and *transitus* ('transitions'), both of which, of course, are similarly important for his letter collection; in relation to the *Panegyricus*, at least, it is made plain that these are distinctively civilized features, produced and appreciated only by the cultured audience. The same letter recommends shifts of tone and mode (*ut in pictura lumen non alia res magis quam umbra commendat, ita orationem tam summittere quam attollere decet*, 'just as, in a picture, nothing so much sets off light as shade, so it is proper to lower as well as to raise the tone of an oration', 3.13.4) – an image easily as appropriate, one might think, to the twists and turns of the letter collection as of the speech.[19] Variety, then, and the intelligent disposition of even exiguous or hackneyed material make for effective oratory – and although we might think letters as *individual* items are a different kind of thing, these features are especially valuable in letter *collections*.

---

[18] One might almost see this '*otium*' as the reader/listener's intellectual equivalent of the *otium* of 7.9 which Fuscus is supposed to use to hone his technical skills. For stylistic sophistication as the true marker of learning in a letter-writer, too, see 7.13, where Pliny dismisses Ferox's claim not to be studying by admiring the polished style of the very letter in which he made the claim ('it is so elegant it could only have been written by one who is studying [*a studente*]', 7.13.2).

[19] Cf. Pliny's acknowledgement that circumstances might force him reluctantly to write letters which are *umbraticas* ('from the shade of the closet'), 9.2.3.

LENGTH, REPETITION AND THE COMMITMENT TO VARIETY

The difficulty for the writer of making lengthy works both attractive and effective for all kinds of readers/audiences is a recurring anxiety in the collection from 1.20 onwards, and the issue is early associated with themes of effort which we have already highlighted in Chapter 6. In 1.20 Pliny notes for the first time that the enormous range of possible responses from an audience should prompt the conscientious speaker to undertake lengthy, varied and sometimes challengingly elevated treatment of his topic. Here he reports that Regulus once contrasted the crisp aggression of his own style with Pliny's more ploddingly thorough approach:

dixit aliquando mihi Regulus, cum simul adessemus: 'tu omnia quae sunt in causa putas exsequenda; ego iugulum statim uideo, hunc premo.' (1.20.14)

Regulus once said to me, when we were acting together: 'You think you must follow up every element of the suit. I at once see the throat of the case and grasp *that.*'

In his own defence, Pliny invokes variety on the one hand and persistence on the other. At 1.20.16 an image of agricultural diversification illustrates the benefits of a multi-faceted approach: a good farmer will cultivate several kinds of crops in order to ensure a good harvest. Pliny then moves on in 1.20.17–19 to elucidate Eupolis' image of the 'sting' left in an audience by Pericles' oratory.[20] Just as Pliny dismisses the self-confidence of a contemporary rival who claims to be able to know just how and where to 'go for the throat' in his pleading, here he makes sure that we understand Pericles' 'sting' correctly: 'leaving a sting in a listener' is neither a swift nor a casual process for Pliny, but demands effort, concentration and even repetitiveness. One cannot expect results from a pinprick – one needs to hammer one's 'point' home:

nam delectare persuadere copiam dicendi spatiumque desiderat, relinquere uero aculeum in audientium animis is demum potest qui non pungit sed infigit. (1.20.18)

For to delight and persuade demands copiousness of speech and time for speaking. Moreover, he alone is able to 'leave a sting' in the minds of his hearers who not only pricks with it, but fixes it in.

At 2.5.11, in a covering letter for a draft speech, Pliny returns to his manifesto of oratorical variety as a means of pleasing as many people as possible:

---

[20] Quint. *Inst.* 12.10.65. For the image of a 'sting' in oratory, cf. 4.5.3. For a revealing contrast, however, between the 'sparing style' of Spurinna and the 'effusive supplication' of Regulus in 1.5, see Hoffer (1999) 79.

adnisi certe sumus, ut quamlibet diuersa genera lectorum per plures dicendi species teneremus, ac sicut ueremur, ne quibusdam pars aliqua secundum suam cuiusque naturam non probetur, ita uidemur posse confidere, ut uniuersitatem omnibus uarietas ipsa commendet. (2.5.7)

I have at any rate striven to interest readers of the most opposite characters, by a great variety of styles, and just as I fear that particular parts will not, in accordance with individual tastes, be approved by some, so I am pretty confident that this very variety will commend the book to all as a whole.

He goes on to illuminate his practice with an image drawn this time not from the agricultural sphere but from the culinary/social world: a dinner host should offer a variety of dishes, in order that something may suit the taste of every diner.[21] 2.5 then meditates further upon the pros and cons of reading selectively instead of comprehensively. Pliny acknowledges that the addressee cannot come to a final judgement of the speech without reading its entirety, but still defends his decision to send only selections of the work for comment:

in praesentia tamen et ista tibi familiariora fient, et quaedam ex his talia erunt ut per partes emendari possint. etenim, si auulsum statuae caput aut membrum aliquod inspiceres, non tu quidem ex illo posses congruentiam aequalitatemque deprendere, posses tamen iudicare, an id ipsum satis elegans esset; nec alia ex causa principiorum libri circumferuntur, quam quia existimatur pars aliqua etiam sine ceteris esse perfecta. (2.5.10–12)

For the present, however, what I have sent will become more familiar to you, and in this there will be certain corrections capable of being made in the parts. For if you were to inspect a head broken off from a statue, or some limb or other, though of course you could not gather from it its harmony and proportion to the rest, yet you might judge whether, taken by itself, it was a work of art or not. For this and no other reason, books of selected extracts are circulated, because it is believed that a part may be complete in itself without the remainder.

Here, although full understanding requires diligent examination of the whole, taste might be usefully and properly exercised in the reading of selections. Once again, there is a ready analogy with letters – carefully crafted items in themselves, but available to the anthologizing reader to be temporarily detached from the larger artwork.

Pliny's poetic efforts arouse similar concerns about pleasing a disparate readership. In 4.14.3, for example, he depends upon variety to charm all of his readers some of the time:

---

[21] Cf. also 6.33.8, where the lengthy speech *pro Attia Viriola* is said to be made palatable by its variety and organization. Cf. 4.14.3 (on Pliny's poetic efforts).

his iocamur ludimus amamus dolemus querimur irascimur, describimus aliquid modo pressius modo elatius, atque ipsa uarietate temptamus efficere, ut alia aliis quaedam fortasse omnibus placeant.

In these I am jokey and playful, I make love, grieve, complain, am angry, indulge in descriptions, at times in a homely, at others in a more elevated strain, and, by the very variety of treatment, aim at this result, that while different parts may please different people, there may be some parts which will possibly please everybody.

At 8.21 he expresses gratitude that his audience of select friends listened patiently to an entire collection of his poetry (in a variety of metres, as usual), because it means that he can be equally diligent in revising the whole collection ('I read the whole that I may correct the whole, and this cannot be the case with those who recite extracts [*electa recitantibus*]', 8.21.4). At the same time, he lets us know that he had been engaged in law-court business on the very day the recitation was due to begin, a fact which should not be taken, he says, as undermining his commitment to his poetic work, but as evidence of his philosophy that work on behalf of friends must come before literary relaxation, business before pleasure. This in itself illustrates the principle which opens the letter:

Ut in uita sic in studiis pulcherrimum et humanissimum existimo seueritatem comitatemque miscere, ne illa in tristitiam, haec in petulantiam excedat. (8.21.1)

Just as in life, so in literature, I deem it the most excellent course, and the one most in accord with human nature, to mingle the grave with the gay, lest the former should degenerate into morbidness and the latter into sauciness.

Pliny takes a coherent and well-integrated approach to life's variety, and represents his work (here his poetry) as a most faithful representation of the variety of his own emotions (4.14.3), while his letters about the verse illustrate and explain how they fit into the variety of his own activities and how they might win the hearts of his disparate audiences. He also, of course, insists that even a variegated work should ultimately be considered as a whole.

By Book 9, Pliny's commitment to variety will be linked to his own persona as the man who puts only modest valuation upon his talent: in 9.29.1 Pliny justifies his own great variety of compositional styles and genres by offering them as a respectable alternative to the single great talent he claims to lack (*ego uariis me studiorum generibus nulli satis confisus experior*, 'I try my hand at various kinds of literature, not being sufficiently confident about any of them'). Once again, this has consequences for the reader, who is advised to take each literary item in the context of Pliny's wider literary output (*proinde, cum hoc uel illud leges, ita singulis ueniam ut non singulis dabis*, 'so when you read this or that of mine, allow for each single composition as not standing by itself', 9.29.2).[22]

So, although Pliny says very little explicitly about his epistolary work, by 9.40 the reader should be aware that all the works he does talk about are built upon compositional practices and principles which apply just as well to the letter collection, and Pliny's concerns about length and variety, as well as his conscious assessment of an audience's requirements, are handled in a remarkably consistent way across multiple genres. Pliny builds a manifesto of variety, balance, *studia* and hard work throughout the collection and designs the letter collection itself to embody and endorse these qualities; along the way, he acknowledges and allows for a natural anthologizing tendency among his readers, each of whom (according to temperament or time constraints) will engage with some different part of his work, but he also encourages sustained reading both of sequences at the local level and of whole works from start to finish.

Pliny's understated encouragement to re-read and revise implicitly echoes the instructions of his teacher, Quintilian, to chew over what one has read, in order to digest it properly and commit it to memory; indeed the freedom to do this is one of the advantages of reading over hearing a text read aloud (*repetere saepius licet*, 'we can re-read a passage again and again', Quint. *Inst.*10.1.19). Moreover, he insists upon the value of re-reading a work as a whole:

nec per partes modo scrutanda omnia, sed perlectus liber utique ex integro resumendus, praecipueque oratio . . . saepe enim praeparat, dissimulat, insidiatur orator, eaque in prima parte actionis dicit, quae sunt in summa profutura. itaque suo loco minus placent, adhuc nobis quare dicta sunt ignorantibus, ideoque erunt cognitis omnibus repetenda. (Quint. *Inst.* 10.1.20–1)

Nor must we study it merely in parts, but must read through the whole work from cover to cover and then read it afresh, a precept which applies more especially to speeches . . . For the orator frequently prepares his audience for what is to come, dissembles and sets a trap for them and makes remarks at the opening of his speech which will not have their full force until the conclusion. Consequently what he says will often seem comparatively ineffective where it actually occurs, since we do not realize his motive, and it will be necessary to re-read the speech after we have acquainted ourselves with all that it contains.

Such are the practices of the mature reader, in Quintilian's programme, and Pliny's habit of revealing new perspectives or imparting fresh information

---

[22] For variety in Book 9, and a sequential reading of the book, see Goetzl (1952).

late in the collection reflects and supports good reading practices of this kind.[23]

LIFE/LETTERS AND MANAGED MISCELLANEITY

At the same time, Pliny shows a marked commitment to variety, for a purpose seemingly greater than purely aesthetic satisfaction in the design of his letter collection.[24] The variety in the letters reflects the full and well-lived life which Pliny represents as the ideal, in which *otium* and *studia* regularly punctuate public work, and laborious literary production in 'serious' genres is interspersed with speedy composition of shorter, lighter works. In such a life one maintains friendships with those who have chosen very different paths: the great senators who spend their lives on the front line of political and military events, the northern grandees who have eschewed urban ambition and the pursuit of consular office, the scholars, the philosophers, the professional poets and the unexpectedly cultured farmers who people this collection and make up its first audience. Life for Pliny is cumulative – an accumulation of tasks both brief and lengthy, many of them repeated or cyclical, a 'mixed portfolio' of lasting friendships, and a body of literary work which includes, miniaturizes or alludes to most elite genres.

The best life, in these terms, is one of 'managed miscellaneity' and Pliny's complex epistolary programme teaches the members of his circle how to design and execute such a life for themselves. Pliny's collection offers a worldly curriculum in practical living for the littérateur and public servant; it teaches its readers, by example and by exhortation, how (and when and what) to write, how to participate in a literary community, how to fulfil ambition under one-man rule, how to run private friendships, how to be a local benefactor (and how to record and commemorate one's munificence), how to remember the great men of the past, how to be a governor, what to do with an emperor's letters – and so on.

Success in applying Pliny's varied lessons, however, depends upon successful acquisition of a skill which we have considered from a number of

---

[23] We might note that one of the few items of furniture mentioned in Pliny's villa letters is a bookcase containing books which are not just to be read but to be read many times over (*non legendos... sed lectitandos*, 2.17.8). Cf. 6.7.2, where he is *re-reading* (*lectito*) Calpurnia's letters.

[24] It is interesting that one of Pliny's primary objections to the games is the lack of variety and novelty they offer to their audience: *nihil nouum nihil uarium, nihil quod non semel spectasse sufficiat*, 'there is no novelty, no variety about them, nothing which one is not satisfied with having seen once only' (9.6.1). Once is enough for the games; there is no invitation to revisit.

different perspectives in this book already: time management. Life's variety is ordered and made meaningful in Pliny's collection by means of careful division of one's days and years in the pursuit of a consciously selected set of activities, many of which are described, as we have argued earlier, in alternating letters within a book or alternating books within the collection. The short-term goal is to achieve healthy balance in life; the medium-term goal is to support the effective conduct of *negotium*; the long-term (and most important) goal is to ensure that one has done enough to achieve some kind of immortality.

LETTERS AND TIME

The selection of the letter form to deal with the issue of time was particularly apt: not only did Seneca's epistolary curriculum begin with an exhortation to Lucilius to take control of his time (*Ep.* 1.1), but letters more generally have a special relationship with time, being not only rooted in the moment of composition, but acting as a record of past or recent events.[25] Pliny's habit of emphasizing the universal applicability of his letters by stripping out standard epistolary time-markers serves to make them almost timeless artefacts when considered as individual items. The *collection*, however, gives the reader the sensation of being plunged *in medias res*, of entering Pliny's life when it is already up and running; moreover, within that collection, the letter sequences which structure and guide the reader's experience often depend upon the subtlest of quasi-chronological markers, many of them designed to be in some sense creatively misleading.

It is upon this disruption of time that Pliny plays at the very beginning of his collection, where we seem to break in in the middle of a long-standing conversation. *Frequenter hortatus es*, 'you have frequently urged me', says Pliny in 1.1 to his dedicatee – and we are away upon a project which is only – at last – coming into being after a series of (possibly epistolary?) exchanges upon the subject.[26] Then in 1.2 we immediately

---

[25] The beginning of a letter collection may be located anywhere in a life of epistolary writing. In Cicero's hands, in particular, they also became the ideal medium for projections of the future; cf. e.g. Cic. *Fam.* 2.8.1–2, Nep. *Att.* 16.4. Letters act as pledges for future action, or as moral guides which encapsulate exemplary behaviour of all kinds and reach forward to guide future action.

[26] In a collection each letter itself also emerges out of a broad but shadowy hinterland of 'lost' or 'discarded' letters. The 'hinterland' of the letters is also important and some letters put themselves in a context of other letters which are not in the collection, while still others refer back only to conversations: 4.7, to Catius Lepidus, for example, begins *saepe tibi dico* ('I often tell you'), but is the only letter to this man.

'arrive late' to another epistolary conversation, as Pliny sends his addressee the book *quem prioribus epistulis promiseram*, 'which I promised in my earlier letters'.[27] Here, as we suggested in our study of Pliny's manipulation of his Ciceronian models in Chapter 3, the reader is forced into a moment of confusion as to which book Pliny is referring to (the letter collection itself, which was the topic of letter 1.1, or some other of his works); we need to 'solve the riddle' quickly as more details emerge in the letter. He tells his addressee that he has composed nothing else *eodem ζήλῳ* ('in precisely the same spirit of emulation/zeal/style') – an ambivalent formula which appears to echo (and trump) the *paulo curatius* ('with rather more than usual care') of 1.1.1, but also forms the first clue for solving the riddle, since it echoes the more common technical critical terms (especially εὔζηλος, 'in correct taste') which belong properly to the sphere of oratory;[28] this, as the next sentence finally indicates, is the genre to which Pliny has turned in the 'interval' between the end of 1.1. and the beginning of 1.2.

The slipperiness of epistolary time, combined with the possibilities offered by a poetic model of book design, helps Pliny convey a loose chronology for the work, a vague sense both of quasi-historical record and of forward movement through a life. Pliny sometimes seems to reinforce this by the most fleeting of suggestions; so, for example, the decision to open Book 2 with the time-marker *post aliquot annos* gives the linear reader a momentary sense that time has passed since the end of Book 1, although once we get our bearings we realize that we are looking back once more at an exemplary life which began long before the Domitianic horrors which still loom (if only in the form of a tactful silence) over Book 1.

Above all, the collection's design allows Pliny to portray the development of a persona, as we see him gaining the confidence to admit to the poetic pastimes he has pursued since his teens, to refer more consistently to the success of his published works among his readers, to move towards more of the disciplined and managed *otium* for which Spurinna's fruitful and green old age provides the model and towards which his closing letters on his own routines in *otium* clearly point (9.36 and 9.40) and to claim his position as the equal in reputation even of Tacitus.

---

[27] We have a similar pairing at the beginning of the final book of 'private' letters, as 9.1, a letter urging publication of his addressee's attack on the Egyptian prefect Pompeius Planta, is followed by a letter in reply to Sabinus' request for more and longer letters (*facis iucunde quod non solum plurimas epistulas meas uerum etiam longissimas flagitas*, 'you are very obliging in pressing me not only for frequent letters, but for very long ones into the bargain').

[28] Cf. 7.12.2. See Sherwin-White (1966) 86–9.

FINISHING THE COLLECTION: BOOK 10

All of this, however, ignores the presence of Book 10 in the collection.[29] This final book is different in tone and style from the nine books of 'private and literary letters' which precede it, and it makes a new departure in its organizational principles too, since it gathers together letters exchanged between Pliny and just one addressee: the emperor Trajan. Trajan's replies are also included, and most of the letters are about a single (though multi-faceted) task: Pliny's tour of duty as the proconsular governor of Bithynia.

Until relatively recently, this book was seen as the work of an unknown editor, who collected such letters between Pliny and Trajan as remained available after Pliny's death, arranging them neatly (where possible) in question-and-answer pairs, as a posthumous 'appendix' to the nine books compiled and published by Pliny himself before departure for Bithynia.[30] However, in recent years Woolf, Stadter and Noreña have all argued in different ways for a more integral place for Book 10 within the letter collection;[31] like Books 1–9, it shows marked interest in self-representation, in the 'deft reworking of Ciceronian themes',[32] and in familiar issues of imperial justice and good administration, friendship and patronage. As Greg Woolf puts it, 'not only does it offer a quasi-narrative of Pliny's first year in office but it also conforms to a principle well established in the first nine books of the Letters, that of *uarietas* – varying the subject matter frequently in an apparently random fashion, one which conceals some significant juxtapositions'.[33]

Readers are now, in consequence, beginning to entertain the possibility that Book 10 was designed and published by Pliny himself. Definitive proof of the editor's identity is beyond our reach, and likely to remain so.[34] Nevertheless, it may be fruitful to explore some interpretative consequences of reading Book 10 within the grand design of the collection, as the crowning resolution of sub-narratives and themes which have been developed throughout the earlier nine-book collection. In particular, we suggest that this book, in which the key topic of Pliny's (or any Good Senator's) relationship with emperors is pulled together into the synecdochic tale of a single relationship with Trajan, provides an implicit answer to the problem

[29] For bibliography on Bithynia-Pontus and Pliny's stint as governor there, and on his treatment of the local Christian community (neither topic is covered in this volume), see Appendix 3.

[30] On the nature and publication of Book 10, see Sherwin-White (1966) 525–55. Cf. Ludolph (1997) 49–56 on differences between Book 10 and the other letter books.

[31] Woolf (2006a), Stadter (2006), Noreña (2007).

[32] Woolf (2006a) 104.   [33] Woolf (2006a) 103.

[34] But see Appendix 1 for further suggestions of artistry in the arrangement of Book 10.

of how, given Cicero's dominance in the letter genre, one can write letters at all under an imperial system which precludes 'Ciceronian' engagement with high politics.

Book 10 begins, appropriately, with a short letter in celebration of Trajan's accession, which functions as dedication and preface for the new book. Book 1 also situated itself chronologically in relation to an emperor's death (*post Domitiani mortem*, 'after the death of Domitian,' 1.5.1), but ignored Trajan's accession, offering instead an implied continuity between Nerva and Trajan in the better days after Domitian's assassination. Book 10, by contrast, 'restarts the clock' on the collection, beginning from a happier point in the story. Thereafter, the opening fourteen ('pre-Bithynian') letters of the book fill in some of the details of Pliny's career (as we have already seen in our biographical reading of the letters in Chapter 1) and return to two subjects in particular which were important to Pliny in Books 1–9: his health (a topic now revisited from a new perspective as he seeks rewards for his medical attendants)[35] and the welfare and promotion of some, at least, of his closest friends who appeared in earlier books, including Suetonius, Rosianus Geminus and Voconius Romanus.[36] We find more evidence that Pliny liked to think himself a punctilious public servant, that Good Emperors approved of his actions when in court (7.33, 10.3B), and that Pliny had had a fruitful relationship with Nerva in particular, and was now keen to build on the association with Trajan of which we have seen glimpses in Books 1–9.[37]

Above all, as we noted in Chapter 2, Pliny's presence in Bithynia after the nine books of 'private' letters makes the reader realize at last how peculiarly prominent this province had already been in Pliny's professional life, providing the subject matter for a short but central sequence of letters about Pliny's defence of Bassus and then of Varenus against Bithynian prosecutions in Books 4–7, some of them (particularly 4.9 and 7.6) among Pliny's longest and most complex letters about his professional activities.[38] Yet again, one might reasonably think, Pliny has used a

---

[35] See Chapter 1.

[36] Key addressees/subjects from 1–9: Voconius Romanus, 10.4; his own hopes of the augurate, 10.13; his doctors, unnamed in the letters which mention health in Books 1–9, but for whose relatives he asks favours and citizenship in Book 10; Rosianus Geminus, 10.26; Suetonius, 10.94.

[37] On Book 10 as an advertisement for good relations between Pliny and Trajan, see Noreña (2007) esp. 254–61.

[38] 4.9, 5.20, 6.13, 7.6, 7.10.

later gathering of letters to re-illuminate important features of the earlier collection.[39]

Above all, Book 10 is a book of *negotium*, in which Pliny provides variety by describing, in 107 distinctively short letters, the vast range of challenges facing the governor of a disparate and financially chaotic province. In Books 1–9, although Pliny's emphasis was on variety in the management of one's life (and so we do find in those books some lengthy letters describing Pliny's legal cases, or his service on the emperor's *consilium*, or his delivery of the *Panegyricus*), the primary setting for letters was the time of *otium* in which public activity could be recalled in tranquillity and cast in epistolary form for his friends. Indeed, at two important points in the collection, 3.20.10–12 and 9.2.2–3, Pliny claims that any desire on his part to produce letters of importance – long, Ciceronian letters about public matters – is frustrated by the constraints of the contemporary political system. Readers of Book 9 who share Sherwin-White's disappointment at its large number of relatively short letters on matters of little or no political interest see Pliny as giving accidental confirmation of the truth of such claims – and one might see Book 10 as further evidence that on public service Pliny does indeed write only the *litterae inlitteratissimae* ('most unliterary letters') he bemoans in 1.10.9.

However, once one reads 3.20 and 9.2 first in the immediate context of their respective books (looking in particular at what kinds of letters Pliny juxtaposes with them) and then as part of a cycle in which Pliny reflects upon and experiments with the letter form in new political circumstances, we find enough to suggest that the significance of both these letters for our understanding of Book 10's surprising, even revolutionary, qualities needs careful unpacking, and that Book 10, in its turn, once again forces us to re-read earlier books and re-interpret Pliny's agenda.

LETTER 3.20 AND THE EPISTOLARY MUSE

The bulk of letter 3.20 concerns the history of balloting procedures on election day. Pliny builds his account around a conventional contrast between the supposed dignity and sobriety of such events in 'the old days' and the intemperance of 'today' which has necessitated the introduction of the secret ballot. In the last section of the letter, however, Pliny explains why he has written on this subject, and offers one of his relatively rare explicit meditations on the nature of epistolary opportunity and inspiration:

---

[39] On the Bithynia saga in the earlier books of the collection, see Chapter 2.

haec tibi scripsi, primum ut aliquid noui scriberem, deinde ut non numquam de
re publica loquerer, cuius materiae nobis quanto rarior quam ueteribus occasio,
tanto minus omittenda est. et hercule quousque illa uulgaria? 'quid agis? ecquid
commode uales?' habeant nostrae quoque litterae aliquid non humile nec sordidum, nec priuatis rebus inclusum. sunt quidem cuncta sub unius arbitrio, qui
pro utilitate communi solus omnium curas laboresque suscepit; quidam tamen
salubri temperamento ad nos quoque uelut riui ex illo benignissimo fonte decur-
runt, quos et haurire ipsi et absentibus amicis quasi ministrare epistulis possumus.
uale. (3.20.10–12)

I have written this to you, first, in order to write of something new; next that I
may occasionally speak of public affairs: the occasions for which, as they are rarer
for us than for our ancestors, so they are the less to be neglected. And, by Hercules,
when shall we cease hearing those commonplaces, 'What are you up to? I hope
you are tolerably well?' Let our letters too contain something out of the ordinary
and the paltry, and whatever is confined to private interests. All things, to be sure,
are at the disposal of one who, for the common advantage, has taken on himself
single-handed the cares and labours of all; yet by a healthful dispensation of them
there flow down even to us certain rills, so to speak, from that bounteous source,
such as we cannot only drink in ourselves, but also in a manner supply to our
absent friends through the medium of letters. Farewell.

This passage is dense and its references complex. Pliny makes a familiar
distinction between the material of great public importance available to
the *ueteres*, and the ordinary topics of private life to which contemporary
writers are restricted. He appears to privilege the reporting of political
news as the primary function of letters (although this has indeed been
relatively unimportant in his collection so far), and to reject their more
'private' role in providing reassuring updates about a friend's daily activities
and physical health (in fact a far more characteristic topic, most recently
treated, for example, at 3.17). Cicero is the unnamed but tangible presence
here, and the reader will naturally recall all the letters in which Cicero
wrote explicitly about the *res publica* (that such letters were often written
in a tone of complaint and despair is not highlighted).

Pliny's focus here is upon content rather than style, and (unusually) upon
letters as opposed to any other form of writing. Nevertheless, his complaints
here and in 9.2.3 (*nos quam angustis terminis claudamur*, 'how narrow are
the limits in which *I* am enclosed') about the restrictions imposed upon
letter-writers should be read in conjunction with the conventional characterization of letters themselves as inherently of restricted scope and length.
In fact Pliny tends to apologize for any lengthy treatment of a topic of political or historical interest on the grounds that he has transgressed against
the natural *angustiae* of the genre: 4.17, for example, closes by defending

the letter's lengthy exposition of Pliny's responsibilities to Corellia's daughter (*latius scilicet et uberius quam epistularum angustiae sinunt*, 'of course with greater detail and fullness than the narrow limits of a letter permit', 4.17.11).[40]

Within (and despite) such generic *angustiae*, however, Pliny's collection has presented a consistent message about the importance of *cura* and *labor* in the production of letters and other kinds of writing as well as in the responsible management of one's days. As we have noted in Chapter 6, Pliny begins his collection by emphasizing his natural *desidia* but he does so partly in order to urge himself and his addressees on to effort, a message which is subtly reinforced by, for example, the linked allusions in 1.2.2 and 1.3.3 to Vergil's Sibyl's strictures about the heroic *labor* required of those who wish to cheat death.[41] 3.20.12 returns to the value of *curae laboresque*, and confirms, it seems, that the *cura* and *labor* of the elite now belong in the private sphere and the world of *otium* alone, while the emperor has undertaken them in the public sphere on everyone's behalf, allowing only a few public responsibilities to trickle down to the senatorial class. The consequence for letters is a dearth of material which one might think fatally exacerbates the inherently restricted scope of the genre itself. In three and a half sentences, then (*haec scripsi . . . suscepit*), Pliny has apparently told a tidily packaged epistolographical version of a tale of decline more familiar (from the *Dialogus*, in particular) in relation to oratory.[42]

In the letter's final tantalizing and rather enigmatic *tamen* sentence, however, Pliny constructs an image of epistolary *materia* as water which the writer draws from the spring of the emperor's beneficence and then serves to his friends, with the unconventional twist that an epistolary writer must serve his refreshing draughts of inspiration from a distance – a touch which disrupts the conventional image to which it seems to claim kinship, since water being drawn from a spring and then served to friends *at a distance* seems otherwise an *adynaton*, or at the very least an odd conflation of images and genres, as Pliny's self-conscious *quasi ministrare* ('in a manner supply', 3.20.12) seems to acknowledge.

We should not downplay the oddity of the last few sentences of 3.20, nor fail to notice Pliny's dexterity in expressing in so short a passage both nostalgia on the one hand for opportunities under the republic which are now lost and grateful relief on the other for the emperor's provisions in this area. There is a drought, as it were, in the news which letter-writers can both participate in and write about, but somehow the emperor makes sure the

---

[40] Cf. 6.16.22.   [41] See Marchesi (2008) 27–33.   [42] Tac. *Dial.* 1.

writers (and their addressees) do not die of thirst.[43] The emperor becomes a kind of epistolary Muse,[44] and Pliny 'renovates' a potentially negative position to serve a panegyrical agenda: any letters on *political* matters (which have been restricted by the imperial system) paradoxically depend upon the emperor's beneficent presence which, it turns out, provides a compensatory source of epistolary inspiration. At all events, the provision of these metaphorical *riui*, 'in a healthy blend' (Henderson's felicitous translation of *salubri temperamento*,[45] 3.20.12), certainly suggests that they are to be counted as quasi-physical amenities of the new, settled regime.[46]

The link Pliny makes between the presence of a Good Emperor and the lifting of 'today's' famine in epistolary material prepares us for some of what will come later in the collection. At 7.33, for example, Pliny really does provide an emperor's letter as material for someone else's work, while at the same time advertising openly that he has already been an emperor's addressee on at least one occasion:

diuus quidem Nerua (nam priuatus quoque attendebat his quae recte in publico fierent) missis ad me grauissimis litteris non mihi solum, uerum etiam saeculo est gratulatus, cui exemplum (sic enim scripsit) simile antiquis contigisset. (7.33.9)

The late Emperor Nerva (for even while a private citizen he paid attention to exhibitions of uprightness in public affairs), in a very weighty communication which he addressed to me, congratulated not only me, but the age, on being blessed with an example (it was thus that he wrote) of the antique kind.

Such letters provide another way into the history books. Above all, however, Book 10 provides a demonstration of what is possible in the way of 'public' letters on topics related to *negotium publicum*, at least, if not to *res publica*

---

[43] A possible aqueduct metaphor in 3.20 is potentially an important link also to Book 10 – where Pliny is himself the physical representative of the emperor and makes decisions about water supply and bath houses. It is an especially appropriate image, of course (better than the cup-bearer image), for use in and of letters, which are modes of communication in absence and at distance, just as aqueducts deliver water to people who are at a distance from a fresh spring. Cf. Frontin. *Aq.* 2.129.11 for *haurire* used of drawing water from fountains or arches for private use.

[44] Cf. Lucil. 1008, Lucr. 1.927–8. For *e fontibus haurire* ('to drink from springs') used of the process of inspiration, cf. also Stat. *Theb.* 4.38. Statius writes of shared inspiration at *Silu.* 1.2.259, and the image of 'drinking from the same spring' is used by Cicero in a letter to Plancus advising him how best to achieve glory and success in his public life (*Fam.* 10.3.4), referring to their shared intellectual training and outlook, but the image in 3.20 of Pliny passing on inspiration at long distance seems to be an aptly epistolary adaptation of his own.

[45] Henderson (2002a) 145.

[46] The phrase *salubri temperamento* is used elsewhere of the sophisticated and technologically advanced steam heating system at Pliny's villa, 2.17.9, though the notion of compromise is also strongly suggested (cf. 1.7.3 *tenebo ergo hoc temperamentum*, 'I will therefore preserve this mean' – and this in a context in which Pliny is the quasi-divine source of favours). For *temperamentum* used of Trajan's moderation and also of his respect for traditional offices, see *Pan.* 10.3, 55.5, 79.5.

in the sense Cicero might have recognized. In this book, we find that although it is no longer possible to write letters of public importance to one's peers (and in the 'private' context one has to apologize for being able to write only short letters due to the lack of material, as we see in 9.2), nevertheless it *is* possible to write short letters about state business to the emperor, and Book 10 demonstrates, indeed, that stripped-down, 'miniaturized' versions of Cicero's Cilician letters, at least, are still possible. Moreover, Pliny becomes in this book not just an epistolary Ganymede, serving cooling draughts of epistolary inspiration to his friends, but rather the physical representative of the emperor himself, the living proof of Trajan's care for those of his subjects who live at a distance from Rome:

prouinciales, credo, prospectum sibi a me intellegent. nam et tu dabis operam, ut manifestum sit illis electum te esse, qui ad eosdem mei loco mittereris. (10.18.2)

The provincials will, I trust, understand that I have had their interests in view. For you, for your part, will take care to make it plain to them that you have been selected to be sent to them as representing me.

The addition of Book 10 to the collection, moreover, crowns the didactic agenda. Pliny has shown how to write literary letters, and referred only by way of contrast to the *inlitteratissimae litterae* required of him by his job (1.10.9); he has also, in the final books of the 'private' collection, offered advice to friends on their conduct on tours of duty in a province (8.24, 9.5);[47] Book 10 then provides the extended practical lesson in the details of provincial management.

In addition, it serves to represent Pliny not only as the trusted correspondent of Trajan, thus associating him permanently in posterity's mind with the Good Emperor, but also as editor, custodian and even historian, in a minor way, of emperors' letters. This is, after all, the one book in which we hear epistolary voices other than Pliny's, most of which are emperors' voices – Trajan's, of course, above all, but Pliny also cites administrative letters relating to Bithynia by Domitian and Nerva. The actual texts of some of the letters themselves are also included in the collection (almost exactly halfway through) in 10.58, while in 10.65 Pliny depicts himself listening to readings of imperial letters of general relevance to problems of

---

[47] On Maximus' assignment in Achaia, like Pliny's in Bithynia, in Trajan's new disposition of gubernatorial posts (both were selected by Trajan personally and given a special mandate in their otherwise senatorial provinces), see Bodel (unpublished) 99–100. Bodel suggests too that 8.24 is supposed to remind knowledgeable readers of Pliny's own provincial assignment. Bodel (unpublished) 100 is important on the 'accident of history' which took Pliny to the province which he had dismissed as servile in 8.24.9 – Bodel thinks 'the irony is Pliny's own'.

provincial management: Vespasian to the Lacedaemonians, Titus to the Lacedaemonians and Achaeans, and Domitian to Avidius Nigrinus and Armenius Brocchus. Past emperors both good and bad are, in a sense, now all filed in an epistolary archive for the convenience and instruction of their successor and his letter-writing governor in Bithynia.

In Book 10, we find ourselves deep in Pliny's *negotium* in Bithynia, and the old themes of work and effort reappear, but take on a different colour. If we read Book 10, as we now suggest one might, as the crowning book of the collection, we will see that Pliny has developed his persona and his activities in relation to *cura* very carefully, moving from stylistic *cura* at the beginning of Book 1 to the first mention of the emperor's removal of 'real' *cura* from all the elite in 3.20, to the final instantiation of such *cura* in Book 10. Anxiety about (for example) the appropriate length of a speech or – especially – of a letter in earlier books, and the *cura* of writing and *negotium* are swept away in Book 10 by the real pressure which produces short letters from the representative and ambassador of an emperor's *cura*.

Finally, the flurry of letters between consular governor and emperor not only serves a competitive agenda which we will discuss next, but also emphasizes Trajan's effectiveness as the provider of material for letters which matter for the welfare of the Roman state and its dominions. Thus it may give further assistance in understanding the message of the end of 3.20: under a benevolent emperor the dearth of material for letters is relieved by the *riui ex illo benignissimo fonte*, 'rills from that most bounteous source' (3.20.12). Conversely, the apparent absence of letters in Books 1–9 which were composed during the era of Domitian only confirms Pliny's implied assertion that letters could be choked off altogether under repressive regimes. The shock of hearing Domitian's imperial voice in a single letter safely archived at the heart of a book which is devoted to a fruitful and practical correspondence with Trajan only accentuates the silence of this voice in the earlier books;[48] that Book 10, like Book 1, locates itself in time by reference to an emperor's recent death – this time that of Nerva (10.1), rather than of Domitian (1.5) – also helps to make the point that we have consigned the tyrant to a past which was remembered in the 'private' letters only for the sake of its great resistance heroes but which has now altogether disappeared.

Book 10, moreover, serves to crown Pliny's efforts to outdo all his epistolary predecessors, a point which may be illustrated by revisiting Pliny's echo

[48] Other emperors' voices are occasionally audible in Books 1–9 (e.g. Claudius in 1.13.3, or Nerva in 7.33.9).

of Ovid's epistolary exile poetry in 1.1 and assessing where Pliny stands in relation to Ovid, as well as Seneca and Cicero, by the end of the ten-book collection.

Let us return to the beginning at last, to the famous dedicatory opening letter:

frequenter hortatus es, ut epistulas, si quas paulo curatius scripsissem, colligerem publicaremque. collegi non seruato temporis ordine (neque enim historiam componebam), sed ut quaeque in manus uenerat. superest ut nec te consilii nec me paeniteat obsequii. ita enim fiet, ut eas quae adhuc neglectae iacent requiram et si quas addidero non supprimam. uale. (1.1)

You have frequently urged me to collect and publish such of my letters as had been written with rather more than usual care. I *have* collected them, without preserving the order of dates (since it was not a history that I was compiling), but just as each came to hand. It remains that you should have no cause to repent your advice, nor I my compliance. The result, in that case, will be that I shall hunt up such other letters as still lie neglected, and if I write any fresh ones, I will not withhold them. Farewell.

Here, one thinks, is a clear (if brief) statement of the principles upon which the work is built:

1. It contains the letters upon which Pliny has lavished special care.
2. There is no editorial attempt to reflect the chronological order of composition. Rather, by retaining the sequence in which the letters came to his hand when he began his work of collecting them together, Pliny turns himself, in a sense, into the first reader/recipient of the letters.
3. There is no claim to up-to-date comprehensiveness (some publishable letters may have been overlooked and might be included in future volumes).
4. If Pliny composes any new letters of special merit he will not keep them back. This is, then, not a chronologically arranged work, but it is potentially one which will end only upon Pliny's death.

As Henderson says, all this is a 'gesture towards informality' – and it is, of course, part of the point here to contrast the care lavished upon the letter as an individual item against the relaxed informality of the editorial process and of the letters as a collection.[49]

---

[49] Henderson (2002a) 21. On the seemingly disordered autobiographical fragments generated by this approach, see Chapter 1. For Pliny's design at book level (which reveals that his claim that he arranged his letters 'as they came to hand' is creatively misleading), see Chapter 2.

It is well over two decades since Ronald Syme noted the echo in Pliny 1.1 of Ovid's *Pont.* 3.9.51–4:[50]

> nec liber ut fieret, sed uti sua cuique daretur
> littera, propositum curaque nostra fuit.
> postmodo conlectas utcumque sine ordine iunxi:
> hoc opus electum ne mihi forte putes.

Not that a book might come out of it, but to send the appropriate letter to each person – *this* was my project and my care. These letters I later collected, put them together somehow, without order – please don't think this work involved any *choice* by me! (trans. P. Green, adapted)

We find here the same emphasis on the care lavished upon each individual letter in contrast to the casual disposition of multiple letters within a book collection. There is, of course, as much false modesty in Ovid's assertion of informality in collection as there is in Pliny's, and, as Marchesi has recently pointed out, Pliny has taken a highly sophisticated approach to applying multiple organizational systems within his collection – all of them, as she says, 'poetic in nature'.[51]

Marchesi plays out some of the significance of the Ovidian allusion in 1.1 for the letters of Books 1–9, comparing their 'fragmented narrative' with Ovid's version of such an endeavour in the first of his exile books, too, *Tristia* 1. All together the letters of *Tristia* 1 present a broken narrative of Ovid's journey out of the city, across the sea, then across land and finally across the Black Sea. Pliny too encourages us to read for an epistolary story in Books 1–9 in various ways (as Marchesi says, 'the mere presence of epistles that develop successive stages of a plot [invite] a sequential reading of his work'), but the overall effect is different – and even Marchesi concludes on a negative position: 'To be sure', she says, 'Pliny has nothing that even comes close to the strict narrativity of *Tristia* 1.'[52]

In relation to Books 1–9 Marchesi is quite correct. Book 10, however, is another matter, and we suggest that some of its many oddities start to make more sense when we read the book in terms of the Ovidian agenda Marchesi detects in the arrangement of Books 1–9. Space precludes exhaustive exploration of the issue here, and the following remarks are suggestions only, but let us take as an example just one of those oddities, namely the inclusion in 10.15 of the more tedious details of Pliny's journey to Bithynia – by boat, on land, then by boat again:

---

[50] Syme, *RP* 5.478 [= (1985b) 176]; cf. the brief discussion of this echo in Chapter 2.
[51] Marchesi (2008) 22; cf. Mayer (2003) 232.   [52] Marchesi (2008) 26.

quia confido, domine, ad curam tuam pertinere, nuntio tibi me Ephesum cum omnibus meis ὑπὲρ Μαλέαν nauigasse quamuis contrariis uentis retentum. nunc destino partim orariis nauibus, partim uehiculis prouinciam petere. nam sicut itineri graues aestus, ita continuae nauigationi etesiae reluctantur. (10.15)

As I am convinced, sir, that the news will be of interest to you, I beg to announce that I have sailed past the promontory of Malea and reached Ephesus, with all my entourage, though retarded by contrary winds. Now I propose to make for my province, partly by coasting-boats, partly by land conveyances. For as the excessive heats are an impediment to a land journey, so in like manner the Etesian winds oppose continuous navigation.

When Pliny arrives in Bithynia, he lists his modes of transport again (10.17A). If we think the letters were simply gathered together by the Unknown Editor, then we might accept that these rather dull items were found in a file and retained in the published version for the sake of completeness. But if we assume that there is a design in Book 10 and that it could have been masterminded by Pliny himself, then it is all the odder that the author of all the carefully crafted, allusive, literary letters of Books 1–9 would care to include such material – even in this very different kind of book at the end of his collection.

Why could we not think, however, that Pliny is taking full advantage of the epistolary opportunities of his journey – not just any journey, after all, but a journey to the Black Sea – and playing upon the works of an entirely different letter-writer, one who wrote back from the Black Sea to a hostile emperor or to those who could help him approach that angry Jupiter? Fitzgerald has recently suggested that Martial, too, constructs his work as a kind of echo of Ovid, a more positive version of the playful poet's relationship with an emperor; this approach develops and adds further colour to the work of Roger Pitcher, who argues that 'by referring back to aspects of Ovid's exile poetry Martial is able to present himself as the superior of Ovid, and acceptable to the emperor'.[53] It seems possible that something similar is going on in Pliny's work.

We start in 1.1, then, in the world of Ovid's *Epistulae ex Ponto*, with an apparently casual collection of letters in the private or semi-private world. Pliny's first letter alludes to the last poem in Ovid's collection (as it was first planned, at least, before another book got added) of poetic letters *ex Ponto*.[54] But we suggest that Pliny ends his work in a chiastic pattern of allusion, bringing his reader back to the beginning of Ovid's

---

[53] Fitzgerald (2007b) 187; Pitcher (1998) 71–2.
[54] On the likely publication of the fourth book after Ovid's death, see Froesch (1968) 53–4.

exilic letters with an implicit engagement in Book 10 with the situations and some of the motifs of *Tristia* 1. This is, as students of poetic allusion have noted, a characteristic feature of neoteric book design,[55] and it is Pliny's revolutionary step to demonstrate the applicability of such design principles to such a prosaic (in all senses) genre as the collected letters of a consular lawyer.

It is the contrasts in situation, of course, which are important, and which are so piquantly illuminated in Pliny's combination of quasi-poetic design and images on the one hand and (often – and especially in Book 10) relentlessly workaday material on the other. In Ovid's case most of the letters are addressed to individuals other than the emperor, since a direct approach to an angry emperor is – or is presented as – difficult. Pliny, by contrast, writes directly to the emperor, in a manner and using language which, as Noreña has demonstrated, blurs the public/private distinction and suggests a friendly (although not intimate) relationship between them.[56] Moreover, Pliny has neatly reversed the situation we find in Ovid, writing to all and sundry from within Italy in Books 1–9, but addressing only the emperor from his travels towards the Black Sea region.

Further, Ovid presents, in the poems in which he talks about the environment and people of Tomis, a highly coloured, frightening and alien picture. Pliny, by contrast, as Woolf has pointed out, strips away anything worrying[57] and largely (though not totally) ignores non-Roman elements of the place and of his experience there. He reports his journey to the province in prosaic, unexciting, even bland terms – but as a man whose welfare on this journey might have been desirable for his courteous and patient addressee.[58] The province, when he gets there, is in *financial* chaos, but the colourful, even garish, barbarism of the Black Sea, which was so prominent a feature in other writers who mention the region, is virtually eliminated.

Sceptical readers might object that a sustained allusion to Ovid might make sense for Martial who, as Fitzgerald says, 'as a writer of risqué verse, which may fall foul of the emperor, . . . must hope that he does not go the way of Ovid'.[59] Ovid is, one might think, a far cry from our respectable, even priggish, administrator, who knows his way around a set of accounts

---

[55] Zetzel (1983) 261.   [56] Noreña (2007) 246.
[57] Cf. Woolf (2006a) 105 on the characterlessness of the province.
[58] Note, however, the Odyssean quality of 10.15, where Pliny notes that he has rounded Malea with his entire entourage (perhaps a subtly contrastive allusion to Menelaus' and Odysseus' crucial journeys past Malea at *Od.* 3.286–92 and 9.74–6); for Odysseus as a significant figure for Ovid, see e.g. Gaertner (2005) 243–4.
[59] Fitzgerald (2007b) 189.

like no one else, and parades his position as part of the establishment elite. Nevertheless, Pliny has already carefully built up a persona over the course of nine books of letters addressed to everyone BUT the emperor. Martial himself was posthumously invoked in 3.21 to vouch for Pliny's appreciation for a naughty poet – right after the only reference in the first nine books to the emperor's role as an inspiration for letters (3.20.12). And Pliny himself has devoted key letters to defending his decision to write naughty poetry himself, a pastime which is acceptable if you are not someone like Ovid but a genuinely respectable orator, lawyer, consul and administrator – or even potentially an emperor. 5.3, for example, offers a list (beginning with Cicero) of worthy public men (including emperors) who were known to write verse, a list which should remind the reader of Ovid's incendiary exempla in *Tristia* 2 of respectable writers who have written risqué verse, culminating at *Tr.* 2.442 with self-justification for following in their footsteps.[60]

The structuring allusion to the *Epistulae ex Ponto* in 1.1, combined with the detailed coverage of Pliny's journey eastwards in Book 10, should be read as suggestive of Pliny's debt to Ovid. In Book 10 Pliny *has*, in the most literal manner of speaking, 'gone the way of Ovid', but as a successful agent of a friendly emperor rather than an exile disgraced for his naughty verse and an unidentifiable *error*. These can, of course, be only suggestions, given the state of our evidence about the circumstances of publication of this final book, but given Pliny's close and subtle engagement with poets as well as with Cicero in the nine-book collection, it seems interpretatively fruitful to consider the effects of including Book 10 within the boundaries of a planned and balanced collection.

CONCLUSION

In Pliny the Younger's letter collection, then, we have a long work made up of lots of short items casually collected into nine books, within which Pliny explores a nexus of themes, including the importance of *cura* and *labor*, and the movement of a successful and well-planned life towards deserved literary *otium*. These are crowned by the one extra book at the end, which functions both as a kind of Ciceronian coda and as the climax of a collection in which Pliny began as the lazy pleasure seeker and ended up on the Black Sea as not only a new and better prose Ovid, but a new and better Cicero, trumping both his predecessors by getting on well with

[60] Cf. 5.3.5.

the sole ruler, and documenting his service to the state in the short letters for which he seemed to apologize in 1.10 and 9.2.

In this collection, then, as we have seen throughout this book, the reader will find not just Pliny. One can read these letters as a fractured narrative about a single life, but they are also a steadily developed narrative about a fractured persona. The collection builds coherence and direction by adding allusive complexity to Pliny's persona(e), as we find in its pages an Ovid in prose, a Cicero in verse, a 'Senecan' philosopher in public life, and Tacitus' touchy equal. Above all, the collection's 'grand design' invites readers to think carefully about how the whole collection, as well as each book, begins and ends, and about the number of reading strategies to which it is hospitable. And we can see that best if we keep reading, from the beginning right to the very end – and then start from the beginning again.

A Pliny timeline and the great Comum inscription

Events during Pliny's lifetime are catalogued below, with some artificiality, according to three categories: major political events; events in Pliny's life and career; and events in Pliny's 'circle' (very broadly conceived). Many dates are provisional,[1] particularly the dating of public offices (e.g. Pliny's praetorship under Domitian or period of service in Bithynia). We follow – in the main – the account provided by Birley (2000a) 1–17, supplemented for political events by *CAH*[2] 11.1009–11.[2] (Birley provides full information on controversies in Pliny's career and notice of alternative datings.) Stages in the lives of Pliny and his circle are studied in Chapters 1 (AD 96–8) and 4 (Pliny's early manhood) of this volume. The main source for our knowledge of Pliny's life outside the *Letters*, the great Comum inscription, is printed and briefly discussed below.

CAH[2] 11.1–131 provides an authoritative narrative of political events during Pliny's adult life. Articles on Pliny's early career and on the lives of those in his circle (e.g. Verginius Rufus, Vestricius Spurinna) are collected in Syme, *RP* 7. For further articles on the latter group, including the Elder Pliny, see Syme, *RP* 2.477–95 [= (1960)], 2.694–723 [= (1968)], 2.743–73 [= (1969b)] and 5.431–39 [= (1985e)], 5.440–77 [= (1985a)]. See also Birley (2000b) for the career of Tacitus (some of Birley's dates are adopted below).[3] Further context is provided by biographies of Nerva, Trajan and the early career of Hadrian authored (respectively) by Grainger (2003), Bennett (2001) and Birley (1997) 1–76.

---

[1] As will be evident in differences from similar tables in Griffin (1999) 157–8, Lefèvre (2009) 20–1.

[2] See also e.g. Vidman *PIR*[2] P 490; Syme, *RP* 7.551–67, (1958) 75–85; Sherwin-White (1966) 69–82. Known inscriptions relating to Pliny are listed in Vidman *PIR*[2] P 490; for the *tegulae* inscriptions from the vicinity of Tifernum Tiberinum referred to there as 'unpublished', see now Uroz Sáez (1999a), (2008). The more important inscriptions have been widely reprinted, e.g. in the editions of Guillemin (1927–28), Schuster (1958), Radice (1969), Zehnacker (2009); also Sherwin-White (1966) 732–3.

[3] For a comparison of the careers of Pliny and Tacitus, see Griffin (1999); for their relationship in the *Letters*, see Chapter 5 of this volume.

The timeline below may also be read against the broad dates for letters in Books 1–9 as suggested by Sherwin-White (1966) 27–41: Books 1–2 (late 96–Sept. 100); 3 (Sept. 100–103, excepting 3.4 and 3.9 which belong respectively to 99 and mid-100); 4 (104–5); 5 (105–6, except possibly 5.20, which may be early 107); 6 (106–7); 7 (107); 8 (107–8), 9 (106–8, except 9.4, 9.8, and 9.26, which may be 100–1, 104–5, and 96–8 respectively). These dates do not differ greatly from the scheme developed by Syme (1958) 660–4, except in some minor details: Book 1 (97–8); 2 (97–100, with the exception of 2.9, which may belong to 101); 3 (101–2); 4 (103–5); 5 (105–6); 6 (106–7); and 7 (107). The dating of letters in Books 8–9 has always proved particularly difficult – significant in itself, of course – and Syme devoted later separate study to the issue (*RP* 5.478–89 [= (1985b)]). He argued that Book 8 contains letters mostly from 107–8, but with some as late as 108–9; and that Book 9 covers the years 107–9. For discussion of dating issues, see further Chapters 1 and 2 in this volume.[4]

A TIMELINE

Particular uncertainty or controversy over dating is marked by the use of 'c.' or '?'. The question-mark sign is not used to query matters of fact. P. = Pliny the Younger

Date	Events		
Approx. Year	Political	In Pliny's life	In Pliny's 'circle'
c. 58	Nero emperor since 54.		Birth of Tacitus.
61–2		Birth of P.	
68–9	Death of Nero (68); civil war, brief reigns of Galba, Otho and Vitellius (68–9), accession of Vespasian (69).		Ambiguous role of Verginius Rufus in insurrection against Nero in 68; Silius Italicus consul in 68 and Verginius consul in 69.
Before 76		Death of P.'s father (L. Caecilius Secundus); appointment of Verginius Rufus as P.'s guardian.	Elder Pliny holds series of equestrian procuratorships, including Hispania Tarraconensis (73–4?).

---

[4] See also e.g. Cova (1966) 126–36, Aubrion (1989).

Date	Events		
Approx. Year	Political	In Pliny's life	In Pliny's 'circle'
c. 70			Birth of Suetonius
c. 77		P. studying in Rome with Quintilian.	Elder Pliny's *Natural History* finished; Corellius Rufus consul (78).
79	Accession of Titus.	Probable testamentary adoption of P. by Elder Pliny.	Death of Elder Pliny during eruption of Vesuvius while commanding fleet at Misenum.
80–1	Great plague in Rome (80); accession of Domitian (81).	P. appointed *decemvir stlitibus iudicandis*; first appears in court as advocate; co-opted as *patronus* of Tifernum Tiberinum.	Tacitus *quaestor Augusti* (81?).
c. 82		P. *tribunus militum* in Syria.	
c. 84		P. *seuir equitum Romanorum*; marries for first time; defends Iunius Pastor in Centumviral courts.	
85–6	Dacian war (85–8).		Tacitus *tribunus plebis* (85?); Martial begins to publish epigrams (86).
c. 87		P. enters senate as *quaestor Augusti*.	
88			Tacitus praetor.
c. 89	Domitian proclaims edict against philosophers.		
c. 91		P. *tribunus plebis*.	Publication of *Thebaid* of Statius (91–2).

(*cont.*)

Date	Events		
Approx. Year	Political	In Pliny's life	In Pliny's 'circle'
93	Trials of Baebius Massa, then of members of the 'Stoic opposition': Herennius Senecio, Helvidius Priscus, Arulenus Rusticus.	P. praetor (?); in tandem with Herennius Senectio P. undertakes public prosecution of Baebius Massa.	Statius begins to publish *Siluae*.
94–6	Domitian expels philosophers from Italy (95?).	P. *praefectus aerari militaris* (?).	Publication of Quintilian's *Institutio Oratoria* (95–6?).
96	Assassination of Domitian (Sept. 96); accession of Nerva.	Probable date of earliest P.'s *Letters*; death of P.'s wife (daughter of Pompeia Celerina) now or in 97.	Deaths of Statius and Quintilian (?).
97	Increasing unrest with Nerva; riot of Praetorian guard, adoption of Trajan (Oct.?).	P. attempts prosecution of Publicius Certus; sets up library and alimentary scheme in Comum; suffers serious illness.	Verginius Rufus consul for 3rd time, but dies the same year; Tacitus consul at time of funeral (Nov.?); Vestricius Spurinna governor of Germania Inferior; suicide of Corellius Rufus (?).
98	Death of Nerva (Jan. 98); accession of Trajan.	P. *praefectus aerari Saturni* with Cornutus Tertullus, for two years (?); marries Calpurnia (?); gains *ius trium liberorum* from Trajan; in tandem with Tacitus begins lengthy public prosecution of Marius Priscus.	Vestricius Spurinna consul for second time; Tacitus publishes *Agricola* and *Germania* (?); Martial leaves Rome.
c. 99	Trajan finally enters Rome as emperor (autumn).	P. undertakes public prosecution of Caecilius Classicus on behalf of province of Baetica.	

Date	Events		
Approx. Year	Political	In Pliny's life	In Pliny's 'circle'
100	Trajan *consul ordinarius*.	P. *consul suffectus* with Cornutus Tertullus (Sept. – Oct.); publishes *Panegyricus* (?).	Iulius Frontinus consul for second time.
101			Death of Silius Italicus (?).
102	First Dacian war (begins 101): Trajan absent from Rome.	P. undertakes public defence of Iulius Bassus, governor of Bithynia.	Tacitus publishes *Dialogus* (?); Martial's last book of epigrams.
103		P. finally achieves co-option as augur in succession to Iulius Frontinus.	
104–6	Second Dacian war 105–6: Trajan again absent from Rome.	P. *curator aluei Tiberis et riparum et cloacarum urbis*.	Tacitus returns to Rome (104/105) possibly after governing consular province; death of Regulus (105?).
106		Publication of earliest books of *Letters* (?); P. undertakes public defence of Varenus Rufus, governor of Bithynia.	
108–9			Tacitus publishes *Histories* (?).
109/10–111/12	Dedication of Trajan's forum (112).	P. *legatus pro praetore* in Bithynia and Pontus.	Tacitus proconsul of Asia (112–13).
113	Parthian war; dedication of Trajan's column.		
115			Tacitus writing the *Annals*.
117	Death of Trajan; accession of Hadrian.		

In letter 10.120, following the death of Calpurnia's grandfather, Pliny informs Trajan that his wife, wishing to be with her aunt, has been provided with passes for official transport to speed her journey to Italy. In 10.121 – the final letter of the book – Trajan replies to confirm the grant. From the book's closure at this point, many have concluded that Pliny died soon after Calpurnia's departure for Italy. The assumption is understandable, although equally these Calpurnia letters offer an artistically satisfying end to the book, with their reassertion of a family connection which bulked large in the later instalments of the nine-book correspondence, and the reference here to a journey home to Italy which reverses, in thematic terms, the journey out from Italy described at the start of the Bithynia sequence (10.15–17b) – even if the return journey is not Pliny's.[5] At any rate, Pliny clearly died before Trajan (the great Comum inscription implies the emperor is alive: see below), and the celebration of Trajan's accession day of 28 January is repeated twice (10.52, 102) but not three times. A tempting – but not overwhelmingly necessary – inference is that Pliny died before he could offer thanks and celebration on a third occasion.[6] See Chapter 8 for further possible evidence in Book 10 of artistic design (by the author?).

THE GREAT COMUM INSCRIPTION

Only one original fragment remains of this famous inscription: the rest is known from a fifteenth-century manuscript copy.[7] Estimates of the size of the full inscription vary, but at around 3 metres long it must have been an imposing sight.[8] Its location in Comum is unknown, but clearly it was intended for public viewing on a monument or building associated with Pliny, perhaps his library there (or even his 'tomb').[9] Its restored text runs as follows:[10]

---

[5] For further comments on the closure to the collection provided by 10.120–1, see Whitton (2011).

[6] See Sherwin-White (1966) 82, Vidman *PIR*² P 490 (pp. 207–8), Williams (1990) 13.

[7] For the fate of the inscription and its transportation at some point in the middle ages from Como to Milan and incorporation there in the church of St. Ambrose, see Alföldy (1999a) 222.

[8] See Eck (1997) 99 n. 80, Alföldy (1999a) 227; the surviving portion measures 87 × 85 cm.

[9] See Eck (1997) 99, (2001) 234–5.

[10] *CIL* 5.5262 = Alföldy (1999a) = Alföldy (1999b), with full commentary. The text here is reproduced from Krieckhaus (2006) 216 following Alföldy's reconstruction – which affects most notably the status of Pliny's power as legate of Trajan in Bithynia: *proconsulari potestate* not *consulari potestate*; cf. Birley (2000a) 5–6. For a summary of debates on aspects of the inscription, see Krieckhaus (2006) 44–7.

C(aius) Plinius L(uci) f(ilius) Ouf(entina tribu) Caecilius [Secundus co(n)s(ul)]
augur legat(us) pro pr(aetore) prouinciae Pon[ti et Bithyniae pro]
consulari potesta[te] in eam prouinciam e[x senatus consulto ab]
Imp(eratore) Caesar(e) Nerua Traiano Aug(usto) German[ico Dacico p(ater) p(atriae) missus]
curator aluei Tiberis et riparum et [cloacarum urbis]
praef(ectus) aerari Saturni praef(ectus) aerari mil[itaris pr(aetor) trib(unus) plebis]
quaestor Imp(eratoris) seuir equitum [Romanorum]
trib(unus) milit(um) leg(ionis) [III] Gallica[e in prouincia Syria Xuir stli]
tib(us) iudicand(is) therm[as ex HS - - -] adiectis in
ornatum HS $\overline{CCC}$ [– et eo amp]lius in tutela[m]
HS $\overline{CC}$ t(estamento) f(ieri) i(ussit) [item in alimenta] libertor(um) suorum homin(um) C
HS |XVIII|LXVI DCLXVI rei [p(ublicae) legauit quorum in]crement(a) postea ad epulum
[pl]eb(is) urban(ae) uoluit pertin[ere item uiuu]s dedit in aliment(a) pueror(um)
et puellar(um) pleb(i) urban(ae) HS [$\overline{D}$ item bybliothecam HS ? et] in tutelam bybliothe
cae HS C(milia)

Gaius Plinius Caecilius Secundus, son of Lucius, of the tribe Oufentina, consul; augur; praetorian commissioner with proconsular power for the province of Pontus and Bithynia, sent to that province in accordance with the senate's decree by the emperor Nerva Trajan Augustus, victor over Germany and Dacia, the Father of his country; curator of bed and banks of the Tiber and sewers of Rome; prefect of the treasury of Saturn; prefect of the military treasury; praetor; tribune of the people; quaestor of the emperor; commissioner for the Roman knights; military tribune of the third Gallic legion in the province of Syria; magistrate on board of ten; left by will public baths at a cost of... and an additional 300,000 sesterces for furnishing them, with interest on 200,000 for their upkeep... and also to his city capital of 1,866,666 sesterces to support a hundred of his freedmen, and subsequently to provide an annual dinner for the people of the city... Likewise in his lifetime he gave 500,000 sesterces for the maintenance of boys and girls of the city, and also 100,000 for the upkeep of the library... (Trans. B. Radice, adapted)

The inscription gives, in the summary of Birley (2000a) 5, Pliny's '*cursus honorum*', in descending order, modified (as often in such inscriptions) by the consulship and priesthood (augurship in his case), being placed straight after the name, out of chronological order'.[11] This is followed by a listing of gifts given both in life and by will to the town of Comum and its citizens and to Pliny's freedmen.[12] The generous testamentary donations by Pliny to his home town include public baths and cash for their furnishing and upkeep, funds for the maintenance of his freedmen and for an annual dinner for the citizens of Comum, in addition to lifetime donations to an

---

[11] On the function of such inscriptions, see Eck (2009). Compare Pliny's epistolary version of his *cursus* at 7.16.2–3, where he sets out his career in comparison with that of his friend Calestrius Tiro. (In this race, Pliny is the clear winner.) On Tiro, see further Chapter 5.

[12] For Pliny's relationship with Comum in general, see Gasser (1999) 186–216, Krieckhaus (2004).

alimentary scheme also recorded here, plus money for the upkeep of his library.[13]

Eck (1997) 98–9 emphasizes the grammatical form of this testamentary inscription:

no one has yet pointed out the fact that the inscription, although it was set up after Pliny's death, does not directly name anyone as responsible for carrying this out. It must in fact have been Pliny himself, since he is named in the nominative. Pliny would have given the instructions for the text, as is shown by the use of the nominative case. He did not want to rely on other people, whether private persons or indeed the magistrates of the community.[14]

In Eck's view, this inscription – with its 'mixture of offices and *beneficia*' – is nothing less than the *res gestae Plinii Secundi*.[15] Various major posts – consul, praetor, tribune of the plebs – are restored to its text from other surviving inscriptions (e.g. from a fragment of another testamentary inscription which originally covered his whole career: *CIL* 6.1552 = 11.5272,[16] from Hispellum), as well as from allusions in the *Letters*. Some of the information provided in the Comum inscription is absent from the *Letters*, including not only some early posts and associated details (*decemuir stlitibus iudicandis*, the name of Pliny's legion where he was military tribune, *seuir equitum Romanorum*), but – most notably – Pliny's term at the *aerarium militare* or military treasury. As noted above pp. 34–5 and p. 35 n. 98, Pliny is silent in the *Letters* and *Panegyricus* on this post; but his tenure here can be used to question Pliny's narrative about

---

[13] For Pliny's public gifts as listed both in inscriptions and the *Letters*, see Duncan-Jones (1982) 27–32, also Manuwald (2003), Krieckhaus (2006) 45–8. For the donation of baths – perhaps inspired by Trajan's baths at Rome – see Patterson (2006) 148–60, esp. 154–7. For the donation of a banquet – effected also by Pliny in the context of dedication of a temple at Tifernum (4.1.6) – see Patterson (2006) 169–76.

[14] For Pliny's concern with proper monuments and memorialization in the letters, cf. 3.6, 6.10, 9.19.

[15] For another view, see Alföldy (1999a) 221, and for a revised view from Eck, see Eck (2001) 232ff., also Krieckhaus (2006) 44–5.

[16] For commentary on this inscription and its history, see Alföldy (1999a) 223–5, 229–33. A conjectural text of the fuller inscription is offered by Alföldy (1999a) 233, 243 (cf. Birley (2000a) 5–6); but the fragments as they survive offer (with Alföldy's supplements):

[quaestor imperatori]s trib(unus) plebis pr(aetor) | [cur(ator) aluei] Tiberis ex s(enatus) c(onsulto) pro|[consulari potestate legatus pr(o) pr(aetore) prouinciae Ponti] et Bithyniae et legatus | [testame]nto [fieri] iussit

quaestor of the Emperor; tribune of the people; praetor; . . . curator of the bed of the Tiber; in accordance with the senate's decree praetorian commissioner with proconsular power for the province of Pontus and Bithynia, and as commissioner . . . ordered in his will . . .

For the significance of a lengthy testamentary inscription set up in Hispellum (an Umbrian town with little role to play in the *Letters*), see Champlin (2001), and above p. 204, with n. 8.

personal dangers and a stalled career during the last years of Domitian. On the other hand, another post – consular curator of the bed and banks of the Tiber (listed in the timeline above for 104–6) – is not mentioned explicitly in the *Letters* and appears only as a subject of possible allusion at 5.14.2–3 (cf. 8.17). Accordingly, some suggest that Pliny's silence on the military treasury post is not significant.[17]

---

[17] Thus Vidman *PIR²* P 490 (p. 205): 'officium hoc non tanti fuit'.

Letters *1–9: Catalogue of contents and addressees*

For an explanation of the purposes – and limitations – of this catalogue, see the Introduction to this volume. Below, we give the names of the addressees strictly in the form in which they appear in the heading to each letter in Mynor's Oxford Classical Text (including occasional restorations, all marked as such), rather than supply their fuller nomenclature, since this is very often missing in the manuscripts. The manuscript sources for the names of each addressee are as follows. Two medieval mss., B and F, erratically preserve some double names of correspondents in Books 1 and 3–5, as far as letter 5.6 (where both give out, by apparent coincidence). These can be supplemented from the letter headings in two late manuscripts and the 1508 Aldine edition (as far as Book 4), as well from the 'indices' pre-served in B (Robbins (1910) 480). These indices – which feature in the arguments of Chapters 2 and 5 of this volume – cover the first five books and list addressees and opening words separately from the text of the let-ters, with substantial provision of double names in Books 3–5 alongside sparser fare in Book 1 (where single names predominate) and none at all in Book 2 (where single names alone are catalogued); see Robbins (1910) 476–8, also Stangl (1886), Merrill (1895). The indices can be traced back to the late antique New York Pierpont Morgan Library M.462 (transcribed in Lowe and Rand (1922)), as documented in Chapter 2. The fragmen-tary New York manuscript, the ancestor of B and F, preserves the end of Book 2 (2.20.13–14), followed by an index for the whole of Book 3 (with double names for addressees), then the text of that book as far as 3.5.4 (with single names in the letter heading, whether *gentilicium* or *cognomen*).

As a result of this state of affairs, we have single names only for addressees in Books 2 and 6–9. Nevertheless, for authoritative discussion of the prob-able fuller names of many of the addressees in Books 2 and 6–9 (and indeed the entire collection), see the onomasticon of Birley (2000a); cf. the select index in Appendix 4 of this volume. In the core of the present book we do not hesitate to accept many of the identifications made there. For conventions governing which names of a correspondent are used (and where) in the collection, see Chapter 5 of this volume, Birley (2000a) 21–34, and Bodel (unpublished), Chapter 2. For developments in the Roman system of naming individuals in the early imperial period, see Salway (1994).

Book 1		
	Addressee	Subject
1.1	Septicius <Clarus>	A response to the addressee's request for the collection and publication of Pliny's letters.
1.2	<Maturus> Arrianus	A request for comments on a recent unnamed speech written in the style of Demosthenes, Calvus and Cicero, with a view to satisfying the demands of the book trade in which Pliny's previously published work has already apparently enjoyed some success.
1.3	Caninius Rufus	Praise of the addressee's villa in Comum, and encouragement that he give himself over to study and produce some lasting work.
1.4	Pompeia Celerina, socrus	A return invitation to Pliny's mother-in-law to make use of Pliny's homes, and comparison of the domestic staff of their respective households.
1.5	Voconius Romanus	A report that Regulus is desperate for reconciliation with Pliny now that Domitian is dead; narration of past hostilities between the pair; and Pliny's refusal in person of a reconciliation until the return of Mauricus from exile.
1.6	Cornelius Tacitus	Pliny reports that he has been hunting and caught three boars while making notes in his tablets.
1.7	Octavius Rufus	A response to a request that Pliny not represent the province of Baetica in a court case; Pliny details his past services to and connections with the Baetici.
1.8	Pompeius Saturninus	A response to a request for recent work: Pliny toys with the idea of sending a speech delivered at Comum on his establishment of a library and *alimenta* scheme there, but worries about the negative effects of self-praise.
1.9	Minicius Fundanus	On the pointless activity of the city versus honourable time spent reading and writing at the Laurentine villa.
1.10	Attius Clemens	In praise of the philosopher Euphrates; Pliny's desire to spend more time with him, away from onerous official duties.
1.11	Fabius Iustus	An anxious letter about the length of time since the addressee's last letter to Pliny; encouragement to write, even if there is no news to pass on.
1.12	Calestrius Tiro	A report of the long illness and honourable suicide of Corellius Rufus, who nevertheless fulfilled his desire to outlive Domitian.

(cont.)

	Book 1	
	Addressee	Subject
1.13	Sosius Senecio	On the flourishing of the literary scene this April with a new crop of poets; the disrespectful habits of modern recitation audiences in contrast with times past.
1.14	Iunius Mauricus	A response to a request that Pliny seek out a husband for the addressee's niece: Pliny recommends Minicius Acilianus.
1.15	Septicius Clarus	Pliny 'passes sentence' on the addressee for failing to attend Pliny's simple dinner party (and choosing more lavish entertainment elsewhere).
1.16	Erucius	Praise of Pompeius Saturninus for his oratory, history, verses in the style of Catullus and Calvus, and letters written either by himself or his wife.
1.17	Cornelius Titianus	Praise of Titinius Capito (who keeps busts of Brutus, Cassius and Cato at home) for obtaining Nerva's permission to erect a statue of Lucius Silanus in the forum.
1.18	Suetonius Tranquillus	The addressee has requested adjournment of his court case after a dream; Pliny recounts his own similarly disturbing dream before the case in the Centumviral court which made his reputation as a young man.
1.19	Romatius Firmus	Pliny declares a gift of money to the addressee – a fellow townsman – in order to raise his status from *decurio* to *eques*.
1.20	Cornelius Tacitus	A long letter on the proper style and length of a speech, attacking the affectation of *breuitas*.
1.21	Plinius Paternus	Pliny thanks the addressee for recommendations in a recent purchase of slaves.
1.22	Catilius Severus	On the severe illness of the lawyer Titius Aristo, Pliny's constant presence at his bedside and Aristo's contemplation of suicide.
1.23	Pompeius Falco	A response to a request for advice on the question whether a man should continue to practise law while holding the office of tribune.
1.24	Baebius Hispanus	A request that the addressee ensure that Suetonius pays a reasonable price for the small estate he wishes to buy.

	Book 2	
	Addressee	Subject
2.1	Romanus	A report of the public funeral of Verginius Rufus (where the *laudatio* is given by Tacitus), along with a rehearsal of Verginius' life and long-standing support of Pliny.
2.2	Paulinus	Pliny is angry with the addressee for failing to correspond; Pliny demands more letters – no other recompense or excuse will do.

	Book 2	
	Addressee	Subject
2.3	Nepos	Praise of the professional Greek orator Isaeus for his impressive extempore performances, along with a plea to the addressee to come to Rome to hear Isaeus.
2.4	Calvina	Pliny reports that he has paid off the debts owed to others by the addressee's deceased father, and that he now also cancels the debt owed to himself.
2.5	Lupercus	Pliny sends part of an unnamed but highly varied speech to the addressee for comment, adding a plea for indulgence towards the more poetic passages.
2.6	Avitus	A report of a vulgar dinner party where a host distinguishes his grades of guest by serving differing qualities of food and drink to each.
2.7	Macrinus	Pliny celebrates a vote by the senate to erect a triumphal statue for Spurinna and a consolatory statue for his much-lamented son Cottius.
2.8	Caninius	An enquiry after the addressee's leisure at his Comum villa – by way of contrast with the increasing business piling up for Pliny.
2.9	Apollinaris	Pliny expresses concern and solicits aid for his young protégé Sextius Erucius in the forthcoming senatorial elections to the tribunate.
2.10	Octavius	A plea to the addressee to release his verses for publication at last, or at least to give readings, so that he may garner the reputation he deserves.
2.11	Arrianus	A lengthy report of Pliny's prosecution, along with Tacitus, of Marius Priscus, governor of Africa, in front of the emperor in the senate.
2.12	Arrianus	A shorter report of the sequel to the trial of Marius Priscus: the appearance of Marius Priscus' *legatus* Hostilius Firminus before the senate on related charges.
2.13	Priscus	A request that the addressee confer a provincial post on Pliny's friend Voconius Romanus.
2.14	Maximus	A lament for the decline of standards in the Centumviral court: the irruption of young men without introduction and the use of paid audiences are symptomatic.
2.15	Valerianus	An enquiry about the pleasure given the addressee by the purchase of new estates; Pliny's troubles with the estate inherited from his mother.
2.16	Annius	A reply to a correspondent on the legality of Pliny's inheritance of some property through a will; Pliny wants to respect the testator's wishes and accept the legacy.

(cont.)

Book 2		
	Addressee	Subject
2.17	Gallus	A detailed description of Pliny's Laurentine villa.
2.18	Mauricus	A reply to a request to search out and review some possible tutors for the children of the addressee's brother; Pliny reports a gratifying visit to the schools of rhetoric.
2.19	Cerialis	Pliny accepts an invitation to read a legal speech to an audience, but underlines the drop in dramatic temperature at a recitation by comparison with a courtroom, and the demanding nature and technicalities of the speech.
2.20	Calvisius	On Regulus' disgraceful legacy-hunting: three anecdotes.

Book 3		
	Addressee	Subject
3.1	Calvisius Rufus	A description of the fixed but varied daily routine of the elderly Vestricius Spurinna: Pliny hopes to adopt a similar mode of retirement, at the appropriate moment.
3.2	Vibius Maximus	A request to the addressee to offer advancement to the knight Arrianus Maturus.
3.3	Corellia Hispulla	An assertion that a teacher of rhetoric must be found for the son of the addressee: Pliny is pleased to recommend Iulius Genitor, who displays none of the usual vices.
3.4	Caecilius Macrinus	A request for the addressee's opinion on Pliny's decision to act again – with the senate's encouragement, but despite employment at the treasury – on behalf of the Baetici, this time in a case of provincial corruption against Caecilius Classicus.
3.5	Baebius Macer	A response to a request for a complete list of the works written by the Elder Pliny, plus an explanation of the daily schedule which allowed the Elder to write so much, despite the burden of office.
3.6	Annius Severus	An instruction that the addressee arrange a marble base for Pliny's (recently purchased) bronze statue of an old man – to be set up in the temple of Jupiter in Comum, with an inscription of Pliny's honours.
3.7	Caninius Rufus	A report of the death of Silius Italicus and a review of his life and achievements, from a tarnished career under Nero to a leisure-filled retirement.
3.8	Suetonius Tranquillus	A reply to Suetonius' request that Pliny transfer the tribunate originally obtained for Suetonius to the latter's kinsman.
3.9	Cornelius Minicianus	A report on the difficulties Pliny overcame in his prosecution of Caecilius Classicus on behalf of the province of Baetica.

	Book 3	
	Addressee	Subject
3.10	Vestricius Spurinna, Cottia	An acknowledgement that Pliny has written a memoir of the deceased son of the addressees, which he now sends for comment and approval.
3.11	Iulius Genitor	A report of the philosopher Artemidorus' generous account of Pliny's risky services to him when Pliny was praetor under Domitian.
3.12	Catilius Severus	Pliny agrees to come to dinner, but on condition that the dinner not be costly and end in timely fashion: they both have early-morning duties.
3.13	Voconius Romanus	Pliny forwards to the addressee a copy of his recently delivered speech of thanks to the emperor in his capacity as consul (= the *Panegyricus*), asking for comments.
3.14	Acilius	A report of the murder of Larcius Macedo at the hands of his own slaves.
3.15	Silius Proculus	Reply to a request to comment on the addressee's poetry (as Cicero did for the members of his generation).
3.16	Nepos	Pliny passes on, from Fannia, three less well-known stories about her grandmother Arria.
3.17	Iulius Servianus	Pliny anxiously enquires after the well-being of his addressee, from whom he has not heard for some time.
3.18	Vibius Severus	A report that Pliny has decided to expand and publish his speech of thanks to the emperor as consul (= the *Panegyricus*); plus an account of Pliny's recitation of this longer version to an enthusiastic audience over three days.
3.19	Calvisius Rufus	Request to the addressee for advice on the purchase of an estate adjoining Pliny's, whose resources the previous owner ran down.
3.20	Maesius Maximus	A report on the introduction of the secret ballot in senatorial elections: Pliny will not forgo this rare opportunity to write to his correspondent about political matters.
3.21	Cornelius Priscus	A report of the death of Martial, whose poem in honour of Pliny is quoted.

	Book 4	
	Addressee	Subject
4.1	\<Calpurnius\> Fabatus, prosocer	Pliny confirms that he and his wife are hastening preparations for a journey to see the addressee (his wife's grandfather); but they must make one stop at Tifernum Tiberinum near Pliny's Tuscan estate for the dedication of a temple which he has funded.

(*cont.*)

	Book 4	
	Addressee	Subject
4.2	Attius Clemens	A report of the death of Regulus' son, Regulus' extravagant grief and express desire to marry again in old age.
4.3	Arrius Antoninus	Praise of the addressee's achievements as twice consul and proconsul of Asia, but still greater praise of his literary achievements with epigrams and mimes.
4.4	Sosius Senecio	A request that the addressee bestow a tribunate on Varisidius Nepos.
4.5	Iulius Sparsus	Pliny sends to the addressee a copy of a speech which, when recited over two days to an audience, received an enthusiastic response (comparable to the reception of Aeschines on Rhodes).
4.6	Iulius Naso	A report that, while none of Pliny's estates is prospering financially, the Laurentine villa is rich in a harvest of literary studies.
4.7	Catius Lepidus	A report on Regulus' extravagant grief for his dead son: now he has written a memoir and sent copies throughout the empire. Regulus' energy is misdirected and his talent as a speaker non-existent.
4.8	Maturus Arrianus	A reply to congratulations on finally achieving co-option as an augur: Pliny became augur and consul at a younger age than Cicero, but cannot hope to emulate his genius.
4.9	Cornelius Ursus	An extended account of Pliny's successful defence of Iulius Bassus on charges of provincial corruption as governor of Bithynia; a copy of the speech will follow, once Pliny has completed substantial revisions.
4.10	Statius Sabinus	A reply to a request for advice on legal problems arising from incomplete instructions in a will pertaining to the manumission of a slave and his right to a legacy.
4.11	Cornelius Minicianus	News that Valerius Licinianus is teaching rhetoric in Sicily: the story of his connection with the execution, under Domitian, of the Vestal Virgin Cornelia.
4.12	Maturus Arrianus	A request that the addressee offer his congratulations to Egnatius Marcellinus for his scruples in raising with the senate the issue of a deceased secretary's salary.
4.13	Cornelius Tacitus	An account of Pliny's decision, on a recent trip home to his native town, to help fund a school there: Tacitus is asked to recommend teachers from among his own pupils.
4.14	[Decimus] Paternus	Pliny sends his hendecasyllabic verse to the addressee for comment and approval, but with an assurance that his verse avoids explicit language.
4.15	Minicius Fundanus	A request that the addressee – in his predicted consulship – adopt Asinius Bassus as his quaestor.

	Book 4	
	Addressee	Subject
4.16	Valerius Paulinus	A report of Pliny's recent success with a seven-hour speech before a packed Centumviral courthouse.
4.17	Clusinius Gallus	An assurance that the addressee's request that Pliny defend Corellia in a forthcoming case is superfluous: Pliny is in any case obliged by his long-standing admiration of, and connection with, her deceased father, Corellius.
4.18	Arrius Antoninus	A report of Pliny's failure to reflect in Latin translation the quality of the addressee's Greek epigrams.
4.19	Calpurnia Hispulla	Pliny assures his young wife's aunt of the worthiness of her niece: she studies Pliny's works, follows his performances in court or recitation and cherishes his *gloria*.
4.20	Novius Maximus	Pliny has previously given his opinion of the addressee's individual books, and now praises the work as a whole.
4.21	Velius Cerealis	A report of the deaths in childbirth of the two daughters of Helvidius Priscus the younger.
4.22	Sempronius Rufus	A report of Pliny's service on an imperial *consilium* devoted to the issue of the Greek games at Vienne; Iunius Mauricus spoke frankly on the issue, just as he had done once, in the company of Nerva, in a conversation about Catullus Messalinus.
4.23	Pomponius Bassus	Congratulations to the addressee on his active retirement in leisure after a lifetime of public service; reflections on the appropriate pursuits at different stages of life.
4.24	Fabius Valens	Pliny reflects on changes in fortune, in both his own life and those of other orators, since his first appearance before a four-panel session of the Centumviral court as a youth.
4.25	Maesius Maximus	A further report on secret ballots in the senate: Pliny conveys his anger that some papers were despoiled by witty obscenities.
4.26	Maecilius Nepos	Pliny happily agrees to revise his own works for the addressee: they will not be superfluous baggage for the appointed governor of so important a province.
4.27	Pompeius Falco	A report of an excellent recent poetry recitation by Sentinus Augurinus, one of whose pieces (quoted) concerns Pliny's own career as a poet.
4.28	Vibius Severus	Pliny passes on a request from Herennius Severus that the addressee make copies of portraits of Cornelius Nepos and Titius Catus for display in a library.
4.29	Romatius Firmus	A report of the severity of the new praetor Licinius Nepos, who would not allow even a senator to excuse himself from jury duty.
4.30	Licinius Sura	A natural history curiosity for the learned addressee to explain: a spring on Lake Como whose level within an artificial grotto rises and falls three times each day.

(cont.)

	Book 5	
	Addressee	Subject
5.1	Annius Severus	Narrative of an inheritance disputed, under Domitian, by a son whose mother had previously disinherited him; Pliny (one of the beneficiaries) helped to settle the dispute, and has now received a legacy from the son.
5.2	Calpurnius Flaccus	In return for the addressee's gift of thrushes, Pliny can send back only a letter of thanks.
5.3	Titius Aristo	Pliny defends his composition of light verse on senatorial precedent, and his practice of reciting them on the ground of critical usefulness.
5.4	Iulius Valerianus	Report of an incident at the senate, involving the praetor Nepos, where the citizens of Vicetia have complained of the abandonment of a prosecution case by an advocate, who – it now emerges – took a fee for his services.
5.5	Novius Maximus	A report of the death of Gaius Fannius, who leaves his history of the victims of Nero unfinished (an eventuality Fannius foresaw after an apparition of Nero).
5.6	Domitius Apollinaris	A detailed description of Pliny's Tuscan villa.
5.7	Calvisius Rufus	Upon receiving an inheritance, Pliny asserts to the addressee (a co-beneficiary) his intention to respect the wishes of the deceased Saturninus and pay his legacy to Comum out of their share in the will; it is assumed that Rufus will do the same.
5.8	Titinius Capito	A reply to a request to write a work of history: despite family precedent for such an endeavour, Pliny asserts that it is difficult to work on oratory and history simultaneously, and that both ancient and modern history present problems of subject matter.
5.9	Sempronius Rufus	A report of an adjournment of a trial occasioned by an edict from the praetor Nepos which stipulated that counsel must not receive a fee before a trial (but may do so afterwards).
5.10	Suetonius Tranquillus	A plea to the addressee to publish his completed work at long last, or to expect an attack from Pliny's satiric verse.
5.11	Calpurnius Fabatus, prosocer	A response to the welcome news of the generous dedication in Comum of a public colonnade by the addressee, Pliny's grandfather-in-law.
5.12	Terentius Scaurus	Pliny explains the stimulus (and useful revisions) to be gained from recitation. Now that his current work has been through that process, he is sending it on for comment.
5.13	\<Iulius\> Valerianus	A further report on the case of the citizens of Vicetia: it turns out that their advocate gave up the case at the last minute for fear of opposing a senator; after some discussion he is acquitted; an imperial decree on accepting fees results.

	Book 5	
	Addressee	Subject
5.14	Pontius Allifanus	A report that, while in Comum, Pliny has heard the good news of the award of the curatorship of the Aemilian road to Cornutus Tertullus, his colleague both at the treasury and in the consulship; Pliny himself must soon return to Rome.
5.15	Arrius Antoninus	An assertion that the qualities of the addressee's verse are best appreciated through (failed) attempts to imitate them.
5.16	Aefulanus Marcellinus	A lament for the death of the young daughter of Fundanus, whose virtues and charms were many; any consolation sent to Fundanus should be gently expressed.
5.17	Vestricius Spurinna	A report of a successful poetry reading by the young Calpurnius Piso: Pliny himself congratulated the author, and is eager for noble families to achieve literary distinction.
5.18	Calpurnius Macer	Pliny, hunting and writing on his Tuscan estates, sends greetings to his addressee, who is enjoying the retirement of his own estate.
5.19	Valerius Paulinus	Pliny confesses his indulgence towards his slaves, and his affection for his 'literary' slave Zosimus. The previous ill health of the latter has now recurred, and Pliny requests a visit for him to the addressee's estate at Forum Iulii, to assist his convalescence.
5.20	Cornelius Ursus	A report that, following their prosecution of Iulius Bassus, the Bithynians have now proceeded against Varenus Rufus. Pliny gives an account of the preliminary proceedings and his own speech.
5.21	Pompeius Saturninus	Pliny is glad to hear the addressee has been detained in Rome, but is sorry to hear of the serious illness of Iulius Valens and the death of the young writer Iulius Avitus.

	Book 6	
	Addressee	Subject
6.1	Tiro	A request to the addressee to follow him south to Rome; Pliny misses him keenly.
6.2	Arrianus	Pliny misses the dead Regulus in court because he took his occupation so seriously – unlike today's courts, where time for speaking is severely curtailed and speakers are lazy.
6.3	Verus	An expression of satisfaction that the farm belonging to Pliny's nurse – his gift to her – is now managed by the addressee, after a period of diminishing returns.
6.4	Calpurnia	An expression of anxious concern for the addressee, Pliny's wife, who has gone off to Campania for the sake of her health, while Pliny is delayed by his duties in Rome.

(*cont.*)

	Book 6	
	Addressee	Subject
6.5	Ursus	Report of an 'ugly' altercation in the senate between the praetors Nepos and Celsus over an aspect of the Bithynian prosecution of Varenus Rufus, already settled at an earlier meeting.
6.6	Fundanus	The addressee is urged to come to Rome immediately to support the candidature of Pliny's protégé, Iulius Naso.
6.7	Calpurnia	A reply to his wife's report that she misses him: he longs for her and is inflamed by her letters.
6.8	Priscus	A request that the addressee – on behalf of Pliny's intimate, Atilius Crescens – recover from a third party a debt owed to Crescens by an estate to which the third party is now heir.
6.9	Tacitus	A reply to Tacitus' request that Pliny support the candidature of the latter's own protégé, Iulius Naso.
6.10	Albinus	A report of Pliny's visit to the former home of Verginius Rufus: 10 years after his death, Verginius' tomb, lamentably, is still not finished.
6.11	Maximus	An account of Pliny's encounter with the young orators Ummidius Quadratus and Fuscus Salinator in the court of the city prefect: their gratifying wish to adopt Pliny as their model.
6.12	Fabatus, prosocer	An acceptance of a frankly expressed request from his wife's grandfather that Pliny aid an associate in court.
6.13	Ursus	A further report on skirmishes in the senate over an aspect of the Bithynian prosecution of Varenus Rufus.
6.14	Mauricus	Pliny agrees to visit the addressee at Formiae, on condition that the addressee not put himself out.
6.15	Romanus	A report of the elegist Passenus Paulus' humiliation, during a recitation, at the hands of his friend Iavolenus Priscus.
6.16	Tacitus	A lengthy narrative, at the addressee's request, of the death of the Elder Pliny during the eruption of Vesuvius.
6.17	Restitutus	An expression of indignation at the cool reception given a friend's literary work at a recitation: one must learn to praise all who make literary efforts.
6.18	Sabinus	Pliny agrees to appear as an advocate for the addressee's home town of Firmum.
6.19	Nepos	A report on the economic consequences of recent imperial decrees on elections, particularly of the injunction that all candidates must invest one-third of their wealth in Italian property.
6.20	Cornelius Tacitus	A further narrative (again at the addressee's request) of events during the eruption of Vesuvius, now concentrating on the experiences of the Younger Pliny and his mother.

(*cont.*)

	Book 7	
	Addressee	Subject
7.1	Geminus	Advice on conducting oneself resolutely when ill, illustrated by Pliny's own strict abstinence in accordance with the advice of doctors.
7.2	Iustus	A promise to send some writings to the addressee, but only when the latter has time to read them.
7.3	Praesens	A plea to the addressee to return to Rome and vary his prolonged leisure with the normal round of duties.
7.4	Pontius	A reply to a request for more information about Pliny's career as a poet: an account of Pliny's output, from an early Greek tragedy at the age of 14 right up to his most recent hendecasyllables.
7.5	Calpurnia	An assertion of Pliny's yearning for Calpurnia during an unaccustomed separation.
7.6	Macrinus	An account of the latest twist in the Bithynian prosecution of Varenus Rufus: Pliny, by his silence at a recent hearing, has achieved more than through elaborate oratory.
7.7	Saturninus	Pliny expresses his delight that Priscus and the addressee have become friends.
7.8	Priscus	Pliny expresses his delight at the continuing friendship between Saturninus and the addressee.
7.9	Fuscus	A detailed reply to a request for advice on literary exercises suitable for a prolonged period of leisure time.
7.10	Macrinus	A further short update on the progress of the Bithynian prosecution of Varenus Rufus: it appears likely that the whole operation will be dropped.
7.11	Fabatus, prosocer	A reply to Pliny's grandfather-in-law, justifying the sale, at below market value, of recently inherited land near Lake Como to the sister of Corellius Rufus.
7.12	Minicius	Pliny sends the addressee the work he has been asking for, which combines the lower style the addressee prefers and the more high-flown style he does not like so well.
7.13	Ferox	An assertion that the polish of the addressee's letter undermines his claim therein to have given no time to literary studies recently.
7.14	Corellia	A reply rejecting the addressee's offer to pay a higher price for the estate she is buying from Pliny.
7.15	Saturninus	Pliny commiserates with his addressee that they are both distracted by their duties; but is pleased to hear that Priscus continues to be a delightful companion.
7.16	Fabatus, prosocer	Pliny assures his grandfather-in-law that his old friend and colleague Calestrius Tiro – on his way as proconsul to Baetica – will only be too pleased to divert his journey to confirm manumission for the addressee's slaves.

	Book 7	
	Addressee	Subject
7.17	Celer	A reply to the addressee's report that others criticize Pliny for giving recitals of his speeches: Pliny defends his practice at length on the ground of its usefulness for effecting revisions.
7.18	Caninius	At the addressee's request, Pliny explains how best to ensure the long-term effectiveness of a financial gift to one's home community.
7.19	Priscus	A report that Fannia has contracted a serious illness while attending to a sick Vestal Virgin: Pliny reviews her life (and that of her mother).
7.20	Tacitus	Pliny reflects on his exchange of work and comments with the addressee: he rejoices in their shared fame in the field of literary achievement.
7.21	Cornutus	Pliny assures the addressee he is following his advice to take care of an eye problem while at his villa.
7.22	Falco	In reply to the addressee's promise to confer a tribunate on a friend of the writer, Pliny reveals the identity of the friend: Cornelius Minicianus, ornament of Pliny's homeland.
7.23	Fabatus, prosocer	Despite his grandfather-in-law's willingness to travel to Milan to meet Calestrius Tiro, Pliny begs him to wait for Tiro at home in Comum.
7.24	Geminus	A report of the death of Ummidia Quadratilla: her respectful and responsible treatment of her promising grandson Quadratus, whom she sent off to concentrate on his studies when she herself wished to watch her troupe of actors.
7.25	Rufus	Pliny conveys his delight at discovering the unsuspected literary talents of Terentius Iunior, country neighbour and recently retired procurator of Narbonensis.
7.26	Maximus	Reflections on our improved character when ill: we should try to be the kind of persons we promise to be when ill.
7.27	Sura	A request to the addressee to consider the reality of apparitions, with three examples given: the appearance of 'Africa' to Curtius Rufus; a visitation by a ghost to the philosopher Athenodorus in Athens; and the ghostly cutting of the hair of Pliny's slaves (just as he was being secretly accused by Carus before Domitian).
7.28	Septicius	Pliny replies to criticisms received by the addressee that Pliny praises his friends excessively.
7.29	Montanus	Pliny reports his recent discovery of a monument to Pallas whose inscription will provoke both indignation and laughter from the addressee.
7.30	Genitor	Pliny commiserates with the addressee on the death of his pupil, and reports on his own various duties, which leave him little time for literary studies.

(cont.)

	Book 7	
	Addressee	Subject
7.31	Cornutus	A commendation of Claudius Pollio, who served in the army at the same time as Pliny and is now seeking the friendship of the addressee.
7.32	Fabatus, prosocer	Pliny expresses his delight at hearing from his grandfather-in-law of the successful visit of Calestrius Tiro to Comum to enact the manumission of slaves.
7.33	Tacitus	Pliny conveys his wish to appear in Tacitus' histories, and offers the story of his role, alongside Herennius Senecio, in the prosecution of Baebius Massa under Domitian.

	Book 8	
	Addressee	Subject
8.1	Septicius	A report on Pliny's journey to his country estate: several of the entourage have taken ill on the road because of the heat, most worryingly Encolpius, Pliny's reader.
8.2	Calvisius	A report of the losses made by various dealers on Pliny's grape harvest: Pliny has enacted a policy of partial remission of losses.
8.3	Sparsus	A response to the addressee's opinion that the work of Pliny lately sent him is the best yet: Pliny says that he always prefers to consider his newest work his best.
8.4	Caninius	Encouragement of the addressee in his arduous task of writing an epic poem in celebration of Trajan's Dacian victories.
8.5	Geminus	A eulogy of the recently deceased wife of Macrinus, and expression of concern for Macrinus himself.
8.6	Montanus	A further report on the provoking inscription to Pallas: Pliny has now looked up the original *senatus consultum* in honour of Pallas, and analyses it at length.
8.7	Tacitus	A response to the book the addressee has sent for comment: Pliny will comment on it the more freely, as he has nothing to send Tacitus for comment in return.
8.8	Romanus	A detailed description of the source of the Clitumnus river.
8.9	Ursus	A report that Pliny is so harassed by duties to friends that he has no time for leisure or study.
8.10	Fabatus, prosocer	Pliny consoles his grandfather-in-law for the disappointments of not yet becoming a great-grandfather; but assures him of Calpurnia's recovery from her miscarriage.

	Book 8	
	Addressee	Subject
8.11	Hispulla	Pliny assures the addressee, aunt of Calpurnia, of the latter's recovery from her miscarriage, and requests that she excuse the incident to Pliny's grandfather-in-law.
8.12	Minicianus	Pliny asks to be excused: Titinius Capito – a great patron of literary endeavour – is reading today from his work on the deaths of famous men.
8.13	Genialis	Pliny conveys his delight that the addressee is reading Pliny's works with his own father, who is the most excellent of teachers.
8.14	Aristo	Expressing the view that ignorance of senatorial procedure is now widespread (thanks to the slavery of past times), Pliny requests the expert opinion of the addressee on his conduct in a recent debate in the senate concerning the fate of the freedmen of the consul Afranius Dexter, allegedly murdered by his slaves.
8.15	Iunior	The grape harvest for both Pliny and the addressee is poor, and Pliny has sent him multiple volumes, knowing he will have the time now to read them.
8.16	Paternus	A report of deaths among Pliny's slaves: Pliny explains his habit of manumission and of respecting the wills of slaves within the community of his household.
8.17	Macrinus	News of disaster: the Tiber and its tributaries have burst their banks, causing devastation worsened by continual bad weather; Pliny begs the addressee to give information on his own condition.
8.18	Rufinus	An analysis of the will of Domitius Tullus: he has made his adopted daughter his heir, thus evading the legacy-hunters (and he has not neglected his wife), with the result that the dead man cuts a better figure in death than in life.
8.19	Maximus	With his wife ill and with deaths and illness among his slaves, Pliny reports he has taken refuge in literary studies.
8.20	Gallus	On the wonders and delights of Lake Vadimon.
8.21	Arrianus	A report on Pliny's recent recitation of a new book of 'varied' poetry to select friends: the revised result will soon be with the addressee.
8.22	Geminus	An explanation of Pliny's attitude towards the forgiveness of errors in self and others.
8.23	Marcellinus	A lengthy lament for the death of Pliny's protégé, the young aedile designate Iunius Avitus.
8.24	Maximus	Detailed advice for the addressee, the newly appointed governor of Achaia, on the particular task of governing the cradle of culture and civilization.

	Book 9	
	Addressee	Subject
9.1	Maximus	A plea to the addressee not to be put off publishing his works concerning Planta by the sudden death of the latter.
9.2	Sabinus	A response to the request of the addressee for more and longer letters: Pliny does not have Cicero's genius or his copious material.
9.3	Paulinus	An expression of the opinion that people should either strive for lasting fame or eschew pointless work and enjoy their leisure in peace.
9.4	Macrinus	Pliny is sending the addressee a speech which can be easily understood at whatever point the reader chooses to start.
9.5	Tiro	Advice to the addressee in his capacity as provincial governor on the importance of preserving the distinction of ranks among his charges.
9.6	Calvisius	A report that Pliny, despite being in Rome, is spending all his time on literary studies: the circus races are on, which hold no interest for Pliny.
9.7	Romanus	Pliny responds to the news that the addressee is building with his own report of work being done on a pair of his villas on Lake Como, named Comedy and Tragedy.
9.8	Augurinus	A eulogy of the excellent writings of the addressee – especially those which are about Pliny himself.
9.9	Colonus	Pliny consoles the addressee on the death of young Pompeius Quintianus.
9.10	Tacitus	A report to the addressee on the difficulty of combining boar-hunting and literary studies at Pliny's country estate this summer.
9.11	Geminus	A reply to the addressee's wish to have something dedicated to him for inclusion in Pliny's works.
9.12	Iunior	A reminder to a father not to treat his son too harshly: Pliny has been forced to criticize another man for rebuking his son for spending too much on dogs and horses.
9.13	Quadratus	The addressee, after reading Pliny's *de Helvidi ultione*, asks to know more of the background and context to the speech: Pliny provides a detailed account of his attack on Publicius Certus in the aftermath of the assassination of Domitian.
9.14	Tacitus	Pliny asserts that he does not know whether posterity will care for himself or the addressee; but both certainly deserve some such notice.
9.15	Falco	A report that Pliny has fled to his Tuscan estate in order to revise his speeches; but he is so disturbed by complaints from his tenants that he can do very little.

	Book 9	
	Addressee	Subject
9.16	Mamilianus	A report that Pliny has no time for hunting: the grape harvest is at hand, although it is poor and Pliny must make new verses instead of new wine.
9.17	Genitor	In reply to a complaint about the presence of jesters at a dinner, Pliny advises the addressee to loosen up and realize how many people are bored by the kind of literary entertainment they themselves enjoy at dinner.
9.18	Sabinus	In reply to a request for more of Pliny's work, Pliny promises to send more – but piecemeal, so as not to overwhelm the addressee.
9.19	Ruso	The addressee, after reading one of Pliny's letters, compares the memorial inscription of Verginius Rufus unfavourably with the example of Frontinus, who forbade any monument to himself and preferred to trust to 'memory': Pliny replies with a vigorous defence of Verginius.
9.20	Venator	Pliny responds with delight to the addressee's letter about Pliny's writings, reporting also on the better than expected progress of the grape harvest.
9.21	Sabinianus	A report that the addressee's freedman, sorry for what he has done, has requested that Pliny intercede with the addressee on his behalf; Pliny has already reprimanded the freedman himself, and recommends forgiveness.
9.22	Severus	On the recent ill health of Passenus Paulus, descendant and imitator of Propertius (and now of Horace): joy at the eventual recovery of this literary man.
9.23	Maximus	A report of two recent incidents which have given Pliny particular pleasure: a conversation at the races recounted by Tacitus (which implies that they have equal fame for literary studies), and another at a dinner at which Pliny himself was present (where he was recognized solely from a description of his literary efforts).
9.24	Sabinianus	Pliny conveys his delight that the addressee has taken his advice and welcomed the erring freedman back into his household.
9.25	Mamilianus	Despite the demands of military business, the addressee has asked for more of Pliny's light poetry: in consequence, Pliny is beginning to hope for fame from his verse.
9.26	Lupercus	In response to the addressee's adverse comments on the high style of Pliny's writings, Pliny defends himself at some length in high style, with particular reference to the example of Demosthenes.
9.27	Paternus	A report of a recent incident in which a certain person, having begun to recite his history, was begged by audience members not to continue the next day, through shame of hearing the account of their own deeds.

(cont.)

	Book 9	
	Addressee	Subject
9.28	Romanus	Informing the addressee that he has received three letters from him at the same time, Pliny replies to each in turn. A further letter has not arrived.
9.29	Rusticus	Lacking confidence in any single genre, Pliny explains that he has always tried his hand at various types of writing (and would like to be judged on that basis).
9.30	Geminus	Pliny responds to the addressee's praise of Nonius' beneficence with a definition of true generosity: to give to a variety of people with special regard for the less well off.
9.31	Sardus	Pliny reports that he has read the addressee's work with pleasure, especially the parts about Pliny himself.
9.32	Titianus	Living the life of complete leisure, Pliny asserts he does not want to write long letters, but he does want to read them.
9.33	Caninius	The one about the dolphin.
9.34	Tranquillus	Hearing that he reads his own poetry badly, and wondering whether to use his inexperienced freedman as reader, Pliny asks the addressee for advice.
9.35	†Atrius†	Pliny reports that he has not yet had time to read work sent him by the addressee, and recommends that the addressee put a limit to the revision of his own works.
9.36	Fuscus	At the addressee's request, Pliny outlines his daily routine in summer at his Tuscan villa.
9.37	Paulinus	Pliny reports that he cannot attend the addressee on the first day of his consulship because he must attempt a radical solution to the continuing problems of his tenants, by accepting rent in kind.
9.38	Saturninus	Pliny confirms his praise of Rufus' book, which is perfect.
9.39	Mustius	Pliny, required to rebuild a temple of Ceres on his estates, with a new portico and statue of the goddess, gives instructions for relevant purchases and for construction.
9.40	Fuscus	Further to the account of his summer routine in Tuscany, Pliny now supplies the addressee, at his request, with an account of his winter routine at the Laurentine villa.

Popular topics in the Letters: Bibliographical help

For the function of this appendix within the present volume, see the Introduction. Below we provide bibliographical pointers on selected popular topics in Pliny, plus (where possible) an indication of some relevant letters. Neither the list of topics nor accompanying bibliography is designed to be exhaustive. In the case of the bibliography, we point readers towards selected items: by dipping in, readers will soon be able to discover the fuller bibliography for themselves, including numerous classic items not listed below for reasons of space. In listing 'starter' items we concentrate on bibliography in English; contributions in other languages are usually found in the 'further items' section immediately underneath. In both cases we list bibliography with the most recent items first, since these are in theory likely to include a more up-to-date (further) bibliography of their own. Inevitably, topics often overlap, as e.g. in the instance of 'Benefactor/patron (Pliny as)', 'Comum and Pliny', and 'Estates: Pliny as landowner'. Since we have tried to reduce repetition between entries, readers should check all entries relevant to their chosen theme.

We have not included our own contributions in the present volume to the topics listed below; for such contributions (where they exist), please consult the indices to this volume.

In this appendix, the Harvard system of citation by author surname plus date of publication (standard in the main text of the present volume) is supplemented by an abbreviated publication title (occasionally consisting of the book or article subtitle, since these are sometimes more revealing of actual content). Abbreviated book titles are indicated in italics, abbreviated article titles are contained in quotation marks. Full title details of all items can be found in the 'References' section of this volume. For topics not listed below, the reader may consult the following bibliographical surveys up to 1989:[1]

---

[1] A more recent update to selected topics in Pliny is provided by Anguissola (2007).

Hanslik R. (1955) and (1964). 'Plinius der Jüngere', *AAHG* 8: 1–18 and *AAHG* 17: 1–16.

Beaujeu, J. (1961). 'Pline le Jeune 1955–1960', *Lustrum* 6: 272–303.

Cova, P. (1974). 'Sette anni di studi su Plinio il Giovane (1966–1973)', *BStudLat.* 4: 274–91.

Römer, F. (1975) and (1987). 'Plinius d. J. III. Bericht', *AAHG* 28: 153–200 and 'IV. Bericht', *AAHG* 40: 153–98.

Aubrion, E. (1989). 'La "Correspondance" de Pline le Jeune: problèmes et orientations actuelles de la recherche', *ANRW* II 33.1: 304–74.

LIST OF TOPICS

1. Addressees, family and friends of Pliny
2. Benefactor/patron (Pliny as)
3. Bithynia-Pontus and Book 10: Pliny as governor
4. Christians in Book 10
5. Chronology of the *Letters*
6. Cicero and Pliny
7. Comum and Pliny
8. Elder Pliny and Younger Pliny
9. Estates : Pliny as landowner
10. Historiography (Pliny and)

11. Individual letters: Selected readings
12. Latinity and style of the *Letters*
13. Letters (epistolographical studies)
14. Martial and Pliny
15. *Otium* (leisure) and Pliny
16. *Panegyricus*
17. Poetry/Pliny as poet
18. Reception of Pliny
19. Revision and authenticity in the *Letters*
20. Rhetoric and rhetorical style (Pliny's views on)
21. Seneca and Pliny

22. Slavery in Pliny
23. Statius and Pliny
24. 'Stoic Opposition', Domitian and Pliny
25. Suetonius and Pliny
26. Tacitus and Pliny
27. Trajan and Pliny
28. Transmission and textual tradition of the *Letters*
29. Vesuvius letters
30. Villa letters
31. Women in Pliny (incl. Calpurnia)

1. ADDRESSEES, FAMILY AND FRIENDS OF PLINY

Select letters: *passim.*

Start with: Champlin 'Pliny's other country' (2001); Birley *Onomasticon* (2000a) 1–4, 17–21; Syme 'Consular friends of the Elder Pliny' *RP* 7.496–511; Syme 'Verginius Rufus' *RP* 7.512–20; Syme 'Vestricius Spurinna' *RP* 7.541–50; Syme 'Correspondents of Pliny' *RP* 5.440–77 [= (1985a)]; Syme 'Pliny the procurator' *RP* 2.742–73 [= (1969b)]; Syme 'People in Pliny' *RP* 2.694–723 [= (1968)]; Jones 'New commentary on the letters' (1968b); Syme 'Pliny's less successful friends' *RP* 2.477–96 [= (1960)].

Further items: Krieckhaus *Senatorische Familien* (2006) 31–50; Gonzalès *Esclaves et affranchis* (2003) 51–65, 77–105; Mratschek '*Illa nostra Italia*' (2003); Bacchiega 'Gli altri Plinii' (1993).
See also: 2. Benefactor/patron (Pliny as); **7.** Comum and Pliny; **25.** Suetonius and Pliny; **26.** Tacitus and Pliny; **31.** Women in Pliny (incl. Calpurnia).

2. BENEFACTOR/PATRON (PLINY AS)

Select letters: 1.7, 1.8, 3.6, 3.9, 3.21, 4.1, 5.7, 6.18, 7.18, 9.39; cf. *CIL* 5.5262 (reprinted in Appendix 1).

Start with: Patterson *Landscapes and Cities* (2006) 154–7, 169–76; Hoffer *Anxieties* (1999) 93–110; Duncan-Jones *Economy of the Roman Empire* (1982) 27–32; Nicols 'Pliny and the patronage of communities' (1980); White 'Friends of Martial, Statius and Pliny' (1975).

Further items: Krieckhaus *Senatorische Familien* (2006) 45–8; Manuwald 'Eine schule für Novum Comum' (2003); Ludolph *Epistolographie* (1997) 179–93.
See also: 1. Addressees, family and friends of Pliny; **7.** Comum and Pliny; **9.** Estates: Pliny as landowner; **14.** Martial and Pliny; **25.** Suetonius and Pliny.

3. BITHYNIA-PONTUS AND BOOK 10 : PLINY AS GOVERNOR

Select letters: 10.15–121; cf. 6.22, 8.24, 9.5, 9.28.4; also 4.9, 5.20, 6.5, 6.13, 7.6, 7.10.

Start with: Madsen *Eager to be Roman* (2009) 11–26; Noreña 'Social economy of Pliny's correspondence with Trajan' (2007); Stadter 'Pliny and the ideology of empire' (2006); Woolf 'Pliny's province' (2006a); Millar 'Trajan: government by correspondence' (2004a); Williams *Correspondence with Trajan* (1990); Gamberini *Stylistic Theory and Practice* (1983) 332–76; Talbert 'Pliny as governor' (1980); Levick 'Pliny in Bithynia' (1979).

Further items: Mazzoli 'Tra *Panegirico* e libro X dell' *epistolario* pliniano' (2003); Alföldy 'Die Inschriften des jüngeren Plinius' (1999a) 221–44 [= (1999b)]; Instinsky 'Formalien im Briefwechsel mit Trajan' (1969); Vidman *Étude sur la correspondance de Pline avec Trajan* (1960).
See also: 4. Christians in Book 10; **27.** Trajan and Pliny.

4. CHRISTIANS IN BOOK 10

Select letters: 10.96, 10.97.

Start with: Peper and DelCogliano 'Pliny and Trajan correspondence' (2006); Fishwick 'Pliny and the Christians' (1990); Williams *Correspondence with Trajan* (1990) 138–44; Johnson *'De conspiratione delatorum'* (1988); Sherwin-White *Commentary* (1966) 691–712, 772–87.

Further items: Lefèvre *Vom Römertum zum Ästhetizismus* (2009) 176–80; Reichert 'Durchdachte Konfusion' (2002); Muth 'Plinius d. J. und Kaiser Trajan über die Christen' (1982); Wlosok *Rom und die Christen* (1970) 27–39.

See also: 3. Bithynia-Pontus and Book 10: Pliny as governor ; **18.** Reception of Pliny; **27.** Trajan and Pliny.

5. CHRONOLOGY OF THE *LETTERS*

Select letters: 1.1 *et passim.*

Start with: Bodel *Publication of Pliny's Letters* (unpublished; cf. Marchesi *Art of Pliny* (2008) 12 n. 1); Murgia 'Pliny's letters and the *Dialogus*' (1985) 191–202; Syme 'Dating of Pliny's latest letters' *RP* 5.478–89 [= (1985b)]; Syme *Tacitus* (1958) 660–64; Sherwin-White *Commentary* (1966) 20–41, 62–5, 529–32.

Further items: Gonzalès *Esclaves et affranchis* (2003) 50–6; Asbach 'Zur Chronologie' (1881); Mommsen 'Zur Lebensgeschichte' (1869) 31ff.

See also: 13. Letters (epistolographical studies); **19.** Revision and authenticity in the *Letters*; **28.** Transmission and textual tradition of the *Letters*.

6. CICERO AND PLINY

Select letters: 1.2, 1.5, 1.20, 3.15, 3.21, 4.8, 5.3, 7.4, 7.17, 9.2, 9.26.

Start with: Gibson and Steel 'Indistinct literary careers of Cicero and Pliny' (2010); Marchesi *Art of Pliny* (2008) 207–40, 252–57; Morello 'Pliny and the art of saying nothing' (2003); Riggsby 'Pliny on Cicero and oratory' (1995); Rudd 'Cicero *ad Familiares* 5.12 and Pliny's Letters' (1992).

Further items: Lefèvre *Vom Römertum zum Ästhetizismus* (2009) 111–22 [= (1996b)]; Méthy 'La correspondence de Pline le Jeune' (2006); Wolff 'Pline et Cicéron' (2004); Wolff *Refus du pessimisme* (2003) 92–5; Wenskus 'Rhetorik als Briefthema bei Cicero und Plinius' (1999); Weische 'Plinius d. J. und Cicero' (1989); Guillemin *La vie littéraire* (1929) 67–99, 113–17.

See also: 10. Historiography (Pliny and); **12.** Latinity and style of the *Letters*; **20.** Rhetoric and rhetorical style (Pliny's views on).

7. COMUM AND PLINY

Select letters: 1.3, 1.8, 1.19, 2.8, 3.6, 4.1, 4.13, 4.30, 5.7, 5.11, 5.14, 6.24, 7.11, 7.14, 7.18, 9.7.

Start with: Henderson *Pliny's Statue* (2002a) 167–71; Hoffer *Anxieties* (1999) 31–3.

Further items: Krieckhaus '*Duae patriae?*' (2004); Gasser *Germana Patria* (1999) 186–216; Luraschi 'Aspetti di vita pubblica' (1999); Alföldy 'Ein Tempel des Herrscherkultes in Comum' (1983) [= (1999a) 211–19].

See also: 1. Addressees, family and friends of Pliny; **2.** Benefactor/patron (Pliny as); **9.** Estates: Pliny as landowner.

8. ELDER PLINY AND YOUNGER PLINY

Select letters: 1.19, 3.5, 4.30, 5.8, 6.16, 6.20, 9.32.

Start with: R. Gibson 'Elder and better' (2011a); Stevens 'Pliny and the dolphin' (2009); Henderson *Pliny's Statue* (2002a) 69–102; Henderson 'Pliny on uncle Pliny (*Epistles* 3.5)' (2002b).

Further items: Lefèvre *Vom Römertum zum Ästhetizismus* (2009) 123–41 [= (1996a)]; Cova 'Plinio il Giovane contro Plinio il Vecchio' (2001).

See also: 1. Addressees, family and friends of Pliny; **10.** Historiography (Pliny and); **15.** *Otium* (leisure) and Pliny; **29.** Vesuvius letters.

9. ESTATES : PLINY AS LANDOWNER

Select letters: 1.9, 2.15, 2.17, 3.19, 4.1, 4.6, 5.6, 5.18, 6.3, 6.19, 8.2, 8.15, 8.17, 9.7, 9.10, 9.15, 9.16, 9.20, 9.37, 9.39.

Start with: Kehoe *Law and the Rural Economy* (2007) 105–9; Kehoe 'Investment in estates' (1993); de Neeve 'A Roman landowner and his estates' (1992 [1990]); Kehoe 'Approaches to economic problems' (1989); Kehoe 'Allocation of risk' (1988); Duncan-Jones *Economy of the Roman Empire* (1982) 19–24.

Further items: Braconi 'Territorio e paesaggio dell' alta valle del Tevere' (2008); Anguissola 'Plinio il Giovane tra letteratura e archeologia: aggiornamento bibliografico (1936–2006)' (2007); Lo Cascio 'L'economia dell'Italia Romana' (2003); Andermahr *Totus in Praediis* (1998) 384–6.

See also: 1. Addressees, family and friends of Pliny; **7.** Comum and Pliny; **30.** Villa letters.

10. HISTORIOGRAPHY (PLINY AND)

Select letters: 1.1, 3.5, 5.5, 5.8, 6.16, 6.20, 7.33, 8.4, 8.12, 9.27.

Start with: Woodman 'Pliny on writing history: *Epistles* 5.8' (forthcoming); Marchesi *Art of Pliny* (2008) 144–206; Tzounakas 'Pliny's first epistle and his attitude towards historiography' (2007); Ash 'Pliny the historian?' (2003); Gamberini *Stylistic Theory and Practice* (1983) 58–81; Traub 'Pliny's treatment of history' (1955).

Further items: Baier 'Plinius über historischen und rhetorischen Stil' (2003); Ludolph *Epistolographie* (1997) 71–6; Ussani 'Leggendo Plinio il Giovane, II (*Oratio–historia*)' (1971).

See also: 8. Elder Pliny and Younger Pliny; **12.** Latinity and style of the *Letters*; **20.** Rhetoric and rhetorical style (Pliny's views on); **26.** Tacitus and Pliny; **29.** Vesuvius letters.

11. INDIVIDUAL LETTERS: SELECTED READINGS

Select letters: 1.1, 1.6 (and 9.10), 1.19, 3.11, 3.14, 4.22, 5.6, 5.10, 5.16, 6.31, 7.31, 8.14, 8.20, 10.1–2; also 4.28, 6.15, 7.33.

Start with: 1.1: Tzounakas 'Pliny's first epistle and his attitude towards historiography' (2007); **1.6** and **9.10:** Edwards 'Hunting for boars' (2008); **1.19:** Henderson 'Funding homegrown talent' (2002c); **3.11:** Shelton 'Rhetoric and autobiography' (1987); **3.14:** Williams 'Pliny and the murder of Larcius Macedo' (2006); **4.22:** Woolf 'Playing games with Greeks' (2006b); **5.6:** Chinn '5.6 and the ancient theory of ekphrasis' (2007); **5.10:** Power 'Pliny 5.10 and the literary career of Suetonius' (2010); **5.16:** Bodel 'Minicia Marcella' (1995); **6.31** Saylor 'Emperor as *insula*' (1972); **7.31:** Baker 'Persistence of a theme' (1985); **8.14:** Whitton 'Pliny 8.14' (2010); **8.20:** Saylor 'Overlooking lake Vadimon' (1982); **9.33:** Stevens 'Pliny and the dolphin' (2009); **10.1–2:** Hoffer 'Accession propaganda in Pliny' (2006).

Further items: 4.28: Radicke 'Der öffentliche Privatbrief' (2003); **6.15:** Schröder 'Literaturkritik oder *Fauxpas*?' (2001); **7.33:** Hennig 'Zu Plinius *Ep*. 7,33' (1978).

See also: 4. Christians in Book 10; **6.** Cicero and Pliny; **8.** Elder Pliny and Younger Pliny; **14.** Martial and Pliny; **26.** Tacitus and Pliny; **29.** Vesuvius letters; **30.** Villa letters; **31.** Women in Pliny (incl. Calpurnia).

12. LATINITY AND STYLE OF THE *LETTERS*

Select letters: *passim.*

Start with: Hoffer *Anxieties* (1999) 13–14; von Albrecht *Masters of Latin Prose* (1989) 160–4; Gamberini *Stylistic Theory and Practice* (1983) 161–75, 180–376, 449–529.

Further items: Lefèvre *Vom Römertum zum Ästhetizismus* (2009) *passim*; Wolff *Refus du pessimisme* (2003) 87–91; Hausler 'Parenthesen im Lateinischen am Beispiel der Pliniusbriefe' (2000); Guerrini 'I diminutivi' (1997); Melzani 'Elementi della lingua d'uso' (1992); Cova 'Arte allusiva e stilizzazione retorica' (1972); Trisoglio *La personalità di Plinio* (1972) 211–44; Strube 'II 7: eine sprachliche und stilistische Analyse' (1964); Pliszczynska *De elocutione Pliniana* (1955); D'Agostino 'I diminutivi in Plinio' (1931); Guillemin *La vie littéraire* (1929) 146–55; Deane 'Greek in Pliny' (1918); Kukula *Epistularum libri novem* (1912) vii–xv.

See also: 10. Historiography (Pliny and); **20.** Rhetoric and rhetorical style (Pliny's views on); **26.** Tacitus and Pliny; **29.** Vesuvius letters.

13. LETTERS (EPISTOLOGRAPHICAL STUDIES)

Select letters: 1.1 *et passim.*

Start with: Ebbeler 'Letters' (2010); Porter and Adams *Paul and the Ancient Letter Form* (2010); White *Cicero in Letters* (2010) 3–29, 63–86; Gunderson 'S.V.B; E.V.' (2007); Gibson and Morrison 'What is a letter?' (2007); Morello and Morrison *Ancient Letters* (2007); Poster 'Epistolary theory in Greco-Roman antiquity' (2007); Trapp 'Biography in letters' (2007); Klauck *Ancient Letters and the New Testament* (2006); Edwards 'Epistolography' (2005); Ebbeler 'Caesar's letters and the ideology of literary history' (2003); Trapp *Greek and Latin Letters* (2003) 1–46; de Pretis *'Epistolarity' in the First Book of Horace's Epistles* (2002); Wilson 'Seneca's Epistles reclassified' (2001); Malherbe *Ancient Epistolary Theorists* (1988); Wilson 'Seneca's epistles to Lucilius: a revaluation' (1987); Stowers *Letter Writing in Greco-Roman Antiquity* (1986); Altman *Epistolarity* (1982).

Further items: Laurence-Guillaumont *Epistulae Antiquae* V (2008); Laurence-Guillaumont *Epistulae Antiquae* IV (2006); Nadjo and Gavoille

Epistulae Antiquae III (2004); Nadjo and Gavoille *Epistulae Antiquae* I (2002a); Nadjo and Gavoille *Epistulae Antiquae* II (2002b); Cugusi *Evoluzione e forme dell' epistolografia latina* (1983).

See also: 5. Chronology of the *Letters*; **19.** Revision and authenticity in the *Letters*.

14. MARTIAL AND PLINY

Select letters: 3.21

Start with: Marchesi *Art of Pliny* (2008) 62–8; Henderson *Pliny's Statue* (2002a) 47–57; Henderson 'On Pliny on Martial' (2001); Pitcher 'Pliny and Martial reconsidered' (1999); Gowers *Loaded Table* (1993) 250–79; Adamik 'Pliny and Martial' (1976); Vessey 'Pliny, Martial and Silius Italicus' (1974).

Further items: Lefèvre *Vom Römertum zum Ästhetizismus* (2009) 157–9.

See also: 2. Benefactor/patron (Pliny as); **17.** Poetry/Pliny as poet; **23.** Statius and Pliny.

15. OTIUM (LEISURE) AND PLINY

Select letters: 1.3, 1.6, 1.9, 1.19, 2.8, 2.17, 3.1, 3.5, 4.23, 5.6, 5.18, 7.3, 7.9, 8.9, 9.3, 9.6, 9.10, 9.32, 9.36, 9.40.

Start with: Johnson *Readers and Reading Culture in the High Roman Empire* (2010) 32–62; Fitzgerald 'The letter's the thing (in Pliny Book 7)' (2007a); Myers 'Garden ownership in Statius and Pliny' (2005); Leach '*Otium* as *luxuria*' (2003); Connors 'Literature of leisure' (2000); Hoffer *Anxieties* (1999) 111–18.

Further items: Méthy *Les Lettres de Pline* (2007) 353–78; Pani 'Sviluppa della tematica dell'*otium* in Plinio' (1993); Ussani '*Otium e pax* in Plinio il Giovane' (1981); André *L'otium dans la vie morale* (1966).

See also: 8. Elder Pliny and Younger Pliny; **17.** Poetry/Pliny as poet; **21.** Seneca and Pliny; **30.** Villa letters.

16. PANEGYRICUS

Select letters: 3.13, 3.18; cf. 6.27 and *Paneg.*

Start with: Roche 'Pliny's thanksgiving: an introduction to the *Panegyricus*' (2011a); Noreña 'Self-fashioning in the *Panegyricus*' (2011); B. Gibson 'Contemporary contexts' (2011); Manolaraki 'Political and rhetorical seascapes in Pliny's *Panegyricus*' (2008); Morford 'Pliny's *Panegyricus* and liberty' (1992); Gamberini *Stylistic Theory and Practice* (1983) 377–448; Radice 'Pliny and the *Panegyricus*' (1968); Bruère 'Tacitus and Pliny's *Panegyricus*' (1954).

Further items: Strobel 'Plinius und Domitian' (2003); Beutel *Vergangenheit* (2000) 37–127; Fedeli 'Il *Panegirico* di Plinio nella critica moderna' (1989).

See also: 20. Rhetoric and rhetorical style (Pliny's views on); **24.** 'Stoic Opposition', Domitian and Pliny; **27.** Trajan and Pliny.

17. POETRY/PLINY AS POET

Select letters: 1.13, 1.16, 2.10, 3.15, 3.21, 4.3, 4.14, 4.18, 4.19, 4.27, 5.3, 5.15, 5.17, 6.15, 6.21, 7.4, 8.4, 8.21, 9.22, 9.25, 9.34.

Start with: Marchesi *Art of Pliny* (2008) 53–96; Roller 'Pliny's Catullus' (1998); Hershkowitz 'Pliny the poet' (1995); Courtney *Fragmentary Latin Poets* (1993) 367–70; Gamberini *Stylistic Theory and Practice* (1983) 82–118.

Further items: Höschele *Die blütenlesende Muse* (2010) 46–52; Auhagen 'Plinius' *hendecasyllabi*' (2003); Cova *La critica letteraria di Plinio* (1966) 48–59, 72–94.

See also: 2. Benefactor/patron (Pliny as); **14.** Martial and Pliny; **15.** *Otium* (leisure) and Pliny; **20.** Rhetoric and rhetorical style (Pliny's views on); **23.** Statius and Pliny.

18. RECEPTION OF PLINY

Select letters: *passim.*

Start with: Gibson 'Pliny and the letters of Sidonius' (forthcoming a); Cain *Letters of Jerome* (2009) 18–19; Liebeschuetz *Ambrose of Milan* (2005) 31–6; du Prey *Villas of Pliny from Antiquity to Posterity* (1994); Cameron 'Fate of Pliny's *Letters* in the late Empire' (1965).[2]

Further items: Lefèvre *Vom Römertum zum Ästhetizismus* (2009) 252–72 [= (1988)]; Römer 'Eine poetische Gestaltung von *Epist.* 3,5' (2003); Wolff *Refus du pessimisme* (2003) 95–8; Kemper 'Plinius Minor van Oudheid tot Renaissance' (2000); Zelzer '*Plinius Christianus:* Ambrosius' (1989);

---

[2] For a selection of modern novels which feature Pliny as a character, see above p. 18 n. 38.

Meulemans *Plinius' Fontein* (1913); Allain *Pline le Jeune et ses héritiers*, vol. III (1901) 229–409; Geisler 'Loci similes auctorum Sidonio anteriorum' (1887).

See also: 4. Christians in Book 10; **28**. Transmission and textual tradition of the *Letters*; **29**. Vesuvius letters; **30**. Villa letters.

19. REVISION AND AUTHENTICITY IN THE *LETTERS*

Select letters: 1.1 *et passim*.

Start with: Henderson *Pliny's Statue* (2002a) 20–2; Hoffer *Anxieties* (1999) 17–18, 26–7, 87; Bell 'Revision and authenticity' (1989); Gamberini *Stylistic Theory and Practice* (1983) 122–61; Winniczuk 'Ending phrases in Pliny's letters' (1975); Lilja 'Nature of Pliny's letters' (1970).

Further items: Gonzalès *Esclaves et affranchis* (2003) 37–50; Wolff *Refus du pessimisme* (2003) 31–54; Ludolph *Epistolographie* (1997) 40–59; Sherwin-White 'The man and his letters' (1969b); Sherwin-White *Commentary* (1966) 11–20; Zelzer 'Zur Frage des Charakters der Briefsammlung des jüngeren Plinius' (1964).

See also: 5. Chronology of the *Letters*; **12**. Latinity and style of the *Letters*; **13**. Letters (epistolographical studies); **20**. Rhetoric and rhetorical style (Pliny's views on); **28**. Transmission and textual tradition of the *Letters*.

20. RHETORIC AND RHETORICAL STYLE (PLINY'S VIEWS ON)

Select letters: 1.2, 1.16, 1.20, 2.3, 2.5, 2.11–12, 2.14, 2.19, 4.5, 4.16, 4.24, 6.2, 6.11, 6.29, 6.33, 7.6, 7.9, 7.12, 7.17, 9.4, 9.26, 9.29.

Start with: Innes '*Panegyricus* and rhetorical theory' (2011); Dominik 'Tacitus and Pliny on oratory' (2007); Mayer '*Gloria dicendi*' (2003); Starr 'Pliny on private recitations' (1990); Gamberini *Stylistic Theory and Practice* (1983) 12–57; Orentzel 'Declamation in the age of Pliny' (1968); Syme *Tacitus* (1958) 668–70.

Further items: Cova 'Plinio il giovane contra Quintiliano' (2003); Cugusi 'Idee retoriche di Plinio' (2003); Cova *La critica letteraria di Plinio* (1966) 60–107; Guillemin *La vie littéraire* (1929) 67–111; Norden *Kunstprosa* (1915) 318–21.

See also: 6. Cicero and Pliny; **10**. Historiography (Pliny and); **12**. Latinity and style of the *Letters*; **17**. Poetry/Pliny as poet; **19**. Revision and authenticity in the *Letters*; **26**. Tacitus and Pliny.

21. SENECA AND PLINY

Select letters: 1.12, 3.7, 9.3.

Start with: Tzounakas 'Seneca's presence in Pliny's epistle 1.12' (2011); Marchesi *Art of Pliny* (2008) 14–20, 234–6; Griffin 'Pliny's debt to moral philosophy' (2007); Griffin '*De Beneficiis* and Roman society' (2003); Henderson *Pliny's Statue* (2002a) 118–23; Griffin 'Seneca and Pliny' (2000).

Further items: Cova 'Presenza di Seneca in Plinio' (1997); Lausberg 'Cicero – Seneca – Plinius' (1991).

See also: 6. Cicero and Pliny; **12.** Latinity and style of the *Letters*; **15.** *Otium* (leisure) and Pliny; **20.** Rhetoric and rhetorical style (Pliny's views on); **30.** Villa letters.

22. SLAVERY IN PLINY

Select letters: 1.4, 1.21, 3.14, 4.10, 5.19, 6.28, 7.16, 7.29, 7.32, 8.1, 8.6, 8.14, 8.16, 8.19, 9.21, 9.24.

Start with: Carlon *Pliny's Women* (2009) 119–21; Williams 'Murder of Larcius Macedo' (2006); Hoffer *Anxiety* (1999) 45–52.

Further items: Lefèvre *Vom Römertum zum Ästhetizismus* (2009) 181–94; Gonzalès *Esclaves et affranchis* (2003) 109–249; Bonelli 'Plinio il Giovane e la schiavitù' (1994); Yuge 'Die einstellung Plinius des Jüngeren zur Sklaverei' (1986).

See also: 2. Benefactor/patron (Pliny as); **9.** Estates: Pliny as landowner.

23. STATIUS AND PLINY

Select letters: 2.17, 5.6, 6.16, 6.20.

Start with: Newlands 'Vesuvius in Statius and Pliny' (2010); Pagán 'Epistolary preface from Statius to Pliny' (2010); Marchesi *Art of Pliny* (2008) 140–2; Myers 'Garden ownership in Statius and Pliny' (2005); Leach '*Otium* as luxuria' (2003) 152–6; White 'Friends of Martial, Statius and Pliny' (1975).

Further items: Aricò 'Plinio e la poesia' (1995); Guillemin *La vie littéraire* (1929) 125–7.

See also: 14. Martial and Pliny; **17.** Poetry/Pliny as poet; **29.** Vesuvius letters; **30.** Villa letters.

24. 'STOIC OPPOSITION', DOMITIAN AND PLINY

Select letters: 1.5, 1.12, 1.14, 2.18, 3.11, 3.16, 4.11, 4.22, 5.5, 6.2, 7.19, 7.27, 7.33, 9.13, 9.27.

Start with: Whitton "'Let us tread our path together'" (2012); Roche 'Pliny's thanksgiving: an introduction to the *Panegyricus*' (2011a); Carlon *Pliny's Women* (2009) 18–67; Freudenburg *Satires of Rome* (2001) 215–34; Birley *Onomasticon* (2000a) 10–16; Hoffer *Anxieties* (1999) 55–91; Syme 'Pliny's early career' *RP* 7.551–67; Syme 'A political group' *RP* 7.568–87; Shelton 'Letter 3.11' (1987); Orentzel 'Pliny and Domitian' (1980); Sherwin-White *Commentary* (1966) 763–71.

Further items: Lefèvre *Vom Römertum zum Ästhetizismus* (2009) 49–65; Strobel 'Plinius und Domitian?' (2003); Beutel *Vergangenheit* (2000) 175–237; Ludolph *Epistolographie* (1999) 44–9; Soverini 'Aspetti e problemi del rapporto con Domiziano e Traiano' (1989).

See also: 16. *Panegyricus*; **26.** Tacitus and Pliny; **27.** Trajan and Pliny; **31.** Women in Pliny.

25. SUETONIUS AND PLINY

Select letters: 1.18, 1.24, 3.8, 5.10, 9.34, 10.94–5.

Start with: Gibson 'Suetonius and the *uiri illustres* of Pliny' (forthcoming b); Power 'Pliny 5.10 and the literary career of Suetonius' (2010); Henderson *Pliny's Statue* (2002a) 24–6; Hoffer *Anxieties* (1999) 211–25; Wallace-Hadrill *Suetonius* (1983) 4–5, 26–38, 162–71; Syme 'Travels of Suetonius Tranquillus' *RP* 3.1337–49 [= (1981)].

Further items: Méthy 'Suétone vu par un contemporain' (2009); Lefèvre *Vom Römertum zum Ästhetizismus* (2009) 160–8.

See also: 2. Benefactor/patron (Pliny as); **10.** Historiography (Pliny and).

26. TACITUS AND PLINY

Select letters: 1.6, 1.20, 2.1, 2.11, 4.13, 4.15, 5.8, 6.9, 6.16, 6.20, 7.20, 7.33, 8.7, 9.10, 9.14, 9.23, 9.27.

Start with: Whitton "'Let us tread our path together'" (2012); Johnson *Readers and Reading Culture in the High Roman Empire* (2010) 63–73; Woodman 'Tacitus and the contemporary scene' (2009); Marchesi *Art of Pliny* (2008) 97–143; Edwards 'Hunting for boars with Pliny and

Tacitus' (2008); Dominik 'Tacitus and Pliny on oratory' (2007); Griffin 'Pliny and Tacitus' (1999); Murgia 'Pliny's Letters and the *Dialogus* (1985); Syme 'Juvenal, Pliny, Tacitus' *RP* 3.1135–57 [= (1979a)]; Syme *Tacitus* (1958) 59–129; Bruère 'Tacitus and Pliny's *Panegyricus*' (1954).

Further items: Lefèvre *Vom Römertum zum Ästhetizismus* (2009) 145–56, 246–50 [(= 1978)]; Vielberg 'Plinius d.J. und Tacitus' (1988); Cova *La critica letteraria di Plinio* (1966) 94–9.

See also: 10. Historiography (Pliny and); **20.** Rhetoric and rhetorical style (Pliny's views on); **24.** 'Stoic Opposition', Domitian and Pliny; **29.** Vesuvius letters.

27. TRAJAN AND PLINY

Select letters: 2.11–12, 3.13, 3.18, 4.22, 6.19, 6.22, 6.27, 6.31, 8.4, 8.17, 9.2, 10.1–121 *et passim.*

Start with: Carlon *Pliny's Women* (2009) 143–5, 201–4; Marchesi *Art of Pliny* (2008) 199–203; Noreña 'Social economy of Pliny's correspondence with Trajan' (2007); Hoffer 'Accession propaganda in Pliny' (2006); Henderson *Pliny's Statue* (2002a) 146–51; Rees 'Pliny's paradoxical Trajan' (2001); Coleman 'Literature after AD 96: change or continuity?' (2000); Leach 'The politics of self-representation' (1990); Syme 'Pliny and the Dacian wars' *RP* 6.142–9 [= (1964)]; Sherwin-White 'Trajan's replies to Pliny' (1962).

Further items: Lefèvre *Vom Römertum zum Ästhetizismus* (2009) 76–9; Biffino 'Il *temperamentum* e l' uomo ideale dell' età Traianea' (2003); Soverini 'Aspetti e problemi del rapporto con Domiziano e Traiano' (1989); Trisoglio *La personalità di Plinio* (1972) 50–96.

See also: 3. Bithynia-Pontus and Book 10: Pliny as governor; **4.** Christians in Book 10; **16.** *Panegyricus*; **24.** 'Stoic Opposition', Domitian and Pliny.

28. TRANSMISSION AND TEXTUAL TRADITION OF THE *LETTERS*

Start with: R. Gibson '<Clarus> confirmed?' (2011b); Reynolds *Texts and Transmission* (1983) 316–22; Mynors *C. Plini Caecili Secundi Epistularum Libri Decem* (1963) v–xxii; Stout *Scribe and Critic at Work in Pliny's Letters* (1954); Lowe and Rand *A Sixth-Century Fragment of the Letters of Pliny* (1922); Johnson 'MSS of Pliny's *Letters*' (1912); Robbins 'Tables of contents in MSS of Pliny's *Letters*' (1910); Merrill 'The codex Riccardianus of Pliny's letters' (1895).

Further items: Barwick 'Zwei antike Ausgaben der Pliniusbriefe?' (1936); Stangl 'Zur kritik der briefe Plinius' (1886).

See also: 18. Reception of Pliny; **19.** Revision and authenticity in the *Letters*.

29. VESUVIUS LETTERS

Select letters: 6.16 and 6.20.

Start with: Hales and Paul *Pompeii in the Public Imagination* (2011); Scarth *Vesuvius* (2009) 38–85; Marchesi *Art of Pliny* (2008) 171–89; Berry 'Pliny's Vesuvius narratives' (2008); Marturano and Varone 'A.D. 79 eruption' (2005); Augoustakis 'Style in 6.20' (2005); Sigurdsson and Carey 'Eruption of Vesuvius' (2002); Jones 'Vesuvius letters' (2001); Eco 'Portrait of the Elder as a Young Pliny' (1994); Sigurdsson, Carey, Cornell and Pescatore 'The eruption of Vesuviur in AD 79' (1985); Sigurdsson, Cashdollar and Sparks 'Eruption of Vesuvius' (1982).

Further items: Lefèvre *Vom Römertum zum Ästhetizismus* (2009) 126–41 [= (1996a)]; Cova 'Una rilettura critica delle lettere vesuviane' (2005); Cova 'Probleme e orientamenti della critica recente sulle lettere vesuviane' (2004); Schönberger 'Vesuv-Briefe' (1990); Gigante 'Racconto Pliniano' (1979); Görler 'Zum literarischen Hintergrund' (1979); Lillge 'Literarische form' (1918).

See also: 8. Elder Pliny and Younger Pliny; **10.** Historiography (Pliny and); **18.** Reception of Pliny; **26.** Tacitus and Pliny.

30. VILLA LETTERS

Select letters: 2.17, 5.6, 9.7, 9.36, 9.40.

Start with: Chinn 'Pliny *Epistulae* 5.6 and the ancient theory of ekphrasis' (2007); Marzano *Roman Villas in Central Italy* (2007) 110–14, 150–1, 306–9, 312–29, 736–7; Riggsby 'Pliny in space' (2003); Rossiter 'Building for the seasons at Pliny's villas' (2003); Claridge 'Villas of the Laurentine shore' (1997–8); Bergmann 'Visualising Pliny's villas' (1995); du Prey *Villas of Pliny* (1994).

Further items: Lefèvre *Vom Römertum zum Ästhetizismus* (2009) 223–34 [= (1977)]; Braconi and Uroz Sáez 'La villa di Plinio il Giovane a San Giustino' (2008); Anguissola 'Plinio il Giovane tra letteratura e archeologia: aggiornamento bibliografico (1936–2006)' (2007); Braconi and Uroz Sáez *La villa di Plinio il Giovane a San Giustino: primi risultati* (1999);

Purcell 'Il *litus Laurentinum* e l' archaeologia dell' *otium*' (1998); Ramieri 'La villa di Plinio a Castel Fusano' (1995); Scivoletto '*Urbs, municipia, villae* e *studia* nell' epistolario di Plinio' (1989). **See also: 9.** Estates: Pliny as landowner; **15.** *Otium* (leisure) and Pliny; **18.** Reception of Pliny; **23.** Statius and Pliny.

31. WOMEN IN PLINY (INCLUDING CALPURNIA)

Select letters: 1.4, 2.4, 3.16, 4.1, 4.11, 4.17, 4.19, 4.21, 5.16, 6.3, 6.4, 6.7, 6.24, 6.32, 6.33, 7.5, 7.11, 7.14, 7.19, 7.24, 8.5, 8.10, 8.11, 10.120–1.

Start with: Carlon *Pliny's Women* (2009); de Pretis 'Approaches to Pliny's epistles to Calpurnia' (2003); Sick 'Ummidia Quadratilla' (1999); de Verger 'Erotic language in Pliny, *Ep.* 7.5' (1999); Bodel 'Minicia Marcella' (1995); Shelton 'Pliny and the ideal wife' (1990); Dobson 'Pliny's depiction of women' (1982).

Further items: Lefèvre *Vom Römertum zum Ästhetizismus* (2009) 195–217; Wenskus 'Wie schreibt man einer Dame?' (2001); Maniet 'Pline le Jeune et Calpurnia' (1966). **See also: 1.** Addressees, family and friends of Pliny; **7.** Comum and Pliny; **24.** 'Stoic Opposition', Domitian and Pliny.

List of main characters in the Letters

For an explanation of the purpose and strict limitations of this index to a select number of those who appear in the *Letters*, see the Introduction to this volume. In keeping with established practice, names of characters are alphabetized below (largely, but not invariably) according to *nomen* rather than *cognomen*. Thus Vestricius (*nomen*) Spurinna (*cognomen*) is listed below under V rather than S, and Cornelius Tacitus under C. This convention inevitably creates some difficulties for the reader, inasmuch as characters – according to a second established practice – sometimes have their names shortened to *cognomen* alone in the body of the present volume (and so are identified as simply Spurinna or Tacitus, etc.); however, in order to minimize difficulties, we have provided cross-references along the lines of 'Tacitus: see Cornelius Tacitus'. One (conventional) exception to this second practice is where the *cognomen* of a character lacks distinctiveness, as in the cases of Verginius Rufus or Corellius Rufus. Their names are regularly shortened in this volume to Verginius and Corellius, respectively. Other exceptions proliferate alongside this, as e.g. in the case of Pliny himself, who was known to contemporaries both as Plinius (a name taken after adoption) and as Secundus (his *cognomen*). The former has prevailed as a means of identification (as in the body of this volume), for various reasons; for these and other matters of nomenclature, see Appendix 2 and above pp. 109–10 with nn. 23–7. The majority of women are identified by one name only.

Emperors are not included in the index. Below, P. = Pliny the Younger.

AFRANIUS DEXTER: consul of 105, murdered while in office.
ALBINUS: see Lucceius Albinus.
ALLIFANUS: see Pontius Allifanus.
ANNIUS SEVERUS: correspondent of P., from Comum.
ANTEIA: widow of Helvidius the Younger.
ANTONINUS: see Arrius Antoninus.

APOLLINARIS: see Domitius Apollinaris.

AQUILIUS REGULUS: consul (year unknown), leading orator of Centumviral court, rival of P., informer under Nero and Domitian.

ARISTO: see Titius Aristo.

ARRIA THE ELDER: mother of Arria the Younger, wife of Caecina Paetus, with whom she committed suicide in 42 after revolt against emperor Claudius.

ARRIA THE YOUNGER: daughter of Arria the Elder and Caecina Paetus, wife of Thrasea Paetus, mother of Fannia, and exiled by Domitian.

ARRIANUS: see Maturus Arrianus.

ARRIUS ANTONINUS: twice consul (69, 97), and poet admired by P.

ARTEMIDORUS: philosopher, friend of P. from time in Syria (like Euphrates), exiled by Domitian.

ARULENUS RUSTICUS (Iunius Arulenus Rusticus): Stoic senator, brother of Iunius Mauricus, executed by Domitian in connection with Thrasea Paetus and Helvidius Priscus.

ATILIUS CRESCENS: boyhood friend of P., from the Transpadane regions.

AUGURINUS: see Sentius Augurinus.

AVIDIUS NIGRINUS: consul of 110, involved in trial of Varenus Rufus.

AVITUS: see Iulius Avitus or Iunius Avitus.

BAEBIUS MACER: friend of P., possibly from Comum, consul in 103.

BAEBIUS MASSA: prosecuted by P. and Herennius Senecio after term as proconsul of Baetica under Domitian.

BASSUS: see Iulius Bassus or Pomponius Bassus.

BRUTTIUS PRAESENS: twice consul (118, 139), with connections via his mother to the Transpadane regions.

CAECILIUS CLASSICUS: proconsul of Baetica under Nerva/Trajan, whose associates were prosecuted by P. after the death of Classicus.

CAECILIUS MACRINUS: correspondent of P., perhaps from the Transpadane regions.

CAECINA PAETUS: father of Arria the Younger, husband of Arria the Elder, with whom he committed suicide in 42 after revolt against emperor Claudius.

CALESTRIUS TIRO: old friend and colleague of P., praetorian governor of Baetica under Trajan.

CALPURNIA: wife of P., from Comum, niece of Calpurnia Hispulla, granddaughter of Calpurnius Fabatus.

CALPURNIA HISPULLA: aunt of P.'s wife Calpurnia, perhaps related to Hispulla, wife of Corellius Rufus.

CALPURNIUS FABATUS: grandfather of P.'s wife Calpurnia, from Comum.

CALPURNIUS MACER: consul of 103, possibly from the Transpadane regions.

CALVISIUS RUFUS: friend of P., from Comum.

CANINIUS RUFUS: literary friend of P., from Comum.

CAPITO: see Titinius Capito.

CARUS: see Mettius Carus.

CATILIUS SEVERUS: twice consul (110, 120), perhaps from Bithynia.

CATIUS FRONTO: consul of 96, involved in trials of Marius Priscus, Iulius Bassus and Varenus Rufus.

CELERINA: see Pompeia Celerina.

CERTUS: see Publicius Certus.

CLARUS: see Erucius Clarus or Septicius Clarus.

CLASSICUS: see Caecilius Classicus.

CLUSINIUS GALLUS: correspondent of P., perhaps from the Transpadane regions.

CORELLIA: sister of Corellius Rufus.

CORELLIA HISPULLA: daughter of Corellius Rufus, perhaps related via Hispulla (wife of Corellius Rufus) to Calpurnia Hispulla, the aunt of P.'s wife.

CORELLIUS RUFUS: consul of 78, patron and supporter of P., father of Corellia Hispulla, brother of Corellia.

CORNELIUS MINICIANUS: Roman knight, from the Transpadane regions.

CORNELIUS PRISCUS: consul of 104 (?), from the Transpadane regions.

CORNELIUS TACITUS: the historian, consul of 97.

CORNELIUS URSUS: friend and correspondent of P., recipient of letters on trials of governors of Bithynia.

CORNUTUS TERTULLUS: friend and supporter of P., colleague with him both as prefect of the treasury of Saturn and as consul of 100.

COTTIA: wife of Vestricius Spurinna.

CREMUTIUS RUSO: aspiring orator and young protégé of P.

CRESCENS: see Atilius Crescens.

DELPHINUS: unidentified, from the environs of Hippo.

DEXTER: see Afranius Dexter.

DOMITIUS APOLLINARIS: northern Italian senator and friend of P., consul of 97.

ERUCIUS CLARUS: the father (M. Erucius Clarus) is a knight from the Transpadane regions; the son (Sex. Erucius Clarus) is twice consul (117, 146) and nephew of Septicius Clarus.

EUPHRATES: Stoic philosopher, from Tyre, friend of P. from time in Syria (like Artemidorus).

FABATUS: see Calpurnius Fabatus.

FABIUS IUSTUS: consul of 102, and friend of Cornelius Tacitus.

FABIUS QUINTILIANUS: see Quintilian.

FALCO: see Pompeius Falco.

FANNIA: daughter of Arria the Younger and Thrasea Paetus, granddaughter of Arria the Elder, wife of Helvidius Priscus the Elder (whose *Life* she asks Herennius Senecio to write), and exiled by Domitian.

FIRMUS: see Romatius Firmus.

FRONTINUS: see Iulius Frontinus.

FRONTO: see Catius Fronto.

FUNDANUS: see Minicius Fundanus.

FUSCUS SALINATOR (Pedanius Fuscus Salinator): aristocratic young orator, protégé of P., friend of Ummidius Quadratus, marries daughter of Iulius Servianus.

GALLUS: see Clusinius Gallus.

GEMINUS: see Rosianus Geminus.

GENITOR: see Iulius Genitor.

HELVIDIAE: daughters of Helvidius the Younger; both die in childbirth.

HELVIDIUS PRISCUS THE ELDER: husband of Fannia, son-in-law of Thrasea Paetus, praetorian senator and member of 'Stoic opposition', executed by Vespasian *c.* 74; *Life* written by Herennius Senecio at request of Fannia.

HELVIDIUS THE YOUNGER: son of Helvidius Priscus the Elder, husband of Anteia, consul of *c.* 87, executed by Domitian in 93 with the intrigue of Publicius Certus; his memory 'vindicated' by P. with an attack on Certus in the senate in 97.

HERENNIUS SENECIO: senator from Baetica, fellow prosecutor with P. of Baebius Massa (whose counter-action for treason he survives); writes *Life* of Helvidius Priscus the Elder at request of Fannia, and is executed in 93 after prosecution by Mettius Carus.

HISPULLA: wife of Corellius Rufus; see also Calpurnia Hispulla or Corellia Hispulla.

IAVOLENUS PRISCUS: consul of 86 and leading jurist.

ITALICUS: see Silius Italicus.

IULIUS AVITUS: brother of Iulius Naso, both sons of Iulius Secundus the Gallic orator.

IULIUS BASSUS: proconsul of Bithynia-Pontus *c.* 100–1; defended by P. against Bithynians.

IULIUS FRONTINUS: three-time consul (*c.* 73, 98, 100) and supporter of P., author of *De Aquaeductu Urbis Romae*; P. succeeds him as augur.

IULIUS GENITOR: rhetorician, recommended by P. as teacher for son of Corellia Hispulla.

IULIUS NASO: young protégé of P., son of orator Iulius Secundus, supported by both P. and Tacitus for quaestorship; brother of Iulius Avitus.

IULIUS SABINUS: correspondent of P. and perhaps first commander of garrison of Dacia.

IULIUS SERVIANUS: three-time consul (90, 102, 134), husband of sister of Hadrian, father-in-law of Fuscus Salinator; gains *ius trium liberorum* from Trajan for P.

IULIUS SPARSUS: perhaps consul of 88 and patron of Martial.

IULIUS VALERIANUS: unidentified correspondent of P.

IUNIOR: see Terentius Iunior.

IUNIUS AVITUS: correspondent of P., dies while aedile designate; do not confuse with Iulius Avitus.

IUNIUS MAURICUS: Stoic senator, brother of (Iunius) Arulenus Rusticus, and exiled by Domitian; P. recommends bridegroom and teachers for children of his late brother.

IUSTUS: see Fabius Iustus or Minicius Iustus.

LIBERALIS: see Salvius Liberalis.

LICINIUS NEPOS: consul of perhaps 127, praetor in 105, gently mocked by Pliny in the latter office.

LICINIUS SURA: three-time consul (*c.* 93, 102, 107), from Tarraconensis; correspondent with P. on 'scientific' matters.

LUCCEIUS ALBINUS: consul of *c.* 102, fellow prosecutor of Caecilius Classicus and defender of Iulius Bassus with P.

MACER: see Baebius Macer or Calpurnius Macer.

MACRINUS: see Caecilius Macrinus.

MAESIUS MAXIMUS: correspondent of P., from the Transpadane regions.

MAMILIANUS: see Pomponius Mamilianus.

MARIUS PRISCUS: proconsul of Africa, prosecuted by P., with Tacitus as co-prosecutor.

MASSA: see Baebius Massa.

MATURUS ARRIANUS: Roman knight, from Altinum: frequent correspondent with P. on a wide range of matters.

MAURICUS: see Iunius Mauricus.

MAXIMUS: there are at least five correspondents or characters in the letters insecurely identified as a Maximus; see Birley (2000a) 70–1 s.v. See also Maesius Maximus or Novius Maximus.

METILIUS NEPOS: twice consul (103, 128), correspondent of P., perhaps from the Transpadane regions.

METTIUS CARUS: informer, under Domitian, and prosecutor of Herennius Senecio.

METTIUS MODESTUS: consul of 82(?), exiled under Domitian.

MINICIANUS: see Cornelius Minicianus.

MINICIUS FUNDANUS: consul of 107, friendly with both P. and Plutarch.

MINICIUS IUSTUS: husband of Corellia.

MONTANUS: perhaps L. Venuleius Montanus Apronianus, consul of 92.

NASO: see Iulius Naso.

NEPOS: see Licinius Nepos or Metilius Nepos.

NERATIUS PRISCUS: consul of 97, and possibly governor of Germany in 98–9.

NIGRINUS: see Avidius Nigrinus.

NOVIUS MAXIMUS: literary correspondent of P., possibly from the Transpadane regions.

OCTAVIUS RUFUS: literary correspondent of P., origin unknown.

PAETUS: see Caecina Paetus or Thrasea Paetus.

PALLAS: freedman of the emperor Claudius.

PASSENUS PAULUS: Roman knight, from Asisium, descendant and imitator of Propertius.

PATERNUS: see Plinius Paternus.

PAULINUS: see Valerius Paulinus.

PAULUS: see Passenus Paulus.

PLANTA: see Pompeius Planta.

PLINIUS PATERNUS: literary correspondent from Comum, perhaps related to P.'s mother and uncle.

PLINY THE ELDER (Plinius Secundus): adoptive father and maternal uncle of P., equestrian administrator, historian and author of the *Natural History*; died during eruption of Vesuvius in 79.

POMPEIA CELERINA: mother of P.'s wife (immediately prior to Calpurnia).

POMPEIUS FALCO: consul of 108 (?), married to a daughter of Sosius Senecio.

POMPEIUS PLANTA: Roman knight, prefect of Egypt *c.* 98–100.

POMPEIUS SATURNINUS: poet and orator, literary correspondent of P.; not to be confused with the man of same name from Comum (5.7).

POMPONIUS BASSUS: consul of 94.

POMPONIUS MAMILIANUS: consul of 100 and correspondent of P.

POMPONIUS RUFUS: consul of 98, involved in trials of Caecilius Classicus and Iulius Bassus.

PONTIUS ALLIFANUS: literary friend of P. and resident of Campania.

PRAESENS: see Bruttius Praesens.

PRISCUS: there are perhaps as many as three insecurely identified correspondents named Priscus in the letters; see Birley (2000a) 83 s.v.; not
to be confused with Cornelius Priscus, Helvidius Priscus, Iavolenus
Priscus, Marius Priscus or Neratius Priscus (for whom see above).

PUBLICIUS CERTUS: praetorian prefect of the treasury of Saturn,
attacked by P. in the senate in 97 for his part in the prosecution
of Helvidius the Younger.

QUADRATILLA: see Ummidia Quadratilla.

QUADRATUS: see Ummidius Quadratus.

QUINTILIAN (Fabius Quintilianus): teacher of P., author of the *Institutio
Oratoria*.

REGULUS: see Aquilius Regulus.

ROMANUS: see Voconius Romanus.

ROMATIUS FIRMUS: correspondent of P., from Comum.

ROSIANUS GEMINUS: P.'s quaestor as consul in 100 (and eventually consul himself *c.* 125).

RUFUS: see Calvisius Rufus, Caninius Rufus, Corellius Rufus, Octavius
Rufus, Pomponius Rufus, Sempronius Rufus, Varenus Rufus, or
Verginius Rufus; for other Rufi in the correspondence, see Birley
(2000a) 85 s.v.

RUSO: see Cremutius Ruso.

RUSTICUS: unidentified correspondent of P.; see also Arulenus Rusticus.

SABINIANUS: unidentified correspondent of P., but perhaps consul of 112.

SABINUS: see Iulius Sabinus or Statius Sabinus.

SALINATOR: see Fuscus Salinator.

SALVIUS LIBERALIS: consul of *c.* 85, orator banished by Domitian,
involved in trials of Marius Priscus and Caecilius Classicus.

SARDUS: possibly Asconius Sardus from the Transpadane regions.

SATURNINUS: see Pompeius Saturninus.

SEMPRONIUS RUFUS: possible consul of 113.

SENECIO: see Herennius Senecio or Sosius Senecio.

SENTIUS AUGURINUS: poet, possibly from Verona, and relation of
Vestricius Spurinna.

SEPTICIUS CLARUS: dedicatee of the *Letters*, Guard Prefect of Hadrian
from 119, perhaps from the Transpadane regions.

SERVIANUS: see Iulius Servianus.

SEVERUS: see Annius Severus, Catilius Severus, Vettenius Severus, or Vibius Severus.

SILIUS ITALICUS: consul of 68, perhaps from the Transpadane regions, orator and poet, author of epic *Punica*.

SOSIUS SENECIO: consul of 99 and 107, related by marriage to both Iulius Frontinus and Pompeius Falco.

SPARSUS: see Iulius Sparsus.

SPURINNA: see Vestricius Spurinna.

STATIUS SABINUS: correspondent of P., from Firmum.

SUETONIUS TRANQUILLUS: the biographer, sometime protégé of P., Roman knight, *ab epistulis* to Hadrian.

SURA: see Licinius Sura.

TACITUS: see Cornelius Tacitus.

TERENTIUS IUNIOR: Roman knight, former procurator of Narbonese Gaul.

TERTULLUS: see Cornutus Tertullus.

THRASEA PAETUS: consul of 56, leader of Stoic opposition under Nero, father of Fannia, son-in-law of Caecina Paetus and Arria.

TIRO: see Calestrius Tiro.

TITINIUS CAPITO: Roman knight, writer, patron of the arts, *ab epistulis* to Domitian, Nerva and Trajan.

TITIUS ARISTO: a legal expert, frequently cited in the *Digest*.

TRANQUILLUS: see Suetonius Tranquillus.

UMMIDIA QUADRATILLA: grandmother of Ummidius Quadratus, owner of a troupe of actors.

UMMIDIUS QUADRATUS: rising aristocratic orator, consul of 118.

URSUS: see Cornelius Ursus.

VALERIANUS: see Iulius Valerianus.

VALERIUS PAULINUS: consul of 107, involved in trial of Iulius Bassus.

VARENUS RUFUS: proconsul of Bithynia *c.* 105–6, defended by P. on charges of corruption.

VERGINIUS RUFUS: three-time consul (63, 69, 97) and legal guardian of P.

VESTRICIUS SPURINNA: twice consul (?, 98), admired elder and literary correspondent of P.

VETTENNIUS SEVERUS: consul of 107, correspondent of P.

VIBIUS SEVERUS: otherwise unknown literary correspondent of P., apparently from the Transpadane regions.

VOCONIUS ROMANUS: Roman knight from Tarraconensis, boyhood friend of P. and favoured correspondent.

References

Adamik, T. (1976). 'Pliny and Martial', *Annales Universitatis Scientiarum Budapestensis Sect. Class.* 4: 63–72.

Albrecht, M. von (1989). *Masters of Latin Prose from Cato to Apuleius*, trans. N. Adkin (*ARCA* Classical and Medieval Texts, Papers and Monographs 23), Leeds.

Alföldy, G. (1983). 'Ein Tempel des Herrscherkultes in Comum', *Athenaeum* 61: 362–73.

—— (1999a). *Städte, Eliten und Gesellschaft in der Gallia Cisalpina: Epigraphisch-historische Untersuchungen*, Stuttgart.

—— (1999b). 'Die Inschriften des jüngeren Plinius und seine Mission in Pontus und Bithynia', *Acta Archaeologica Academiae Scientiarum Hungaricae* 39: 21–44.

Allain, E. (1901–2). *Pline le Jeune et ses héritiers*, 4 vols. Paris.

Altman, J.G. (1982). *Epistolarity: Approaches to a Form*, Columbus, Ohio.

Andermahr, A.M. (1998). *Totus in Praediis: Senatorischer Grundbesitz in Italien in der frühen und hohen Kaiserzeit*, Bonn.

André, J.-M. (1966). *L'otium dans la vie morale et intellectuelle romaine*, Paris.

Anguissola, A. (2007). 'L'epistolario di Plinio il Giovane tra letteratura e archeologia: aggiornamento bibliografico (1936–2006)', in K. Lehmann Hartleben, *Plinio il Giovane: lettere scelte con commento archeologico* (rev. edn), Pisa, unnumbered pages.

Aricò, G. (1995). 'Plinio il Giovane e la poesia', in *Storia Letteratura e Arte nel Secolo dopo Christo: Atti del Convegno, Mantova, October 1992*, Florence, 27–42.

Asbach, I. (1881). 'Zur Chronologie der Briefe des jüngeren Plinius', *Rheinisches Museum* 36: 38–49.

Ash, R. (2003). '"Aliud est enim epistulam, aliud historiam ... scribere" (*Epistles* 6.16.22). Pliny the historian?', in Morello and Gibson (2003), 211–25.

Aubrion, E. (1989). 'La "Correspondance" de Pline le Jeune: problèmes et orientations actuelles de la recherche', *Aufstieg und Niedergang der römischen Welt* II.33.1: 304–74.

Augoustakis, A. (2005). '*Nequaquam historia digna?* Plinian style in *Ep.* 6.20', *Classical Journal* 100: 265–73.

Auhagen, U. (2003). '*Lusus* und *Gloria* – Plinius' *hendecasyllabi* (*Ep.* 4,14; 5,3 und 7,4)', in Castagna and Lefèvre (2003), 3–13.

Bablitz, L. (2007). *Actors and Audience in the Roman Courtroom*, Abingdon and New York.

Bacchiega, S. (1993). 'Gli altri Plinii', in G. Sena Chiesa, P. Angelo Donati and A. Sartori (eds.), *Novum Comum 2050: Atti del Convegno celebrativo della Fondazione di Como romana, 1992*, Como, 269–90.

Baier, T. (2003). 'κτῆμα oder ἀγώνισμα: Plinius über historischen und rhetorischen Stil', in Castagna and Lefèvre (2003), 66–81.

Baker, R.J. (1985). 'Pliny, *Epistulae* 7.31 and the persistence of a theme', *Maia* 37: 49–54.

Baldwin, B. (1983). *Suetonius*, Amsterdam.

Barchiesi, A. (2005). 'The search for the perfect book', in Gutzwiller (2005b), 320–42.

Baroin, C. (1998). 'La maison romaine comme image et lieu de mémoire', in C. Auvray-Assayas (ed.), *Images romaines*, Paris, 177–91.

Barwick, K. (1936). 'Zwei antike Ausgaben der Pliniusbriefe?', *Philologus* 91: 423–48.

　(1958). 'Zyklen bei Martial und in der kleinen Gedichten des Catull', *Philologus* 102: 284–318.

Batstone, W.W. (1998). 'Dry pumice and the programmatic language of Catullus 1', *Classical Philology* 93: 125–35.

Beagon, M. (2005). *The Elder Pliny on the Human Animal: Natural History Book 7*, Oxford.

Beard, M. (2002). 'Ciceronian correspondences: making a book out of letters', in T.P. Wiseman (ed.), *Classics in Progress*, London, 103–44.

　(2008). *Pompeii: the Life of a Roman Town*, London.

Bell, A.A. (1989). 'A note on revision and authenticity in Pliny's Letters', *American Journal of Philology* 110: 460–6.

　(2002). *All Roads Lead to Murder: A Case from the Notebooks of Pliny the Younger*, Boone, North Carolina.

　(2008). *The Blood of Caesar: A Second Case from the Notebooks of Pliny the Younger*, Boone, North Carolina.

Bennett, J. (2001). *Trajan: Optimus Princeps*, 2nd edn, London.

Bergmann, B. (1991). 'Painted perspectives of a villa visit: landscape as status and metaphor', in E. Gazda (ed.), *Roman Art in the Private Sphere: New Perspectives on the Architecture and Décor of the Domus, Villa, and Insula*, Ann Arbor, Michigan, 49–70.

　(1994). 'The Roman house as memory theatre: the house of the Tragic Poet in Pompeii', *Art Bulletin* 76: 225–56.

　(1995). 'Visualising Pliny's villas', *Journal of Roman Archaeology* 8: 406–20.

Bernstein, N.W. (2008a). 'Each man's father served as his teacher: constructing relatedness in Pliny's *Letters*: in loving memory of Harry Bernstein (1913–2008)', *Classical Antiquity* 27.2: 203–30.

　(2008b). Review of Méthy (2007), *Bryn Mawr Classical Review* 2008.1.12.

Berriman, A. and M. Todd (2001). 'A very Roman coup: the hidden war of imperial succession', *Historia* 50: 312–31.

Berry, D. (2008). 'Letters from an advocate: Pliny's "Vesuvius" narratives (*Epistles* 6.16, 6.20)', *Papers of the Langford Latin Seminar* 13: 297–313.

Beutel, F. (2000). *Vergangenheit als Politik: neue Aspekte im Werk des jüngeren Plinius*, Frankfurt am Main.

Bickel, E. (1958). 'Die beiden Villenstrassen im Baiae, die am Berghang und die am Strand', *Rheinisches Museum* 101: 287–8.

Biffino, G.G. (2003). 'Il *temperamentum* e l'uomo ideale dell'età Traianea', in Castagna and Lefèvre (2003), 173–87.

Birley, A.R. (1997). *Hadrian: Restless Emperor*, London.

(2000a). *Onomasticon to the Younger Pliny*, Munich.

(2000b). 'The life and death of Cornelius Tacitus', *Historia* 49: 230–47.

Bispham, E. (2007). 'Pliny the Elder's Italy', in E. Bispham, G. Rowe and E. Matthews (eds.), *Vita Vigilia Est: Essays in Honour of Barbara Levick* (*BICS* Supplement 100), London, 41–67.

Bodel, J. (1995). 'Minicia Marcella: taken before her time', *American Journal of Philology* 116: 453–60.

(1997). 'Monumental villas and villa monuments', *Journal of Roman Archaeology* 10.5–35.

(unpublished). *The Publication of Pliny's Letters*.

Bollansée, J. (1994). '*P. Fay.* 19, Hadrian's memoirs, and imperial epistolary auto-biography', *Ancient Society* 25: 279–302.

Bonelli, G. (1994). 'Plinio il Giovane e la schiavitù', *Quaderni Urbinati di Cultura Classica* 3: 141–8.

Bonomi Ponzi, L. (1999). 'Introduzione storico-topografica', in Braconi and Uroz Sáez (1999), 9–17.

Braconi, P. (1998). 'Paysage et aménagement: un domaine de Pline le Jeune', in M. Clavel-Leveque and A. Vignot (eds.), *Cité et Territoire II*, Paris, 155–64.

(1999a). 'Introduzione', in Braconi and Uroz Sáez (1999), 19–20.

(1999b). 'La villa di Plinio a San Giustino', in Braconi and Uroz Sáez (1999), 21–42.

(2001). 'La pieve 'vecchia' di San Cipriano e la villa *in Tuscis* di Plinio il Giovane', in *Umbria cristiana: Dalla diffusione del culto al culto dei Santi*, Spoleto, vol. II: 737–47.

(2003). 'Les premiers propriétaires de la *villa* de Pline le Jeune *in Tuscis*', *Histoire et Sociétés Rurales* 19.1: 37–50.

(2008). 'Territorio e paesaggio dell'alta valle del Tevere in età romana', in Coarelli and Parker (2008), 87–104.

Braconi, P. and J. Uroz Sáez (eds.) (1999). *La villa di Plinio il Giovane a San Giustino: primi risultati di una ricerca in corso*, Perugia.

(2001). 'Il tempio della tenuta di Plinio il Giovane "*in Tuscis*"', *Eutopia* n.s. I.1–2: 203–17.

(2008). 'La villa di Plinio il Giovane a San Giustino', in Coarelli and Parker (2008), 105–21.

Breed, B.W. (2009). 'Perugia and the plots of the *Monobiblos*', *Cambridge Classical Journal* 55: 24–48.

Bruère, R.T. (1954). 'Tacitus and Pliny's *Panegyricus*', *Classical Philology* 49: 161–179.

(1956). 'Pliny the Elder and Virgil', *Classical Philology* 51: 228–46.

Bulwer-Lytton, E. (1834). *The Last Days of Pompeii*, London.

Burridge, R.A. (2004). *What are the Gospels? A Comparison with Graeco-Roman Biography*, 2nd edn, Grand Rapids, Michigan.

Bütler, H.-P. (1970). *Die geistige Welt des jüngeren Plinius: Studien zur Thematik seiner Briefe*, Heidelberg.

Cain, A. (2009). *The Letters of Jerome: Asceticism, Biblical Exegesis, and the Construction of Christian Authority in Late Antiquity*, Oxford.

Cameron, A. (1965). 'The fate of Pliny's *Letters* in the late Empire', *Classical Quarterly* 15: 289-98 (with addendum in *Classical Quarterly* 17 (1967) 421–2).

Carlon, J.M. (2009). *Pliny's Women: Constructing Virtue and Creating Identity in the Roman World*, Cambridge.

Castagna, L. and E. Lefèvre (eds.) (2003). *Plinius der Jüngere und seine Zeit*, Munich and Leipzig.

Champlin, E. (1974). 'The chronology of Fronto', *Journal of Roman Studies* 64: 136–59.

(2001). 'Pliny's other country', in M. Peachin (ed.), *Aspects of Friendship in the Graeco-Roman World: Proceedings of a conference held at the Seminar für Alte Geschichte, Heidelberg on 10–11 June, 2000* (*JRA* supplement 43), Portsmouth, Rhode Island, 121–8.

Chinn, C.M. (2007). 'Before your very eyes: Pliny *Epistulae* 5.6 and the ancient theory of ekphrasis', *Classical Philology* 102: 265–80.

Claridge, A. (1985). 'Il vicus di epoca imperiale nella tenuta di Castelporziano: indagini archeologiche 1984', in *Castelporziano I: campagna di scavo e restauro 1984*, Rome, 71–88.

(1988). 'Il vicus di epoca imperiale: indagini archeologiche nel 1985 e 1986', in *Castelporziano II: campagna di scavo e restauro 1985–1986*, Rome, 61–73.

(1997–8). 'The villas of the Laurentine shore', *Rendiconti della Pontificia Accademia Romana di Archaeologia* 70: 307–17.

(1998). 'Il vicus di epoca imperiale: campagne di ricerche 1987–91', in Lauro (1998), 115–36.

(forthcoming a). 'Nuovi scavi al vicus de epoca imperiale 1995–98. Rapporto preliminare', in Lauro (forthcoming).

(forthcoming b). 'Thomas Ashby nell' Ager Laurens. Appunti e carte topografici inediti nell' archivio della British School at Rome', in Lauro (forthcoming).

Clark, A. (2007). 'The city in epistolography', *Oxford University Research Archive*, http://ora.ouls.ox.ac.uk/objects/uuid:ce2ad6d6–5093–4c12-b5b1-fab 38e4a826c

Coarelli, F. and H. Parker (eds.) (2008). *Mercator Placidissimus: the Tiber Valley in Antiquity; New research in the upper and middle river valley* (Proceedings of the Conference held at the British School at Rome, 27–8 Feb. 2004), Rome.

Coleman, K. (1988). *Statius, Siluae IV: Text, Translation, and Commentary*, Oxford.

(2000). 'Latin literature after AD 96: change or continuity?', *American Journal of Ancient History* 15 [1990]: 19–39.

Connors, C. (2000). 'Imperial space and time: the literature of leisure', in O. Taplin (ed.), *Literature in the Roman World*, Oxford, 492–518.

Conybeare, C. (2000). *Paulinus Noster: Self and Symbol in the Letters of Paulinus of Nola*, Oxford.

Courtney, E. (1993). *The Fragmentary Latin Poets*, Oxford.

Cova, P.V. (1966). *La critica letteraria di Plinio il Giovane*, Brescia.

——— (1972). 'Arte allusiva e stilizzazione retorica nelle lettere di Plinio', *Aevum* 46: 16–36.

——— (1997). 'La presenza di Seneca in Plinio il Giovane', *Paideia* 52: 95–107.

——— (1999). 'I viaggi di Plinio il Giovane', *Bollettino di Studi Latini* 29: 136–40.

——— (2001). 'Plinio il Giovane contro Plinio il Vecchio', *Bollettino di Studi Latini* 31: 55–67.

——— (2003). 'Plinio il giovane contra Quintiliano', in Castagna and Lefévre (2003), 83–94.

——— (2004). 'Probleme e orientamenti della critica recente sulle lettere vesuviane di Plinio', *Bollettino di Studi Latini* 34: 609–17.

——— (2005). 'Per una rilettura critica delle lettere vesuviane di Plinio', *Bollettino di Studi Latini* 35: 87–96.

Cugusi, P. (1983). *Evoluzione e forme dell'epistolografia latina nella tarda repubblica e nei primi due secoli dell'impero, con cenni sull'epistolografia preciceroniana*, Rome.

——— (2003). 'Qualche riflessione sulle idee retoriche di Plinio il Giovane', in Castagna and Lefévre (2003), 95–122.

D'Agostino, V. (1931). 'I diminutivi in Plinio il Giovane', *Atti dell'Accademia delle Scienze di Torino* 66: 93–130.

D'Arms, J. (1970). *Romans on the Bay of Naples*, Cambridge.

Deane, S.N. (1918). 'Greek in Pliny's letters', *Classical World* 12: 41–54.

Dickey, E. (2002). *Latin Forms of Address from Plautus to Apuleius*, Oxford.

Dobson, E.S. (1982). 'Pliny the Younger's depiction of women', *Classical Bulletin* 58: 81–5.

Dominik, W. (2007). 'Tacitus and Pliny on oratory', in W. Dominik and J. Hall (eds.), *A Companion to Roman Rhetoric*, Oxford and Malden, MA, 323–38.

Doody, A. (2010). *Pliny's Encyclopaedia: The Reception of the Natural History*, Cambridge.

Duncan-Jones, R. (1982). *The Economy of the Roman Empire*, 2nd edn, Cambridge.

Ebbeler, J. (2003). 'Caesar's letters and the ideology of literary history', *Helios* 30: 3–19.

——— (2010). 'Letters', in A. Barchiesi and W. Scheidel (eds.), *The Oxford Handbook of Roman Studies*, Oxford, 464–76.

——— (2012). *Disciplining Christians: Correction and Community in Augustine's Letters*, Oxford.

Eck, W. (1997). 'Rome and the outside world: senatorial families and the world they lived in', in B. Rawson and P. Weaver (eds.), *The Roman Family in Italy: Status, Sentiment, Space*, Oxford, 73–99.

(2001). 'Die grosse Pliniusinschrift aus Comum: Funktion und Monument', in A. Bertinelli and A. Donati (eds.), *Varia Epigraphica: Atti del Colloquio Internazionale di Epigrafia, Bertinoro, 8–10 giugno 2000*, Faenza (*Epigrafia e Antichità* 17), 225–35.

(2002). 'An emperor is made: senatorial politics and Trajan's adoption by Nerva in 97', in G. Clark and T. Rajak (eds.), *Philosophy and Power in the Graeco-Roman World: Essays in Honour of Miriam Griffin*, Oxford, 211–26.

(2009). 'There are no *cursus honorum* inscriptions. The function of the *cursus honorum* in epigraphic communications', *Scripta Classica Israelica* 28: 79–92.

Eco, U. (1994). 'A portrait of the Elder as a Young Pliny', in *The Limits of Interpretation*, Bloomington, Indiana, 123–36.

Edwards, C. (1997). 'Self-scrutiny and self-transformation in Seneca's *Letters*', *Greece & Rome* 44: 23–38. Reprinted (2008) in J.G. Fitch (ed.), *Oxford Readings in Classical Studies: Seneca*, Oxford, 84–101.

(2005). 'Epistolography', in S.J. Harrison (ed.), *A Companion to Latin Literature*, Oxford and Malden, Massachusetts, 270–83.

Edwards, R. (2008). 'Hunting for boars with Pliny and Tacitus', *Classical Antiquity* 27: 35–58.

Fedeli, P. (1989). 'Il *Panegirico* di Plinio nella critica moderna', *Aufstieg und Niedergang der römischen Welt* II.17.2: 387–514.

Ferri, R. (2007). 'The Epistles', in S. Harrison (ed.), *The Cambridge Companion to Horace*, Cambridge, 121–31.

Finamore, J.T. (1984). 'Catullus 50 and 51: friendship, love and *otium*', *Classical World* 78: 11–19.

Fishwick, D. (1990). 'Pliny and the Christians', *American Journal of Ancient History* 9: 123–30.

Fitzgerald, W. (2007a). 'The letter's the thing (in Pliny, Book 7)', in Morello and Morrison (2007), 191–210.

(2007b). *Martial: The World of the Epigram*, Chicago.

Förtsch, R. (1993). *Archäologischer Kommentar zu den Villenbriefen des jüngeren Plinius*, Mainz.

Fowler, D. P. (1995). 'Martial and the book', *Ramus* 24: 31–58.

Franceschini, M. de (2005). *Ville dell' agro romano*, Rome.

Freudenburg, K. (2001). *Satires of Rome: Threatening Poses from Lucilius to Juvenal*, Cambridge.

Frischer, B.D. (2001). 'Ramsay's enquiry: text and context', in Frischer and Brown (2001), 73–104.

Frischer, B.D. and I.G. Brown (eds.) (2001). *Allan Ramsay and the Search for Horace's Villa*, Aldershot.

Froesch, H. H. (1968). *Ovids Epistulae ex Ponto I-III als Gedichtsammlung*, Diss., Bonn.

Gaertner, J.F. (2005). *Ovid, Epistulae ex Ponto, Book 1*, Oxford.

Gamberini, F. (1983). *Stylistic Theory and Practice in the Younger Pliny*, Zurich and New York.

Garthwaite, J. (1998). 'Putting a price on praise: Martial's debate with Domitian in Book 5', in F. Grewing (ed.), *Toto notus in orbe: Perspektiven der Martial-Interpretation*, Stuttgart, 157–73.

Gasser, F. (1999). *Germana Patria: Die Geburtsheimat in den Werken römischer Autoren der späten Republik und der frühen Kaiserzeit*, Stuttgart and Leipzig.

Gazich, R. (2003). 'Retorica dell'esemplarità nelle *Lettere* di Plinio', in Castagna and Lefèvre (2003), 123–41.

Gee, E. (2001). 'Cicero's Astronomy', *Classical Quarterly* 51: 520–36.

Geisler, E. (1887). 'Loci similes auctorum Sidonio anteriorum', *Monumenta Germaniae Historica, Auctores Antiquissimi*, Berlin, Vol. VIII, 353–83.

Giannotti, F. (2001). 'Criteri organizzativi nell'epistolario di Sidonio Apollinare. Il caso del terzo libro', *Annali della Facoltà di lettere e filosofia dell' Università di Siena* 22: 27–38.

Gibson, B. (2006). *Statius, Siluae 5*, Oxford.

   (2011). 'Contemporary contexts', in Roche (2011c), 104–24.

Gibson, R.K. (2003). 'Pliny and the art of (in)offensive self-praise', in Morello and Gibson (2003), 235–54.

   (2007). *Excess and Restraint: Propertius, Horace, and Ovid's Ars Amatoria* (*BICS* Supplement 89), London.

   (2011a). 'Elder and better: the *Naturalis Historia* and the *Letters* of the Younger Pliny', in Gibson and Morello (2011), 187–206.

   (2011b). '<Clarus> confirmed? Pliny, *Epistles* 1.1 and Sidonius Apollinaris', *Classical Quarterly* 61.2: 653–7.

   (2012). 'On the nature of ancient letter collections', *Journal of Roman Studies* 102.

   (forthcoming a). 'Pliny and the letters of Sidonius: from Constantius and Clarus to Firminus and Fuscus', in B.J. Gibson and R.D. Rees (eds.), *Pliny in Late Antiquity*.

   (forthcoming b). 'Suetonius and the *uiri illustres* of Pliny the Younger', in T.J. Power and R.K. Gibson (eds.), *Suetonius the Biographer: Thirteen Studies*, Oxford.

Gibson, R.K. and R. Morello (eds.) (2011). *Pliny the Elder: Themes and Contexts* (*Mnemosyne Supplements* 329), Leiden.

Gibson, R.K. and A.D. Morrison (2007). 'Introduction: what is a letter?', in Morello and Morrison (2007), 1–16.

Gibson, R.K. and C. Steel (2010). 'The indistinct literary careers of Cicero and Pliny the Younger', in P. Hardie and H. Moore (eds.), *Classical Literary Careers and their Reception*, Cambridge, 118–37.

Gigante, M. (1979). 'Il racconto Pliniano dell'eruzione del Vesuvio dell' a. 79', *La Parola del Passato* 188-9: 321–76.

Giovio, B. (1982). *Historiae Patriae Libri Duo*, Como (= New Press reprint of 1887 edition by the Società storica Comense, Como; *editio prima* 1629, Venice).

Goalen, M. (2001). 'Describing the villa: *un rêve virgilien*', in Frischer and Brown (2001), 37–50.

Goetzl, J. (1952). '*Variatio* in the Plinian epistle', *Classical Journal* 47: 265–99.

Goldberg, S. (2009). 'The faces of eloquence: the *Dialogus de oratoribus*', in A.J. Woodman (ed.), *The Cambridge Companion to Tacitus*, Cambridge, 73–84.

Gonzalès, A. (2003). *Pline le Jeune: esclaves et affranchis à Rome*, Paris.

Görler, C. (1979). 'Kaltblutiges Scharchen: Zum literarischen Hintergrund der Vesuvbriefe des jüngeren Plinius', in G.W. Bowersock, W. Burber and M.J. Putnam (eds.), *Arktouros: Hellenic Studies presented to Bernard M.W. Knox on the occasion of his 65th birthday*, Berlin and New York, 427–33.

Gowers, E. (1993). *The Loaded Table: Representations of Food in Roman Literature*, Oxford.

(2003). 'Fragments of autobiography in Horace, *Satires* 1', *Classical Antiquity* 22: 55–92.

Gowing, A. (2005). *Empire and Memory: The Representation of the Roman Republic in Imperial Culture*, Cambridge.

Grainger, J.D. (2003). *Nerva and the Roman Succession Crisis of AD 96–99*, London.

Griffin, M. (1976). *Seneca: A Philosopher in Politics*, Oxford (2nd edn, 1992).

(1995). 'Philosophical badinage in Cicero's letters to his friends,' in J.G.F. Powell (ed.), *Cicero the Philosopher: Twelve Papers*, Oxford, 325–46.

(1999). 'Pliny and Tacitus', *Scripta Classica Israelica* 18: 139–58.

(2000). 'Seneca and Pliny', in C. Rowe and M. Schofield (eds.), *The Cambridge History of Greek and Roman Political Thought*, Cambridge, 532–58.

(2003). '*De Beneficiis* and Roman society', *Journal of Roman Studies* 93: 92–113.

(2007). 'The Younger Pliny's debt to moral philosophy', *Harvard Studies in Classical Philology* 103: 451–81.

Guerrini, C. (1997). 'I diminutivi nell' epistolario di Plinio il Giovane. Una nota stilistica', in *Discentibus obvius: Omaggio degli allievi a Domenico Magnino*, Como, 53–71.

Guillemin, A.M. (1927–8). *Pline le Jeune. Lettres I–IX*, 3 vols., Paris.

(1929). *Pline et la vie littéraire de son temps*, Paris.

Gunderson, E. (1997). 'Catullus, Pliny, and love-letters', *Transactions of the American Philological Association* 127: 201–31.

(2007). 'S.V.B.; E.V.', *Classical Antiquity* 26: 1–48.

Gutzwiller, K. (2005a). 'The literariness of the Milan papyri, or what difference a book?', in Gutzwiller (2005b), 287–319.

(ed.) (2005b). *The New Posidippus: A Hellenistic Poetry Book*, Oxford.

Hales, S. and J. Paul (eds.) (2011). *Pompeii and the Public Imagination: From its Rediscovery to Today*, Oxford.

Hall, J. (2009). *Politeness and Politics in Cicero's Letters*, Oxford.

Hardy, H. (ed.) (2004). *Isaiah Berlin: Flourishing; Letters 1926–46*, London.

Harries, J. (1994). *Sidonius Apollinaris and the Fall of Rome, AD 407–85*, Oxford.

Harrington, J. (2006). *Letters from Calpurnia, Pliny's Wife A.D. 110–113*, Palmer Lake, Colorado.

Harris, R. (2003). *Pompeii*, London.

Hausler, S. (2000). 'Parenthesen im Lateinischen am Beispiel der Pliniusbriefe, *Glotta* 76: 202–31.

Haywood, R.M. (1952–3). 'The strange death of Pliny the Elder', *Classical World* 46: 1–3.

Henderson, J. (2001). 'On Pliny on Martial on Pliny on anon ... (*Epistles* 3.21 / *Epigrams* 10.10)', *Ramus* 30: 56–87.

(2002a). *Pliny's Statue: The Letters, Self-Portraiture and Classical Art*, Exeter.

(2002b). 'Knowing someone through their books: Pliny on uncle Pliny (*Epistles* 3.5)', *Classical Philology* 97: 256–84.

(2002c). 'Funding homegrown talent: Pliny, *Letters* 1.19', *Greece & Rome* 49: 212–26.

(2003). 'Portrait of the artist as a figure of style: P.L.I.N.Y's LETTERS', in Morello and Gibson (2003), 115–25.

(2004). *Morals and Villas in Seneca's Letters: Places to Dwell*, Cambridge.

Hennig, D. (1978). 'Zu Plinius *Ep.* 7,33', *Historia* 27: 246–9.

Hershkowitz, D. (1995). 'Pliny the Poet', *Greece & Rome* 42: 168–81.

Heyworth, S.J. (ed.) (2007). *Classical Constructions: Papers in Memory of Don Fowler*, Oxford.

Hinds, S.E. (2001). 'Cinna, Statius, and "immanent literary history" in the cultural economy', in *L'histoire littéraire immanente dans la poésie latine* (*Entretiens Hardt* 47), Geneva, 221–65.

Hodkinson, O. (2006). 'Novels in the Greek letter: inversions of the written–oral hierarchy in the Briefroman "Themistocles"', in V. Rimell (ed.), *Seeing Tongues, Hearing Scripts: Orality and Representation in the Ancient Novel* (*Ancient Narrative* Supplement 7), Groningen, 257–78.

(2007). 'Better than speech: some advantages of the letter in the Second Sophistic', in Morello and Morrison (2007), 283–300.

Hoffer, S.E. (1999). *The Anxieties of Pliny the Younger*, Atlanta.

(2006). 'Divine comedy? Accession propaganda in Pliny, *Epistles* 10.1–2 and the *Panegyric*', *Journal of Roman Studies* 96: 73–87.

Holzberg, N. (ed.) (1994). *Der griechische Briefroman: Gattungstypologie und Textanalyse* (*Classica Monacensia* 8), Tübingen.

(2004–5). 'Martial, the book, and Ovid', *Hermathena* 177/178: 209–224.

Höschele, R. (2010). *Die blütenlesende Muse: Poetik und Textualität antiker Epigrammsammlungen* (*Classica Monacensia* 37), Tübingen.

Howe, N. P. (1985). 'In defense of the encyclopedic mode: on Pliny's *Preface* to the *Natural History*', *Latomus* 46: 561–76.

Hunt, J.D. (2001). 'Some reflections on the idea of Horace's farm', in Frischer and Brown (2001), 27–36.

Hutchinson, G. (1984). 'Propertius and the unity of the book', *Journal of Roman Studies* 74: 99–106.

(1998). *Cicero's Correspondence: A Literary Study*, Oxford.

(2008). *Talking Books: Readings in Hellenistic and Roman Books of Poetry*, Oxford.

Innes, D. (2011). 'The *Panegyricus* and rhetorical theory', in Roche (2011c), 67–84.

Instinsky, H.U. (1969). 'Formalien im Briefwechsel des jüngeren Plinius mit Kaiser Trajan', *Abhandlungen der Akademie der Wissenschaften Mainz* 12: 387–406.

Inwood, B. (2007). 'The importance of form in Seneca's philosophical letters', in Morello and Morrison (2007), 133–48.

Janson, T. (1964). *Latin Prose Prefaces*, Stockholm.

Jardine, L. (1993). *Erasmus, Man of Letters: The Construction of Charisma in Print*, Princeton.

Jashemski, W.M. and F. Meyer (eds.) (2002). *The Natural History of Pompeii*, Cambridge.

Johannsen, N. (2006). *Dichter über ihre Gedichte: Die Prosavorreden in den Epigrammaton libri Martials und in den Silvae des Statius* (*Hypomnemata* 166), Göttingen.

Johnson, D. (1912). 'The MSS of Pliny's *Letters*', *Classical Philology* 7: 66–75.

Johnson, G.J. (1988). '*De conspiratione delatorum*. Pliny and the Christians revisited', *Latomus* 47: 417–22.

Johnson, W.A. (2000). 'Towards a sociology of reading in classical antiquity', *American Journal of Philology* 121: 593–627.

(2005). 'The Posidippus papyrus: bookroll and reader', in Gutzwiller (2005b), 70–80.

(2010). *Readers and Reading Culture in the High Roman Empire: A Study of Elite Communities*, Oxford.

Jones, C.P. (1968a). 'Julius Naso and Julius Secundus', *Harvard Studies in Classical Philology* 72: 279–88.

(1968b). 'A new commentary on the Letters of Pliny', *Phoenix* 22: 111–42.

Jones, N.F. (2001). 'Pliny the Younger's Vesuvius letters (6.16 and 6.20)', *Classical World* 95: 31–48.

Kaster, R. (1995). *C. Suetonius Tranquillus, de Grammaticis et Rhetoribus*, Oxford.

(1998). 'Becoming "CICERO"', in P.E. Knox and C. Foss (eds.), *Style and Tradition: Studies in Honour of Wendell Clausen*, Stuttgart, 250–65.

Kehoe, D.P. (1988). 'Allocation of risk and investment on the estates of Pliny the Younger', *Chiron* 18: 15–42.

(1989). 'Approaches to economic problems in the Letters of Pliny the Younger: the question of risk in agriculture', *Aufstieg und Niedergang der römischen Welt* II.33.1: 555–90.

(1993). 'Investment in estates by upper-class landowners in early imperial Italy: the case of Pliny the Younger', in H. Sancisi-Weerdenburg, R.J. van der Spek, H.C. Teitler, H.T. Wallinga (eds.), *De Agricultura: In Memoriam Pieter Willem de Neeve* (Dutch Monographs on Ancient History and Archaeology 10), Amsterdam, 214–37.

(2007). *Law and the Rural Economy in the Roman Empire*, Ann Arbor.

Kemper, S. (2000). '*Neglegit carpitque posteritas*: Plinius Minor van Oudheid tot Renaissance', in Z. von Martels, P. Steenbakkers, and A. Vanderjagt (eds.), *Limae Labor et Mora: Opstellen voor Fokke Akkerman ter gelegenheid van zijn zeventigste verjaardag*, Leende, 8–19.

Kennedy, D.F. (1984). 'The epistolary mode and the first of Ovid's *Heroides*', *Classical Quarterly* 34: 413–22. Reprinted (2006) in P. Knox (ed.), *Oxford Readings in Ovid*, Oxford, 69–85.

Ker, J. (2004). 'Nocturnal writers in Imperial Rome: the culture of lucubration', *Classical Philology* 99: 209–42.

Klauck, H.-J. (2006). *Ancient Letters and the New Testament: A Guide to Context and Exegesis*, Waco, Texas.

König, J. (2007a). 'Alciphron's Epistolarity', in Morello and Morrison (2007), 257–82.

(2007b). 'Fragmentation and coherence in Plutarch's *Sympotic Questions*', in König and Whitmarsh (2007), 43–68.

König, J. and T. Whitmarsh (eds.) (2007). *Ordering Knowledge in the Roman Empire*, Cambridge.

Konstan, D. (1995). 'Patrons and friends', *Classical Philology* 90: 328–42.

(1997). *Friendship in the Classical World*, Cambridge.

Korfmacher, W.C. (1946–7). 'Pliny and the gentleman of Cicero's *Offices*', *Classical World* 40: 50–3.

Krevans, N. (2005). 'The editor's toolbox: strategies for selection and presentation in the Milan Epigram Papyrus', in Gutzwiller (2005b), 81–96.

(2007). 'The arrangement of epigrams in collections', in P. Bing and J.S. Bruss (eds.), *Brill Companion to Hellenistic Epigram: Down to Philip*, Leiden, 131–64.

Krieckhaus, A. (2004). '*Duae patriae*? C. Plinius Caecilius Secundus zwischen *germana patria* und *urbs*', in L. de Light, E.A. Hemelrijk, and H.W. Singor (eds.), *Roman Rule and Civic Life: Local and Regional Perspectives (Proceedings of the Fourth Workshop of the International Network, Impact of Empire)*, Amsterdam, 299–314.

(2006). *Senatorische Familien und ihre patriae (1./2. Jahrhundert n. Chr.)* (Studien zur Geschichtsforschung des Altertums 14), Hamburg.

Kukula, R.C. (1912). *C. Plinii Caecili Secundi Epistularum libri novem, Epistularum ad Traianum liber, Panegyricus*, 2nd edn, Leipzig.

Lanciani, R.A. (1909). *Wanderings in the Roman Campagna*, London.

Laurence, P. and F. Guillaumont (eds.) (2006). *Epistulae Antiquae IV: Actes du IVe Colloque 'Le Genre Épistolaire Antique et ses Prolongements Européens'* (Université François-Rabelais, Tours, 2–3 December 2004), Louvain and Paris.

(eds.) (2008). *Epistulae Antiquae V: Actes du Ve Colloque 'Le Genre Épistolaire Antique et ses Prolongements Européens'* (Université François-Rabelais, Tours, 6–8 September 2006), Louvain and Paris.

Lauro, M.G. (ed.) (1998). *Castelporziano III: campagne di scavo e restauro 1987–91*, Rome.

(ed.). (forthcoming). *Castelporziano IV*.

Lauro, M.G. and Claridge, A. (1998). '*Litus Laurentinum*: carta archaeologia della zona litoranea a Castelporziano', in Lauro (1998), 39–61.

Lausberg, M. (1991) 'Cicero – Seneca – Plinius. Zur Geschichte des römischen Prosabriefes', *Anregung* 37: 82–100.

Lauterbach, I. (1996). 'The gardens of the Milanese "villeggiatura" in the mid-sixteenth century', in J.D. Hunt (ed.), *The Italian Garden: Art, Design, and Culture*, Cambridge, 127–59.

Lawrence, C. (2001). *The Secrets of Vesuvius*, London.

(2003). *The Dolphins of Laurentum*, London.

(2007). *The Roman Mysteries Treasury*, London.

(2008–9). *Roman Mysteries: the Complete Series 1–2* (BBC DVD: Lace / Revelations Films Ltd).

Leach, E. (1990). 'The politics of self-representation: Pliny's *Letters* and Roman portrait sculpture', *Classical Antiquity* 9: 14–39.

(2003). '*Otium* as *luxuria*: economy of status in the younger Pliny's letters', in Morello and Gibson (2003), 147–66.

(2006). '*An gravius aliquid scribam*: Roman *seniores* write to *iuvenes*', *Transactions of the American Philological Association* 136: 247–67.

Lee, B.T. (2008). 'The potentials of narrative: the rhetoric of the subjective in Tibullus', in Liveley and Salzman-Mitchell (2008), 196–220.

Leeman, A.D. (1963). *Orationis Ratio*, 2 vols., Amsterdam.

Lee-Stecum, P. (1998). *Powerplay in Tibullus: Reading Elegies Book One*, Cambridge.

Lefèvre, E. (1977). 'Plinius-Studien I: Römische Baugesinnung und Landschaftsauffassung in den Villenbriefen (2,17; 5,6)', *Gymnasium* 84: 519–41.

(1978). 'Plinius-Studien II: Diana und Minerva. Die beiden Jagd-Billette an Tacitus (1,6; 9,10)', *Gymnasium* 85: 37–47.

(1987). 'Plinius-Studien III: Die Villa als geistiger Lebensraum (1,3; 1,24; 2,8; 6, 31; 9, 36)', *Gymnasium* 94: 247–62.

(1988). 'Plinius-Studien IV: Die Naturauffassung in den Beschreibungen der Quelle am *Lacus Larius* (4,30), des *Clitumnus* (8,8) und des *Lacus Vadimo* (8,20)', *Gymnasium* 95: 236–69.

(1989). 'Plinius-Studien V: Vom Römertum zum Ästhetizismus. Die Würdigungen des älteren Plinius (3,5), Silius Italicus (3,7) und Martial (3,21)', *Gymnasium* 96: 113–28.

(1996a). 'Plinius-Studien VI: Der große und der kleine Plinius. Die Vesuv-Briefe (6, 16; 6, 20)', *Gymnasium* 103: 193–215.

(1996b). 'Plinius-Studien VII: Cicero das unerreichbare Vorbild (1,2; 3,15; 4,8; 7,4; 9,2)', *Gymnasium* 103: 333–53.

(2009). *Vom Römertum zum Ästhetizismus: Studien zu den Briefen des jüngeren Plinius*, Berlin and New York.

Lejeune, P. (1989). *On Autobiography*, Minneapolis.

Levick, B. (1979). 'Pliny in Bithynia – and what followed', *Greece & Rome* 26: 119–31.

Liebeschuetz, J.H.W.G. (2005). *Ambrose of Milan: Political Letters and Speeches*, with the assistance of C. Hill (Translated Texts for Historians 43), Liverpool.

Lilja, S. (1970). 'On the nature of Pliny's letters', *Arctos* 6: 61–79.

Lillge, F. (1918). 'Die literarische Form der Briefe Plinius des jüngeren über den Ausbruch des Vesuvius', *Sokrates* 6: 209–34, 273–97.

Littlewood, A.R. (1987). 'Ancient literary evidence for the pleasure gardens of Roman country villas', in MacDougall (1987), 9–30.

Liveley, G. and P. Salzman-Mitchell (eds.) (2008). *Latin Elegy and Narratology: Fragments of a Story*, Columbus, Ohio.

Lo Cascio, E. (2003). 'L' economia dell' Italia Romana nella testimonianza di Plinio', in Castagna and Lefèvre (2003), 281–302.

Lorenz, S. (2004). 'Waterscape with black and white: epigrams, cycles, and webs in Martial's *epigrammaton liber quartus*', *American Journal of Philology* 125: 255–78.

Lowe, E.A. and E.K. Rand (1922). *A Sixth-Century Fragment of the Letters of Pliny the Younger*, Washington, D.C.

Lowe, N.J. (2000). *The Classical Plot and the Invention of Western Narrative*, Cambridge.

Lowrie, M. (2007). 'Making an *exemplum* of yourself: Cicero and Augustus', in Heyworth (2007), 91–112.

Ludolph, M. (1997). *Epistolographie und Selbstdarstellung: Untersuchungen zu den 'Paradebriefen' Plinius des Jüngeren* (*Classica Monacensia* 17), Tübingen.

Luraschi, G. (1999). 'Aspetti di vita pubblica nella Como dei Plini', in *Storia di Como antica*, Como, 461–504 (= Luraschi (1984). *Plinio, i suoi luoghi, il suo tempo*, Como, 71–105).

MacBain, B. (2010). *Roman Games: A Plinius Secundus Mystery*, Scottsdale, Arizona.

McDermott, W.C. (1971). 'Pliny the younger and inscriptions', *Classical World* 65: 84–94.

McDermott, W.C. and A.E. Orentzel (1977). 'Silius Italicus and Domitian', *American Journal of Philology* 98: 24–34.

MacDougall, E.B. (ed.) (1987). *Ancient Roman Villa Gardens* (Dumbarton Oaks Colloquium on the History of Landscape Architecture 10), Washington, D.C.

McEwen, I.K. (1995). 'Housing Fame: in the Tuscan villa of Pliny the Younger', *Res* 27: 11–24.

McHam, S.B. (2005). 'Renaissance monuments to favourite sons', *Renaissance Studies* 19: 458–86.

Macé, A. (1900). *Essai sur Suétone*, Paris.

Madsen, J.M. (2009). *Eager to be Roman: Greek Response to Roman Rule in Pontus and Bithynia*, London.

Malherbe, A.J. (1988). *Ancient Epistolary Theorists*, Atlanta.

Maniet, A. (1966). 'Pline le Jeune et Calpurnia', *L'Antiquité Classique* 35: 149–85.

Manolaraki, E. (2008). 'Political and rhetorical seascapes in Pliny's *Panegyricus*', *Classical Philology* 103: 374–94.

Manuwald, G. (2003). 'Eine schule für Novum Comum. Aspekte der *liberalitas* des Plinius', in Castagna and Lefèvre (2003), 203–17.

Marchesi, I. (2008). *The Art of Pliny's Letters: A Poetics of Allusion in the Private Correspondence*, Cambridge.

Marcus, L. (1994). *Auto/biographical Discourses: Theory, Criticism, Practice*, Manchester.

Marturano, A. and A. Varone (2005). 'The A.D. 79 eruption: seismic activity and effects of the eruption on Pompeii', in M.S. Balmuth, D.K. Chester and P.A. Johnston (eds.), *Cultural Responses to the Volcanic Landscape: The Mediterranean and Beyond*, Boston, 241–60.

Marzano, A. (2007). *Roman Villas in Central Italy: A Social and Economic History* (Columbia Studies in the Classical Tradition 30), Leiden.

Matthews, J.F. (1974). 'The letters of Symmachus', in J.W. Binns (ed.), *Latin Literature of the Fourth Century*, London and Boston, 58–99.

Mayer, R.G. (1991). 'Roman historical *exempla* in Seneca', in P. Grimal (ed.), *Sénèque et la prose latine* (Entretiens Hardt 36), 141–69. Reprinted (2008) in J.G. Fitch (ed.), *Oxford Readings in Classical Studies: Seneca*, Oxford, 299–315.

(1994). *Horace, Epistles Book I*, Cambridge.

(2001). *Tacitus, Dialogus de Oratoribus*, Cambridge.

(2003). 'Pliny and *gloria dicendi*', in Morello and Gibson (2003), 227–34.

Mazzoli, G. (2003). '"E il principe risponde": tra *Panegirico* e libro X dell'epistolario pliniano', in Castagna and Lefèvre (2003), 257–66.

Melzani, G. (1992). 'Elementi della lingua d'uso nelle lettere di Plinio il Giovane', in P. V. Cova (ed.), *Letteratura latina dell' Italia settentrionale: cinque studi*, Brescia, 197–244.

Merrill, E.T. (1895). 'The codex Riccardianus of Pliny's letters', *American Journal of Philology* 16: 468–90.

Méthy, N. (2003). '*Ad exemplar antiquitatis*. Les grandes figures du passé dans la correspondance de Pline le Jeune', *Revue des Études Latines* 81: 200–14.

(2006). 'La correspondance de Pline le Jeune ou un autre définition de la lettre', in Laurence and Guillaumont (2006), 171–81.

(2007). *Les lettres de Pline le Jeune: Une représentation de l'homme*, Paris.

(2009). 'Suétone vu par un contemporain', *Gérion* 27: 219–29.

Meulemans, A. (1913). *Plinius' Fontein*. (Moscow Symphony Orchestra, conducted by F. Devreese: Marco Polo 8.223776, 1996).

Millar, F. (1964). 'The *aerarium* and its officials under the Empire', *Journal of Roman Studies* 54: 33–44.

(2004a). 'Trajan: government by correspondence', in *Government, Society and Culture in the Roman Empire* (eds. H.M. Cotton and G.M. Rogers), Chapel Hill and London, 23–46.

(2004b). 'The *aerarium* and its officials under the Empire', in *Government, Society and Culture in the Roman Empire* (eds. H.M. Cotton and G.M. Rogers), Chapel Hill and London, 73–88 [= Millar (1964)].

Momigliano, A. (1993). *The Development of Greek Biography*, 2nd edn, Cambridge, Massachusetts.

Mommsen, Th. (1869). 'Zur Lebensgeschichte des jüngeren Plinius', *Hermes* 3: 31–139. Reprinted (1906) in *Gesammelte Schriften von Theodor Mommsen*, vol. 4, Berlin, 366–468.

Monsigny, J. (1988). *Toutes les vies mènent à Rome*, Paris.

Morello, R. (2003). 'Pliny and the art of saying nothing', in Morello and Gibson (2003), 187–209.

(2007). 'Confidence, *invidia* and Pliny's epistolary curriculum', in Morello and Morrison (2007), 169–89.

Morello, R. and R.K. Gibson (eds.) (2003). *Re-Imagining Pliny the Younger*, *Arethusa* 36.2.

Morello, R. and A. Morrison (eds.) (2007). *Ancient Letters: Classical and Late Antique Epistolography*, Oxford.

Morford, M.P.O. (1992). '*Iubes esse liberos*: Pliny's *Panegyricus* and liberty', *American Journal of Philology* 113: 575–93.

Morgan, L. (2007). '*Natura narratur*: Tullius Laurea's elegy for Cicero', in Heyworth (2007), 113–40.

Morgan, T. (2007). *Popular Morality in the Early Roman Empire*, Cambridge.

Morrison, A. (2007). 'Didacticism and epistolarity in Horace's *Epistles* 1', in Morello and Morrison (2007), 107–31.

Most, G.W. (1989). 'The stranger's stratagem: self-disclosure and self-sufficiency in Greek culture', *Journal of Hellenic Studies* 109: 114–33.

Mratschek, S. (2003). '*Illa nostra Italia*: Plinius und die Wiedergeburt der Literatur in der Transpadana', in Castagna and Lefèvre (2003), 219–41.

Murgia, C.E. (1985). 'Pliny's letters and the *Dialogus*', *Harvard Studies in Classical Philology* 89: 171–206.

Murison, C.L. (2003). 'M. Cocceius Nerva and the Flavians', *Transactions of the American Philological Association* 133: 147–57.

Muth, R. (1982). 'Plinius d. J. und Kaiser Trajan über die Christen. Interpretationen zu Plin. *Ep.* X. 96,97', in P. Neukam (ed.), *Information aus der Vergangenheit* (Dialog Schule – Wissenschaft 16), Munich, 96–128.

Myers, K.S. (2005). '*Docta otia*: garden ownership and configurations of leisure in Statius and Pliny the Younger', *Arethusa* 38: 103–29.

Mynors, R.A.B. (1963). *C. Plini Caecili Secundi Epistularum Libri Decem*, Oxford.

Nadjo, L. and E. Gavoille (eds.) (2002a). *Epistulae Antiquae I: Actes du Ier Colloque 'Le Genre Épistolaire Antique et ses Prolongements'* (Université François-Rabelais, Tours, 18–19 September 1998), Louvain and Paris.

(eds.) (2002b). *Epistulae Antiquae II: Actes du IIe Colloque 'Le Genre Épistolaire Antique et ses Prolongements Européens'* (Université François-Rabelais, Tours, 28–30 September 2000), Louvain and Paris.

(eds.) (2004). *Epistulae Antiquae III: Actes du IIIe Colloque 'Le Genre Épistolaire Antique et ses Prolongements Européens'* (Université François-Rabelais, Tours, 25–7 September 2002), Louvain and Paris.

Neeve, Pieter W. de (1992). 'A Roman landowner and his estates: Pliny the Younger', *SIFC* 10: 335–44. Longer version published in *Athenaeum* 78 (1990): 363–402.

Newlands, C. (2002). *Statius' Silvae and the Poetics of Empire*, Cambridge.

(2009). 'Statius' prose prefaces', *Materiali e Discussioni* 61: 91–104.

(2010). 'The eruption of Vesuvius in the epistles of Statius and Pliny', in A.J. Woodman and J. F. Miller (eds.), *Proxima Poetis: Latin Historiography and Poetry in the Early Empire*, Leiden, 206–21.

(2011). *Statius, Silvae Book 2*, Cambridge.

Nicholson, J. (1998) 'The survival of Cicero's letters', in C. Deroux (ed.), *Studies in Latin Literature and Roman History* 9, Brussels, 63–105.

Nicols, J. (1980). 'Pliny and the patronage of communities', *Hermes* 108: 365–85.

Norden, E. (1915). *Die antike Kunstprosa: vom VI. Jahrhundert v. Chr. bis in die Zeit der Renaissance*, 3rd edn, Leipzig and Berlin.

Noreña, C. (2007). 'The social economy of Pliny's correspondence with Trajan', *American Journal of Philology* 128: 239–77.

(2011). 'Self-fashioning in the *Panegyricus*', in Roche (2011c), 29–44.

Orentzel, A. (1968). 'Declamation in the age of Pliny', *Classical Bulletin* 54: 65–8.

(1980). 'Pliny and Domitian', *Classical Bulletin* 56: 49–51.

Pagán, V. (2010). 'The power of the epistolary preface from Statius to Pliny', *Classical Quarterly* 60: 194–201.

Pani, M. (1993). 'Sviluppi della tematica dell'*otium* in Plinio il Giovane', in M. Pani (ed.), *Potere e valori a Roma fra Augusto e Traiano* (Documenti e Studi: Collana del Dipartimento de Scienze dell'antichità dell'Università di Bari, Sezione Storica 14), 2nd edn, Bari, 181–92.

Patterson, J.R. (1985). 'Il vicus di epoca imperiale nella tenuta presidenziale di Castelporziano: contesto storico', in *Castelporziano I: campagna di scavo e restauro 1984*, Rome, 67–70.

(2006). *Landscapes and Cities: Rural Settlement and Civic Transformation in Early Imperial Italy*, Oxford.

Pelling. C. (2009). 'Was there an ancient genre of "autobiography"? Or, did Augustus know what he was doing?', in C. Smith and A. Powell (eds.), *The Lost Memoirs of Augustus and the Development of Roman Autobiography*, Swansea, 41–64.

Penwill, J. (2010). 'Evolution of an assassin: the Letters of Chion of Heraclea', *Ramus* 39: 24–52.

Peper, B.M. and M. DelCogliano (2006). 'The Pliny and Trajan correspondence', in A.J. Levine, D.C. Allison Jr., and J.D. Crossan (eds.), *The Historical Jesus in Context*, Princeton, 366–71.

Pitcher, R.A. (1998). 'Martial's debt to Ovid', in F. Grewing (ed.), *Toto Notus in Orbe: Perspektiven der Martial-Interpretation* (Palingenesia 65), Stuttgart, 59–76.

(1999). 'The hole in the hypothesis: Pliny and Martial reconsidered', *Mnemosyne* 52: 554–61.

Pliszczynska, J. (1955). *De elocutione Pliniana*, Lublin.

Porter, S.E. and S.A. Adams (eds.) (2010). *Paul and the Ancient Letter Form*, Leiden.

Poster, C. (2007). 'A conversation halved: epistolary theory in Greco-Roman antiquity', in C. Poster and L.C. Mitchell (eds.), *Letter-Writing Manuals and Instruction from Antiquity to the Present*, Columba, South Carolina, 21–51.

Power, T.J. (2010). 'Pliny, *Letters* 5.10 and the literary career of Suetonius', *Journal of Roman Studies* 100: 140–62.

Pretis, A. de (2002). '*Epistolarity' in the First Book of Horace's Epistles*, Piscataway, New Jersey.

(2003). '"Insincerity," "facts," and "epistolarity": approaches to Pliny's Epistles to Calpurnia', in Morello and Gibson (2003), 127–46.

Prey, Pierre de la Ruffinière du (1994). *The Villas of Pliny from Antiquity to Posterity*, Chicago.

Purcell, N. (1998). 'Alla scoperta di una costa residenziale romana: il *litus Laurentinum* e l'archaeologia dell'*otium*', in Lauro (1998), 11–32.

Radice, B. (1968). 'Pliny and the *Panegyricus*', *Greece & Rome* 15: 166–72.

——— (1969). *Pliny: Letters and Panegyricus*, 2 vols., London and Cambridge, Massachusetts.

Radicke, J. (1997). 'Die Selbstdarstellung des Plinius in seinen Briefen', *Hermes* 125: 447–69.

——— (2003). 'Der öffentliche Privatbrief als "kommunizierte Kommunikation" (Plin. *Epist.* 4.28)', in Castagna and Lefèvre (2003), 23–34.

Ramieri, A.M. (1995). 'La villa di Plinio a Castel Fusano', *Archeologia Laziale* 12.2: 407–16.

Rees, R.D. (2001). 'To be and not to be: Pliny's paradoxical Trajan', *Bulletin of the Institute of Classical Studies* 45: 149–68.

——— (2007). 'Letters of recommendation and the rhetoric of praise', in Morello and Morrison (2007), 149–68.

Reeve, M.D. (2011). 'The *Vita Plinii*', in Gibson and Morello (2011), 207–22.

Reichel, M. (ed.) (2005). *Antike Autobiographien: Werke, Epochen, Gattungen*, Cologne.

Reichert, A. (2002). 'Durchdachte Konfusion: Plinius, Trajan und das Christentum', *Zeitschrift für die neutestamentliche Wissenschaft* 93: 227–50.

Reynolds, L.D. (1983). *Texts and Transmission: A Survey of the Latin Classics*, Oxford.

Richardson-Hay, C. (2006). *First Lessons: Book 1 of Seneca's Epistulae Morales*, Bern.

Ricotti, E. Salza Prina (1983). 'La villa laurentina di Plinio il Giovane: un'ennesima ricostruzione', in *Lunario romano*, Rome, 229–51.

——— (1984). 'La c.d. Villa Magna: il Laurentinum di Plinio il Giovane', *Atti Acc. Naz. Dei Lincei Rend.* S. VIII, vol. 39, fasc. 7–12: 339–58.

——— (1985). 'La Villa Magna a Grotte di Piastra', in *Castelporziano I: campagna di scavo e restauro 1984*, Rome, 53–66.

——— (1987). 'The importance of water in Roman garden triclinia', in E.B. MacDougall (ed.), *Ancient Roman Villa Gardens*, Washington, D.C., 138–83.

——— (1988). 'Il Laurentino: scavi del 1985', in *Castelporziano II: campagna di scavo e restauro 1985–1986*, Rome, 45–56.

Riggsby, A. (1995). 'Pliny on Cicero and oratory: self-fashioning in the public eye', *American Journal of Philology* 116: 123–35.

——— (1997). '"Public" and "private" in Roman culture: the case of the *cubiculum*', *Journal of Roman Archaeology* 10: 36–56.

——— (1998). 'Self and community in the Younger Pliny', *Arethusa* 31: 75–97.

——— (2003). 'Pliny in space (and time)', in Morello and Gibson (2003), 167–86.

——— (2007). 'Guides to the wor(l)d', in König and Whitmarsh (2007), 88–107.

Robbins, F.E. (1910). 'Tables of contents in the MSS of Pliny's Letters', *Classical Philology* 5: 476–87.

Roche, P. (2011a). 'Pliny's thanksgiving: an introduction to the *Panegyricus*', in Roche (2011c), 1–28.

—— (2011b). 'The *Panegyricus* and the monuments of Rome', in Roche (2011c), 45–66.

—— (ed.) (2011c). *Pliny's Praise: The Panegyricus in the Roman World*, Cambridge.

Roller, M. (1998). 'Pliny's Catullus: the politics of literary appropriation', *Transactions of the American Philological Association* 128: 265–304.

—— (2004). 'Exemplarity in Roman culture: the cases of Horatius Cocles and Cloelia', *Classical Philology* 99: 1–56.

Römer, F. (2003). 'Eine poetische Gestaltung von *Epist.* 3,5 aus dem 16. Jahrhundert', in Castagna and Lefèvre (2003), 327–40.

Rosenmeyer, P.A. (2001). *Ancient Epistolary Fictions: The Letter in Greek Literature*, Cambridge.

—— (2006). *Ancient Greek Literary Letters: Selections in Translation*, London and New York.

Rossi, O. (2010). *Letters from Far Away: Ancient Epistolary Travel Writing and the Case of Cicero's Correspondence*, Diss., Yale.

Rossiter, J.J. (2003). 'A shady business: building for the seasons at Pliny's villas', *Mouseion* 3: 355–62.

Rudd, N. (1992). 'Stratagems of vanity: Cicero *ad Familiares* 5.12 and Pliny's letters', in A.J. Woodman and J. Powell (eds.), *Author and Audience in Latin Literature*, Cambridge, 18–32.

Salomies, O. (1992). *Adoptive and Polyonymous Nomenclature in the Roman Empire* (Commentationes humanarum litterarum 97), Helsinki.

Salway, B. (1994). 'What's in a name? A survey of Roman onomastic practice from c. 700 B.C. to A.D. 700', *Journal of Roman Studies* 84: 124–45.

Saylor, C. (1972). 'The Emperor as *Insula*: Pliny *Epist.* 6.31', *Classical Philology* 67: 47–51.

—— (1982) 'Overlooking lake Vadimon. Pliny on tourism (*Epist.* VIII, 20)', *Classical Philology* 77: 139–44.

Scarth, A. (2009). *Vesuvius: a Biography*, Princeton and Oxford.

Scherf, J. (2008). '*Epigramma longum* and the arrangement of Martial's book', in A.M. Morelli (ed.), *Epigramma longum: Da Marziale alla tarda antichità / From Martial to Late Antiquity* (Cassino), Vol. I, 195–216.

Schönberger, O. (1990). 'Die Vesuv-Briefe des jüngeren Plinius (VI 16 und 20)', *Gymnasium* 97: 526–48.

Schröder, B.J. (2001). 'Literaturkritik oder *Fauxpas*? Zu Plin. *Epist.* 6.15', *Gymnasium* 108: 241–47.

Schuster, M. (1958). *C. Plini Caecili Secundi Epistularum libri novem, Epistularum ad Traianum liber, Panegyricus*, rev. R. Hanslik, Stuttgart and Leipzig.

Scivoletto, N. (1989). '*Urbs, municipia, villae* e *studia* nell' epistolario di Plinio', *Giornale Italiano di Filologia* 41: 179–93.

Shackleton Bailey, D.R. (1965–70). *Cicero's Letters to Atticus*, 6 vols., Cambridge.

—— (1977). *Cicero: Epistulae ad Familiares*, 2 vols., Cambridge.

Sharrock, A.R. (2000). 'Intratextuality: texts, parts, and (w)holes in theory', in A.R.
 Sharrock and H. Morales (eds.), *Intratextuality: Greek and Roman Textual
 Relations*, Oxford, 1–39.
 (2006). 'Love in parentheses: digression and narrative hierarchy in Ovid's ero-
 todidactic poems', in R.K. Gibson, S.J. Green and A.R. Sharrock (eds.), *The
 Art of Love: Bimillennial Essays on Ovid's Ars Amatoria and Remedia Amoris*,
 Oxford, 23–39.
Shelton, J.A. (1987). 'Pliny's letter 3.11: rhetoric and autobiography', *Classica et
 Mediaevalia* 38: 121–39.
 (1990). 'Pliny the Younger, and the ideal wife', *Classica et Mediaevalia* 41: 163–86.
Sherwin-White, A.N. (1962). 'Trajan's replies to Pliny: authorship and necessity',
 Journal of Roman Studies 52: 114–25.
 (1966). *The Letters of Pliny: A Historical and Social Commentary*, Oxford.
 (1969a). *Fifty Letters of Pliny*, 2nd edn, Oxford.
 (1969b). 'Pliny, the man and his letters', *Greece and Rome* 16: 76–90.
Shotter, D.C.A. (1967). 'Tacitus and Verginius Rufus', *Classical Quarterly* 17: 370–
 81.
 (2001). 'A considered epitaph', *Historia* 50: 253–5.
Sick, D. (1999). 'Ummidia Quadratilla. Cagey businesswoman or lazy pantomime
 watcher?', *Classical Antiquity* 18: 330–48.
Sigurdsson, H. and S. Carey (2002). 'The eruption of Vesuvius in A.D. 79', in
 Jashemski and Meyer (2002), 37–64.
Sigurdsson, H., S. Carey, W. Cornell and T. Pescatore (1985). 'The eruption of
 Vesuvius in A.D. 79', *National Geographic Research* 1: 332–87.
Sigurdsson, H., S. Cashdollar and R.S.J. Sparks (1982). 'The eruption of Vesuvius
 in A.D. 79: reconstruction from historical and vulcanological evidence',
 American Journal of Archaeology 86: 39–51.
Sisani, S. (2008). '*Dirimens Tiberis?* I confini tra Etruria e Umbria', in Coarelli
 and Parker (2008), 45–86.
Sogno, C. (2006). *Q. Aurelius Symmachus: A Political Biography*, Ann Arbor.
Soverini, P. (1989). 'Imperio e imperatori nell' opera di Plinio il Giovane: aspetti
 e problemi del rapporto con Domiziano e Traiano', *Aufstieg und Niedergang
 der römischen Welt* II.33.1: 515–54.
Stadter, P.A. (2006). 'Pliny and the ideology of empire: the correspondence with
 Trajan', *Prometheus* 32: 61–76.
Stangl, Th. (1886). 'Zur kritik der briefe Plinius des jüngeren', *Philologus* 45:
 642–79.
Starr, R. (1990). 'Pliny the Younger on private recitations and C. Titius on irre-
 sponsible judges', *Latomus* 49: 464–72.
Stevens, B. (2009). 'Pliny and the dolphin – or a story about storytelling', *Arethusa*
 42: 161–79.
Stinchcomb, J. (1935–6). 'The literary tastes of the younger Pliny', *Classical World*
 29: 161–5.
Stout, S.E. (1954). *Scribe and Critic at Work in Pliny's Letters*, Bloomington.

Stowers, S.K. (1986). *Letter Writing in Greco-Roman Antiquity*, Philadelphia.

Strawson, G. (2004). 'Against narrativity', *Ratio* 17: 428–52.

Strobel, K. (2003). 'Plinius und Domitian: Der willige Helfer eines Unrechtssystems? Zur Problematik historischer Aussagen in den Werken des jüngeren Plinius', in Castagna and Lefèvre (2003), 303–14.

Strube, N. (1964). 'Plinius der Jüngere II 7: eine sprachliche und stilistische Analyse', *Wiener Studien* 77: 185–91.

Sturrock, J. (1993). *The Language of Autobiography: Studies in the First Person Singular*, Cambridge.

Syme, R. (1958). *Tacitus*, Oxford.

(1960). 'Pliny's less successful friends', *Historia* 9: 362–79 [= *RP* 2.477–96].

(1964). 'Pliny and the Dacian wars', *Latomus* 23: 750–9 [= *RP* 6.142–9].

(1968). 'People in Pliny', *Journal of Roman Studies* 58: 135–51 [= *RP* 2.694–723].

(1969a). 'Legates of Cilicia under Trajan', *Historia* 18: 352–66 [= *RP* 2.774–89].

(1969b). 'Pliny the procurator', *Harvard Studies in Classical Philology* 73: 201–36 [= *RP* 2.742–73].

(1970). *Ten Studies in Tacitus*, Oxford.

(1979a). 'Juvenal, Pliny, Tacitus', *American Journal of Philology* 100: 250–78 [= *RP* 3.1135–57].

(1979b). 'Ummidius Quadratus, *capax imperii*', *Harvard Studies in Classical Philology* 82: 287–310 [= *RP* 3.1158–78].

(1981). 'The travels of Suetonius Tranquillus', *Hermes* 109: 105–17 [= *RP* 3.1337–49].

(1982). 'Partisans of Galba', *Historia* 31: 460–83 [= *RP* 4.115–39].

(1983). 'Eight consuls from Patavium', *Proceedings of the British School at Rome* 51: 102–24 [= *RP* 4.371–96].

(1984). 'Hadrian and the senate', *Athenaeum* 62: 31–60 [= *RP* 4.295–324].

(1985a). 'Correspondents of Pliny', *Historia* 34: 324–59 [= *RP* 5.440–77].

(1985b). 'The dating of Pliny's latest letters', *Classical Quarterly* 35: 176–85 [= *RP* 5.478–89].

(1985c). 'The paternity of polyonomous consuls', *Zeitschrift für Papyrologie und Epigraphik* 61: 191–8 [= *RP* 5.639–47].

(1985d). 'The Testamentum Dasumii: some novelties', *Chiron* 15: 41–63 [= *RP* 5.521–45].

(1985e). 'Transpadana Italia', *Athenaeum* 63: 28–36 [= *RP* 5.431–39].

Talbert, R.J.A. (1980). 'Pliny the Younger as Governor of Bithynia-Pontus', in C. Deroux (ed.), *Studies in Latin Literature and History II*, Brussels, 412–35.

Tanzer, H. (1924). *The Villas of Pliny the Younger*, New York.

Tola, E. (2008). 'Chronological segmentation in Ovid's *Tristia*: the implicit narrative of elegy', in Liveley and Salzman-Mitchell (2008), 51–67.

Trapp, M.B. (2003). *Greek and Latin Letters: An Anthology with Translation*, Cambridge.

(2007). 'Biography in letters; biography and letters', in B.M. McGing and J. Mossman (eds.), *The Limits of Ancient Biography*, London, 335–50.

Traub, H.W. (1955). 'Pliny's treatment of history in epistolary form', *Transactions of the American Philological Association* 86: 213–32.

Trisoglio, F. (1972). *La personalità di Plinio il Giovane nei suoi rapporti con la politica, la società e la letteratura* (Memoria dell' accademia delle scienze di Torino: classe di scienze morali, storiche e filologiche, 4.25), Turin.

Tzounakas, S. (2007). '*Neque enim historiam componebam*: Pliny's first epistle and his attitude towards historiography', *Museum Helveticum* 64: 42–54.

——— (2011). 'Seneca's presence in Pliny's epistle 1.12', *Philologus* 155.2: 346–60.

Uroz Sáez, J. (1999a). 'I bolli laterizi', in Braconi and Uroz Sáez (1999), 43–50.

——— (1999b). '*Domini* e proprietà agraria', in Braconi and Uroz Sáez (1999), 191–208.

——— (2008). 'Fundiary property and brick production in the high Tiber valley', in Coarelli and Parker (2008), 123–42.

Ussani, V. (1971). 'Leggendo Plinio il Giovane, II (*Oratio – historia*)', *Rivista di Cultura Classica e Medioevale* 13: 70–135.

——— (1974–5). *Plinio il Giovane: Documenti critici e testi raccolti da Vincenzo Ussani jr.*, Rome.

——— (1981). '*Otium* e *pax* in Plinio il Giovane', *Romanitas* 14–20: 37–58.

Verger, A.M. de (1999). 'Erotic language in Pliny, *Ep.* 7.5', *Glotta* 74: 114–16.

Vessey, D.W.T. (1974). 'Pliny, Martial and Silius Italicus', *Hermes* 102: 109–16.

Vidman, L. (1960). *Étude sur la correspondance de Pline le Jeune avec Trajan*, Prague.

——— (1980). *Fasti Ostienses*, 2nd edn, Prague.

Vielberg, M. (1988). 'Bemerkungen zu Plinius d.J. und Tacitus', *Würzburger Jahrbücher für die Altertumswissenschaft* 14: 171–83.

Waarden, J.A. van (2011). 'Episcopal self-presentation: Sidonius Apollinaris and the Episcopal election in Bourges A.D. 470', in J. Leemans, P. van Nuffelen, S.W.J. Keough, and C. Nicolaye (eds.), *Episcopal Elections in Late Antiquity*, Berlin, 555–61.

Wallace-Hadrill, A. (1983). *Suetonius: The Scholar and his Caesars*, London.

Weische, A. (1989). 'Plinius d. J. und Cicero. Untersuchungen zur römischen Epistolographie in Republik und Kaiserzeit', *Aufstieg und Niedergang der römischen Welt* II.33.1: 375–86.

Wenskus, O. (1999). '"Gespräche" unter Freunden. Rhetorik als Briefthema bei Cicero und Plinius', in L. Döpp (ed.), *Antike Rhetorik und ihre Rezeption*, Stuttgart, 29–40.

——— (2001). 'Wie schreibt man einer Dame? Zum Problem der Sprachwahl in der römischen Epistolographie', *Wiener Studien* 114: 215–31.

White, P. (1975). 'The friends of Martial, Statius, and Pliny, and the dispersal of patronage', *Harvard Studies in Classical Philology* 79: 265–300.

——— (1993). *Promised Verse: Poets in the Society of Augustan Rome*, Cambridge, Massachusetts, and London.

——— (2010). *Cicero in Letters: Epistolary Relations of the Late Republic*, Oxford.

Whitton, C.L. (2010). 'Pliny, *Epistle* 8.14: senate, slavery and the *Agricola*', *Journal of Roman Studies* 100: 118–39.

(2011). 'Trapdoors: the falsity of closure in Pliny's *Epistles*', in F. Grewing and
B. Acosta-Hughes (eds.), *The Door Ajar: False Closure in Greek and Roman
Literature and Art*, Heidelberg.

(2012). '"Let us tread our path together": Tacitus and the younger Pliny', in
V.E. Pagán (ed.), *Blackwell Companion to Tacitus*, Oxford and Malden, MA,
345–68.

Wilkinson, L.P. (1982). 'Cicero and the relationship of oratory to literature', in
E.J. Kenney (ed.), *The Cambridge History of Latin Literature*, Cambridge,
230–67.

Will, E.J. (1982). 'Ambiguity in Horace, *Odes* 1.4', *Classical Philology* 77: 240–5.

Williams, K.F. (2006). 'Pliny and the murder of Larcius Macedo', *Classical Journal*
101: 409–24.

Williams, W. (1990). *Pliny: Correspondence with Trajan from Bithynia (Epistles
X.15–121)*, Warminster.

Wilson, M. (1987). 'Seneca's Epistles to Lucilius: a revaluation', *Ramus* 16: 102–21.

(2001). 'Seneca's Epistles reclassified', in S.J. Harrison (ed.), *Texts, Ideas and the
Classics*, Oxford, 164–87.

Winniczuk, L. (1975). 'The ending phrases in Pliny's letters', *Eos* 63: 319–28.

Wlosok, A. (1970). *Rome und die Christen: Zur Auseinandersetzung zwischen Christentum und römischen Staat* (*Der altsprache Unterricht*, Beiheft 13.1), Stuttgart.

Wolff, E. (2003). *Pline le jeune, ou le refus du pessimisme*, Rennes.

(2004). 'Pline et Cicéron: quelques remarques', in Nadjo and Gavoille (2004),
441–7.

Woodman, A.J. (1974). 'Sleepless poets: Catullus and Keats', *Greece & Rome* 21:
51–3.

(1988). *Rhetoric in Classical Historiography*, London.

(1989). 'Virgil the historian', in J.Diggle, J.B. Hall and H.D. Jocelyn (eds.),
Studies in Latin Literature and its Tradition in Honour of C.O. Brink (*PCPS*
Supplement 15), Cambridge, 132–45.

(2009). 'Tacitus and the contemporary scene', in A.J. Woodman (ed.), *The
Cambridge Companion to Tacitus*, Cambridge, 31–43.

(forthcoming). 'Pliny on writing history: *Epistles* 5.8', in *From Poetry to History:
Selected Papers*, Oxford.

Woodman, A.J. and R.H. Martin (1996). *The Annals of Tacitus Book 3*, Cambridge.

Woolf, G. (2003). 'The city of letters', in C. Edwards and G. Woolf (eds.), *Rome
the Cosmopolis*, Cambridge, 203–21.

(2006a). 'Pliny's province', in T. Bekker-Nielsen (ed.), *Rome and the Black Sea
Region: Domination, Romanisation, Resistance* (Black Sea Studies 8), Aarhus,
93–108.

(2006b). 'Playing games with Greeks: one Roman on Greekness', in D. Konstan
and S. Said (eds.), *Greeks on Greekness: Viewing the Greek Past Under the
Roman Empire* (*PCPS* Supplement 29), Cambridge, 162–78.

Yuge, T. (1986). 'Die einstellung Plinius des Jüngeren zur Sklaverei', in H. Kalyck,
B.B. Gullath and A. Graeber (eds.), *Studien zur Alten Geschichte: Festschrift
S. Lauffer* (Historica 2), Rome, vol. III, 1089–1102.

Zehnacker, H. (2009). *Pline le Jeune: Lettres. Volume I. Livres I–III*, Paris.

Zelzer, K. (1964). 'Zur Frage des Charakters der Briefsammlung des jüngeren Plinius', *Wiener Studien* 77: 144–61.

(1989). '*Plinius Christianus*: Ambrosius als Epistograph', *Studia Patristica* 23: 203–8.

(1990). *Sancti Ambrosii opera: Pars x: Epistulae et acta; Tom. II: Epistularum libri VII–VIII (CSEL 5.82)*, Vienna.

Zetzel, J. (1983). 'Catullus, Ennius, and the poetics of allusion', *Illinois Classical Studies* 8: 251–66.

Zimmerman, T.C.P. (1995). *Paolo Giovio: The Historian and the Crisis of Sixteenth-Century Italy*, Princeton.

Index of passages

General index

Made in the USA
Middletown, DE
16 October 2017